영어 1등급
프로젝트

READING

메가스터디

절대
평가

큐

영어
기본

유형독해

Structure

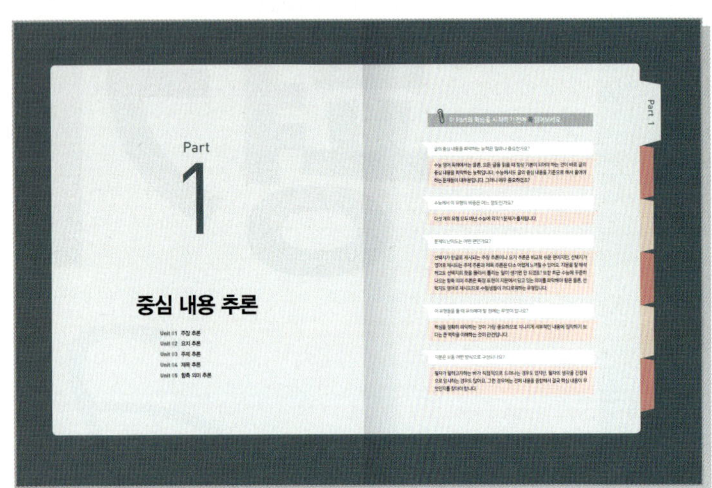

수능에 출제되는 다양한 영어·독해 문제를 유형에 따라 분류하여, 유형별로 필요한 독해 능력을 기준으로 총 6개의 Part로 나누었습니다. 각 Part에 대한 **종합적인 소개**, **수능에서의 비중**, **지문 구성 방식**, **문제 난이도**, **유의점** 등을, 수능 독해에 익숙하지 않은 학습자들에게 **질문과 응답** 형식으로 쉽게 알려줍니다.

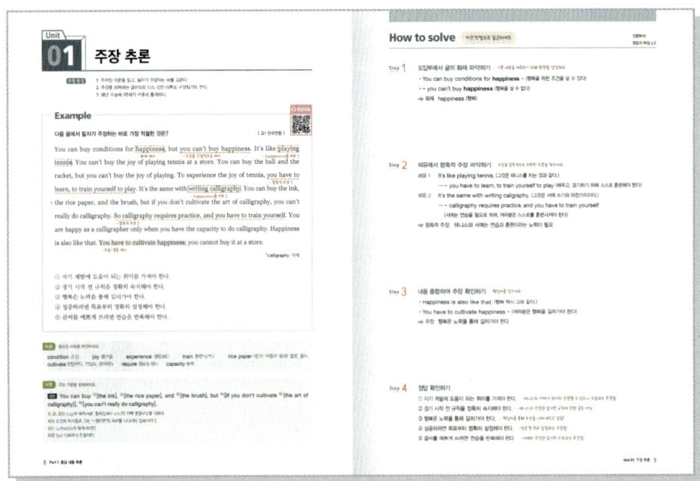

유형 대표 Example & How to Solve

각 유형의 세부적인 특징에 대해 소개하며 최신 기출 문제를 유형 대표 Example로 제시합니다. 지문에 대한 상세 분석을 첨삭식으로 제공하며 핵심 어휘 및 구문 풀이를 확인할 수 있습니다. How to Solve에서는 체계적인 Step에 따라 지문과 선택지를 분석하고 정답을 찾아가는 방법을 설명합니다.

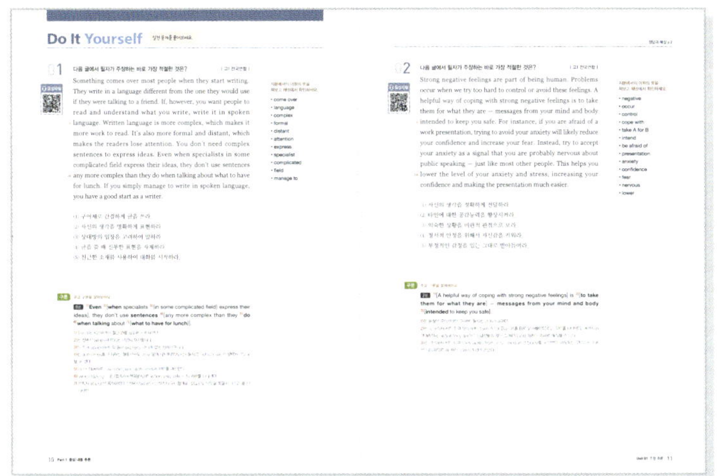

Do It Yourself

유형마다 총 **4개의 실전 문제**를 풀어봅니다. 첫 두 문제는 최신 출제 경향을 파악하고 학습 방향을 잡을 수 있는 **기출 문제**로 구성되며, 뒤의 두 문제는 재미있고 신선한 소재를 다루는 **신출 문제**로 구성됩니다.

지문에 쓰인 **핵심 어휘**의 뜻을 써보도록 하며, 다소 어려운 문장에 대해서는 **해석을 돕는 구문 풀이**를 제공하여 문장 해석에 어려움이 있는 학생들에게 독해의 방향을 잡도록 합니다. 지문마다 QR코드를 넣어 원어민 음성을 들을 수 있도록 하였습니다.

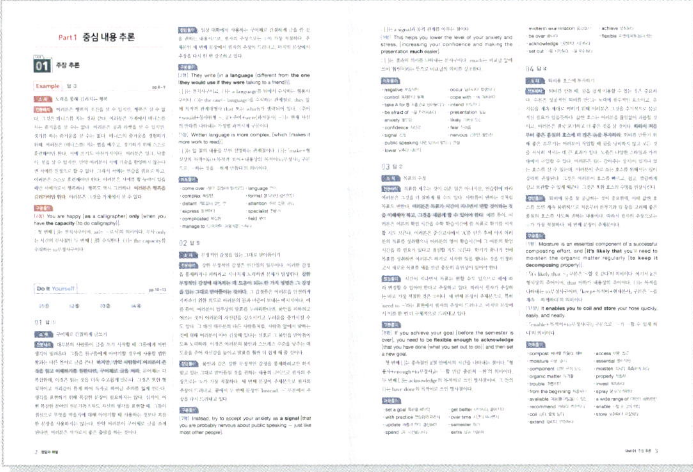

How was it?

2~3개의 Unit이 끝날 때마다 배운 내용을 **복습**할 수 있는 **확인 문제**를 제공합니다.

학습한 어휘의 뜻과 스펠링을 써보는 **어휘 문제**, 그리고 앞서 배운 지문에서 뽑은 문장을 통해 구문 풀이 능력과 해석 능력을 집중하여 기를 수 있는 다양한 유형의 **어법 문제**를 풀어 봅니다.

정답과 해설

문제의 **정답**, **소재**, 정확한 **전문해석**, 자세한 **해설**, 꼭 짚고 넘어가야 할 **오답풀이**, 해석의 기초가 되는 **구문풀이**, 상세한 **어휘풀이**를 제공합니다.

Contents

Part 4   빈칸 추론

Part 5   논리 추론

Part 6   장문 독해

지문 음성 파일 다운받는 법

• 본 교재에 수록된 지문의 음성 파일은 메가북스 홈페이지(http://www.megabooks.co.kr) → [자료실] → [듣기파일]
  에서 무료로 다운로드받으실 수 있습니다.
• 스마트폰 어플리케이션으로 지문 옆의 QR코드를 찍으면 음성을 바로 들으실 수 있습니다.

Part

1

중심 내용 추론

이 Part의 학습을 시작하기 전에 꼭 읽어보세요.

글의 중심 내용을 파악하는 능력은 얼마나 중요한가요?

수능 영어 독해에서는 물론, 모든 글을 읽을 때 항상 기본이 되어야 하는 것이 바로 글의 중심 내용을 파악하는 능력입니다. 수능에서도 글의 중심 내용을 기준으로 해서 풀어야 하는 문제들이 대부분입니다. 그러니 매우 중요하겠죠?

수능에서 이 유형의 비중은 어느 정도인가요?

다섯 개의 유형 모두 매년 수능에 각각 1문제가 출제됩니다.

문제의 난이도는 어떤 편인가요?

선택지가 한글로 제시되는 주장 추론이나 요지 추론은 비교적 쉬운 편이지만, 선택지가 영어로 제시되는 주제 추론과 제목 추론은 다소 어렵게 느껴질 수 있어요. 지문을 잘 해석하고도 선택지의 뜻을 몰라서 틀리는 일이 생기면 안 되겠죠? 또한 최근 수능에 꾸준히 나오는 함축 의미 추론은 특정 표현이 지문에서 담고 있는 의미를 파악해야 함은 물론, 선택지도 영어로 제시되므로 수험생들이 까다로워하는 유형입니다.

이 유형들을 풀 때 유의해야 할 점에는 무엇이 있나요?

핵심을 정확히 파악하는 것이 가장 중요하므로 지나치게 세부적인 내용에 집착하기 보다는 큰 맥락을 이해하는 것이 관건입니다.

지문은 보통 어떤 방식으로 구성되나요?

필자가 말하고자하는 바가 직접적으로 드러나는 경우도 있지만, 필자의 생각을 간접적으로 암시하는 경우도 많아요. 그런 경우에는 전체 내용을 종합해서 결국 핵심 내용이 무엇인지를 찾아야 합니다.

Unit 01 주장 추론

유형 특징
1. 주어진 지문을 읽고, 필자가 주장하는 바를 고른다.
2. 주장을 피력하는 글이므로 다소 강한 어투로 구성되기도 한다.
3. 매년 수능에 1문제가 꾸준히 출제된다.

Example

다음 글에서 필자가 주장하는 바로 가장 적절한 것은? | 고1 전국연합 |

You can buy conditions for happiness, but you can't buy happiness. It's like playing
→ 화제 제시   → 주장을 간접적으로 제시   → happiness를 비유 1
tennis. You can't buy the joy of playing tennis at a store. You can buy the ball and the
racket, but you can't buy the joy of playing. To experience the joy of tennis, you have to
→ 함축적 주장 1
learn, to train yourself to play. It's the same with writing calligraphy. You can buy the ink,
→ happiness를 비유 2
5 the rice paper, and the brush, but if you don't cultivate the art of calligraphy, you can't
really do calligraphy. So calligraphy requires practice, and you have to train yourself. You
→ 함축적 주장 2
are happy as a calligrapher only when you have the capacity to do calligraphy. Happiness
is also like that. You have to cultivate happiness; you cannot buy it at a store.
→ 주장=결론 제시

*calligraphy 서예

① 자기 계발에 도움이 되는 취미를 가져야 한다.
② 경기 시작 전 규칙을 정확히 숙지해야 한다.
③ 행복은 노력을 통해 길러가야 한다.
④ 성공하려면 목표부터 명확히 설정해야 한다.
⑤ 글씨를 예쁘게 쓰려면 연습을 반복해야 한다.

어휘 중요한 어휘를 확인하세요.

condition 조건   joy 즐거움   experience 경험하다   train 훈련시키다   rice paper (한지·닥종이 등의) 얇은 종이
cultivate 함양하다, 기르다, 경작하다   require 필요로 하다   capacity 능력

구문 주요 구문을 살펴보아요.

4행 You can buy 1) [the ink], 2) [the rice paper], and 3) [the brush], but 4) [if you don't cultivate 5) {the art of calligraphy}], 6) [you can't really do calligraphy].

1), 2), 3)은 buy의 목적어로, 등위접속사 and로 인해 병렬구조를 이룬다.
4)는 조건의 부사절로, if는 '~한다면'의 의미를 나타내는 접속사이다.
5)는 cultivate의 목적어이다.
6)은 but 이하에서 주절이다.

How to solve   이런 방법으로 접근하세요.

Step 1   **도입부에서 글의 화제 파악하기**   지문 내용을 예측하기 위해 방향을 설정해요.

- You can buy conditions for **happiness** ~ (행복을 위한 조건을 살 수 있다)
- ~ you can't buy **happiness** (행복을 살 수 없다)
- ➡ **화제** happiness (행복)

Step 2   **비유에서 함축적 주장 파악하기**   주장을 함축적으로 표현한 부분을 찾으세요.

비유 1   It's like playing tennis. (그것은 테니스를 치는 것과 같다.)
→ ~ you have to learn, to train yourself to play (배우고, 경기하기 위해 스스로 훈련해야 한다)

비유 2   It's the same with writing caligraphy. (그것은 서예 쓰기와 마찬가지이다.)
→ ~ calligraphy requires practice, and you have to train yourself
(서예는 연습을 필요로 하며, 여러분은 스스로를 훈련시켜야 한다)

➡ **함축적 주장** 테니스와 서예는 연습과 훈련이라는 노력이 필요

Step 3   **내용 종합하여 주장 확인하기**   핵심어를 찾으세요.

- Happiness is also like that. (행복 역시 그와 같다.)
- You have to cultivate happiness ~ (여러분은 행복을 길러가야 한다)
- ➡ **주장** 행복은 노력을 통해 길러가야 한다.

Step 4   **정답 확인하기**

① 자기 계발에 도움이 되는 취미를 가져야 한다. → 테니스와 서예가 취미와 관련될 수 있으나 주장과는 무관함
② 경기 시작 전 규칙을 정확히 숙지해야 한다. → 테니스와 관련은 있지만 규칙에 관한 글은 아님
③ 행복은 노력을 통해 길러가야 한다. → 핵심어를 통해 주장을 나타내므로 정답!
④ 성공하려면 목표부터 명확히 설정해야 한다. → 성공 및 목표 설정과는 무관함
⑤ 글씨를 예쁘게 쓰려면 연습을 반복해야 한다. → 서예와 관련은 있지만 주장과는 무관함

Do It Yourself

01 다음 글에서 필자가 주장하는 바로 가장 적절한 것은? | 고1 전국연합 |

Something comes over most people when they start writing. They write in a language different from the one they would use if they were talking to a friend. If, however, you want people to read and understand what you write, write it in spoken language. Written language is more complex, which makes it more work to read. It's also more formal and distant, which makes the readers lose attention. You don't need complex sentences to express ideas. Even when specialists in some complicated field express their ideas, they don't use sentences any more complex than they do when talking about what to have for lunch. If you simply manage to write in spoken language, you have a good start as a writer.

① 구어체로 간결하게 글을 쓰라.
② 자신의 생각을 명확하게 표현하라.
③ 상대방의 입장을 고려하여 말하라.
④ 글을 쓸 때 진부한 표현을 자제하라.
⑤ 친근한 소재를 사용하여 대화를 시작하라.

지문에서의 어휘의 뜻을 써보고 해설에서 확인하세요.

- come over
- language
- complex
- formal
- distant
- attention
- express
- specialist
- complicated
- field
- manage to

구문 주요 구문을 살펴보아요.

8행 1)**Even** 2)[**when** specialists 3){in some complicated field} express their ideas], they don't use **sentences** 4)[any more complex than they 5)**do** 6)**when talking** about 7){**what to have for lunch**}].

1) Even은 시간의 부사절인 2)를 강조하는 부사이다.

2)는 접속사 when이 이끄는 시간의 부사절이다.

3)은 주어 specialists와 동사 express 사이에 있는 전치사구이다.

4)는 sentences를 수식하는 형용사구로, any 앞에 〈관계대명사+be동사〉인 which are가 생략된 것으로 볼 수 있다.

5) do는 대동사로, use complex sentences의 의미를 대신한다.

6) when talking ~은 〈접속사+현재분사〉로 'when they talk ~'의 의미를 나타낸다.

7) 전치사 about의 목적어이며, 「의문사(what)+to부정사(구)」 형태로 '점심으로 무엇을 먹을지'의 의미를 나타낸다.

02 다음 글에서 필자가 주장하는 바로 가장 적절한 것은?

| 고1 전국연합 |

Strong negative feelings are part of being human. Problems occur when we try too hard to control or avoid these feelings. A helpful way of coping with strong negative feelings is to take them for what they are — messages from your mind and body
5 intended to keep you safe. For instance, if you are afraid of a work presentation, trying to avoid your anxiety will likely reduce your confidence and increase your fear. Instead, try to accept your anxiety as a signal that you are probably nervous about public speaking — just like most other people. This helps you
10 lower the level of your anxiety and stress, increasing your confidence and making the presentation much easier.

① 자신의 생각을 정확하게 전달하라.
② 타인에 대한 공감능력을 향상시켜라.
③ 익숙한 상황을 비판적 관점으로 보라.
④ 정서적 안정을 위해서 자신감을 키워라.
⑤ 부정적인 감정을 있는 그대로 받아들여라.

지문에서의 어휘의 뜻을
써보고 해설에서 확인하세요.

- negative
- occur
- control
- cope with
- take A for B
- intend
- be afraid of
- presentation
- anxiety
- confidence
- fear
- nervous
- lower

구문 주요 구문을 살펴보아요.

2행 [1)][A helpful way of coping with strong negative feelings] is [2)][**to take them for what they are**] — **messages from your mind and body** [3)][**intended** to keep you safe].

1)은 문장의 주어인 명사구이며, 동사는 그 뒤의 is이다.
2)는 to부정사구로, 주격 보어이며, 「take A for B」는 'A를 B로 받아들이다'라는 의미를 나타낸다. 여기서 B에 해당하는 what they are는 '그 감정들의 있는 그대로의 모습'이라는 의미로 해석할 수 있다.
3)은 과거분사구로, 앞의 messages from your mind and body를 수식한다. 의도되는 것이라는 수동의 의미이므로 과거분사 intended가 쓰였다.

Do It Yourself

03 다음 글에서 필자가 주장하는 바로 가장 적절한 것은?

Setting goals is not an easy task, but you will get better at it with practice. Goals change just as people do. You need to understand that your goals will change over time, and you need to be able to update them. For example, you may begin the semester with a
5 goal of spending extra study time on your math class. After you earn an "A" on your midterm examination, you may decide that you already have achieved your goal and that you need to spend that extra study time on your English class. If you achieve your goal before the semester is over, you need to be flexible enough
10 to acknowledge that you have done what you set out to do and then set a new goal.

① 목표를 성취할 때까지 지속적으로 노력해야 한다.
② 상황과 필요에 따라 목표를 변경할 수 있어야 한다.
③ 때에 따라 과목별로 적정한 학습시간을 할애해야 한다.
④ 처음부터 성취할 수 있는 적당한 수준의 목표를 세워야 한다.
⑤ 목표는 노력하면 반드시 성취할 수 있다는 점을 인식해야 한다.

구문 주요 구문을 살펴보아요.

5행 After you earn an "A" on your midterm examination, 1)[you may decide 2){that you already have achieved your goal} and 3){that you need to spend 4)**that** extra study time on your English class}].

1)이 주절이며, 주절의 주어는 you이고, 동사는 may decide이다.
2)와 3)은 모두 decide의 목적어인 명사절로, 등위접속사 and로 인해 병렬 연결되었다.
4)의 that은 지시어로 쓰였다.

04 다음 글에서 필자가 주장하는 바로 가장 적절한 것은?

In composting, easy access to water is important. Moisture is an essential component of a successful composting effort, and it's likely that you'll need to moisten the organic matter regularly to keep it decomposing properly. A cheap hose will trouble you forever, and you'll finally give up and buy a better one. Thus invest more money in a good-quality hose from the beginning. For composting, a fine spray works great to gently moisten everything without wasting water as you work. Nozzles are available in a wide range of styles and prices. You can buy hoses with or without reels, but for your main hose a reel is strongly recommended. It enables you to coil and store your hose quickly, easily, and neatly. It also extends the life of the hose.

*decompose 썩다, 분해하다 **nozzle 노즐, (호스 등의) 발사구

***reel 릴, 감아주는 도구

① 퇴비에 적당량의 물과 햇빛을 공급하라.
② 작물 종류에 따라 퇴비 비율을 조절하라.
③ 농기구를 사용한 직후에 바로 관리를 하라.
④ 처음부터 좋은 품질의 퇴비용 호스를 구입하라.
⑤ 좋은 퇴비를 만들기 위해서 시기를 잘 선택하라.

지문에서의 어휘의 뜻을 써보고 해설에서 확인하세요.

- compost
- access
- moisture
- essential
- component
- moisten
- organic matter
- properly
- trouble
- invest
- from the beginning
- spray
- available
- a wide range of
- enable
- coil
- store
- extend

구문 주요 구문을 살펴보아요.

7행 1)**For composting**, a fine spray 2)[**works great**] 3)[to gently moisten everything 4)**without wasting** water] 5)[**as you work**].

1)은 전치사구로, 「for -ing」은 '~하기 위해'의 의미이다.
2) 〈자동사+부사〉로, work는 '효과가 있다'의 의미이며, great은 '크게, 잘'의 의미를 나타내는 부사로 쓰였다.
3)은 목적을 나타내는 to부정사구이다.
4) 「without -ing」는 '~하지 않고서'의 의미이다.
5)는 시간의 부사절로, as는 '~할 때'의 의미를 나타내는 접속사이다.

유형 특징
1. 주어진 지문을 읽고, 글의 요지를 고른다.
2. 글의 핵심을 파악하는 것이 가장 중요하다.
3. 매년 수능에 1문제가 꾸준히 출제된다.

Example

음성파일

다음 글의 요지로 가장 적절한 것은?

| 고1 전국연합 |

Certainly praise is critical to a child's sense of self-esteem, but when given too often for too little, it kills the impact of real praise when it is called for. Everyone needs to know they are valued and appreciated, and praise is one way of expressing such feelings — but only after something *praiseworthy* has been accomplished. Awards are supposed to be rewards — reactions to positive actions, honors for *doing something well*! The ever-present danger in handing out such honors too lightly is that children may come to depend on them and do only those things that they know will result in prizes. If they are not sure they can do well enough to earn merit badges, or if gifts are not guaranteed, they may avoid certain activities.

① 올바른 습관은 어린 시절에 형성된다.
② 칭찬은 아이의 감성 발달에 필수적이다.
③ 아이에게 칭찬을 남발하지 않는 것이 중요하다.
④ 물질적 보상은 학습 동기 부여에 도움이 되지 않는다.
⑤ 아이에게 감정 표현의 기회를 충분히 줄 필요가 있다.

어휘 중요한 어휘를 확인하세요.

certainly 분명히, 확실히　　praise 칭찬　　critical 중요한, 결정적인　　self-esteem 자존감　　impact 효과, 영향, 충격　　call for ~을 필요로 하다　　appreciate (~의 진가를) 인정하다, 감상하다　　praiseworthy 칭찬할 만한　　accomplish 성취하다　　be supposed to ~해야 하다, ~하기로 되어 있다　　reward 보상, 보답　　reaction 반응, 반작용　　positive 긍정적인　　honor 명예, 상　　ever-present 상존하는, 항상 존재하는　　hand out ~을 부여하다, ~을 나누어 주다　　come to ~하게 되다　　earn 벌다, 받다　　merit badge 칭찬[공훈] 배지　　guarantee 보장하다, 보증하다

How to solve 이런 방법으로 접근하세요.

Step 1 **글 전반부에서 핵심어 찾기** 핵심어는 반복해서 나와요.

- Certainly **praise** is critical to a child's sense of self-esteem ~ (분명 칭찬은 아이의 자존감에 중요하다)
- ~ it kills the impact of real **praise** ~ (그것은 진정한 칭찬의 효과를 없앤다)
- ~ **praise** is one way of expressing such feelings ~ (칭찬은 그러한 느낌을 표현하는 하나의 방법이다)

➡ **핵심어** praise (칭찬)

Step 2 **주제문 파악하기** 주제문은 보통 글의 전반부 혹은 후반부에 나와요.

- ~ when given too often for too little, it kills the impact of real praise ~

  (사소한 일에 칭찬을 너무 자주하면 진정한 칭찬의 효과가 사라진다)

➡ **주제문** 필자의 견해 · 중심 생각이 드러나므로 요지 예측 가능

Step 3 **근거 종합해 요지 도출하기**

근거 1 ~ only after something *praiseworthy* has been accomplished

  (칭찬할 만한 일을 성취한 뒤여야만 한다)

근거 2 ~ reactions to positive actions, honors for *doing something well*

  (긍정적인 행동에 대한 반응, 어떤 일을 잘한 것에 대한 상)

근거 3 ~ children may come to depend on them ~ (아이들이 그것에 의존할 수도 있다)

근거 4 ~ they may avoid certain activities (아이들이 그러한 활동을 피할 지도 모른다)

➡ **요지** 아이에게 칭찬을 남발하지 않는 것이 중요하다.

Step 4 **정답 확인하기**

① 올바른 습관은 어린 시절에 형성된다. → 습관 형성과는 무관함

② 칭찬은 아이의 감성 발달에 필수적이다. → 칭찬에 관한 것이지만 감성 발달과는 무관함

③ 아이에게 칭찬을 남발하지 않는 것이 중요하다. → 핵심어, 주제문, 근거를 통해 추론한 요지이므로 정답!

④ 물질적 보상은 학습 동기 부여에 도움이 되지 않는다. → 칭찬이나 보상에 관한 것이지만 학습 동기 부여와는 무관함

⑤ 아이에게 감정 표현의 기회를 충분히 줄 필요가 있다. → 감정 표현 기회와는 무관함

구문 주요 구문을 살펴보아요.

5행 1)[The ever-present danger **in handing** out such **honors** too lightly] is 2)[**that** children **may come** to depend on 3)**them** and 4)**do** only **those things** 5){**that** 6)(they know) will result in prizes}].

1) 문장의 주어이며, 「in -ing」은 '~할 때'의 의미이다.

2) 문장의 동사 is의 보어로 쓰인 명사절이다. that은 명사절을 이끄는 접속사이다.

3) 복수 대명사 them이 가리키는 것은 앞에 나온 honors이다.

4) 조동사 may에 동사원형 come과 공통으로 연결되어 병렬구조를 이룬다.

5) 관계대명사 that이 이끄는 관계절로, those things를 수식한다.

6) 관계절인 5) 안에 삽입된 절이다. '~ do only those things + They know (that) only those things will result in prizes'에서 온 것으로 생각하면
   이해하기 쉽다.

Do It Yourself 실전 문제를 풀어보세요.

01 다음 글의 요지로 가장 적절한 것은?

| 고1 전국연합 |

Too many companies advertise their new products as if their competitors did not exist. They advertise their products in a vacuum and are disappointed when their messages fail to get through. Introducing a new product category is difficult, especially if the new category is not contrasted against the old one. Consumers do not usually pay attention to what's new and different unless it's related to the old. That's why if you have a truly new product, it's often better to say what the product is not, rather than what it is. For example, the first automobile was called a "horseless" carriage, a name which allowed the public to understand the concept against the existing mode of transportation.

① 과도한 광고 경쟁이 제품의 가격을 상승시킨다.
② 기존 제품과의 대비가 신제품 광고에 효과적이다.
③ 신제품 개발을 위해 정확한 수요 예측이 필요하다.
④ 수익 향상을 위해 새로운 고객 관리 방식이 요구된다.
⑤ 제품에 대한 올바른 정보 제공이 소비자의 신뢰를 높인다.

지문에서의 어휘의 뜻을 써보고 해설에서 확인하세요.

- advertise
- competitor
- vacuum
- get through
- category
- contrast
- consumer
- pay attention to
- automobile
- carriage
- concept
- existing
- transportation

구문 주요 구문을 살펴보아요.

7행 That's [1)][why 2){if you have a truly new product}, 3)it's often better 4){to say 5)(**what** the product is not), 6)**rather than** 7)(**what** it is)}].

1)은 문장의 보어 역할을 하는 명사절로서, why 앞에 the reason이 생략되어 있다.
2)는 명사절 내의 조건의 부사절이다.
3) it은 명사절 내 주절의 형식상의 주어이다.
4)는 명사절 내의 주절의 내용상의 주어이다.
5)와 7)은 say의 목적어 역할을 하는 명사절로서, 선행사를 포함한 관계대명사 what이 이끌고 있다.
6) 「A rather than B」 구문은 'B라기 보다 A인'의 의미이다.

02

다음 글의 요지로 가장 적절한 것은?　　|　고1 전국연합　|

🎧 음성파일

An interesting study about facial expressions was recently published by the American Psychological Association. Fifteen Chinese people and fifteen Scottish people took part in the study. They viewed emotion-neutral faces that were randomly
5 changed on a computer screen and then categorized the facial expressions as happy, sad, surprised, fearful, or angry. The responses allowed researchers to identify the expressive facial features that participants associated with each emotion. The study found that the Chinese participants relied more on the
10 eyes to tell facial expressions, while the Scottish participants relied on the eyebrows and mouth. People from different cultures perceive happy, sad, or angry facial expressions in different ways. That is, facial expressions are not the "universal language of emotions."

① 문화에 따라 표정을 인식하는 방식이 다르다.
② 동서양을 막론하고 선호하는 표정이 있다.
③ 노력을 통해 좋은 인상을 줄 수 있다.
④ 사람마다 고유한 감정 표현 방식이 있다.
⑤ 지나친 감정 표현은 오해를 불러일으킬 수 있다.

지문에서의 어휘의 뜻을
써보고 해설에서 확인하세요.

- facial expression
- publish
- view
- emotion
- neutral
- randomly
- categorize
- response
- identify
- expressive
- feature
- participant
- associate
- perceive
- universal

구문　주요 구문을 살펴보아요.

6행 The responses ¹⁾**allowed researchers to identify the expressive facial features** ²⁾[that participants associated with each emotion].

1) 「allow+목적어+to부정사」 구문으로 '~가 …하도록 허락하다'의 의미이다.
2)는 바로 앞의 the expressive facial features를 수식하는 관계절로, 목적격 관계대명사 that은 생략할 수 있다.

Do It Yourself

03 다음 글의 요지로 가장 적절한 것은?

Reading great plays provides a more intense experience than most novels can provide, and seeing them is even better. And acting in them brings still greater understanding of their meaning and importance. Whether it's a Shakespearean tragedy or a Feydeau farce, the inner workings of a great play become much clearer when you act in it. What you learn, of course, enhances your understanding of other works of literature. Many college actors have found that, despite the time given over to appearing in a play, their grades in literature and even history courses can improve because of the knowledge they've acquired while rehearsing and performing a classic work.

*Feydeau 페도(프랑스의 극작가) **farce 소극, 익살극

① 연기력은 천부적인 자질보다 연습에 더 좌우된다.
② 자연스러운 연기는 많은 연습과 노력의 결과이다.
③ 다양한 경험은 연기를 하는 데 도움이 될 수 있다.
④ 극에서 연기를 하면 그 작품을 더 잘 이해할 수 있다.
⑤ 고전극에서 연기하는 것은 더 많은 연습을 필요로 한다.

지문에서의 어휘의 뜻을 써보고 해설에서 확인하세요.

- play
- intense
- novel
- act
- understanding
- tragedy
- inner
- enhance
- literature
- appear
- course
- acquire
- rehearse
- classic work

구문 주요 구문을 살펴보아요.

7행 Many college actors have found [1)][that, [2){**despite the time** [3)(given over to appearing in a play)}, their grades in literature and even history courses can improve because of **the knowledge** [4){they've acquired [5)(while rehearsing and performing a classic work)}].

1)은 have found의 목적어 역할을 하는 명사절이고, 2)의 despite은 전치사로 '~에도 불구하고'라는 의미이다.

3)은 앞의 the time을 수식하는 과거분사구로, given은 the time과 수동 관계이며 given 앞에 which is가 생략되었다.

4)는 the knowledge를 수식하는 관계절로, they've 앞에 목적격 관계대명사 that 또는 which가 생략되었다.

5)는 분사구문으로, 의미를 명확히 하기 위해 접속사 while(~하는 동안)을 생략하지 않았다.

04 다음 글의 요지로 가장 적절한 것은?

Sales is an important function for every store. Shops that sell basic products, such as chocolates or magazines do not need to do much selling. Most customers come in to buy something, choose the goods they want, pay, and leave. However, customers expect more help and advice if they want to buy an expensive item, such as a television or car. Stores which sell these types of products therefore need trained sales staff who are friendly and knowledgeable. They must be able to describe and demonstrate their products, and link these to the customer's specific needs. There are many benefits to having well-trained salespeople. They can turn many inquiries into firm sales and build strong links with customers.

① 적절한 시기에 상품을 전시해야 효과를 거둘 수 있다.
② 고가의 상품을 팔 때는 잘 훈련된 판매직원이 필요하다.
③ 고객에 대한 판매원의 태도가 판매 실적에 영향을 미친다.
④ 상품에 대한 직접적인 홍보는 고객과의 관계를 강화할 수 있다.
⑤ 고가 상품 판매 후의 꾸준한 고객 관리가 대량 판매를 촉진한다.

지문에서의 어휘의 뜻을 써보고 해설에서 확인하세요.

- sales
- function
- product
- goods
- staff
- knowledgeable
- describe
- demonstrate
- link
- specific
- need
- benefit
- inquiry
- firm

구문 주요 구문을 살펴보아요.

6행 **Stores** 1)[which sell these types of products] therefore need **trained sales staff** 2)[who are **friendly** and **knowledgeable**].

Stores가 문장의 주어이고, need가 동사로, 1)은 주어인 Stores를 수식하는 관계절이다.
2)는 문장의 목적어인 trained sales staff를 수식하는 관계절이며, who 다음에 are가 쓰인 것은 staff가 형태상은 단수이지만 집합적 의미로 복수로 쓰일 수 있기 때문이다. friendly와 knowledgeable은 be동사 are의 보어로 쓰인 형용사로, and로 인해 병렬구조를 이룬다.

범위 A, B: Unit 01
C, D: Unit 02

A

다음 영어는 우리말로, 우리말은 영어로 옮겨 쓰시오.

01	condition	11	fear
02	train	12	nervous
03	cultivate	13	semester
04	capacity	14	extra
05	complex	15	유연성[융통성] 있는
06	specialist	16	acknowledge
07	complicated	17	access
08	분야	18	properly
09	cope with	19	available
10	불안감	20	extend

B

다음 각 네모 안의 말을 어법에 맞는 순서로 고쳐 쓰시오.

01 They write in a language different from one / the / they / use / would if they were talking to a friend. 🔗 Link p.10 01번

➡ ____

02 This helps you lower the level of your anxiety and stress, increasing your confidence and easier / presentation / making / the / much. 🔗 Link p.11 02번

➡ ____

03 If you achieve your goal before the semester is over, you need to be to / flexible / acknowledge / enough that you have done what you set out to do and then set a new goal. 🔗 Link p.12 03번

➡ ____

04 Moisture is an essential component of a successful composting effort, it's likely that you'll need to moisten the organic matter regularly decomposing / keep / properly / it / to. 🔗 Link p.13 04번

➡ ____

C 다음 영어는 우리말로, 우리말은 영어로 옮겨 쓰시오.

01 critical ____________________   11 identify ____________________

02 self-esteem ____________________   12 universal ____________________

03 earn ____________________   13 tragedy ____________________

04 보장하다, 보증하다 ____________________   14 enhance ____________________

05 competitor ____________________   15 acquire ____________________

06 vacuum ____________________   16 rehearse ____________________

07 contrast ____________________   17 function ____________________

08 existing ____________________   18 goods ____________________

09 중립적인 ____________________   19 describe ____________________

10 randomly ____________________   20 demonstrate ____________________

D 다음 각 문장의 밑줄 친 부분을 어법에 맞게 바르게 고쳐 쓰시오.

01 That's why if you have a truly new product, **which is often better** to say what the product is not, rather than what it is. 🔗 Link p.16 01번

➡ ____________________

02 The responses **allowed researchers identifying** the expressive facial features that participants associated with each emotion. 🔗 Link p.17 02번

➡ ____________________

03 **That you learn**, of course, enhances your understanding of other works of literature. 🔗 Link p.18 03번

➡ ____________________

04 Stores which sell these types of products therefore need trained sales staff who **are friendly and knowledgeably**. 🔗 Link p.19 04번

➡ ____________________

03 주제 추론

유형 특징
1. 주어진 지문을 읽고, 글의 주제를 고른다.
2. 무엇에 관한 글인가를 묻는 문제이며, 핵심 소재에 대한 필자의 관점을 파악한다.
3. 매년 수능에 1문제가 꾸준히 출제된다.

Example

다음 글의 주제로 가장 적절한 것은?

| 고2 전국연합 |

음성파일

The practice of medicine has meant the average age to which people in all nations may expect to live is higher than it has been in recorded history, and there is a better opportunity than ever for an individual to survive serious disorders such as cancers, brain tumors and heart diseases. However, longer life spans mean more people, worsening food and housing supply difficulties. In addition, medical services are still not well distributed, and accessibility remains a problem in many parts of the world. Improvements in medical technology shift the balance of population (to the young at first, and then to the old). They also tie up money and resources in facilities and trained people, costing more money, and affecting what can be spent on other things.

① benefits and losses of medical development
② inequality of medical care around the world
③ constant efforts to fight off serious diseases   ☐ : 소재 예상 가능
④ endless competition to lengthen human life span
⑤ pros and cons regarding increasing medical budgets

어휘 중요한 어휘를 확인하세요.

practice (의료 등의) (전문) 행위   medicine 의료, 의학, 약   mean 결과를 낳다, 의미하다   average age 평균 연령
recorded history 기록된 역사   opportunity 기회   disorder 질병, 질환   cancer 암   tumor 종양   life span 수명
distribute 분배하다   accessibility 접근성, 이용 가능성   improvement 향상, 개선   shift 이동시키다, 이동하다   tie up (돈을 쉽게
쓸 수 없도록) 묶어 두다   resource 자원   facility 시설   affect 영향을 미치다

구문 주요 구문을 살펴보아요.

1행 1)[The practice of medicine has meant **the average age** 2){**to which** people in all nations may expect to live} is higher than it has been in recorded history], and 3)[there is **a better opportunity** than ever 4){for an individual} 5){to survive serious disorders such as cancers, brain tumors and heart diseases}].

1)과 3) 두 개의 절이 등위접속사 and로 인해 병렬 연결되었다.

2)는 the average age를 수식하여 '모든 나라에서 사람들이 살 것이라고 기대하는 평균 연령'이라는 의미를 나타낸다. which 이하가 〈주어+동사〉가 갖추어진 완전한 절이며, '~(세) 까지'라는 의미를 나타내도록 which 앞에 전치사 to가 쓰였다.

5)는 a better opportunity를 수식하는 to부정사구로, 4)를 의미상의 주어로 삼는다.

How to solve　이런 방법으로 접근하세요.

Step 1　선택지를 통해 소재 예상하기　선택지를 먼저 읽고 글의 방향을 예측하세요.

① benefits and losses of **medical development** → 의학 발전과 관련된 것

② inequality of **medical care** around the world → 의료와 관련된 것

③ constant efforts to fight off **serious diseases** → 질병과 관련된 것

④ endless competition to lengthen **human life span** → 인간의 수명과 관련된 것

⑤ pros and cons regarding increasing **medical budgets** → 의료 예산과 관련된 것

➡ **예상 소재**　의료 및 의학 또는 인간 수명이나 질병과 관련된 것

Step 2　반복되는 표현을 통해 핵심 파악하기

· The practice of medicine ~ (의료 행위)

· ~ medical services ~ (의료 서비스)

· ~ medical technology ~ (의료 기술)

➡ **핵심**　의료+의료 기술의 향상

Step 3　핵심에 대한 견해 종합하기

· ~ the average age to which people in all nations may expect to live is higher ~
(모든 나라에서 사람들이 살 것이라고 기대하는 평균 연령이 더 높아진다) → 긍정적 측면 1

· ~ a better opportunity than ever for an individual to survive serious disorders ~
(한 개인이 심각한 질병에서 살아남을 더 높은 가능성) → 긍정적 측면 2

· However, ~ worsening food and housing supply difficulties.
(많아진 사람이 식량과 주택 공급의 어려움을 악화시킨다.) → 역효과 1

· In addition, medical services are still not well distributed ~
(의료 서비스가 여전히 제대로 분배되지 않는다) → 역효과 2

· They also tie up money and resources ~ costing more money ~
(돈과 자원을 묶어 두어 비용을 더 들게 한다)

➡ **견해 종합**　의료 및 의학 발전은 긍정적인 면과 부정적인 면을 모두 가져온다.

Step 4　정답 확인하기

① 의학 발전의 이익과 손실 → 전체 내용을 모두 포괄하므로 정답!

② 세계 전역의 의료 불평등 → 일부 내용에 해당하는 지엽적인 선택지

③ 심각한 질병과 싸우려는 끊임없는 노력 → 글에 언급되었지만 핵심은 아님

④ 인간의 수명을 늘리려는 끊임없는 경쟁 → 일부 내용에 해당하는 지엽적인 선택지

⑤ 의료 예산을 늘리려는 것에 대한 찬성과 반대 → 의료 예산에 관한 찬반 의견은 언급되지 않음

Do It Yourself

01 다음 글의 주제로 가장 적절한 것은?

| 고1 전국연합 |

Have you been abroad? Do you travel a lot? Then you know what I'm talking about. Wherever you go on this globe, you can get along with English. Either most people speak it anyhow, or there is at least somebody around who can communicate in this language. But then, you realize that mostly there's something you may find odd about the way English is used there. If you are abroad, English is likely to be somewhat different from the way you speak it. Well, if you stay there, wherever that is, for a while, you'll get used to this. And if you stay there even longer, you may even pick up some of these features and begin to sound like the locals. What this example teaches us is: English is no longer just "one language."

① pros and cons of travelling abroad
② localization of English in different places
③ necessity for systematic English education
④ various methods to improve English ability
⑤ how to get along with local residents abroad

지문에서의 어휘의 뜻을
써보고 해설에서 확인하세요.

- abroad
- globe
- get along
- communicate
- odd
- get used to
- pick up
- feature
- local
- pros and cons
- localization
- systematic
- method
- get along with
- resident

구문 주요 구문을 살펴보아요.

9행 And 1) [if you stay there **even** longer], you **may** even 2) **pick up** some of these features and 3) **begin** to sound like the locals.

1)은 조건의 부사절이며, 그 안의 even은 비교급을 수식하여 '훨씬'의 의미를 나타낸다.

2) pick up과 3) begin은 조동사 may에 병렬로 연결되며, pick up some of these features는 '이러한 특징의 일부를 배우다'라고 해석할 수 있다.

02 다음 글의 주제로 가장 적절한 것은? | 고1 전국연합 |

Storyteller Syd Lieberman suggests that it is the story in history that provides the nail to hang facts on. Students remember historical facts when they are tied to a story. According to a report, a high school in Boulder, Colorado, is currently experimenting with a study of presentation of historical material. Storytellers present material in dramatic context to the students, and group discussion follows. Students are encouraged to read further. In contrast, another group of students is involved in traditional research/report techniques. The study indicates that the material presented by the storytellers has much more interest and personal impact than that gained via the traditional method.

① why students should learn history
② essential elements of historical dramas
③ advantages of traditional teaching methods
④ benefits of storytelling in teaching history
⑤ importance of having balanced views on history

지문에서의 어휘의 뜻을
써보고 해설에서 확인하세요.

- nail
- hang
- fact
- tie
- according to
- currently
- presentation
- dramatic
- context
- be involved in
- indicate
- via
- method

구문 주요 구문을 살펴보아요.

9행 The study indicates ^1) [that **the material** ^2) {presented by the storytellers} has much more interest and personal impact than ^3) **that** ^4) {gained via the traditional method}].

1)은 indicates의 목적어로 쓰인 명사절이다.
2)는 앞에 있는 the material을 수식하는 분사구이다.
3) that은 the material의 중복을 피하기 위해 쓰인 대명사이다.
4)는 앞에 있는 that을 수식하는 분사구이다.

Do It Yourself

03 다음 글의 주제로 가장 적절한 것은?

A woman can do several unrelated things at the same time. She can talk on a telephone, at the same time as cooking a new recipe and watching television. Or she can drive a car, put on make-up and listen to the radio while talking on a hands-free telephone. In contrast, if a man is cooking a recipe and you talk to him, he is likely to become angry because he can't follow the written instructions and listen at the same time. If a man is shaving and you talk to him he'll cut himself. In some cases, a man might accuse a woman of making him miss a turn on the highway because she was chatting to him at the time. One woman jokingly told us that if she was angry with her husband, she would talk to him while he was hammering a nail.

① gender differences in multitasking
② benefits of sharing household chores
③ things that cause couples to disagree
④ women's favorite activities in everyday life
⑤ the importance of concentration while driving

지문에서의 어휘의 뜻을 써보고 해설에서 확인하세요.

- unrelated
- recipe
- put on make-up
- hands-free
- in contrast
- instructions
- shave
- cut oneself
- accuse A of B
- hammer
- gender
- multitasking
- household chores
- concentration

구문 주요 구문을 살펴보아요.

5행 In contrast, 1)[**if** a man is cooking a recipe and you talk to him], 2)[he is likely to become angry] 3)[**because** he **can't** 4){follow the written instructions} and 5){listen at the same time}].

1)은 if가 이끄는 조건절로, 남자가 동시에 두 가지를 하게 만드는 상황을 말하며, 2)는 주절이다.
3)은 because가 이끄는 부사절이다. 조동사 can't에 4)와 5)가 병렬로 연결되었다.

04 다음 글의 주제로 가장 적절한 것은?

We live in the present and in the future — and we are proud of doing so. But without a strong sense of the past, the present is meaningless and the future will be filled with danger. Hitler is dead, but the spirit he generated is not dead, and will never die. Unless we learn what that spirit means, and how it acts under certain circumstances, we will not be able to cope with its return. Ancient Greece is dead, but its problems remain: especially the one problem that great democracy could not solve — how to achieve both freedom and security at the same time. Learning why Greece failed may help us find some happier solution. We know that in every individual's life the past remains active and influential, even when we are unconscious of it. The same is true of nations: the waves keep widening for centuries.

① the difficulty of predicting the future
② changes in the interpretation of history
③ things to be done for a democratic society
④ the necessity to have a good sense of history
⑤ the relationship between freedom and security

지문에서의 어휘의 뜻을 써보고 해설에서 확인하세요.

- present
- sense
- spirit
- generate
- circumstance
- cope with
- democracy
- solve
- security
- solution
- influential
- unconscious
- be true of
- wave

구문 주요 구문을 살펴보아요.

5행 1)[**Unless** we learn 2){what that spirit means}, and 3){how it acts under certain circumstances}], we 4)**will not be able to** cope with its return.

1)은 '~하지 않으면'이라는 의미를 가진 접속사 Unless가 이끄는 부사절이다. 그 안에서 learn의 목적어로 두 개의 간접의문문 2)와 3)이 쓰였으며, 각각은 '그 망령이 무엇을 의미하는지'와 '그것이 특정한 상황에서 어떻게 작용하는지'라고 해석할 수 있다.

4) 조동사 will과 can은 동시에 나란히 쓰일 수 없으므로 can 대신에 같은 의미를 가진 be able to가 쓰였다.

제목 추론

유형 특징
1. 주어진 지문을 읽고, 적절한 제목을 고른다.
2. 제목 선택지는 보통 함축적이고 상징적인 표현으로 제시된다.
3. 매년 수능에 1문제가 꾸준히 출제된다.

Example

🎧 음성파일

다음 글의 제목으로 가장 적절한 것은?　　　　　　　　　　　　| 고1 전국연합 |

Near an honesty box, in which people placed coffee fund contributions, researchers at
Newcastle University in the UK alternately displayed images of eyes and of flowers. Each
image was displayed for a week at a time. During all the weeks in which eyes were
displayed, bigger contributions were made than during the weeks when flowers were
5 displayed. Over the ten weeks of the study, contributions during the 'eyes weeks' were
almost three times higher than those made during the 'flowers weeks.' It was suggested
that 'the evolved psychology of cooperation is highly sensitive to subtle cues of being
watched,' and that the findings may have implications for how to provide effective nudges
toward socially beneficial outcomes.

*nudge 넌지시 권하기

① Is Honesty the Best Policy?　　　　② Flowers Work Better than Eyes
③ Contributions Can Increase Self-Respect　　④ The More Watched, The Less Cooperative
⑤ Eyes: Secret Helper to Make Society Better

어휘　중요한 어휘를 확인하세요.

honesty box 양심 상자　　fund 값, 자금　　contribution 기부, 공헌　　alternately 번갈아 가며　　display 놓다, 보여 주다
suggest 말하다, 제안하다　　evolved 진전된, 진화된　　psychology 심리　　cooperation 협력, 협동　　sensitive 민감한
subtle 미묘한　　cue 신호　　finding 결과　　implication 암시　　beneficial 이로운　　outcome 결과, 성과

구문　주요 구문을 살펴보아요.

6행　1)It was suggested 2)[that 'the evolved psychology of cooperation is highly sensitive to subtle cues of
being watched],' and 3)[that the findings may have **implications for** 4){**how to** provide effective nudges toward
socially beneficial outcomes}].

1) It은 형식상의 주어이며, 병렬구조로 연결된 2)와 3)이 내용상의 주어로, '~라는 것이 말하여졌다'라는 의미이다.
4)는 전치사 for의 목적어 역할을 한다. 「how to+동사원형」은 '~하는 방법'으로 해석할 수 있다.

How to solve   이런 방법으로 접근하세요.

Step 1   선택지를 통해 소재 예상하기

① Is **Honesty** the Best Policy? → 정직과 관련된 것

② **Flowers** Work Better than **Eyes** → 꽃과 (지켜보는) 눈을 비교

③ **Contributions** Can Increase **Self-Respect** → 기부 및 자기 존중과 관련된 것

④ The More **Watched**, The Less **Cooperative** → 보는 눈이 있는 상황과 협조적인 것의 관계

⑤ **Eyes**: Secret Helper to Make Society Better → (지켜보는) 눈이 사회에 미치는 영향

➡ **예상 소재**   정직과 기부 및 협조에 관한 것

Step 2   글의 구조 파악하기   글이 어떤 흐름으로 전개되는지 파악하세요.

- Near an honesty box, ~ displayed images of eyes and of flowers.

  (커피 값을 기부하는 양심 상자 가까이에 사람의 눈 이미지와 꽃 이미지를 번갈아 가며 놓아두었다.)

➡ **도입부**   연구 방법 소개

- ~ the 'eye weeks' were almost three times higher than those made during the 'flowers weeks.'

  ('눈 주간'의 기부금이 '꽃 주간'의 기부금보다 거의 세 배나 많았다.)

➡ **중반부**   연구 결과

- ~ 'the evolved psychology of cooperation is highly sensitive to ~ of being watched,' ~

  ('진전된 협력 심리가 누군가가 지켜보고 있다는 미묘한 신호에 아주 민감하다.')

- ~ the findings may have implications ~ toward socially beneficial outcomes

  (결과는 사회적으로 이익이 되는 성과를 내게끔 어떻게 효과적으로 넌지시 권할 것인가를 암시한다)

➡ **후반부**   연구 결과 분석 및 시사점

Step 3   내용 종합하여 요지 도출하기

➡ **요지**   지켜보는 눈의 존재 여부가 정직, 기부, 협조, 행동의 차이에 영향을 주어 사회적 성과를 내도록 하는 방법을 암시한다.

Step 4   정답 확인하기

① 정직이 최선의 방책인가? → 양심 상자가 언급되기는 했으나 무관한 내용임

② 꽃이 눈보다 효과가 더 크다 → 연구 결과와 반대되는 내용임

③ 기부는 자기 존중을 증가시킬 수 있다 → 자기 존중에 관한 글은 아님

④ 더 많이 지켜봐질수록, 덜 협력적이다 → 연구 결과와 반대되는 내용임

⑤ 눈: 사회를 더 좋게 만드는 비밀 도우미 → 요지에 부합하는 주제이므로 정답!

Do It Yourself

01 다음 글의 제목으로 가장 적절한 것은? | 고1 전국연합 |

While you are at work, you may dream about a month of Sundays, but your boss wishes for a week of Tuesdays. What makes Tuesday special? Monday is overloaded with meetings to "get things moving," which aren't very productive. Wednesday is
5 "hump day" — just get over it, a worker thinks. On Thursday, people become exhausted; and on Friday, everybody is thinking about the weekend. On Tuesdays, employees hit peak performance because they are very focused on day-to-day activities. Also, Tuesday is usually the first day of the week that
10 they're focused on their own task. In 10 hours, they're doing 20 hours worth of work.

*hump 고비, 난관

① Do You Want to Be More Creative?
② What Your Workers Are Waiting for
③ Weekends Make You More Productive
④ How to Make Your Own Weekly Schedule
⑤ Why Is Tuesday the Most Productive Day?

지문에서의 어휘의 뜻을
써보고 해설에서 확인하세요.

- special
- overloaded
- productive
- get over
- exhausted
- peak
- performance
- task

구문 주요 구문을 살펴보아요.

3행 Monday is overloaded with **meetings to "get things moving,"** [1][which aren't very productive].

[1]은 계속적 용법으로 쓰인 관계절로, meetings to "get things moving"이 관계대명사 which의 선행사이다. 이처럼 관계대명사 which가 계속적 용법으로 쓰인 관계절은 '(그런데) 그것[그것들]은 ~ 하다'라고 해석할 수 있다.

02 다음 글의 제목으로 가장 적절한 것은?

| 고1 전국연합 |

Simply providing students with complex texts is not enough for learning to happen. Assigning students to independently read, think about, and then write about a complex text is not enough, either. Quality questions are one way that teachers can check
5 students' understanding of the text. Questions can also promote students' search for evidence and their need to return to the text to deepen their understanding. Teachers take an active role in developing and deepening students' comprehension by asking questions that cause them to read the text again, resulting in
10 multiple readings of the same text. In other words, these text-based questions provide students with a purpose for rereading, which is critical for understanding complex texts.

① Too Much Homework Is Harmful
② Questioning for Better Comprehension
③ Too Many Tests Make Students Tired
④ Questions That Science Can't Answer Yet
⑤ There Is Not Always Just One Right Answer

지문에서의 어휘의 뜻을
써보고 해설에서 확인하세요.

- provide A with B
- complex
- assign
- independently
- quality
- promote
- evidence
- deepen
- active
- comprehension
- result in
- multiple
- text-based
- purpose
- critical

구문 주요 구문을 살펴보아요.

7행 Teachers take an active role in **developing** and **deepening**
1)[students' comprehension] by asking **questions** 2)[that **cause them to read** the text again], 3)[resulting in multiple readings of the same text].

1)은 동명사 developing과 deepening의 공통 목적어이다.
2)는 questions를 수식하는 관계절이며, 「cause+목적어+to부정사(구)」는 '~을 …하도록 유발하다'의 의미이다.
3)은 앞부분 전체 내용을 의미상 주어로 삼아 그 결과를 설명하는 분사구이다.

Do It Yourself

03 다음 글의 제목으로 가장 적절한 것은?

Humans are naturally programmed to distrust strangers, especially where touching is concerned. Therefore, one man's intention to give out hugs to strangers was unique enough to prompt the crowd to be suspicious. Warily, they watched as he offered free hugs. Could they trust this stranger and his intentions? Was he just having fun? As the first woman approached and hugged the blindfolded man, the crowd's mixed feelings and reactions disappeared, and others followed her lead. Some gave brief hugs; others clung to him as if greeting a long-lost friend. Regardless of the length of the touch, giving each other a hug created an environment for the power of connection and trust.

① Free Hugs: The Courage to Connect
② Why Is It So Hard to Talk to Strangers?
③ What to Do If Approached by a Stranger
④ Hugging Is the Best Way of Acknowledging Others
⑤ What Is the Difference between Intention and Motivation?

지문에서의 어휘의 뜻을 써보고 해설에서 확인하세요.

- be programmed to
- distrust
- hug
- unique
- prompt
- suspicious
- warily
- blindfolded
- lead
- cling to
- long-lost
- connection
- acknowledge
- motivation

구문 주요 구문을 살펴보아요.

1행 Humans are naturally programmed to distrust strangers, [1)][especially **where** touching is concerned].

1)은 부사절이며 where는 접속사 역할을 한다. 접속사 where는 '~한 경우[상황]'라는 뜻으로 '특히 접촉이 연관될 경우에'로 해석한다.

04 다음 글의 제목으로 가장 적절한 것은?

A report has found that more than half of high school students never shower after their physical education(P.E.) classes. Researchers suggest that students don't want to sweat and take a shower, so they are less active in physical education classes.
5 The researchers questioned almost 4,000 students in schools in Essex, England. Lead researcher Dr. Gavin Sandercock said he was surprised at how rarely students showered. He said: "If the unwillingness to shower is a barrier to working up a sweat, we need to tackle this unwillingness to promote physical activity at
10 schools." The report did not look at the exact reasons why the students did not shower after their physical education classes. However, there are other studies that point out that fear of bullying and humiliation may be behind the reluctance of some students to shower. Undressing in front of peers may be too
15 much for some students, and many students have concerns about their body image.

*bully (약자를) 괴롭히다

지문에서의 어휘의 뜻을 써보고 해설에서 확인하세요.

- physical education class
- sweat
- unwillingness
- barrier
- tackle
- promote
- humiliation
- reluctance
- undress
- concern
- academic
- enhance
- address

① Motivation Matters in High School Students
② After P.E. Classes Students Just Don't Shower
③ Effects of Academic Success on Physical Activity
④ Psychological and Social Benefits of Playing Sports
⑤ Enhancing Classroom Approaches for Addressing Barriers to Learning

구문 주요 구문을 살펴보아요.

6행 Lead researcher Dr. Gavin Sandercock said ¹⁾[he was surprised at ²⁾{how **rarely** students showered}].

1)은 said의 목적어로 쓰인 명사절로 he 앞에 접속사 that이 생략되었다.

2)는 전치사 at의 목적어로 쓰인 의문사절인데, 그 안의 rarely는 부정의 의미를 지닌 부사로 '드물게, 좀처럼 ~하지 않다'의 뜻이다.

Unit 05 함축 의미 추론

Example

🎧 음성파일

밑줄 친 at the "sweet spot"이 다음 글에서 의미하는 바로 가장 적절한 것은?　　　| 고1 전국연합 |

For almost all things in life, there can be too much of a good thing. Even the best things
→ 화제 제시: 문제 제기　　　　　　　　　　　　　　　　　　　　　　→ 앞문장 내용 부연 1
in life aren't so great in excess. This concept has been discussed at least as far back as
Aristotle. He argued that being virtuous means finding a balance. For example, people
　　　　　　　　　　　　　　　　　　　　　　　　　　　　　　　　→ 사례 제시
should be brave, but if someone is too brave they become reckless. People should be
→ 사례 1: 용감함에 관한 것　　　　　　　　　　　　　　　　　→ 사례 2: 신뢰에 관한 것
5 trusting, but if someone is too trusting they are considered gullible. For each of these
　　　　　　　　　　　　　　　　　　　　　　→ 주제문
traits, it is best to avoid both deficiency and excess. The best way is to live at the "sweet
　　　　　　　　　　　　　　　　　　　　　　　　　→ 핵심과 관련 있는 표현에 밑줄
spot" that maximizes well-being. Aristotle's suggestion is that virtue is the midpoint,
where someone is neither too generous nor too stingy, neither too afraid nor recklessly
brave.

*excess 과잉　**gullible 잘 속아 넘어가는

① at the time of a biased decision
② in the area of material richness
③ away from social pressure
④ in the middle of two extremes
⑤ at the moment of instant pleasure

어휘　중요한 어휘를 확인하세요.

concept 개념　　Aristotle 아리스토텔레스　　virtuous 미덕이 있는　　brave 용감한　　reckless 무모한　　trusting 신뢰하는
deficiency 부족, 결핍　　spot 장소, 지점　　maximize 극대화하다, 최대화하다　　well-being 행복, 안녕　　suggestion 말, 제안
virtue 미덕　　midpoint 중간 지점　　generous 관대한　　stingy 인색한　　recklessly 무모하게

구문　주요 구문을 살펴보아요.

7행 Aristotle's suggestion is [1][that virtue is **the midpoint**, [2]{where someone is **neither** too generous **nor** too stingy, **neither** too afraid **nor** recklessly brave}].

[1]은 문장의 주격 보어 역할을 하는 명사절이며, 주어와 연결하여 '아리스토텔레스의 제안은 ~라는 것이다'라는 의미로 해석할 수 있다.
[2]는 the midpoint를 수식하는 관계절이며, '그곳에서는 ~하다'라는 의미로 해석할 수 있다. 「neither ~ nor ....」 구문은 '~도 아니며 … 역시 아닌'의 의미이다.

How to solve 이런 방법으로 접근하세요.

Step 1   밑줄 친 말의 표면적 의미 해석하기   우선 해석을 통해 의미를 짐작하세요.

- at the "sweet spot": "달콤한 지점"에서 (좋은 것, 긍정적 의미임을 파악 가능)

Step 2   도입부에서 제기하는 문제 파악하기   무엇에 관해 말하려는 글인지 알아야죠.

- For almost all things in life, there can be too much of a good thing.

  (인생의 거의 모든 것에는, 좋은 것에도 지나침이 있을 수 있다.)
- Even the best things in life aren't so great in excess.

  (심지어 인생에서 최상의 것도 지나치면 그리 좋지 않다.)

Step 3   구체적인 사례 살펴보기

- ~ people should be brave, ~ they become reckless.

  (사람들은 용감해져야 하지만, 너무 용감하다면 그 사람은 무모해진다.)
- People should be trusting, ~ they are considered gullible.

  (사람들은 (타인을) 신뢰해야 하지만, 너무 신뢰한다면 잘 속아 넘어가는 사람으로 여겨진다.)

Step 4   주제문을 토대로 밑줄 친 말의 의미 파악하기

주제문   For each of these traits, it is best to avoid both deficiency and excess.

(이러한 각각의 특성에 있어, 부족과 과잉 둘 다를 피하는 것이 최상이다.)

밑줄 친 말   The best way is to live at the "sweet spot" ~ (최상의 방법은 'sweet spot'에 머무르는 것이다)

➡ at the "sweet spot"   = 최상의 지점에 = 부족과 과잉을 피하는 지점에 = 두 극단의 중간 지점에

Step 5   정답 확인하기

① 편향된 결정의 시기에 → 한쪽으로 치우치지 않는 것에 관한 내용이므로 부적절함

② 물질적 부유함의 지점에 → 내용과 무관함

③ 사회적 압박을 피해 → 내용과 무관함

④ 두 극단의 중간에 → 글의 요지와 연관된 정답!

⑤ 순간적 즐거움의 순간에 → 내용과 무관함

Do It Yourself

01 밑줄 친 information blinded가 다음 글에서 의미하는 바로 가장 적절한 것은?

| 고1 전국연합 |

Technology has doubtful advantages. We must balance too much information versus using only the right information and keeping the decision-making process simple. The Internet has made so much free information available on any issue that we think we have to consider all of it in order to make a decision. So we keep searching for answers on the Internet. This makes us information blinded, like deer in headlights, when trying to make personal, business, or other decisions. To be successful in anything today, we have to keep in mind that in the land of the blind, a one-eyed person can accomplish the seemingly impossible. The one-eyed person understands the power of keeping any analysis simple and will be the decision maker when he uses his one eye of intuition.

*intuition 직관

① unwilling to accept others' ideas
② unable to access free information
③ unable to make decisions due to too much information
④ indifferent to the lack of available information
⑤ willing to take risks in decision-making

지문에서의 어휘의 뜻을 써보고 해설에서 확인하세요.

- doubtful
- balance ~ versus ...
- decision-making process
- consider
- blinded
- accomplish
- seemingly
- analysis
- decision maker

구문 주요 구문을 살펴보아요.

1행 We must balance too much information **1)versus** **2)**[using only the right information] and **3)**[keeping the decision-making process simple].

1) versus는 '~에 대비하여'라는 의미의 전치사이다.
2)와 3)은 versus의 공통 목적어로 쓰인 동명사구이다.

02 밑줄 친 'The body works the same way.'가 다음 글에서 의미하는 바로 가장 적절한 것은?

| 고2 전국연합 |

The body tends to accumulate problems, often beginning with one small, seemingly minor imbalance. This problem causes another subtle imbalance, which triggers another, then several more. In the end, you get a symptom. It's like lining up a series of dominoes. All you need to do is knock down the first one and many others will fall too. What caused the last one to fall? Obviously it wasn't the one before it, or the one before that, but the first one. The body works the same way. The initial problem is often unnoticed. It's not until some of the later "dominoes" fall that more obvious clues and symptoms appear. In the end, you get a headache, fatigue or depression — or even disease. When you try to treat the last domino — treat just the end-result symptom — the cause of the problem isn't addressed. The first domino is the cause, or primary problem.

*accumulate 축적하다

① There is no definite order in treating an illness.
② Minor health problems are solved by themselves.
③ You get more and more inactive as you get older.
④ It'll never be too late to cure the end-result symptom.
⑤ The final symptom stems from the first minor problem.

지문에서의 어휘의 뜻을 써보고 해설에서 확인하세요.

- minor
- imbalance
- subtle
- trigger
- symptom
- line up
- a series of
- knock down
- obviously
- initial
- unnoticed
- clue
- fatigue
- depression
- end-result
- address
- primary

구문 주요 구문을 살펴보아요.

1행 The body tends to accumulate **problems**, 1)[often beginning with one small, seemingly minor imbalance].

1)은 분사구문으로, 앞에 있는 problems를 의미상의 주어로 한다. 즉, 'and they often begin with ~'의 뜻이다.

Do It Yourself

03 밑줄 친 'Garbage In — Garbage Out'이 다음 글에서 의미하는 바로 가장 적절한 것은?

Everyone is agreed that bad logic makes for poor thinking. So naturally it must follow that good logic makes for good thinking. This is, of course, complete nonsense. Good logic is one requirement of good thinking but by no means the only one. Water is a requirement of soup but few would accept a bowl of hot water as a satisfactory soup. Perfect logic can only service the perceptions on which it is required to act. If these are inadequate then the perfectness of the logic will not improve them and will still give a poor answer. No one has ever suggested that a computer that works perfectly well can by itself always produce the correct answer. This is reliant on the input of the data not the machine itself. Hence the word GIGO which means 'Garbage In — Garbage Out'.

① Logic applies differently depending on the situation.
② Almost all facts cannot be fully proved by experiments.
③ Various factors can produce unexpectedly good outcomes.
④ The quality of the input decides the quality of the output.
⑤ The process of logical thinking uses reasoning consistently.

지문에서의 어휘의 뜻을 써보고 해설에서 확인하세요.

- logic
- make for
- poor
- complete
- nonsense
- requirement
- by no means
- satisfactory
- service
- perception
- inadequate
- reliant
- input
- hence
- output

구문 주요 구문을 살펴보아요.

6행 **Perfect logic** can only service **the perceptions** [1)][on which **it** is required to act].

1)은 the perceptions를 수식하는 〈전치사+관계대명사절〉로, 그 안에서 it은 문장의 주어인 Perfect logic을 의미한다. 즉, '완벽한 논리는 그것이 작동하도록 요구되는 인식을 제공할 뿐이다.'로 해석할 수 있다.

04

밑줄 친 the downward trend in work hours has hardly missed a beat이 다음 글에서 의미하는 바로 가장 적절한 것은?

In the United States as a whole, the average work week has remained unchanged for more than half a century. In fact, many experts believe that leisure time has actually been decreasing. Historian Juliet Schor, for example, argues persuasively that the average American has less time to himself or herself than he or she did twenty years ago. This loss of leisure time is not an accident. Schor presents evidence that unions in the United States have focused little attention on the question of working hours, preferring instead to direct their energies toward issues of salary and job security. In Europe, the downward trend in work hours has hardly missed a beat. Organized labor in Europe has kept the issue of shorter working hours at the top of its agenda throughout the postwar period.

① Rights of the workers have been increasingly emphasized.
② The link between leisure time and productivity is not clear.
③ Unions have achieved objectives mainly through political action.
④ The overall situation in Europe is the same as that in the United States.
⑤ Efforts to reduce working hours in Europe have continued to succeed.

지문에서의 어휘의 뜻을 써보고 해설에서 확인하세요.

- expert
- leisure
- persuasively
- loss
- accident
- evidence
- union
- prefer
- direct
- salary
- job security
- miss a beat
- organized
- labor
- agenda

구문 주요 구문을 살펴보아요.

7행 Schor presents **evidence** 1)[that **unions in the United States** have focused little attention on the question of working hours, 2){preferring instead to direct their energies toward issues of salary and job security}].

1)은 evidence와 동격 관계인 절로, '~라는 증거'라고 해석한다.
2)는 동시동작을 표현하는 분사구로, '~하면서'라고 해석한다. 분사구의 주체는 unions in the United States이다.

How was it? 배운 내용을 확인해보세요.

A

다음 영어는 우리말로, 우리말은 영어로 옮겨 쓰시오.

01 disorder		**11** circumstance	
02 distribute		**12** democracy	
03 odd		**13** unconscious	
04 feature		**14** alternately	
05 hang		**15** evolved	
06 극적인		**16** subtle	
07 via		**17** peak	
08 recipe		**18** task	
09 gender		**19** assign	
10 generate		**20** multiple	

B

다음 각 문장의 밑줄 친 부분을 어법에 맞게 바르게 고쳐 쓰시오.

01 **That this example teaches us is**: English is no longer just "one language." 🔗 Link p.24 01번

➡ ______________________________

02 In some cases, a man might accuse a woman of **making him missed** a turn on the highway because she was chatting to him at the time. 🔗 Link p.26 03번

➡ ______________________________

03 Unless we learn **what does that spirit mean**, and how it acts under certain circumstances, we will not be able to cope with its return. 🔗 Link p.27 04번

➡ ______________________________

04 Over the ten weeks of the study, contributions during the 'eyes weeks' were almost **three times higher than that made** during the 'flowers weeks.' 🔗 Link p.28 Example

➡ ______________________________

C

다음 영어는 우리말로, 우리말은 영어로 옮겨 쓰시오.

01 suspicious _______________

02 greet _______________

03 acknowledge _______________

04 장애, 장벽 _______________

05 humiliation _______________

06 reluctance _______________

07 concern _______________

08 virtuous _______________

09 reckless _______________

10 stingy _______________

11 doubtful _______________

12 blinded _______________

13 seemingly _______________

14 trigger _______________

15 initial _______________

16 피로 _______________

17 primary _______________

18 complete _______________

19 inadequate _______________

20 leisure _______________

D

다음 각 네모 안에서 어법상 적절한 것을 고르고, 색칠된 부분을 해석하시오.

01 Monday is overloaded with meetings to "get things moving," what / which aren't very productive. Link p.30 01번

➡ 적절한 것: _______________ 해석: _______________

02 Therefore, one man's intention to give out hugs to strangers was / were unique enough to prompt the crowd to be suspicious. Link p.32 03번

➡ 적절한 것: _______________ 해석: _______________

03 Researchers suggest that / what students don't want to sweat and take a shower, so they are less active in physical education classes. Link p.33 04번

➡ 적절한 것: _______________ 해석: _______________

04 However, there are other studies that point out that / what fear of bullying and humiliation may be behind **the reluctance of some students to shower.** Link p.33 04번

➡ 적절한 것: _______________ 해석: _______________

Part

2

종합적 판단 및 세부 정보

 **이 Part의 학습을 시작하기 전에 꼭 읽어보세요.**

종합적 판단 능력에 대해서 설명해주세요.

문제 유형에 따라 문제 해결을 위한 요소들을 모두 활용해 문제를 해결하는 능력을 말합니다.

문제의 난이도는 어떤 편인가요?

사실, 수능에서 절대 틀려서는 안 되는 유형입니다. 대부분의 문제가 다른 유형에 비해 그다지 어렵지 않은 수준이므로 자신감을 갖고 문제를 대하면 됩니다.

역시 글의 요지를 파악하는 것이 가장 중요한가요?

물론입니다. 하지만 정답을 찾기 위한 요소가 지문 전반에 흩어져 있기 때문에 세부 정보를 빠르게 찾는 것이 더 중요할 때도 많습니다.

그럼 하나하나 꼼꼼하게 읽어야 하겠네요?

반드시 그렇지만은 않습니다. 그 예로, 목적 추론의 경우, 글의 구조를 이해하고 발신인과 수신인, 인물과 배경, 그리고 사건에 대한 이해를 바탕으로 전체적인 흐름, 즉 '숲' 을 볼 수 있어야겠죠.

이 유형을 공부할 때 필요한 점에 대해 알려주세요.

'숲' 과 '나무' 를 함께 볼 수 있는 능력이 필요합니다. 문제 유형에 따라 풀이 전략을 달리하는 것도 좋은 방법입니다. 많은 문제를 풀면서 연습하다보면 점차 요령이 생길 거예요.

Unit 01 목적 추론

1. 주어진 지문을 읽고, 글의 목적으로 적절한 것을 고른다.
2. 글의 종류는 보통 편지글이다.
3. 매년 수능에 1문제가 꾸준히 출제된다.

Example

다음 글의 목적으로 가장 적절한 것은?　　　　| 고1 전국연합 |

Dear Mr. Hane,

Our message to you is brief, but important: Your subscription to *Winston Magazine* will end soon and we haven't heard from you about renewing it. We're sure you won't want to miss even one upcoming issue. Renew now to make sure that the service will continue.

5 You'll get continued delivery of the excellent stories and news that make *Winston Magazine* the fastest growing magazine in America. To make it as easy as possible for you to act now, we've sent a reply card for you to complete. Simply send back the card today and you'll continue to receive your monthly issue of *Winston Magazine*.

Best regards,

10 Thomas Strout

① 무료 잡지를 신청하려고
② 잡지 구독 갱신을 권유하려고
③ 배송 지연에 대해 사과하려고
④ 경품에 당첨된 사실을 통보하려고
⑤ 기사에 대한 독자 의견에 감사하려고

어휘 중요한 어휘를 확인하세요.

brief 간결한　　subscription 구독　　renew 갱신하다　　upcoming 다가오는　　issue (잡지·서적 등의) ~호　　make sure 확실히 ~하다　　delivery 배달　　complete 완성하다　　monthly 월간의

구문 주요 구문을 살펴보아요.

6행 1)[To make **it** as easy as possible 2){for you to act now}], we've sent **a reply card** 3)[for you to complete].

1)은 목적의 의미를 나타내는 to부정사구이다. 그 안에서 it은 형식상의 목적어이고, 2)가 내용상의 목적어이다. for you는 to act ~의 의미상의 주어를 나타낸다.
3)은 a reply card를 수식하는 형용사적 용법의 to부정사구이고, for you는 to complete의 의미상의 주어를 나타낸다.

How to solve 이런 방법으로 접근하세요.

Step 1 글의 종류 파악하기 목적 추론 유형의 지문은 대부분 편지글입니다.

- Dear Mr. Hane, (Hane 씨께,)
- Best regards,
  Thomas Strout (Thomas Strout 드림)
➡ **글의 종류** 편지글

Step 2 등장인물 간의 관계 파악하기

- Your subscription to *Winston Magazine* will end soon and we haven't heard from you about renewing it.

(귀하의 'Winston Magazine' 구독 기간이 곧 만료되는데 저희는 귀하로부터 갱신한다는 말을 듣지 못했습니다.)
➡ **등장인물 간의 관계** 잡지 구독자와 잡지사 관계자

Step 3 필자나 수신인이 처한 상황 파악하기

- We're sure you won't want to miss even one upcoming issue.

(저희는 귀하가 다음의 단 한 호라도 놓치고 싶지 않을 거라고 확신합니다.)
➡ **수신인의 상황** 잡지 구독 갱신을 아직 하지 않음

Step 4 필자의 목적 파악하기 필자가 의도하는 바가 바로 글의 목적이죠.

- Renew now to make sure that the service will continue.

(서비스를 확실히 지속하기 위해 지금 갱신하십시오.)
➡ **필자의 목적** 잡지 구독 갱신 권유

Step 5 정답 확인하기

① 무료 잡지를 신청하려고 → 잡지에 관한 내용이나, 무료 잡지와는 무관함

② 잡지 구독 갱신을 권유하려고 → 내용을 종합해볼 때 정답!

③ 배송 지연에 대해 사과하려고 → 내용과 무관함

④ 경품에 당첨된 사실을 통보하려고 → 내용과 무관함

⑤ 기사에 대한 독자 의견에 감사하려고 → 독자에게 쓴 편지는 맞지만 감사 편지는 아님

실전 문제를 풀어보세요.

01 다음 글의 목적으로 가장 적절한 것은?

| 고2 전국연합 |

Dear Mr. Spencer,

I will have lived in this apartment for ten years as of this coming April. I have enjoyed living here and hope to continue doing so. When I first moved into the Greenfield Apartments, I was told that the apartment had been recently painted. Since that time, I have never touched the walls or the ceiling. Looking around over the past month has made me realize how old and dull the paint has become. I would like to update the apartment with a new coat of paint. I understand that this would be at my own expense, and that I must get permission to do so as per the lease agreement. Please advise at your earliest convenience.

Sincerely,
Howard James

*as per ~에 따라서

① 아파트 안전 진단 결과를 통보하려고
② 아파트 임대차 계약 연장을 논의하려고
③ 아파트 도색 작업에 대한 허락을 받으려고
④ 아파트 수리 비용 부담에 대해 상의하려고
⑤ 아파트 도색에 대한 설문 결과를 알려 주려고

지문에서의 어휘의 뜻을
써보고 해설에서 확인하세요.

- as of
- ceiling
- dull
- update
- coat
- at one's own expense
- permission
- lease
- agreement
- at one's convenience

구문 주요 구문을 살펴보아요.

6행 1)[Looking around over the past month] has **made** me **realize** 2)[how old and dull the paint has become].

1)은 동명사구로 문장의 주어이다. 사역동사 made가 쓰여 목적격 보어로 동사원형 realize가 왔다.
2)는 의문사절로 realize의 목적어이다.

02 다음 글의 목적으로 가장 적절한 것은?

| 고1 전국연합 |

음성파일

My wife and I visited your cinema last month. We purchased two tickets which came to a total of $44. At the time of purchase, the attendant at the information desk told us they were having some problems accepting credit card payments. At that time, I was anxious about my credit card payment, but the attendant told me that there was no problem with my payment. However, when I received my bank statement, I discovered that you charged my card twice. I would be grateful if you could resolve this matter quickly.

① 신용카드 결제 오류의 해결을 요청하려고
② 예매한 영화의 관람시간을 변경하려고
③ 영화 관람료에 대해 문의하려고
④ 신용카드 발급 가능 여부를 확인하려고
⑤ 직원의 불친절한 태도에 대해 항의하려고

지문에서의 어휘의 뜻을 써보고 해설에서 확인하세요.

- purchase
- attendant
- payment
- be anxious about
- receive
- bank statement
- charge
- grateful
- resolve
- matter

구문 주요 구문을 살펴보아요.

2행 At the time of purchase, the attendant at the information desk told us [1)][they were **having some problems accepting** credit card payments].

1)은 접속사 that이 생략된 명사절로, told의 직접목적어 역할을 한다. 「have a problem -ing」는 '~하는 데 문제가 있다'의 의미이다.

Do It Yourself

03

다음 글의 목적으로 가장 적절한 것은?

Recently, I have witnessed many dogs on the loose in the neighborhood. The dogs, which are fierce-looking, are given license to run around the neighborhood. They are frightening, especially to children and the elderly. I am afraid that it's just a
5 matter of time before someone gets seriously injured. The owners of these dogs seem to be unaware of the dangers of letting their pets off the leash and have adopted an indifferent attitude. They have been asked by numerous locals to keep the dogs under control but all requests have been ignored and the
10 situation has not improved. Therefore I ask that you investigate the matter and take appropriate action as soon as possible to prevent the occurrence of more serious problems.

① 유기견 입양 절차에 관해 문의하려고
② 개에게 물린 피해에 대한 보상을 촉구하려고
③ 전문가에 의한 반려견 교육을 신청하려고
④ 어린이가 개에게 물리는 것의 위험성을 알리려고
⑤ 통제 없이 돌아다니는 개들에 대한 조치를 요청하려고

구문 주요 구문을 살펴보아요.

8행 They have **been asked** by numerous locals **to keep** the dogs under control but all requests have been ignored and the situation has not improved.

⟨ask+목적어+to부정사⟩는 '~가 …하도록 요청하다'라는 의미인데, 이것이 수동태인 ⟨be asked+to부정사⟩가 되어 현재완료형과 함께 쓰였다.

04 다음 글의 목적으로 가장 적절한 것은?

You listened to Dr. Buzan's lecture this morning. I appreciate your attention and enthusiasm. During this afternoon's training programs you will learn by doing. For one hour from 1 p.m. you'll learn how to set up a tent. Then, from 2 p.m., you will learn how to use a map. Originally, for one hour from 3:00 p.m., you were scheduled to practice CPR, but it is cancelled owing to the instructor's personal reason. Instead, you'll learn how to use a compass. There'll be recreation time starting at 4:00 p.m.. I'm sure all of these programs will help you to be great instructors for youth outdoor activities. Thank you for your participation and the effort in advance.

*CPR 심폐 소생술

지문에서의 어휘의 뜻을 써보고 해설에서 확인하세요.

- lecture
- attention
- enthusiasm
- set up
- originally
- be scheduled to
- cancel
- owing to
- instructor
- compass
- outdoor
- participation
- in advance

① 오후 실습 일정을 안내하려고
② 일정 취소에 관하여 사과하려고
③ 강연에 관한 보고서 제출을 독려하려고
④ 청소년 야외 활동의 중요성을 강조하려고
⑤ 강사 양성 프로그램 참여 방법을 소개하려고

구문 주요 구문을 살펴보아요.

8행 I'm sure all of these programs will **help you to be** great instructors for youth outdoor activities.

「help+목적어+to부정사구/원형부정사구」는 '~가 …하는 것을 돕다'의 의미이다.

Unit 02 심경 추론

1. 주어진 지문을 읽고, 글에 드러난 등장인물의 심경으로 적절한 것을 고른다.
2. 하나의 심경을 묻기도 하고, 심경 변화를 묻기도 한다.
3. 매년 수능에 1문제가 꾸준히 출제된다.

Example

다음 글에 드러난 Rowe의 심경 변화로 가장 적절한 것은? | 고2 전국연합 |

Rowe jumps for joy when he finds a cave because he loves being in places where so few
→ 변화 전 심경 묘사 1   → 등장인물의 상황 제시

have ventured. At the entrance he keeps taking photos with his cell phone to show off his
→ 변화 전 심경 묘사 2

new adventure later. Coming to a stop on a rock a few meters from the entrance, he sees

the icy cave's glittering view. He says, "Incredibly beautiful!" stretching his hand out to
→ 변화 전 심경 묘사 3   → 변화 전 심경 묘사 4

5 touch the icy wall. Suddenly, his footing gives way and he slides down into the darkness.
→ 상황 반전

He looks up and sees a crack of light about 20 meters above him. 'Phone for help,' he
→ 상황 반전 이후 심경 묘사 1

thinks. But he realizes there's no service this far underground. He tries to move upward
→ 상황 반전 이후 심경 묘사 2   → 상황 반전 이후 심경 묘사 3

but he can't. He calls out, "Is anyone there?" There's no answer.
→ 상황 반전 이후 심경 묘사 4

① delighted → grateful

② disappointed → ashamed

③ indifferent → regretful

④ bored → frightened

⑤ excited → desperate

 중요한 어휘를 확인하세요.

joy 기쁨, 즐거움   cave 동굴   venture 위험을 무릅쓰고 ~하다   entrance 입구   show off ~을 과시하다   adventure 모험
glittering 반짝이는, 빛나는   incredibly 놀랍게, 믿을 수 없게   stretch 뻗치다, 늘이다   slide 미끄러지다   crack 틈, 균열
upward 위로

 주요 구문을 살펴보아요.

1행 1)[Rowe jumps for joy 2){when he finds a cave}] 3)[because he loves being in **places** 4){where so few have ventured}].

1)은 주절이고, 3)은 종속절이다. 2)는 주절 안에 있는 종속절이고, 4)는 places를 수식하는 관계부사절이다.

How to solve

이런 방법으로 접근하세요.

Step 1 **주인공의 상황 파악하기** 이야기의 중심인물과 상황을 파악하세요.

- Rowe jumps for joy ~ (Rowe는 기쁨에 폴짝 뛴다)
- ➡ **주인공** Rowe
- ~ he finds a cave ~ (그는 동굴을 발견한다)
- ➡ **상황** 위험을 무릅쓰고 아무도 해보지 않은 동굴 탐험을 하게 됨

Step 2 **상황 변화 전 심경 파악하기** 변화 이전에 어땠는지 알아야죠.

- Rowe jumps for joy ~ (Rowe는 기쁨에 폴짝 뛴다)
- ~ to show off his new adventure later (나중에 자신의 새로운 모험을 뽐내기 위해)
- ~ he sees the icy cave's glittering view (그는 얼음 동굴의 빛나는 광경을 본다)
- "Incredibly beautiful!" ("믿을 수 없을 정도로 아름다워!")
- ➡ **변화 전 심경** 신나고 설렘

Step 3 **상황 변화 파악하기** 심경에 변화를 가져오는 상황을 파악하세요.

- Suddenly, his footing gives way and he slides down into the darkness.
  (갑자기 그는 발을 헛디뎌 어둠 속으로 미끄러져 들어간다.)
- ➡ **상황 변화** 곤란하고 난감한 일이 발생하는 것으로 반전됨

Step 4 **상황 변화 이후의 심경 파악하기** 상황 반전 이후의 심경이 중요하죠.

- 'Phone for help,' he thinks. ('전화로 도움을 요청해야지,'라고 그는 생각한다.)
- ~ he realizes there's no service this far underground
  (그는 이렇게 깊은 지하에서는 (통화) 서비스가 되지 않는다는 것을 깨닫는다)
- He tries to move upward but he can't. (그는 위로 올라가려고 하지만 올라갈 수 없다.)
- There's no answer. (응답이 없다.)
- ➡ **상황 반전 이후의 심경** 절망적이고 막막함

Step 5 **정답 확인하기**

① 기쁜 → 고마워하는 → ×   ② 실망한 → 수줍어하는 → ×   ③ 무관심한 → 후회하는 → ×

④ 지루해하는 → 무서운 → ×   ⑤ 신난 → 절망적인 → 정답!

심경 문제에 자주 나오는 어휘

- irritated 짜증난
- lonely 외로운
- delighted 기쁜
- pleased 기쁜
- encouraged 용기를 얻은
- depressed 우울한, 의기소침한
- confident 자신감 있는

- bored 지루해 하는
- regretful 후회하는
- anxious 불안한
- relieved 안도한, 진정된
- embarrassed 당황한
- frustrated 좌절한, 낙담한
- refreshed 상쾌한

- envious 부러워하는
- suspicious 의심스러운
- surprised 놀란
- excited 흥분한, 신나는
- sympathetic 동정하는
- scared 무서워하는

- confused 혼란스러운
- indifferent 무관심한
- ashamed 부끄러운
- satisfied 만족한
- disappointed 실망한
- jealous 질투하는

Do It Yourself

01 다음 글에 드러난 'I'의 심경으로 가장 적절한 것은? | 고2 전국연합 |

I'm not sure which one of us did the talking, but it must have been pretty convincing because Mr. Montague agreed to audition us the very next day. We couldn't believe it. We were shocked. Rehearsal was over for the day. After we stopped screaming and hugging and dancing around Jean's basement, I ran all the way home to tell Mom about our "lucky break." She was delighted, and she insisted on going with us to the audition, as much for support as to make sure everything was going smoothly. I felt like a little kid on Christmas Eve. I didn't sleep even an hour that night. That was probably why the next day seemed like a dream.

① sad and depressed
② excited and happy
③ relieved and sympathetic
④ scared and frightened
⑤ ashamed and embarrassed

지문에서의 어휘의 뜻을 써보고 해설에서 확인하세요.

- convincing
- audition
- shocked
- rehearsal
- scream
- basement
- lucky break
- delighted
- insist
- smoothly

구문 주요 구문을 살펴보아요.

1행 I'm not sure 1)[which one of us did the talking], but 2)it 3)must have been pretty convincing because Mr. Montague agreed to audition us the very next day.

1)은 형용사 sure를 보충하는 의문사절로, 앞에 있는 not과 연결되어 '우리 중 누가 그 말을 했는지 확신하지 못하다'는 뜻으로 해석한다.

2) it은 앞에 있는 the talking을 가리킨다.

3) 〈must have p.p.〉는 과거 사실에 대한 추측을 나타내는 표현이며, '~이었음에 틀림없다'의 의미이다.

02 다음 글에 드러난 'I'의 심경 변화로 가장 적절한 것은? | 고2 전국연합 |

Something inside told me that by now someone had discovered my escape. It chilled me greatly to think that they would capture me and take me back to that awful place. So, I decided to walk only at night until I was far from the town. After three nights' walking, I felt sure that they had stopped chasing me. I found a deserted cottage and walked into it. Tired, I lay down on the floor and fell asleep. I awoke to the sound of a far away church clock, softly ringing seven times and noticed that the sun was slowly rising. As I stepped outside, my heart began to pound with anticipation and longing. The thought that I could meet Evelyn soon lightened my walk.

① moved → nervous
② fearful → hopeful
③ lonely → annoyed
④ sympathetic → amused
⑤ sorrowful → frightened

지문에서의 어휘의 뜻을
써보고 해설에서 확인하세요.

- escape
- chill
- capture
- awful
- chase
- deserted
- cottage
- fall asleep
- ring
- step
- pound
- anticipation
- longing
- lighten

구문  주요 구문을 살펴보아요.

2행 1) **It** chilled me greatly 2) [to think 3) {that they would capture me and take me back to 4) **that** awful place}].

1) It은 형식상의 주어이고, to부정사구인 2)가 내용상의 주어이다.
3)은 think의 목적어 역할을 하는 명사절이다.
4)의 that은 지시어로 쓰였다.

Do It Yourself

03 다음 글에 드러난 'I'의 심경으로 가장 적절한 것은?

I gave an impromptu speech to my two best friends at their graduation party in front of about fifty people. I stood up and started speaking but stopped when my cheeks started losing my physical control. I violently shook up and down to the point
5 where people who weren't even that close could see. I kept saying to myself, "Oh, my goodness, why are my cheeks shaking?" I couldn't even really continue because they were shaking so hard that I couldn't talk. My friend's dad walked up to me and jokingly started massaging my cheeks. And then, he
10 took the microphone from me and told me to sit down, which I somehow managed to do. Pretty much ruined my already nonexistent self-confidence when it comes to public speaking.

*impromptu 즉석의, 즉흥의

① hopeful and excited
② jealous and resentful
③ grateful and satisfied
④ indifferent and bored
⑤ nervous and embarrassed

지문에서의 어휘의 뜻을 써보고 해설에서 확인하세요.

- cheek
- physical
- violently
- jokingly
- massage
- microphone
- somehow
- manage to
- pretty much
- ruin
- nonexistent
- self-confidence
- when it comes to
- public speaking

구문 주요 구문을 살펴보아요.

9행 And then, he 1)[took the microphone from me] and 2)[told me **to sit down**], 3)[**which** I somehow managed to do].

1)과 2)는 he를 공통의 주어로 하는 술어동사구로, and로 인해 병렬 연결되었다.

3)은 계속적 용법의 관계대명사절로, to sit down을 부연 설명한다. 관계대명사 which는 의미상 do의 목적어에 해당한다.

04 다음 글에 드러난 'I'의 심경 변화로 가장 적절한 것은?

Late one afternoon I got a call from Michael. "I'm in a tight spot," he told me. "I need a financial brochure laid out and printed by tomorrow afternoon." He said his regular designer was out and that he was under a lot of pressure. I was in the middle of another project, but Michael was my friend, so I dropped everything and worked late into the night on his brochure. Early the next morning Michael gave the go-ahead to have it printed. I was exhausted, but I was glad I'd been able to help him out. Getting back to my office, I discovered this voice-mail message from Michael: "Well, you really screwed this one up! Jack, I know you were under time pressure on this, but the earnings chart isn't presented clearly enough. It's just a disaster. This is an important client. I assume you'll fix it right away." I felt betrayed.

① excited → bored
② satisfied → angry
③ worried → relieved
④ surprised → indifferent
⑤ cheerful → triumphant

지문에서의 어휘의 뜻을 써보고 해설에서 확인하세요.

- tight spot
- financial
- brochure
- lay out
- regular
- pressure
- exhausted
- screw ~ up
- earnings
- disaster
- client
- assume
- betrayed

구문 주요 구문을 살펴보아요.

2행 "I need a financial brochure 1)[laid out and printed by tomorrow afternoon]."

「need+목적어+과거분사(구)」의 구조이며, 목적어인 a financial brochure가 동작의 대상이므로 수동의 의미를 나타내는 과거분사구 1)이 쓰인 것이다. '재무 책자를 내일 오후까지 구성하고 인쇄해야 한다'로 자연스럽게 해석할 수 있다.

How was it? 배운 내용을 확인해보세요.

A 다음 영어는 우리말로, 우리말은 영어로 옮겨 쓰시오.

01 brief _______________
02 subscription _______________
03 갱신하다 _______________
04 (잡지·서적 등의) ~호 _______________
05 ceiling _______________
06 dull _______________
07 permission _______________
08 lease _______________
09 attendant _______________
10 charge _______________

11 resolve _______________
12 목격하다 _______________
13 injured _______________
14 indifferent _______________
15 investigate _______________
16 appropriate _______________
17 enthusiasm _______________
18 취소하다 _______________
19 owing to _______________
20 in advance _______________

B 다음 각 네모 안에서 어법상 적절한 것을 고르고, 색칠된 부분을 해석하시오.

01 I understand that this would be at my own expense, and that / which I must get permission to do so as per the lease agreement. ✐ Link p.46 01번

➡ 적절한 것: _______________ 해석: _______________

02 At the time of purchase, the attendant at the information desk told us they were having some problems accepting / to accept credit card payments. ✐ Link p.47 02번

➡ 적절한 것: _______________ 해석: _______________

03 The owners of these dogs seem / are seemed to be unaware of the dangers of letting their pets off the leash and have adopted an indifferent attitude. ✐ Link p.48 03번

➡ 적절한 것: _______________ 해석: _______________

04 During / While this afternoon's training programs you will learn by doing.

✐ Link p.49 04번

➡ 적절한 것: _______________ 해석: _______________

C

다음 영어는 우리말로, 우리말은 영어로 옮겨 쓰시오.

01 venture ___________

02 show off ___________

03 glittering ___________

04 틈, 균열 ___________

05 convincing ___________

06 delighted ___________

07 insist ___________

08 smoothly ___________

09 chill ___________

10 awful ___________

11 deserted ___________

12 anticipation ___________

13 physical ___________

14 violently ___________

15 manage to ___________

16 ruin ___________

17 brochure ___________

18 exhausted ___________

19 earnings ___________

20 배신감을 느끼는 ___________

D

다음 각 네모 안의 말을 어법에 맞는 순서로 고쳐 쓰시오.

01 Rowe jumps for joy when he finds a cave because he loves being in places few / so / where / have ventured . *Link p.50 Example*

➡ ___________

02 It pretty / have / been / must / convincing because Mr. Montague agreed to audition us the very next day. *Link p.52 01번*

➡ ___________

03 that / I / could meet / the thought / Evelyn soon lightened my walk. *Link p.53 02번*

➡ ___________

04 I need brochure / a / financial / laid out and printed by tomorrow afternoon.

Link p.55 04번

➡ ___________

03 내용 일치

Example

음성파일

James Van Der Zee에 관한 다음 글의 내용과 일치하지 <u>않는</u> 것은? | 고1 전국연합 |

James Van Der Zee was born on June 29, 1886, in Lenox, Massachusetts. The second of
→ 선택지 ①의 내용
six children, James grew up in a family of creative people. At the age of fourteen he
→ 선택지 ②의 내용
received his first camera and took hundreds of photographs of his family and town. By
1906, he had moved to New York, married, and was taking jobs to support his growing
5 family. In 1907, he moved to Phoetus, Virginia, where he worked in the dining room of
→ 선택지 ③의 내용
the Hotel Chamberlin. During this time he also worked as a photographer on a part-time
basis. He opened his own studio in 1916. World War I had begun and many young
→ 선택지 ④의 내용
soldiers came to the studio to have their pictures taken. In 1969, the exhibition, *Harlem*
→ 선택지 ⑤의 내용과 일치하지 않음
On My Mind, brought him international recognition. He died in 1983.

① 여섯 명의 아이들 중 둘째였다.
② 열네 살에 그의 첫 번째 카메라를 받았다.
③ Chamberlin 호텔의 식당에서 일을 했다.
④ 자신의 스튜디오를 1916년에 열었다.
⑤ 1969년에 전시회로 인해 국제적인 비난을 받았다.

어휘 중요한 어휘를 확인하세요.

support 부양하다, 지지하다   dining room 식당   photographer 사진사, 사진작가   on a part-time basis 시간제로
exhibition 전시회   international 국제적인, 세계적인   recognition 인정, 인식

구문 주요 구문을 살펴보아요.

7행 World War I [1)]**had begun** and many young soldiers [2)]**came** to the studio [3)][to **have** their pictures taken].

1) had taken은 〈had p.p.〉의 형태로, 2)의 came보다 앞서 일어난 일임을 나타낸다.
3)은 목적을 나타내는 부사적 용법의 to부정사구이다. 그 안에서 have는 사역동사이며, their pictures가 사진 찍히는 대상이므로 수동태임을 나타내도록 목적격
보어로 과거분사 taken이 쓰였다.

How to solve　　이런 방법으로 접근하세요.

Step 1　　**글의 소재 파악하기**　　질문과 지문 첫 부분을 통해 알 수 있어요.

- 질문: James Van Der Zee에 관해 일치하지 않는 것
- 지문 첫 부분: James Van Der Zee was born on June 29, 1886, in Lenox, Massachusetts.
  (James Van Der Zee는 1886년 6월 29일 Massachusetts주 Lenox에서 태어났다.)
→ **소재**　James Van Der Zee (인물)

Step 2　　**선택지 먼저 읽고 확인할 내용 파악하기**　　주로 인물의 생애에서 구체적인 사실에 관한 내용이 제시됩니다.

① 여섯 명의 아이들 중 둘째였다.　→ the second, six children
② 열네 살에 그의 첫 번째 카메라를 받았다.　→ fourteen, received, first camera
③ Chamberlin 호텔의 식당에서 일을 했다.　→ worked, dining room, Chamberlin
④ 자신의 스튜디오를 1916년에 열었다.　→ opened, studio, 1916.
⑤ 1969년에 전시회로 인해 국제적인 비난을 받았다.　→ 1969, exhibition, recognition

Step 3　　**지문 읽으며 일치 여부 확인하기**　　일치하는 선택지는 바로 지워가세요.

- The second of six children, ~ (여섯 명의 아이들 중 둘째)　→ 선택지 ① 내용 일치
- At the age of fourteen he received his first camera ~
  (열네 살에 첫 번째 카메라를 받음)　→ 선택지 ② 내용 일치
- ~ he worked in the dining room of the Hotel Chamberlin
  (Chamberlin 호텔 식당에서 근무)　→ 선택지 ③ 내용 일치
- He opened his own studio in 1916.
  (1916년에 자신의 스튜디오를 열었음)　→ 선택지 ④ 내용 일치
- In 1969, the exhibition ~ brought him international recognition.
  (1969년 전시회에서 국제적인 인정을 받음)　→ 선택지 ⑤ 내용과 일치하지 않음!

Step 4　　**정답 확인하기**

- In 1969, the exhibition, *Harlem On My Mind*, brought him international recognition.
  (1969년에 'Harlem On My Mind' 전시회는 그에게 국제적인 인정을 가져다주었다.)
→ **일치하지 않는 것**　⑤ 1969년에 전시회로 인해 국제적인 비난을 받았다.　→ 일치하지 않음

Do It Yourself

01 *Star Wreck*에 관한 다음 글의 내용과 일치하는 것은?

| 고1 전국연합 |

Finnish filmmaker Timo Vuorensola came up with the idea for his movie *Star Wreck*, whose original was *Star Trek*. He knew that looking for conventional distribution would be almost impossible. An amateur, science-fiction comedy with an extremely small budget would hardly be attractive to mainstream studios. So Vuorensola took matters into his own hands: he used a social networking site to build up an online fan base, who contributed to the storyline and even offered their acting skills. In return for the help, Vuorensola released *Star Wreck* in 2005 online for free. Seven hundred thousand copies were downloaded in the first week alone, reaching 9 million today.

① 공상과학영화 *Star Trek*의 원작이다.
② 스튜디오 제작 경비가 많이 들었다.
③ 제작 과정에서 팬들의 도움을 받았다.
④ 2005년부터 온라인에서 유료로 배포되었다.
⑤ 지금까지 총 9백만 달러를 벌어들였다.

지문에서의 어휘의 뜻을
써보고 해설에서 확인하세요.

- come up with
- original
- conventional
- distribution
- science-fiction
- budget
- attractive
- mainstream studio
- contribute
- storyline
- release
- copy

구문 주요 구문을 살펴보아요.

6행 So Vuorensola took matters into his own hands[1]: he used a social networking site [2][to build up **an online fan base**], [3][**who** contributed to the storyline and even offered their acting skills].

1)의 콜론(:)은 앞 내용을 부연 설명하는 동격의 기능을 한다.
2)는 결과 또는 목적을 나타내는 to부정사구이다.
3)은 관계절로, 선행사 an online fan base를 부연 설명하며, 이때 who는 and they로 바꿔 쓸 수 있다.

02 Joshua tree에 관한 다음 글의 내용과 일치하지 <u>않는</u> 것은?　| 고1 전국연합 |

Joshua trees are evergreen, with numerous, sharp-pointed leaves at the ends of their branches. The unique appearance of the Joshua tree makes it a very desirable decoration. Unfortunately, many Joshua trees have been dug up to be
5 planted in urban areas, despite a very low rate of survival when removed and planted in other places. Native Americans roasted and ate their flower buds. Young seeds were eaten raw or cooked (and said to taste like bananas). Alcoholic drinks were made from their flowers, too. But Joshua trees are hard to eat by
10 today's standards, and have little possibility of ever becoming a commercial food crop because they are protected by law.

① 뾰족한 잎을 가지고 있다.
② 옮겨 심을 경우 생존율이 매우 낮다.
③ 어린 씨앗은 식용으로 사용되었다.
④ 꽃으로 술을 만들 수 있었다.
⑤ 상업적인 식용 작물이 될 가능성이 크다.

지문에서의 어휘의 뜻을
써보고 해설에서 확인하세요.

- evergreen
- sharp-pointed
- branch
- appearance
- desirable
- dig
- urban
- rate
- roast
- bud
- seed
- raw
- standard
- commercial
- crop

구문　주요 구문을 살펴보아요.

4행 Unfortunately, many Joshua trees 1)**have been dug** up 2)**to be planted** in urban areas, despite a very low rate of survival 3)[**when removed** and **planted** in other places].

1)은 현재완료 수동태 〈have been+p.p.〉이고, 2)는 목적 또는 결과를 나타내는 to부정사구로 be planted 는 수동태이다.
3)은 being이 생략된 분사구문으로, 분사구문의 의미를 명확히 하기 위해 접속사 when을 생략하지 않았다. removed와 planted는 병렬로 연결되어 있으며, when removed and planted를 when they(= Joshua trees) are removed and planted로 바꿔 쓸 수 있다.

Do It **Yourself**

03

Gordon Lightfoot에 관한 다음 글의 내용과 일치하지 <u>않는</u> 것은?

Gordon Lightfoot (1938–) is a Canadian singer, songwriter, and winner of sixteen Juno awards. His singing talent was recognized when he was still a little boy in Orillia, Ontario. Throughout the 1960s and 70s, Lightfoot had a string of hit
5 songs, and he broke records with his sold-out concerts at Toronto's Massey Hall. However, behind the scenes, Lightfoot struggled. In 1972, at the height of his popularity, he suffered a serious illness that paralyzed part of his face. He fought his way through the illness and regained his health. For the next thirty
10 years, Gordon Lightfoot continued to record albums, perform concerts, and appear on television. However, in 2002, he fell ill again, had five operations, and stayed in a hospital for three months. Against all odds, he made a comeback and by 2004, he was recording and touring again. With more than 200 recordings
15 to his credit, he has been considered a song-writing legend by his fellow musicians.

① 어린 소년일 때 노래로 인정받았다.
② 1960년대와 1970년대에 일련의 히트곡을 냈다.
③ 인기 절정기에 얼굴에 마비가 오는 병을 앓았다.
④ 1972년 이후 30년 동안 음악 활동을 계속했다.
⑤ 다섯 차례의 수술을 받고 2002년에 은퇴했다.

구문 주요 구문을 살펴보아요.

14행 1)[**With** more than 200 recordings to his credit], 2)[he **has been considered** a song-writing legend by his fellow musicians].

1)은 With가 이끄는 전치사구이고, 2)는 주절로서, 현재완료와 수동태가 결합된 표현이 쓰였다.

지문에서의 어휘의 뜻을 써보고 해설에서 확인하세요.

• recognize
• a string of
• sold-out
• behind the scene
• struggle
• at the height of
• suffer
• paralyze
• fight one's way through
• regain
• operation
• against all (the) odds
• to one's credit
• legend
• fellow

04 orca에 관한 다음 글의 내용과 일치하지 <u>않는</u> 것은?

Orcas belong to the dolphin family, although they are often referred to as killer whales. Like dolphins, orcas determine the position of an object by measuring how long it takes for an echo to return from the object. Orcas are voluntary breathers; only
5 half of their brain sleeps at one time and the other half remains alert to regulate breathing. They are very social animals who live in stable family groups and display a high level of care for their offspring. Much like wolves, orcas hunt cooperatively in groups for food. Orcas can recognize sounds from members of their
10 own group from several miles away. They live in all oceans in the world; however, their most common habitat is the Arctic and Antarctic Oceans. They are also spotted off the west coast of North America.

① 메아리를 통해 물체의 위치를 측정한다.
② 잠을 잘 때 반쪽 뇌는 정신이 깨어 있다.
③ 안정된 가족 집단을 이루며 생활한다.
④ 단독으로 사냥하기를 좋아한다.
⑤ 남극해와 북극해에서 가장 흔하게 서식한다.

지문에서의 어휘의 뜻을 써보고 해설에서 확인하세요.

- belong to
- refer to
- position
- object
- measure
- echo
- voluntary
- alert
- regulate
- stable
- offspring
- cooperatively
- recognize
- habitat
- spot

구문 주요 구문을 살펴보아요.

4행 Orcas are voluntary breathers; only half of their brain sleeps at one time and 1) **the other** half 2) **remains** alert 3) [to regulate breathing].

1) the other는 '둘 중 나머지 하나'의 의미이다.
2) remain은 상태의 지속 동사로 뒤에 형용사 보어가 이어진다.
3)은 결과나 목적의 의미를 나타내는 to부정사구로, '~하여 호흡하는 것을 조절하다' 또는 '호흡하는 것을 조절하기 위하여' 정도로 해석할 수 있다.

유형 특징
1. 제시된 도표 또는 표를 설명하는 지문에서 일치하지 않는 것을 고른다.
2. 지문의 문장 자체가 선택지를 구성한다.
3. 막대, 원, 선 등의 그래프가 주로 주어지며, 최근 수능에서는 그래프가 아닌 일반적인 표 역시 출제된다.
4. 매년 수능에 1문제가 꾸준히 출제된다.

Example

🎧 음성파일

다음 도표의 내용과 일치하지 <u>않는</u> 것은?

| 고1 전국연합 |

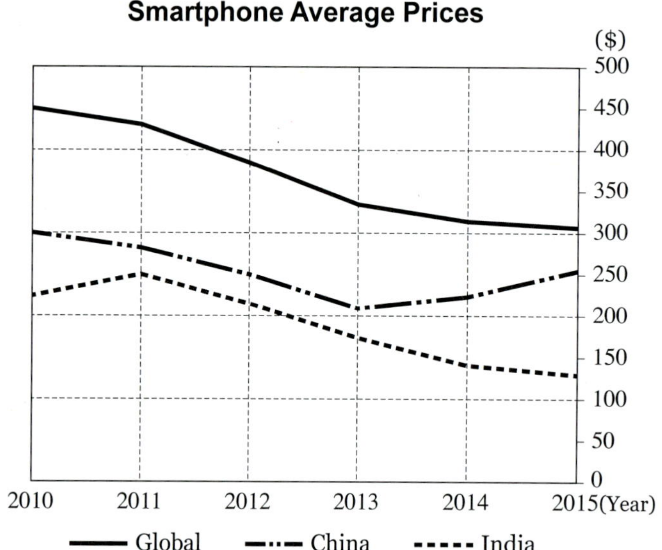

The above graph shows the smartphone average prices in China and India between 2010
→ 도표 지문의 첫 문장: 도표에서 다루는 주제에 대한 개괄적 소개
and 2015, compared with the global smartphone average price during the same period.

① The global smartphone average price decreased from 2010 to 2015, but still stayed the
→ 확인할 사항 1
highest among the three. ② The smartphone average price in China dropped between
→ 확인할 사항 2
2010 and 2013. ③ The smartphone average price in India reached its peak in 2011.
→ 확인할 사항 3
④ From 2013, China and India took opposite paths, with China's smartphone average
→ 확인할 사항 4
price going down and India's going up. ⑤ The gap between the global smartphone
→ 확인할 사항 5
average price and the smartphone average price in China was the smallest in 2015.

How to solve   이런 방법으로 접근하세요.

Step 1

도표 제목 및 세부요소 파악하기

- **제목**　　　Smartphone Average Prices (스마트폰 평균 가격)
- **그래프의 선**　Global, China, India (세계 평균, 중국, 인도)
- **가로축**　　　2010 ～ 2015 (2010년부터 2015년)
- **세로축**　　　$ (달러)

도표 지문의 첫 문장

보통 도표(표) 지문의 첫 문장은 'The graph(table) above shows ~(위 그래프(표)는 ~을 보여준다)'와 같은 도입 표현으로 도표(표) 제목 및 다룰 정보를 간략히 설명하는 문장이다. 따라서 제목과 첫 문장을 거의 동시에 읽으면서 시간을 절약하자.

Step 2

도표와 선택지 내용 비교하며 일치 여부 파악하기

① 전 세계 스마트폰 평균 가격은 2010년부터 2015년까지 하락했지만, 여전히 셋 중에 가장 높게 머물렀다. → 일치

② 중국의 스마트폰 평균 가격은 2010년과 2013년 사이에는 하락했다. → 일치

③ 인도의 스마트폰 평균 가격은 2011년에 최고점에 도달했다. → 일치

④ 2013년부터, 중국의 스마트폰 평균 가격은 하락했고 인도의 스마트폰 평균 가격은 상승하는, 정반대의 모습을 보였다. → 일치하지 않음

⑤ 전 세계 스마트폰 평균 가격과 중국의 스마트폰 평균 가격의 차이는 2015년에 가장 적었다. → 일치

Step 3

정답 확인하기

④ From 2013, China and India took opposite paths, with China's smartphone average price going down and India's going up. → 도표와 일치하지 않음

➡ 2013년부터 중국의 스마트폰 평균 가격은 상승했고, 인도의 스마트폰 가격은 하락했으므로 going down을 going up으로, 그리고 going up을 going down으로 고쳐야 한다.

도표 지문에 자주 나오는 표현과 어휘

도표 문제는 수 또는 비교와 관련된 표현을 얼마나 잘 이해하는지가 핵심이다. 도표 지문에 자주 나오는 다음 표현들을 꼭 익혀두자.

1. 배수 표현 :「배수사 + as ～ as …」와「배수사 + 비교급 + than …」은 '…보다 -배 더 ～한'의 의미
2. '-times'는 '-배'라는 뜻으로 보통 숫자 뒤에 붙이며, 'three times'라고 하면 '3배'라는 의미(단, 2배는 'double'로 표현함)
3. about, approximately, around 등은 '약, 대략'이라는 의미
4. that, those 등의 지시대명사는 보통 앞에서 나온 말의 중복을 피하기 위한 것으로, 무엇을 가리키는지 정확히 파악해야 한다.

Do It Yourself

01 다음 도표의 내용과 일치하지 <u>않는</u> 것은?

| 고1 전국연합 |

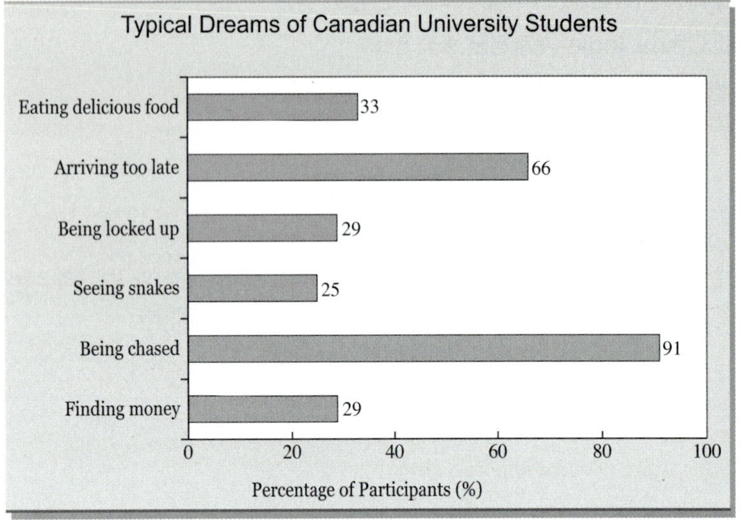

지문에서의 어휘의 뜻을
써보고 해설에서 확인하세요.

- typical
- chase
- frequently
- arrive late
- participant
- percentage
- lock up
- least
- one-third

The above graph shows the typical dreams Canadian university students dream while sleeping. ① Among the six typical dreams, "Being chased" was the most frequently reported dream. ② It was followed by "Arriving too late," which was reported by 66 percent of the participants. ③ The percentage of "Eating delicious food" was half that of "Arriving too late." ④ The percentages of "Being locked up" and "Finding money" were the same. ⑤ "Seeing snakes" was the least frequent dream reported by one-third of the participants.

구문 주요 구문을 살펴보아요.

8행 1)["Seeing snakes"] was 2)[**the least frequent dream** 3){reported by one-third of the participants}].

1)은 동명사구로, 문장의 주어이며, 2)가 주격 보어로 쓰였다. least는 little의 최상급이다.
3)은 과거분사구로, the least frequent dream을 수식한다.

02 다음 도표의 내용과 일치하지 <u>않는</u> 것은?

| 고1 전국연합 |

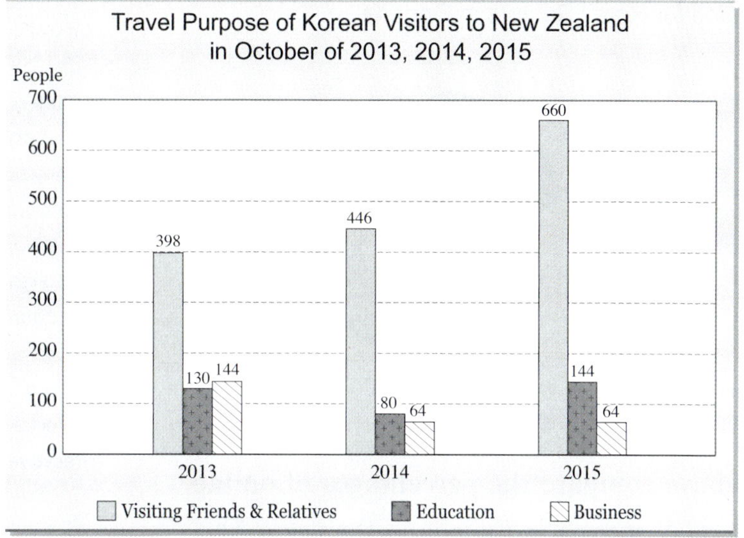

지문에서의 어휘의 뜻을 써보고 해설에서 확인하세요.

- the number of
- visitor
- according to
- purpose
- given period
- relative
- education
- decline
- following
- drop
- compared with
- previous
- double

This graph shows the number of Korean visitors to New Zealand according to their travel purpose in October of 2013, 2014, and 2015. ① Over the given period, the most popular purpose of visiting New Zealand was visiting friends and relatives. ② Visitors for the purpose of education declined from 2013 to 2014, but then increased in the following year. ③ The number of Korean visitors with business interests in 2014 dropped compared with that in the previous year. ④ Education was the least popular travel purpose for all three years. ⑤ The number of people visiting friends and relatives in 2013 was more than double the number of those visiting for business purposes in 2013.

구문 주요 구문을 살펴보아요.

6행 1)[The number of Korean visitors with business interests in 2014] dropped 2)[compared with **that** in the previous year].

1)이 주어이고, 동사는 dropped이다.

2)는 과거분사구이며, that은 중복되는 표현인 the number of Korean visitors with business interests를 대신하여 쓰였다.

Do It Yourself

03 다음 도표의 내용과 일치하지 <u>않는</u> 것은?

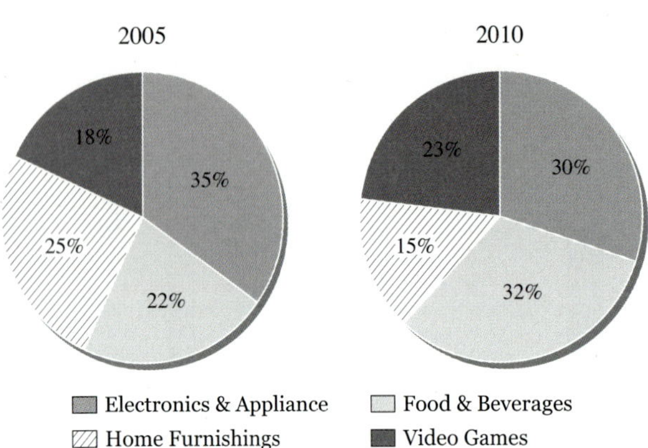

The two pie charts above compare the percentages of online sales across different retail sectors in Canada in the years 2005 and 2010. ① For all of the four sectors, there was a change in their proportion of online transactions over the time frame. ② In 2005, the electronics and appliance sector accounted for 35% of total online sales, but its percentage dropped to 30% in 2010. ③ As an increasing number of people chose to purchase food and beverages online during the given period, the percentage in the sector went from 22% to 32%. ④ The home furnishing industry had 25% of total online sales in 2005, but the figure fell to 15% in 2010. ⑤ Online sales of video games didn't overtake sales of home furnishings in 2010 although video games represented 23% of the market.

구문 주요 구문을 살펴보아요.

11행 1) [Online sales of video games didn't overtake sales of home furnishings in 2010] 2) [although video games represented 23% of the market].

1)은 주절이고, 2)는 '비록 ~이지만'의 의미를 갖는 양보의 부사절이다.

지문에서의 어휘의 뜻을 써보고 해설에서 확인하세요.

• retail
• proportion
• transaction
• time frame
• electronics
• appliance
• account for
• purchase
• figure
• overtake
• represent

04

다음 도표의 내용과 일치하지 <u>않는</u> 것은?

Per Capita Health Care Spending
in the U.S., Canada and Germany from 2011 to 2015

Year \ Country	United States	Canada	Germany
2011	8,508	4,521	4,495
2012	8,745	4,602	4,811
2013	8,713	4,351	4,819
2014	9,024	4,492	5,119
2015	9,507	4,613	5,353

(U.S. Dollars)

The table above shows per capita health care spending in the United States, Canada and Germany from 2011 to 2015. ① Each year, per capita health care spending in the U.S. was a lot higher than that in Canada and Germany respectively. ② Except for a slight decrease in 2013, per capita health care spending in the United States grew each year. ③ However, per capita health care spending in Canada went up and down during the period and the amount spent in 2015 ended up being larger than that in 2011. ④ Per capita health care spending in Germany steadily increased year by year from 2011 to 2015. ⑤ In 2015, per capita health care spending in the U.S. was 9,507 dollars, which was more than twice as much as that in Germany in the same year.

 주요 구문을 살펴보아요.

6행 However, 1)[per capita health care spending in Canada went up and down during the period] and 2)[**the amount** spent in 2015 **ended up being larger than that** in 2011].

1) 두 개의 절 1)과 2)가 and로 인해 병렬 연결되었다.

2)에서 「end up -ing」는 '(결국) ~하게 되다'의 의미이다. 「비교급(larger) than ~」 구문이 쓰였으며, than 뒤의 that은 앞에 나온 the amount spent의 반복을 피하기 위해 쓰인 대명사이다.

지문에서의 어휘의 뜻을 써보고 해설에서 확인하세요.

- per capita
- health care
- spending
- respectively
- except for
- slight
- end up -ing
- steadily
- twice

Unit 05 실용문

1. 안내문을 읽고, 내용과 일치하는 것 또는 일치하지 않는 것을 고른다.
2. 소재는 주로 대회, 행사, 프로그램, 공연, 여행, 모집 등에 관한 것이다.
3. 지문에 언급된 내용의 순서와 선택지의 순서가 일치한다.
4. 매년 수능에 일치와 불일치 유형이 각각 1문제씩 꾸준히 출제된다.

Example

Summer Camp 2019에 관한 다음 안내문의 내용과 일치하는 것은?　　　　| 고1 전국연합 |

Summer Camp 2019
→ 소재: 여름 캠프

This is a great opportunity for developing social skills and creativity!
→ 간략한 소개 및 홍보

Period & Participation → 세부사항 1

• July 1 – 5 (Monday – Friday)

5　• 8 – 12 year olds (maximum 20 students per class)

Programs → 세부사항 2

• Cooking

• Outdoor Activities (hiking, rafting, and camping)

Cost → 세부사항 3

10　• Regular: $100 per person

• Discounted: $90 (if you register by June 15)

Notice → 세부사항 4

• The programs will run regardless of weather conditions.

• To sign up, email us at summercamp@standrews.com.

15　For more information, visit our website: www.standrews.com.

① 참가 연령 제한이 없다.　　　　② 야외 프로그램은 운영되지 않는다.

③ 할인된 가격은 100달러이다.　　　　④ 기상 조건에 관계없이 프로그램이 진행될 것이다.

⑤ 이메일을 통해 등록을 할 수 없다.

 중요한 어휘를 확인하세요.

develop 발달시키다, 계발하다　　social skill 사교기술　　creativity 창의력　　participation 참가　　maximum 최대
outdoor activities 야외활동　　hiking 하이킹, 등산　　rafting 뗏목 타기, 래프팅　　register 등록하다　　notice 공지, 안내
run 진행되다, 운영하다　　regardless of ~와 관계없이　　condition 상태, 조건　　sign up 신청하다　　email 이메일을 보내다; 이메일

How to solve

Step 1 제목과 도입부를 통해 목적 파악하기

- **제목**　Summer Camp 2019 (2019년 여름 캠프)
- **도입부**　This is a great opportunity for developing social skills and creativity!
  (이것은 사교기술과 창의력을 발달시키기 위한 훌륭한 기회입니다!)
- ➡ **목적**　여름 캠프 소개

Step 2 선택지 먼저 읽고 확인할 사항 파악하기

① 참가 연령 제한이 없다. → Period & Participation(세부사항 1) 확인

② 야외 프로그램은 운영되지 않는다. → Programs(세부사항 2) 확인

③ 할인된 가격은 100달러이다. → Cost(세부사항 3) 확인

④ 기상 조건에 관계없이 프로그램이 진행될 것이다. → Notice(세부사항 4) 확인

⑤ 이메일을 통해 등록을 할 수 없다. → Notice(세부사항 4) 확인

Step 3 지문과 선택지 내용 비교하여 정답 확인하기

- 8–12 year olds (8세에서 12세) → 참가 연령에 제한이 있으므로 ①은 불일치
- Outdoor Activities (hiking, rafting, and camping)
  (야외 프로그램 (등산, 래프팅 그리고 캠핑)) → 야외 프로그램이 운영되므로 ②는 불일치
- Discounted: $90 (할인된 가격: 90달러) → 할인된 가격은 90달러이므로 ③은 불일치
- The programs will run regardless of weather conditions.
  (프로그램은 기상 조건에 관계없이 진행될 것이다.) → 기상 조건에 관계없이 진행되므로 ④가 일치!
- To sign up, email us at ~ (등록을 위해서는 ~로 이메일을 보내라)
  → 이메일을 통해 등록할 수 있으므로 ⑤는 불일치

안내문의 주요 구성

1. 전반부: 대회, 행사, 프로그램, 여행, 공연, 모집, 캠페인 등의 취지와 목적 간략 소개
2. 중반부: 시간, 장소, 대상, 마감일, 참가비, 교통편, 요금, 할인, 준비물, 주의사항 안내
3. 후반부: 참가 독려와 추가 정보(등록 및 신청 방법, 이메일, 전화번호, 사이트주소 등) 안내

Do It Yourself

01 Farm Experience Days에 관한 다음 안내문의 내용과 일치하지 <u>않는</u> 것은?

| 고1 전국연합 |

Farm Experience Days

Come and enjoy our Farm Experience Days.

Here are some activities you can enjoy:
- Collect eggs from our hens
- Feed the cows, sheep, and pigs
- Walk around the farm to learn about the animals

– The activities of the day may change according to the weather.

– The fee is $50 per person. This includes a hearty, homemade lunch.

– Reservations are required.

– We're only open on weekdays.

For more information, please call us at 5252 − 7088.

① 소, 양, 돼지에게 먹이를 줄 수 있다.
② 날씨에 따라 당일 체험 활동이 달라질 수 있다.
③ 점심 비용이 참가비에 포함되어 있다.
④ 예약이 필요하다.
⑤ 주말에도 이용할 수 있다.

지문에서의 어휘의 뜻을 써보고 해설에서 확인하세요.

- collect
- feed
- according to
- include
- hearty
- homemade
- reservation
- require
- weekday

구문 주요 구문을 살펴보아요.

3행 **Here are some activities** [1)] [you can enjoy] ~

부사 here가 문두에 와서 주어 some activities ～와 동사 are가 도치된 문장이다.
[1)]은 some activities를 수식하는 관계절이며, 앞에 목적격 관계대명사 that이 생략되어 있다.

02 Night at the Museum에 관한 다음 안내문의 내용과 일치하는 것은?

| 고1 전국연합 |

음성파일

지문에서의 어휘의 뜻을
써보고 해설에서 확인하세요.

- sculpture
- explore
- accommodation
- provide
- book
- sign up
- refund
- up to

Night at the Museum

Have you ever imagined sleeping with Egyptian sculptures or waking up beside mummies? Come to "Night at the Museum"! You can spend a night exploring the museum after dark!

Date & Time
Every third weekend of the month
(Saturday 6:30 p.m. to Sunday 7:30 a.m.)

Admission (Price)
8 to 13-year-olds only ($40 per child)

Including
Materials for activities, overnight accommodations, breakfast (Note: Food will not be provided until breakfast, so you should bring snacks.)

Booking Information
- Book tickets online through the "Night at the Museum" page on the museum website.
- You must sign up as a member on the museum website to book tickets.
- Refunds can only be given up to two weeks before the event.

① 매주 주말에 진행된다.
② 8세 이상이면 누구나 참여할 수 있다.
③ 음식 반입이 불가능하다.
④ 박물관 웹사이트 회원 가입 없이 티켓 예약이 가능하다.
⑤ 행사 2주전까지만 환불이 가능하다.

구문 주요 구문을 살펴보아요.

2행 1)**Have you ever imagined** 2)[sleeping with Egyptian sculptures] or 3)[waking up beside mummies]?

「Have you ever p.p. ~?」 형태의 의문문은 '~한 적이 있는가?' 정도로 해석한다.
or로 병렬 연결된 두 개의 동명사구 2)와 3)이 have ~ imagined의 목적어 역할을 한다.

Do It Yourself

03   Rainbow Basketball Program에 관한 다음 안내문의 내용과 일치하지 <u>않는</u> 것은?

> ### Rainbow Basketball Program
>
> We're open to all Rainbow Elementary School students in grades 1 through 6. A registration night will be held on Wednesday, October 26th from 5:30 p.m. to 7:00 p.m. in the Parks and Recreation Office in Rainbow Town Hall.
>
> • The registration deadline for all participants is Saturday, November 12th.
> • The early registration fee is $25 per child. After November 9th the fee will be $35.
>
> Coaches, assistant coaches and referees are always needed and welcome!
>
> For more information, please call the Parks and Recreation Office at (064) 432 − 1234.

① 1학년부터 6학년까지 참가할 수 있다.
② 등록을 위한 밤 행사가 10월 26일에 개최될 예정이다.
③ 등록 마감시한은 11월 12일이다.
④ 11월 9일 이전에 등록할 경우 등록비가 10달러 더 싸다.
⑤ 코치와 심판으로 지원하는 것은 불가하다.

지문에서의 어휘의 뜻을 써보고 해설에서 확인하세요.

- elementary school
- registration
- be held
- deadline
- participant
- fee
- assistant
- referee

구문 주요 구문을 살펴보아요.

3행 A registration night will **be held** on Wednesday, October 26th ~

hold가 '개최하다'의 의미이므로 수동태인 be held는 '개최되다'의 의미이다. 개최하는 주체보다 개최되는 대상이 중요한 경우는 이렇게 주로 수동태로 표현한다.

04 The Silent Book Contest 2020에 관한 다음 안내문의 내용과 일치하지 <u>않는</u> 것은?

The Silent Book Contest 2020

Deadline: February 15th 2020

Who may enter: The competition is open to illustrators aged 18 and over from around the world.

Description

• The Silent Book Contest 2020 is organized by the Town of Mulazzo, Italy. The competition is exclusively reserved for new, unpublished books with illustrations only. The story must be told by the illustrations, not by words. The subject of the book is open and should not be restricted to any age of readers.

• Submit your work in the form of a digital file.

Entry fee

The entry fee is €50.

Prize

The winner will receive €4,000 in cash and the winning book will be published commercially.

Please visit www.silentbookcontest.com for more information about the contest.

① 전 세계 18세 이상의 삽화가들에게 열려 있다.
② 출판되지 않은 책을 출품해야 한다.
③ 책의 주제는 어린이를 대상으로 해야 한다.
④ 작품은 디지털 파일 형태로 제출해야 한다.
⑤ 수상작은 출판될 예정이다.

지문에서의 어휘의 뜻을 써보고 해설에서 확인하세요.

• silent
• competition
• illustrator
• organize
• exclusively
• reserve
• subject
• restrict
• submit
• entry fee
• publish
• commercially

구문 주요 구문을 살펴보아요.

7행 The competition **is** exclusively **reserved** for new, unpublished books with illustrations only.

주어인 The competition이 reserve(따로 마련하다)의 동작 대상이므로, 술어동사는 수동태 「be+p.p.(과거분사)」가 쓰였다.

How was it? 배운 내용을 확인해보세요.

A 다음 영어는 우리말로, 우리말은 영어로 옮겨 쓰시오.

01 exhibition		11 fellow	
02 recognition		12 alert	
03 come up with		13 regulate	
04 conventional		14 stable	
05 예산		15 offspring	
06 urban		16 평균의; 평균	
07 raw		17 peak	
08 commercial		18 opposite	
09 struggle		19 chase	
10 paralyze		20 participant	

B 다음 각 네모 안의 말을 어법에 맞는 순서로 고쳐 쓰시오.

01 World War I had begun and many young soldiers came to the studio have / taken / to / their pictures . *Link p.58 Example*

➡ ____

02 Unfortunately, many Joshua trees have been dug up to be planted in urban areas, despite a very low rate of survival and planted / other places / in / when / removed .

Link p.61 02번

➡ ____

03 Like dolphins, orcas determine the position of an object by measuring how long an echo / for / it / return / takes / to from the object. *Link p.63 04번*

➡ ____

04 The number of Korean visitors with business interests in 2014 dropped in / that / with / the previous year / compared . *Link p.67 02번*

➡ ____

C

다음 영어는 우리말로, 우리말은 영어로 옮겨 쓰시오.

01 친척 _______________   11 maximum _______________

02 decline _______________   12 condition _______________

03 previous _______________   13 feed _______________

04 retail _______________   14 reservation _______________

05 proportion _______________   15 mummy _______________

06 transaction _______________   16 accommodation _______________

07 account for _______________   17 deadline _______________

08 음료 _______________   18 referee _______________

09 respectively _______________   19 competition _______________

10 slight _______________   20 restrict _______________

D

다음 각 문장의 밑줄 친 부분을 어법에 맞게 바르게 고쳐 쓰시오.

01 Have you ever imagined sleeping with Egyptian sculptures or **wake up** beside mummies? 🔗 Link p.73 02번

➡ ____

02 You can spend a night **explore** the museum after dark! 🔗 Link p.73 02번

➡ ____

03 Refunds can only **give** up to two weeks before the event. 🔗 Link p.73 02번

➡ ____

04 A registration night **will hold** on Wednesday, October 26th from 5:30 p.m. to 7:00 p.m. in the Parks and Recreation Office in Rainbow Town Hall. 🔗 Link p.74 03번

➡ ____

Part

3

어법 · 어휘

독해에서 어법과 어휘는 얼마나 중요한가요?

어법과 어휘는 독해를 위한 기본입니다. 지문을 해석하고 문제를 풀기 위해서는 어법에 대한 지식과 풍부한 어휘력이 반드시 먼저 갖추어져야 해요.

어법과 어휘 유형에서도 결국 독해력이 핵심이라는 거네요?

물론이죠. 글의 맥락을 먼저 파악한 다음, 그것을 중심으로 각 어법 요소와 어휘의 적절성을 판단해야 합니다.

그러면 어떻게 대비해야 하나요?

어법은 기본적인 문장구조 파악 능력이 우선입니다. 주어, 서술어 등 각 문장 성분과 여러 가지 품사의 기능을 반드시 익혀두어야 해요.

어휘는 어떻게 공부해야 할까요?

필수로 알아야 할 어휘들을 바탕으로, 독해를 하면서 모르는 어휘들은 따로 정리해 두고 시간이 날 때마다 틈틈이 외우세요. 반의어, 유의어, 관련 숙어도 함께 외우면 효과가 더 높겠죠?

단기간에 점수를 올리기는 어려울 것 같은데요?

맞습니다. 어법과 어휘는 영어의 기본 실력에 해당하므로 매일 조금씩이라도 꾸준히 공부하는 것이 중요해요. 그렇게 실력이 쌓여야 점수를 올릴 수 있는 영역입니다.

Unit 01 어법성 판단

1. 주어진 지문을 읽고, 어법의 적절성을 판단한다.
2. 밑줄 친 부분 중 어법상 틀린 것을 고르는 유형이 있다.
3. 네모 안의 두 개의 표현 중에서 어법에 맞는 것을 고르는 유형이 있다.
4. 매년 수능에 밑줄과 네모 유형 중 1문제가 꾸준히 출제되며, 최근에는 주로 밑줄 유형이 출제되고 있다.

Example

다음 글의 밑줄 친 부분 중, 어법상 **틀린** 것은?

| 고1 전국연합 |

Bad lighting can increase stress on your eyes, as can light that is too bright, or light that shines ① directly into your eyes. Fluorescent lighting can also be ② tiring. What you may not appreciate is that the quality of light may also be important. Most people are happiest in bright sunshine — this may cause a release of chemicals in the body ③ that bring a feeling of emotional well-being. Artificial light, which typically contains only a few wavelengths of light, ④ do not seem to have the same effect on mood that sunlight has. Try experimenting with working by a window or ⑤ using full spectrum bulbs in your desk lamp. You will probably find that this improves the quality of your working environment.

*fluorescent lighting 형광등

→ ① 부사의 쓰임 확인
→ ② -ing 형태의 쓰임 확인: 동명사/현재분사/진행형 등
→ 핵심 소재
→ ③ that의 쓰임 확인: 관계사/접속사/대명사/지시어 등
→ ④ 동사/조동사/병렬구조/수 일치 등 확인
→ ⑤ (or 이후) 병렬구조 확인

어휘 중요한 어휘를 확인하세요.

appreciate 인식하다 quality 질, 품질 release 배출, 분비 chemical 화학물질 artificial 인공의 typically 전형적으로
contain 포함하다, 담다 wavelength 파장 experiment 실험하다; 실험 spectrum 파장, 분포 범위 environment 환경

구문 주요 구문을 살펴보아요.

1행 1)[Bad lighting can **increase stress on your eyes**], 2)[**as can** 3){**light** 4)(that is too bright)}, or 5){**light** 6)(that shines directly into your eyes)}].

1)은 문장의 주절이고, 2)는 종속절이다.
2)의 can 뒤에는 중복되는 increase stress on your eyes가 생략되었으며, 주어가 길어서 이 생략된 술어동사가 주어인 3) 앞으로 도치된 형태이다. 2) 안에서 3)과 5)가 병렬로 연결되었다. as는 '~처럼'의 의미로 쓰였다.
4)와 6)은 각각 앞에 있는 light를 수식하는 관계절이다.

How to solve 이런 방법으로 접근하세요.

Step 1 글의 주제와 요지 파악하기

- ~ the quality of light may also be important (빛의 질 또한 중요할 수 있다)

➡ **주제** 조명의 질의 중요성

- ~ that bring a feeling of emotional well-being (정서적인 행복감을 주는 체내의 화학물질)
- ~ improves the quality of your working environment (여러분의 작업 환경의 질을 향상시킨다)

➡ **요지** 빛의 질이 중요하며, 이는 정서적인 행복감 및 작업 환경에 영향을 미친다.

Step 2 선택지가 묻고 있는 어법 요소 파악하기

① directly → 부사의 쓰임

② tiring → 형용사처럼 쓰인 현재분사

③ that → 관계대명사

④ do → 주어와 동사의 수 일치

⑤ using → 병렬구조

Step 3 각각 어법에 맞는지 파악하여 정답 확인하기

① 동사인 shines를 수식하는 부사 directly → 적절함

② 주어는 분사가 나타내는 동작(tire)의 행위자로, 형용사 역할을 하는 능동의 현재분사 tiring → 적절함

③ chemicals in the body를 수식하는 관계절을 이끄는 관계대명사 that → 적절함

④ 문장의 술어를 이끄는 조동사로, 단수인 주어 Artificial light과 수 일치를 이루어야 함

   → do는 어법상 틀리며, does로 고쳐야 함!

⑤ 등위접속사 or로 인해 앞에 있는 동명사구 working ~과 병렬을 이루므로, 동명사구를 유도하는 using → 적절함

수능에 자주 출제되는 어법 요소

1. 문장의 구조: 주어 자리에 들어갈 형태 및 동사 자리에 들어갈 형태
2. 동사: 동사의 수 일치, 능동태 vs. 수동태
3. 준동사: to부정사 vs. 원형부정사, 현재분사 vs. 과거분사, 준동사의 능동태 vs. 수동태
4. 품사 구별: 형용사 vs. 부사, 접속사 vs. 관계사, 관계대명사 vs. 관계부사
5. 특수 구문: 병렬구조, 간접의문문, 도치 구조, 대동사 구조

Do It Yourself 실전 문제를 풀어보세요.

01 (A), (B), (C)의 각 네모 안에서 어법에 맞는 표현으로 가장 적절한 것은?

| 고1 전국연합 |

When I was a young girl, my room was always a mess. My mother was always trying to get me to straighten it up, telling me, "Go clean your room!" I resisted her at every opportunity. I hated to (A) tell / be told what to do. I was determined to have my room the way I wanted it. (B) Because / Whether I actually liked living in a messy room or not was another subject altogether. I never stopped to think about the benefits of having a clean room. To me, it was more important to get my own way. And my mother, (C) alike / like most other parents, did not get me to realize the benefits for myself. Instead, she decided on lecturing.

	(A)		(B)		(C)
①	tell	⋯⋯	Because	⋯⋯	alike
②	tell	⋯⋯	Whether	⋯⋯	like
③	be told	⋯⋯	Because	⋯⋯	alike
④	be told	⋯⋯	Because	⋯⋯	like
⑤	be told	⋯⋯	Whether	⋯⋯	like

구문 주요 구문을 살펴보아요.

1행 My mother was always trying to get me 1)[to straighten it up], 2)[telling me, "Go clean your room]!"

1)은 get의 목적격 보어로 쓰인 to부정사구이다. 목적어인 me와 능동의 의미 관계로 연결되어 '내가 방을 정돈하게 하다'라는 뜻으로 해석한다.

2)는 분사구문으로 주절의 주어인 My mother를 의미상의 주어로 삼아 주어의 동시 동작을 표현한다. '나에게 ~라고 말씀하시면서'라는 뜻으로 해석할 수 있다.

02

다음 글의 밑줄 친 부분 중, 어법상 **틀린** 것은?　　　| 고1 전국연합 |

Grateful people are inclined to make healthy decisions. Life and sports present many situations ① where critical and difficult decisions have to be made. Selfish adults or kids do not make sound decisions as well as ② are grateful people. This includes the decision to be self-motivated. Frustrated parents ask: "How do I motivate my child to do sports or continue in sports? Sometimes my child gets ③ discouraged and does not want to put the required effort into his or her sports? What can I, as a parent, do or say to help?" It is difficult and almost impossible ④ to motivate kids or adults who are centered on their own narrow selfish desires. However, kids and adults who live as grateful people are able to motivate ⑤ themselves. They also welcome suggestions from others, even parents.

지문에서의 어휘의 뜻을 써보고 해설에서 확인하세요.

- grateful
- be inclined to
- decision
- present
- critical
- selfish
- sound
- self-motivated
- frustrated
- motivate
- discouraged
- centered on
- narrow

구문　주요 구문을 살펴보아요.

9행　1)It is difficult and almost impossible 2)[to motivate **kids or adults** 3){who are centered on their own narrow selfish desires}].

1) It은 형식상의 주어이고 to부정사구인 2)가 내용상의 주어이다. '~하는 것이 어렵고 거의 불가능하다'라는 뜻으로 해석한다.

3)은 kids or adults를 수식하는 관계절이다.

Do It Yourself

03 (A), (B), (C)의 각 네모 안에서 어법에 맞는 표현으로 가장 적절한 것은?

As soon as you accept that you are not super-human, you will be able to become your best self. (A) Be / Being your best self means loving and accepting all of yourself — and trusting where your heart lies in your lowest times. You can only be great when you are fully aware of yourself and supportive of that self. The best thing you could do at many places (B) are / is keep yourself healthy, balanced and happy, so that you can do more of what "you" do. Never waste your energy on making yourself feel bad. Use all of it to make yourself feel good. Know (C) that / what the bumps in the road are much smaller than they feel.

	(A)		(B)		(C)
①	Be	………	are	………	that
②	Be	………	is	………	what
③	Being	………	is	………	that
④	Being	………	is	………	what
⑤	Being	………	are	………	what

구문 주요 구문을 살펴보아요.

1행 **As soon as** you accept [1)][that you are not super-human], you will be able to become your best self.

As soon as는 시간을 나타내는 접속사 역할을 하며 '~하자마자'로 해석한다.
1)은 accept의 목적어로 쓰인 명사절이다.

04 다음 글의 밑줄 친 부분 중, 어법상 틀린 것은?

Your relationships will work best if you are able to be yourself within them. Relationships where you can be yourself ① <u>are</u> likely to feel more comfortable and to make you happier. This is not to say that you should throw tantrums when you feel like it, and be as ② <u>rudely</u> to people as you wish. Nor ③ <u>is it</u> to suggest that all relationships should be comfortable. Some very good ones can be provocative and ④ <u>challenging</u>. It is rather that relationships tend to become unstable and to be less satisfying when you are not yourself. It follows that it is helpful to be curious about your relationships and ⑤ <u>try</u> to understand them.

*throw a tantrum 성질을 내다

지문에서의 어휘의 뜻을
써보고 해설에서 확인하세요.

- relationship
- be oneself
- be likely to
- comfortable
- rudely
- provocative
- challenging
- unstable
- satisfying
- curious

구문 주요 구문을 살펴보아요.

9행 **It** follows [1)][that **it** is helpful [2)]{to be curious about your relationships} and [3)]{try to understand them}].

1)은 문장 맨 앞의 It을 형식상의 주어로 삼은 내용상의 주어이다. 직역하면 '~라는 결론이 뒤따른다'라는 뜻인데, '결론은 ~가 된다는 것이다'로 자연스럽게 해석할 수 있다.
병렬구조로 연결된 2)와 3)은 1) 안에 있는 it을 형식상의 주어로 삼은 내용상의 주어인데, '여러분의 관계에 대해 궁금해 하고, 그것들을 이해하려고 노력하는 것은 도움이 된다'라는 의미로 해석한다.

100제로 완성하는 어법

1. 동사

Point 1   **수 일치**   [단수 주어, 복수 주어, 수식어-구, 수식어-절, 삽입어구, 부정사 주어, 동명사 주어, 분수 주어, 부분 주어]

 다음 각 네모 안에서 적절한 것을 고르시오.

001   The perfume of wildflowers $\boxed{\text{fill / fills}}$ the air as the grass dances upon a gentle breeze.   수능 응용

002   Those who never make it $\boxed{\text{are / is}}$ the ones who quit too soon.

003   The dead bodies of organisms in the forest, which in turn nourish other organisms, $\boxed{\text{are / is}}$ broken down and turned into soil.

004   To exclude those from voting who are already socially isolated $\boxed{\text{destroy / destroys}}$ our democracy, as it creates a caste system.

005   Building new golf courses $\boxed{\text{are / is}}$ the fastest kind of land development in the world.

006   About three-fifths of the rubber used in the United States $\boxed{\text{go / goes}}$ into tires and tubes.   고3 전국연합 응용

007   Some of my friends $\boxed{\text{think / thinks}}$ I'm silly to work and save for a bike.

어휘   중요한 어휘를 확인하세요.

perfume 향수, 향기   **grass** 풀, 잔디   **gentle** 부드러운   **breeze** 산들바람   **make it** 성공하다   **organism** 생물체, 유기체
nourish 영양분을 공급하다   **soil** 토양, 흙   **exclude** 배제[제외]하다   **isolate** 고립시키다   **democracy** 민주주의
caste system 카스트 제도   **rubber** 고무   **silly** 어리석은

정답   **001** fills   **002** are   **003** are   **004** destroys   **005** is   **006** goes   **007** think

※문장의 해석과 풀이는 해설에서 확인하세요.

Point 2 시제 [과거, 현재, 과거완료, 현재완료, 시간의 부사절]

 다음 각 네모 안에서 적절한 것을 고르시오.

008 Because populations decreased / have decreased a century or so ago, all the koalas in southern Australia today are descended from a small number of recent ancestors.

009 The steamer leaves / left every Tuesday in winter, but in summer both on Tuesdays and Fridays.

010 Later my mother came home and asked me what I have / had been doing.

011 Over the years, I am / have frequently counseled people who wanted better jobs to show more initiative.

012 By the time Jane gets / will get home, her father will have left for Chicago.

Point 3 능동과 수동 [지각동사의 수동태, 명령문의 수동태, 주어와 동사의 관계-능동/수동, 목적어가 절인 경우의 수동태]

 다음 각 네모 안에서 적절한 것을 고르시오.

013 Unlike a stream, a glacier cannot be seen move / to move.

014 Let nothing but your name written / be written on this side.

015 I still remember the awesome feeling I had on that day in May when my little feet carried / were carried me up the stairs into the grandstands at the car racing stadium.

016 Some of our scientific theories are going to prove / be proved false.

017 Acupuncture believes / is believed to be very effective.

어휘 중요한 어휘를 확인하세요.

population 인구 수, 개체 수 descend 내려오다, 전해지다 ancestor 조상, 선조 steamer 기선, 증기선 counsel 상담하다
initiative 주도(권) glacier 빙하 awesome 대단한 grandstand 특별 관람석 theory 이론 prove 입증하다
acupuncture 침술

정답 **008** decreased **009** leaves **010** had **011** have **012** gets **013** to move **014** be written
015 carried **016** be proved **017** is believed
※문장의 해석과 풀이는 해설에서 확인하세요.

Point **4** 동사에 대해 알아야 할 기타 내용 [문장 형성에 있어서 동사의 역할, 자동사 vs. 타동사]

 다음 각 네모 안에서 적절한 것을 고르시오.

018 William Kamkwamba leaving / left school at 14 as his family was unable to pay the school fees. 고3 전국연합 응용

019 With Mom, everything she touched turned / turning to gold.

020 Families in Egypt mourned the death of a cat and had the body of the dead cat wrapped in cloth before it was finally laid / lain to rest.

어휘 중요한 어휘를 확인하세요.

school fee 학비   mourn 애도하다, 슬퍼하다   wrap 싸다   cloth 천, 옷감   lay 놓다, 눕히다, 두다(-laid-laid)

정답 **018** left   **019** turned   **020** laid
※문장의 해석과 풀이는 해설에서 확인하세요.

2. 준동사

Point 1 목적어로 쓰이는 준동사 [동명사, 부정사, 전치사의 목적어]

 다음 각 네모 안에서 적절한 것을 고르시오.

021 These caravans, which can have two to six beds, can be moved and many families enjoy ┃traveling / to travel┃ from place to place on holidays.

022 Situated at an elevation of 1,350m, the city of Kathmandu, which looks out on the sparkling Himalayas, enjoys a warm climate year-round that makes ┃living / to live┃ here pleasant.

023 We tend to believe that our taste in music is a great way of ┃expressing / expressive┃ our individuality.

024 They don't slaughter their cattle for food; but if a cow is killed, then the horns are used for containers; the hides are used ┃making / to make┃ shoes, clothing, and bed coverings.

025 Poor Simba had been shot twice and he did not even raise his head. Finally, Simba stopped ┃breathing / to breathe┃.

어휘 중요한 어휘를 확인하세요.

caravan 이동식 주택, 캐러밴　　from place to place 이리저리, 여기저기　　situate 위치시키다　　elevation 고지대, 고도　　sparkling 반짝이는, 불꽃을 내는　　climate 기후　　year-round 일 년 내내, 연중 내내　　pleasant 즐거운　　individuality 개성　　slaughter 도살하다; 도살　　cattle 소(떼)　　horn 뿔　　container 그릇, 용기　　hide 가죽; 숨기다　　shoot (총을) 쏘다　　raise 들어올리다

정답 **021** traveling　　**022** living　　**023** expressing　　**024** to make　　**025** breathing

※문장의 해석과 풀이는 해설에서 확인하세요.

Point **2**　**목적격 보어로 쓰이는 준동사**　[지각동사-능동, (준)사역동사-수동, 목적어와 능동/수동 관계]

 Check　다음 각 네모 안에서 적절한 것을 고르시오.

026　I watched a man on the Métro try / tried to get off the train and fail.

027　Clauss watched a pair of swimmers waved / waving their arms.

028　Planning is important, but it is action that gets things do / done.

029　You should make your feelings know / known to him.

Point **3**　**분사**　[능동, 수동, 분사구문-능동, 분사구문-수동]

Check　다음 각 네모 안에서 적절한 것을 고르시오.

030　I've always found it disappointed / disappointing that people rather take their time with career than with kids.

031　In some Asian cultures, the act of giving is an important aspect of gift-giving, and this process may appear confused / confusing to Westerners.

032　Birth order may define your role within a family, but as you mature into adulthood, accepted / accepting other social roles, birth order becomes insignificant. 수능 응용

033　The average office worker is scared to leave the office. Terrified / Terrifying that the boss might think they're lazy, they stay at their desks even if they have little to do.

어휘　중요한 어휘를 확인하세요.

Métro (도시의) 지하철　　get off (탈것에서) 내리다　　aspect 측면, 양상　　process 과정　　birth order 출생 순서　　mature 성숙하다, 성장하다　　adulthood 성인기, 성인임　　insignificant 중요하지 않은　　average 평균의; 평균　　office worker 사무실에서 일하는 근무자　　terrify 겁나게 하다

정답　**026** try　　**027** waving　　**028** done　　**029** known　　**030** disappointing　　**031** confusing　　**032** accepting　　**033** Terrified
※문장의 해석과 풀이는 해설에서 확인하세요.

3. 명사, 대명사

Point 1 　**명사와 대명사의 수**　[단수 vs. 복수, 명사의 수, 대명사의 수, 단수 취급 명사, 소유격대명사]

Check　다음 각 네모 안에서 적절한 것을 고르시오.

034　The first thing I notice upon entering this garden is that the ankle-high grass is greener than 〔that / those〕 on the other side of the fence.　수능 응용

035　Things often seem at 〔its / their〕 worst just before they get better.

036　My father is wonderful and I love all 220 pounds of him, but do you think he should sit in the living room in his swimwear when I have 〔company / a company〕?

037　Kathmandu is now the capital of Nepal and, as such, the center of 〔its / it's〕 government, economy, and culture.

Point 2 　**대명사 기타**　[재귀대명사, 부정대명사, 〈동사+부사〉의 대명사 목적어]

Check　다음 각 네모 안에서 적절한 것을 고르시오.

038　Non-English players in the English Premier League are needed to use very basic phrases to introduce 〔them / themselves〕, and ask and answer questions about basic personal details.

039　When a lecturer presents a succession of new concepts, students' faces begin to show signs of frustration; some write furiously in their notebooks, while 〔other / others〕 give up writing in complete discouragement.　고3 전국연합 응용

040　Kids and adults who live as grateful people are able to motivate 〔them / themselves〕.

041　Possibly the most effective way to focus on your goals is to 〔write down them / write them down〕.

어휘　중요한 어휘를 확인하세요.

ankle-high 발목 높이의　　swimwear 수영복　　capital 수도　　government 정부　　economy 경제　　phrase 말, 구절
lecturer 강연자, 강사　　a succession of 연이은, 계속되는　　frustration 좌절　　furiously 맹렬하게, 극단적으로
grateful 감사해하는　　motivate 동기[자극]를 주다

정답　**034** that　　**035** their　　**036** company　　**037** its　　**038** themselves　　**039** others　　**040** themselves
041 write them down
※문장의 해석과 풀이는 해설에서 확인하세요.

4. 형용사, 부사, 비교

Point 1 **형용사, 부사** [almost/most, few/little, many/much, 형용사/부사, high/highly, enough, 형용사 보어]

 **다음 각 네모 안에서 적절한 것을 고르시오.**

042 Many people think the secret is kimchi, a traditional Korean dish served with almost / most every meal.

043 Her clear and elegant prose sets her apart from almost / most other journalists.

044 You may think that moving a short distance is so easy that you can do it in no time with few / little effort. 수능 응용

045 He wasn't a great scholar, but as a teacher he had few / little peers.

046 Perhaps the greatest thing about being a devoted operagoer is that there is so many / much room for growth.

047 The birth rate is low at 1.8 children per woman, and the number of elderly people is growing rapid / rapidly.

048 Feathers help to keep a bird warm / warmly by trapping heat produced by the body close to the surface of the skin.

049 I believe the experiment is high / highly educational.

050 The fact that someone is enough interested / interested enough to give help to poor villagers often works wonders.

051 Your problems and challenges suddenly seem insignificant / insignificantly.

어휘 중요한 어휘를 확인하세요.

elegant 우아한, 고상한   prose 산문(체)   journalist 언론인, 기자   scholar 학자   peer 동료   devoted 헌신적인, 전념[몰두]하는
operagoer 오페라 관람을 자주 다니는 사람   birth rate 출생률   elderly people 노인   rapid 빠른   feather 깃털   trap 가두다
villager 마을 사람, 주민   work wonders 기적을 일으키다   challenge 도전, 난제

정답 **042** almost   **043** most   **044** little   **045** few   **046** much   **047** rapidly   **048** warm   **049** highly
  050 interested enough   **051** insignificant
※문장의 해석과 풀이는 해설에서 확인하세요.

Point 2 비교 [열등비교, 동등비교, 비교급의 강조, 비교구문, 비교급 관용표현]

  다음 각 네모 안에서 적절한 것을 고르시오.

052 I'm the youngest child and thus less aggressive / aggressively than my older brothers and sisters.

053 Without your contributions over the years, we would not be as successful as / than we have been.

054 It can happen that one's memories grow much / very sharper even after a long passage of time.

055 It is better to do mathematics on a blackboard as / than on a piece of paper because chalk is easier to erase, and mathematical research is often filled with mistakes.

056 In quicksand, the more you struggle, the deep / deeper you'll sink.

어휘 중요한 어휘를 확인하세요.

aggressive 공격적인, 적극적인　　contribution 공헌, 기여　　sharp 예리한, 뚜렷한　　mathematics 수학　　mathematical 수학(상)의
be filled with ~로 가득 차다　　quicksand 유사(사람·물건이 빨려 들어가는 유동성 모래)　　struggle 분투하다　　sink 가라앉다

정답 052 aggressive　　053 as　　054 much　　055 than　　056 deeper
※문장의 해석과 풀이는 해설에서 확인하세요.

5. 관계사, 접속사, 전치사

Point 1 **관계사** [관계대명사 that/which/what, 접속사 that, 관계부사, 복합 관계대명사]

 다음 각 네모 안에서 적절한 것을 고르시오.

057 Many social scientists have believed for some time that / what birth order directly affects both personality and achievement in adult life.

058 Although it may be hard for kids to believe such results, they need to learn that they have to be responsible for that / what they eat.

059 Using a specially developed website, they / which offered more than 14,000 people the opportunity to download free music.

060 There are things what / which in a sense I remembered, but which did not strike me as strange or interesting until quite recently.

061 A movie set is the area where / which a motion picture is filmed.

062 At around ten o'clock, twenty people are chosen from the jurors in attendance and are taken to a courtroom where a judge describes how / what the process is going to work.

063 Number one was: "I was born," and you could put however / whatever you liked after that.

어휘 중요한 어휘를 확인하세요.

affect ~에 영향을 미치다   **be responsible for** ~에 대해 책임이 있다   **strike** (생각·주의 등을) 끌다   **motion picture** 영화
juror 배심원   **in attendance** 참석하여   **courtroom** 법정   **judge** 판사

정답 **057** that   **058** what   **059** they   **060** which   **061** where   **062** how   **063** whatever
※문장의 해석과 풀이는 해설에서 확인하세요.

Point 2   접속사, 전치사   [because/because of, whether, like]

 다음 각 네모 안에서 적절한 것을 고르시오.

064   We study philosophy │because / because of│ the mental skills it helps us develop.

고3 모의수능 응용

065   │Whether / That│ the judgment is accurate or not, once you accept it, it will probably influence the way you respond to the neighbor.

066   Falling in love is │like / alike│ being wrapped in a magical cloud.

어휘 중요한 어휘를 확인하세요.

philosophy 철학   **mental** 정신적인, 심리적인   **judgment** 판단   **accurate** 정확한   **influence** ~에 영향을 미치다   **neighbor** 이웃   **wrap** 싸다, 포장하다

정답   **064** because of   **065** Whether   **066** like

※문장의 해석과 풀이는 해설에서 확인하세요.

6. 가정법, 조동사

Point 1 **가정법** [가정법 과거, 가정법 과거완료, as if[though], I wish, unless]

 **다음 각 네모 안에서 적절한 것을 고르시오.**

067 If it were not for the special defenses they have against their enemies, many animals cannot / could not survive.

068 If you turned / had turned a light toward Mars that day, it would have reached Mars in 186 seconds. 수능 응용

069 He wanted actors to perform his plays as if they had been / were musical scores.

070 I wish I could help / could have helped you with the inventory next week, but I'm afraid I'll still be arranging the window displays.

071 Remember, you're writing for people who have not yet read the book, so providing unclear comments won't be helpful unless some specifics are / aren't also included.

어휘 중요한 어휘를 확인하세요.

defense 방어, 수비   **enemy** 적, 원수   **musical score** 악보   **inventory** 재고, 상품 목록   **window display** (쇼 윈도에의) 상품 진열
specific 세부적인[상세한] 것; 구체적인

정답 **067** could not   **068** had turned   **069** were   **070** could help   **071** are
※문장의 해석과 풀이는 해설에서 확인하세요.

Point 2 조동사 [insist that/propose that ~ should, must have p.p., might[may] have p.p., should have p.p.]

 다음 각 네모 안에서 적절한 것을 고르시오.

072 Many witnesses insisted that the accident had taken / should take place on the crosswalk.

073 The gentleman proposed that he give / gave me a ten-dollar reward for my honesty.

074 The police have deduced that Mr. Baker must / should have left his apartment yesterday evening.

075 New scientific evidence shows dinosaurs might / should have been warm-blooded animals that behaved more like mammals than reptiles.

076 I regret having paid little attention to him. In other words, I should be / have paid more attention to him.

어휘 중요한 어휘를 확인하세요.

witness 목격자　　insist 주장하다, 고집하다　　take place 발생하다　　propose 제의[제안]하다　　deduce 추정하다, 추론하다
warm-blooded 온혈의　　mammal 포유동물　　reptile 파충류　　regret 후회하다　　pay attention to ~에게 주목하다[주의를 기울이다]
in other words 다시 말해

정답　**072** had taken　　**073** give　　**074** must　　**075** might　　**076** have
※문장의 해석과 풀이는 해설에서 확인하세요.

7. 특수 구문

Point 1 병렬 [동명사, 동사, 부정사, or, 형용사구, 절]

 **다음 각 네모 안에서 적절한 것을 고르시오.**

077 In case of an emergency, you have to open the doors yourself by pushing a button, depressing a lever or slide / sliding them.

078 As a reviewer, you analyze the book for how it tells a story and evaluate / evaluates the quality of writing and organization.

079 His next goal is to provide enough energy for his entire village and eventually go / goes to college. 고3 전국연합 응용

080 Huge amounts of space are given over to parking lots rather than trees and birds / to trees and birds .

Point 2 생략과 도치 [부사절에서의 생략, 부정어 및 부사구 도치]

다음 각 네모 안에서 적절한 것을 고르시오.

081 If you ever feel ill when travel / traveling in remote foreign parts, just drop some gunpowder into a glass of warm, soapy water, and swallow it.

082 The cattle, though owned / owning by the man, are considered to belong to the man's entire family.

083 Not only this enables / does this enable us to choose our response to particular circumstances, but this encourages us to create circumstances.

084 Only when you are willing to put forth an effort a life is / is a life of value possible.

어휘 중요한 어휘를 확인하세요.

emergency 비상[응급] 상황   depress 끌어내리다, 내리누르다   evaluate 평가하다   organization 조직, 구성   entire 전체의
eventually 결국, 마침내   huge 거대한, 매우 큰   ill 아픈   remote 먼, 멀리 떨어진   gunpowder 화약   soapy water 비눗물
swallow 삼키다   cattle 소(떼)   circumstance 상황, 환경

정답 **077** sliding   **078** evaluate   **079** go   **080** to trees and birds   **081** traveling   **082** owned   **083** does this enable   **084** is a life
※문장의 해석과 풀이는 해설에서 확인하세요.

Point 3 대동사, 간접의문문 [do, 간접의문의 어순]

 다음 각 네모 안에서 적절한 것을 고르시오.

085 You are under the false impression that you do not have as many items to pack as you really are / do . 수능 응용

086 The first thing a doctor will need to know includes what kind and how much of the poisonous plant was eaten, when it was eaten / was it eaten , and what part of the plant was consumed.

087 Almost everyone has heard of Halley's comet, but most people do not know what are comets / what comets are .

Point 4 부정과 강조 [rarely, no, neither ~ nor ... , 부분부정, It ~ that ... 강조, 비교급 강조]

 다음 각 네모 안에서 적절한 것을 고르시오.

088 Troubled by the recent events, he became withdrawn, rare / rarely speaking to even his closest friends.

089 Everyone was willing to participate in the drill, but no / not one was enthusiastic about it.

090 Our policy is to neither confirm or / nor deny information about the company that has not originated from our Public Affairs office.

091 We've always found somewhere to stay before. True, but we may no / not always be so lucky.

어휘 중요한 어휘를 확인하세요.

false 잘못된, 틀린   **impression** 인상   **poisonous** 유독성의   **consume** 소비[소모]하다, 먹어치우다   **comet** 혜성   **withdrawn** 고립한, 수줍어하는, 소심한   **be willing to** 기꺼이 ~하다   **drill** 훈련, 연습   **enthusiastic** 열정적인   **policy** 정책   **confirm** 확인[확정]하다   **deny** 부정[부인]하다   **originate** 유래하다

정답 **085** do   **086** it was eaten   **087** what comets are   **088** rarely   **089** no   **090** nor   **091** not

※문장의 해석과 풀이는 해설에서 확인하세요.

092 Experts say that India realizes it can not necessary / necessarily rely on oil and gas to power its economy.

093 It is while cheese is ripening that is developed / it develops its own special flavor and color.

094 Though some people have much / very less free time than others, nearly everyone has some opportunity to give.

어휘 중요한 어휘를 확인하세요.

expert 전문가　　**rely on** ~에 의존하다　　**power** ~에 힘을 주다, 동력[전력]을 공급하다　　**ripen** 익다, 숙성하다　　**flavor** 맛, 풍미

정답 **092** necessarily　　**093** it develops　　**094** much
※문장의 해석과 풀이는 해설에서 확인하세요.

8. 관용 표현

Point 1 관용 구문 [in that, look forward to -ing, object to -ing, prevent A from -ing, have difficulty -ing, as/like]

 다음 각 네모 안에서 적절한 것을 고르시오.

095 Ice Hockey is unusual among the major sports in such / that teams frequently play with different numbers of players.

096 I look forward to help / helping you solve the problems outlined in our earlier discussion.

097 I strongly object to be / being charged a fee for using my credit card.

098 She said this policy would prevent companies from creating / to create new jobs.

099 I know what you mean. I've been studying Italian for 6 years and have difficulty having / to have a simple conversation.

100 Very hard as / like he works, he can not pass the better university.

어휘 중요한 어휘를 확인하세요.

major 주요한   **frequently** 자주, 빈번히   **look forward to A** A를 기대하다   **solve** 해결하다   **outline** 윤곽을 그리다; 윤곽
object to A A에 반대하다   **charge** (대금을) 청구하다   **policy** 정책   **create** 만들다, 창출하다

정답 **095** that   **096** helping   **097** being   **098** creating   **099** having   **100** as
※문장의 해석과 풀이는 해설에서 확인하세요.

02 어휘 추론

 1. 주어진 지문을 읽고, 어휘의 적절성을 파악한다.
2. 네모 안의 어휘 중 문맥에 맞는 어휘를 고르는 유형이 있다.
3. 밑줄 친 어휘 중 문맥에 맞지 않는 어휘를 고르는 유형이 있다.

Example

(A), (B), (C)의 각 네모 안에서 문맥에 맞는 낱말로 가장 적절한 것은? | 고1 전국연합 |

How does a leader make people feel important? First, by listening to them. Let them
(→ 주제를 담은 문장)
know you respect their thinking, and let them (A) silence / voice their opinions. As an
(→ (A)의 단서 제시)
added bonus, you might learn something! A friend of mine once told me about the CEO

of a large company who told one of his managers, "There's nothing you could possibly tell

5 me that I haven't already thought about before. Don't ever tell me what you think unless I

ask you. Is that understood?" Imagine the (B) improvement / loss of self-esteem that
(→ (B)의 단서 제시)
manager must have felt. It must have discouraged him and negatively affected his

performance. On the other hand, when you make a person feel a great sense of
(→ (C)의 단서 제시)
importance, he or she will feel on top of the world — and the level of energy will

10 (C) decrease / increase rapidly.

	(A)		(B)		(C)
①	silence	········	improvement	········	decrease
②	silence	········	loss	········	increase
③	voice	········	improvement	········	decrease
④	voice	········	loss	········	decrease
⑤	voice	········	loss	········	increase

 중요한 어휘를 확인하세요.

respect 존중하다, 존경하다　　opinion 의견　　added 추가된　　manager 관리자　　self-esteem 자존감　　discourage 낙담시키다
negatively 부정적으로　　performance (업무) 수행　　feel on top of the world 의기양양하다　　rapidly 빠르게

 주요 구문을 살펴보아요.

6행 Imagine [1)][the loss of self-esteem [2)]{that manager [3)]**must have felt**}].

1)은 Imagine의 목적어 역할을 하는 명사구이다.
2)는 the loss of self-esteem을 수식하는 목적격 관계대명사절이다.
3) 〈must have p.p.〉는 과거 사실에 대한 강한 추측을 나타내며, '그 관리자가 틀림없이 느꼈을'로 해석할 수 있다.

How to solve

Step 1 도입부에서 주제 파악하기

· How does a leader make people feel important?

(지도자는 어떻게 사람들이 (자기가) 중요하다고 느끼게 하는가?)

➡ **주제** 상대가 스스로 중요하다고 느끼도록 만드는 지도자의 자질

Step 2 각 어휘의 뜻 파악 후 풀이의 단서 찾기

· (A) 침묵하게 하다 / 소리 내어 말하다 ➡ **단서** Let them know you respect their thinking ~

(여러분이 그들의 생각을 존중한다는 것을 알게 하라)

· (B) 향상 / 상실 ➡ **단서** Don't ever tell me what you think unless I ask you.

(내가 당신에게 묻지 않으면 당신이 생각하는 것을 나에게 절대로 말하지 마라.)

· (C) 감소하다 / 증가하다 ➡ **단서** ~ when you make a person feel a great sense of importance, ~

(여러분이 누군가에게 (그 자신이) 아주 중요한 사람이라는 의식을 느끼게 하면 그 사람은 의기양양해질 것이다)

Step 3 정답 확인하기

➡ (A) 상대의 생각을 존중한다는 것을 알리려면 그들이 의견을 말하게 해야 함 → voice가 적절함

➡ (B) 최고 경영자에게 생각하는 것을 말하지 말라는 얘기를 들은 관리자가 느꼈을 감정 → loss가 적절함

➡ (C) 중요한 사람이라는 의식을 느꼈을 때 그 사람의 활력 수준 → increase가 적절함

자주 나오는 상반된 의미의 어휘

1. 형용사

· limited 제한된 ↔ sufficient 충분한
· frequent 자주 있는 ↔ rare 드문
· favorable 우호적인 ↔ hostile 적대적인
· ordinary 평범한 ↔ luxurious 호화로운
· selfish 이기적인 ↔ unselfish 사심이 없는, 이타적인

· identical 동일한 ↔ opposite 반대의
· valid 유효한 ↔ invalid 무효한
· abundant 풍부한 ↔ scarce 부족한
· permanent 영구적인 ↔ temporary 일시적인
· variable 변동이 심한 ↔ invariable 변하지 않는

2. 동사

· avoid 피하다 ↔ embrace 수용하다
· resist 저항하다 ↔ assist 돕다
· ignore 무시하다 ↔ follow 추종하다
· prevent 막다 ↔ promote 촉진하다
· contract 수축하다 ↔ expand 확장하다

· reveal 드러내다 ↔ conceal 감추다
· decline 쇠퇴하다 ↔ improve 향상되다
· maintain 유지하다 ↔ disturb 방해하다
· release 풀어주다 ↔ reserve 보유하다
· accept 받아들이다 ↔ challenge 이의를 제기하다

3. 명사

· benefit 이익 ↔ loss 손실
· demand 수요 ↔ supply 공급
· lack 부족, 결핍 ↔ presence 있음, 존재
· restriction 제한 ↔ freedom 자유
· maximum 최대(의) ↔ minimum 최소(의)

· reduction 감소 ↔ increase 증가
· appearance 출현 ↔ extinction 소멸
· connection 연결 ↔ disconnection 단절
· surplus 흑자 ↔ deficit 적자

실전 문제를 풀어보세요.

01 (A), (B), (C)의 각 네모 안에서 문맥에 맞는 낱말로 가장 적절한 것은?

| 고1 전국연합 |

Most people assume that if they're going to start on a six-month expedition, they should take a ton of gear to prepare for all the possible challenges. However, the (A) absence / experience of professional backpackers who have explored every corner of the world teaches us the exact opposite: the longer the backpacking trip, the (B) less / more you should carry. It's better to carry a light pack and re-supply every four days or so. Since it's (C) bearable / unbearable for an average backpacker to carry more than 10 days of food, a long distance backpacker must re-supply along the way.

	(A)		(B)		(C)
①	absence	·········	less	·········	bearable
②	absence	·········	more	·········	unbearable
③	experience	·········	less	·········	bearable
④	experience	·········	more	·········	bearable
⑤	experience	·········	less	·········	unbearable

지문에서의 어휘의 뜻을
써보고 해설에서 확인하세요.

- assume
- expedition
- gear
- challenge
- backpacker
- explore
- exact
- opposite
- average
- along the way

구문 수요 구문을 살펴보아요.

1행 Most people assume [1)][that [2)]{if they're going to start on a six-month expedition}, they should take a ton of gear to prepare for all the possible challenges].

1)의 that절이 assume의 목적어 역할을 한다.
2)는 that절 내의 부사절로서, '~한다면'이라는 조건의 의미를 갖는다.

02 다음 글의 밑줄 친 부분 중, 문맥상 낱말의 쓰임이 적절하지 <u>않은</u> 것은?

| 고1 전국연합 |

음성파일

My brother, the mountain climber, once took me and a friend up the 13,776-foot Grand Teton. It was terrifying! As we ① <u>climbed</u>, the mountain went straight up. At that point, we tied ourselves together with ropes to save our lives if one of us ② <u>fell</u>. That rope kept me from taking thousand-foot falls to my death two times. By ③ <u>blocking</u> each other and trusting in the ropes, we finally reached the top safely. You will do a lot more in life if you rope up and ④ <u>borrow</u> strength from others. The more ropes you have, the ⑤ <u>better</u> your chances are for success.

지문에서의 어휘의 뜻을
써보고 해설에서 확인하세요.

- mountain climber
- terrifying
- tie
- save
- borrow
- strength
- chance

구문 주요 구문을 살펴보아요.

1행 **My brother**, 1)[the mountain climber], once took me and a friend up the 13,776-foot Grand Teton.

My brother와 명사구 1)은 콤마로 연결된 동격 관계이며, '산악 등반가인 나의 형'으로 해석할 수 있다.

Do It Yourself

03 다음 글의 밑줄 친 부분 중, 문맥상 낱말의 쓰임이 적절하지 <u>않은</u> 것은?

We have witnessed great leaders ① <u>display</u> their passion, vulnerability and compassion through tears, and often our response is actually to feel a greater connection with them. Witnessing ② <u>raw</u> emotions can connect us together in a way
⁵ that words alone would not achieve. Researcher and expert on shame and vulnerability Brene Brown suggests that our capacity to be ③ <u>vulnerable</u> is the key to living a whole-hearted life. As a manager, leader and colleague it is important that you ④ <u>recognise</u> that tears and sadness are okay. Don't be afraid to
¹⁰ allow others the space to show this and do not be afraid to ⑤ <u>hide</u> your own humanness if the situation arises.

*vulnerability 취약함

지문에서의 어휘의 뜻을 써보고 해설에서 확인하세요.

- witness
- display
- passion
- compassion
- connection
- raw
- expert
- shame
- capacity
- recognise
- humanness
- arise

구문 주요 구문을 살펴보아요.

1행 1) [We have witnessed great leaders 2) {display their passion, vulnerability and compassion through tears}], and 3) [often our response is actually 4) {to feel a greater connection with them}].

첫 번째 절 1)에서 witnessed가 지각동사이고 great leaders가 목적어이며, 원형부정사구인 2)가 목적격 보어이다.

두 번째 절 3)의 안에 있는 4)는 to부정사구로, 주격 보어 역할을 하며, '그들과 더 큰 연결성을 느끼는 것'으로 해석될 수 있다.

04

(A), (B), (C)의 각 네모 안에서 문맥에 맞는 낱말로 가장 적절한 것은?

Looking at pictures actually helps your brain to remember better. Short-term memory, also called working memory, relies heavily on the visual cortex. Words that are read are processed very quickly by our brains. They don't (A) stick / turn around for very long. But recording a picture in your brain takes longer. This means you have to invest your time to remember something. So, the more time spent looking at the picture, the (B) better / worse your memory of it. Saying a word out loud does the same thing. It takes (C) longer / shorter to speak a word than it does to read it. That's why you remember it better when you say it aloud. Therefore, when you are doing last-minute cramming for a test, look at pictures and speak things out loud. Your memory — and your test score — will thank you.

*cortex 대뇌 피질 **cramming 벼락치기, 억지로 쑤셔넣기

지문에서의 어휘의 뜻을 써보고 해설에서 확인하세요.

- actually
- short-term
- rely on
- visual
- process
- record
- invest

	(A)		(B)		(C)
①	stick	········	better	········	longer
②	stick	········	better	········	shorter
③	stick	········	worse	········	longer
④	turn	········	worse	········	shorter
⑤	turn	········	better	········	longer

구문 주요 구문을 살펴보아요.

10행 **That's why** you remember it better when you say it aloud.

「That's why ~」 구문은 '그것이 ~한 이유이다'로 해석할 수 있다.

How was it? 배운 내용을 확인해보세요.

A

다음 영어는 우리말로, 우리말은 영어로 옮겨 쓰시오.

01 appreciate		11 grateful	
02 release		12 selfish	
03 artificial		13 건전한	
04 spectrum		14 frustrated	
05 환경		15 discouraged	
06 mess		16 bump	
07 straighten up		17 rudely	
08 resist		18 provocative	
09 altogether		19 challenging	
10 깨닫다		20 unstable	

B

다음 각 네모 안의 말을 어법에 맞는 순서로 고쳐 쓰시오.

01 I / whether / in a messy room / or not / actually liked living was another subject altogether. Link p.82 01번

➡ ____

02 It is difficult and almost impossible to motivate kids or adults centered on / are / who / narrow selfish desires / their own . Link p.83 02번

➡ ____

03 Use all of it feel / to / yourself / good / make . Link p.84 03번

➡ ____

04 to / nor / it / suggest / is that all relationships should be comfortable. Link p.85 04번

➡ ____

C

다음 영어는 우리말로, 우리말은 영어로 옮겨 쓰시오.

01 self-esteem		**11** strength	
02 negatively		**12** 열정	
03 rapidly		**13** compassion	
04 expedition		**14** achieve	
05 gear		**15** 전문가	
06 탐험하다		**16** capacity	
07 distance		**17** colleague	
08 terrifying		**18** rely on	
09 tie		**19** visual	
10 borrow		**20** process	

D

다음 각 네모 안의 말을 어법에 맞는 순서로 고쳐 쓰시오.

01 Since an average backpacker / it's / for / to carry / unbearable more than 10 days of food, a long distance backpacker must re-supply along the way. *Link p.104 01번*

➡

02 The more ropes you have, your chances / the / are / better for success. *Link p.105 02번*

➡

03 Researcher and expert on shame and vulnerability Brene Brown suggests that to be / capacity / our / vulnerable is the key to living a whole-hearted life. *Link p.106 03번*

➡

04 a word / takes / longer / it / to speak than it does to read it. *Link p.107 04번*

➡

Part

4

빈칸 추론

빈칸 추론은 어떤 유형인가요?

지문의 일부분을 빈칸으로 뚫어 놓고, 그 안에 들어갈 적절한 어휘, 혹은 어구를 고르도록 하는 유형입니다. 지문의 요지나 결론을 요약한 문장 하나를 주고, 그 문장에 들어갈 말을 찾는 요약문 완성 유형도 빈칸 추론과 같은 맥락의 문제라고 볼 수 있습니다.

수능에서 이 유형의 비중은 어느 정도인가요?

매년 수능에서 빈칸 추론은 4문제, 요약문 완성은 1문제가 꾸준히 출제되며, 배점은 주로 3점인 만큼 체감 난이도가 높은 편입니다.

비어있는 곳에 들어갈 말을 찾는 문제라니, 생각만 해도 어려워요.

맞습니다. 수능에서 변별력과 등급을 결정짓는 고난도 문제가 출제되며 수험생들이 가장 어려워하는 유형 중 하나가 바로 빈칸 추론입니다. 글 전체를 이해해야 함과 동시에 각각의 선택지를 세부적으로 따져가면서 빈칸에 적절한지 판단하는 능력을 요구하기 때문입니다.

문제를 풀 때 유의해야할 점에는 무엇이 있나요?

빈칸 추론과 요약문 완성 모두, 먼저 글의 요지를 파악하고, 반복되는 단서를 종합해서 빈칸에 들어갈 말을 결정해야 합니다. 빈칸에 들어갈 말은 대부분 글의 핵심과 관련 있다는 것을 기억해야 합니다.

지문은 보통 어떤 방식으로 구성되나요?

보통 논리를 잘 갖춘 글감이 제시되고, 빈칸 추론은 주로 글의 전반부나 후반부에 빈칸이 제시됩니다. 요약문 완성의 경우, 대부분 지문에는 명확한 주제문이 나타나 있지 않고, 지문의 단서를 바탕으로 주제문을 추론해 내야 합니다.

Part 4

01 빈칸 추론(한 단어/두 단어)

유형 특징
1. 주어진 지문을 읽고, 빈칸에 들어갈 적절한 한 단어 또는 두 단어를 고른다.
2. 글의 주제 및 요지와 관련 있는 핵심어(구)가 빈칸으로 제시된다.
3. 빈칸 추론은 수험생들이 수능에서 가장 어려워하는 유형이다.
4. 빈칸 추론은 매년 수능에 4문제가 꾸준히 출제되며, 그 중 한 단어/두 단어 유형은 1문제 정도 출제된다.

Example

음성파일

다음 빈칸에 들어갈 말로 가장 적절한 것은?　　　　　　| 고1 전국연합 |

Creativity is a skill we usually consider uniquely human. For all of human history, we
→ 화제 제시 = 빈칸의 단서 1
have been the most creative beings on Earth. Birds can make their nests, ants can make
→ 빈칸의 단서 2
their hills, but no other species on Earth comes close to the level of creativity we humans
→ 빈칸의 단서 3
display. However, just in the last decade we have acquired the ability to do amazing
→ 흐름 전환
5　things with computers, like developing robots. With the artificial intelligence boom of the
→ 새로운 화제 제시 = 빈칸의 단서 4
2010s, computers can now recognize faces, translate languages, take calls for you, write
→ 빈칸의 단서 5
poems, and beat players at the world's most complicated board game, to name a few

things. All of a sudden, we must face the possibility that our ability to be creative is not

______________.

① unrivaled　　　　② learned　　　　③ universal

④ ignored　　　　⑤ challenged

어휘 중요한 어휘를 확인하세요.

creativity 창의력　　uniquely 유일하게, 특유하게　　being 존재　　nest 둥지, 보금자리　　species (생물의) 종　　display 보여주다, 전시하다　　decade 10년　　acquire 습득하다, 획득하다　　amazing 놀라운　　artificial 인공의, 인조의　　intelligence 지능　　boom 급속한 발전, 급증　　recognize 인식하다, 인정하다　　translate 번역하다　　poem 시, 운문　　beat 이기다, 물리치다　　complicated 복잡한　　all of a sudden 갑작스럽게, 갑자기　　face 직면하다

구문 주요 구문을 살펴보아요.

2행 [1)[Birds can make their nests], 2)[ants can make their hills], **but** 3)[4){no other species on Earth} comes close to 5){**the level of creativity**} 6){we humans display}].

1), 2), 3)은 모두 등위접속사 but에 의해 병렬로 연결된 절이다.
4)는 절 3)의 주어이다.
5)는 관계절인 6)의 수식을 받는 선행사이다.
6)의 맨 앞에는 목적격 관계대명사인 that 또는 which가 생략되어 있다.

How to solve

이런 방법으로 접근하세요.

Step 1   **도입부에서 글의 화제 파악하기**   글의 전개를 예측하세요.

- Creativity ~ we usually consider uniquely human. (창의력은 우리가 인간만이 가지고 있다고 여기는 것이다.)
- ~ we have been the most creative beings ~ (인간이 가장 창의적인 존재였다)
- ~ no other species on Earth ~ the level of creativity we humans display

  (다른 어떤 종도 인간이 보여주는 창의력 수준에 가까이 도달하지 못한다)

➡ **화제**   인간만이 창의력을 가진다고 여겨진다.

Step 2   **흐름과 화제의 전환 파악하기**   글의 핵심이 드러날 부분입니다!

- **However**, ~ we have acquired the ability to do amazing things with computers ~

  (하지만 우리는 컴퓨터로 놀라운 일을 할 수 있는 능력을 습득하였다) → 역접으로 내용 반전
- ~ computers can now ~ to name a few things (컴퓨터는 얼굴을 인식하고, 언어를 번역하고, 여러분을 대신해 전화를 받고, 시를 쓸 수 있으며, 세계에서 가장 복잡한 보드게임에서 선수들을 이길 수 있다)

➡ **화제 전환**   인간이 아닌 컴퓨터도 창의적인 일을 할 수 있다.

Step 3   **내용 종합해 빈칸에 들어갈 말 추론하기**   빈칸은 요지 중에서 핵심어입니다.

➡ **내용 종합**   창의력에 관한한 이제는 인간만이 유일한 존재가 아닐 수 있다.

- ~ we must face the possibility that our ability to be creative is not ___________.

➡ **빈칸에 들어갈 말**   창의적인 우리의 능력이 경쟁할 상대가 없지 않다는 가능성에 직면해야 한다.

Step 4   **정답 확인하기**

① unrivaled(경쟁할 상대가 없는) → 내용을 종합해 볼 때 정답!

② learned(학식이 있는) → 창의력과 학식이 있는 것의 관계에 관한 내용은 아님

③ universal(보편적인) → 창의력의 보편성에 관한 내용은 언급되지 않음

④ ignored(무시되는) → 창의력이 무시되는지에 관한 내용은 아님

⑤ challenged(도전받는) → 창의력에 있어 컴퓨터에게 도전받고 있으므로 정반대인 오답

Do It Yourself 실전 문제를 풀어보세요.

01 다음 빈칸에 들어갈 말로 가장 적절한 것은?　| 고1 전국연합 |

Let me give you a piece of advice that might change your mind about ______________. Suppose that your doctor said that you have six months to live and recommended that you do everything you ever wanted to do. What would you do? Have you always wanted to sky dive, or climb cliffs, or maybe live alone in the woods for a month but been afraid you might be harmed? What difference would it make if you now attempted it? You'd almost certainly live through it and it would enrich the time you had left. Wouldn't it be nice to go out saying you had faced all your fears? Why do you wait till you have a death sentence? If it's that important to you, do it now.

*death sentence 사형 선고

① being courageous
② helping others
③ making friends
④ recovering health
⑤ encouraging patients

구문 수요 구분를 실퍼보아요.

4행 **Have you** always **wanted** to 1)[sky dive], or 2)[climb cliffs], or maybe 3)[live alone in the woods for a month] but 4)**been afraid** 5)[you might be harmed]?

〈Have you p.p. ~?〉는 경험에 대해 묻는 표현으로, '~했었는가(한 적이 있는가)?'로 해석한다.
1), 2), 3)이 wanted to에 병렬로 연결되었다.
4)는 Have you에 이어지는 wanted와 but으로 인해 병렬로 연결되었다.
5)는 been afraid의 의미상 목적어이다. '~할까봐 두려워했었는가?'로 해석한다. afraid는 형용사지만, 뒤에 절의 형태를 수반해 그것을 목적어처럼 취할 수 있다.

02

다음 빈칸에 들어갈 말로 가장 적절한 것은?　　　| 고1 전국연합 |

The mind is essentially a survival machine. Attack and defense against other minds, gathering, storing, and analyzing information — this is what it is good at, but it is not at all creative. All true artists create from a place of no-mind, from inner stillness. Even great scientists have reported that their creative breakthroughs came at a time of mental quietude. The surprising result of a nationwide inquiry among America's most famous mathematicians, including Einstein, to find out their working methods, was that thinking "plays only a subordinate part in the brief, decisive phase of the creative act itself." So I would say that the simple reason why the majority of scientists are *not* creative is not because they don't know how to think, but because they don't know how to _______________!

*quietude 정적　**subordinate 부수적인

지문에서의 어휘의 뜻을
써보고 해설에서 확인하세요.

- essentially
- defense
- gather
- store
- analyze
- stillness
- breakthrough
- mental
- nationwide
- inquiry
- brief
- decisive
- phase
- majority

① organize their ideas
② interact socially
③ stop thinking
④ gather information
⑤ use their imagination

구문　주요 구문을 살펴보아요.

6행　1)[The surprising result of **a nationwide inquiry among America's most famous mathematicians, including Einstein**, 2){to find out their working methods}], was 3)[that thinking "plays only a subordinate part in the brief, decisive phase of **the creative act** 4)**itself**]."

1)은 문장의 주어인 명사구로, 주어의 핵 The surprising result가 단수이므로, 동사 역시 단수 형태 was가 쓰였다.

2)는 형용사적 용법의 to부정사구로, a nationwide inquiry ∼ including Einstein을 수식한다.

3)은 was의 보어 역할을 하는 명사절이다.

4) itself는 앞의 the creative act를 강조하는 재귀대명사이다.

Do It **Yourself**

03 다음 빈칸에 들어갈 말로 가장 적절한 것은?

Most companies have set guidelines in place for marketing or servicing customers. But you have to remember that guidelines are not permanent rules, but they are just guides. Guidelines need to be allowed to make changes even more easily for
5 existing customers than for new customers. Customers make it easier for you to secure additional business from within their organizations, so you need to make it as easy as possible for them to give you that business. To increase sales productivity, you need to be ____________. For example, if your company's
10 guideline is to pitch products or services at a personal meeting, but your customer does not have the time to meet, try having a phone conference instead.

*pitch 선전하다, 홍보하다

① honest　　　② specific　　　③ flexible
④ creative　　　⑤ inspirational

지문에서의 어휘의 뜻을
써보고 해설에서 확인하세요.

- set ~ in place
- guideline
- market
- customer
- permanent
- allow
- existing
- secure
- additional
- organization
- productivity
- conference
- instead

구문 주요 구문을 살펴보아요.

9행 For example, 1)[if 2){your company's guideline is 3)(to pitch products or services at a personal meeting)}, but 4){your customer does not have **the time** 5)(to meet)}], 6)[**try having** a phone conference instead].

1)은 조건의 부사절이다.
2)와 4)는 등위접속사 but으로 인해 병렬로 연결되었다.
3)은 is의 보어 역할을 하는 명사적 용법의 to부정사구이다.
5)는 the time을 수식하는 형용사적 용법의 to부정사구이다.
6)은 주절로, 명령문이다. 「try -ing」는 '~(하기)를 시도하다'의 의미이다.

04

다음 빈칸에 들어갈 말로 가장 적절한 것은?

🎧 음성파일

Gordon Gallup, an American psychologist, gave a mirror to a group of young chimpanzees. At first, they reacted as though they were seeing other chimpanzees, but after a few days they were using it to look inside their mouths or to inspect other
5 normally hard-to-see parts of their bodies. Watching chimpanzees do this is certainly impressive. It seems obvious from the way they pick their teeth and make funny faces that they ______________ themselves, but can we be sure? To find out Gallup anesthetized them and painted two obvious red spots
10 above one eye and the opposite ear. When they awoke, he let them look in the mirror. You or I, in such a situation, would immediately see the marks and probably try to touch them or rub them off, and so did the chimpanzees.

*anesthetize 마취[마비]시키다

지문에서의 어휘의 뜻을
써보고 해설에서 확인하세요.

- psychologist
- react
- inspect
- normally
- impressive
- obvious
- pick one's teeth
- be sure
- spot
- rub off

① cheat　　　　② protect　　　　③ beautify
④ entertain　　　⑤ recognize

구문 주요 구문을 살펴보아요.

11행 You or I, in such a situation, ¹⁾**would** immediately see the marks and probably try to touch ²⁾**them** or rub them off, and ³⁾[so did the chimpanzees].

1) would는 '~하려고 하다'라는 의미로 습관이나 습성을 나타내는 기능을 한다.
2) them은 앞의 the marks를 대신한다.
3) 「so+동사+주어」 구문은 앞서 나온 내용의 반복을 대신하는 표현이며, so 뒤에 주어와 동사가 도치된다.
'~도 마찬가지다'라는 의미를 나타내므로 '침팬지들도 그렇게 했다'로 해석한다.

빈칸 추론 (짧은 어구)

유형 특징
1. 주어진 지문을 읽고, 빈칸에 들어갈 비교적 짧은 어구를 고른다.
2. 글의 주제 및 요지와 관련 있는 핵심어(구)가 빈칸으로 제시된다.
3. 빈칸 추론 짧은 어구 유형은 매년 수능에 1~2문제 정도 출제된다.

Example

음성파일

다음 빈칸에 들어갈 말로 가장 적절한 것은?　　　　| 고1 전국연합 |

There is a major problem with ＿＿＿＿＿＿＿＿. To determine the number of objects
　→ 화제 제시: ＿＿＿ 에 중대한 문제가 있다　　　　→ 핵심 소재 제시
by counting, such as determining how many apples there are on a table, many children
　　→ 구체적 사례: 탁자 위의 사과 세기　　　　　　→ 사과 숫자를 1부터 셀 경우
would touch or point to the first apple and say "one," then move on to the second apple
and say "two," and continue in this manner until all the apples are counted. If we start at
　　　　　　　　　　　　　→ 숫자를 0부터 셀 경우
5 0, we would have to touch nothing and say "zero," but then we would have to start
touching apples and calling out "one, two, three" and so on. This can be very confusing
　　　　　　　　　　　　　→ This가 가리키는 것 = 앞에 나온 내용
because there would be a need to stress when to touch and when not to touch. If a child
accidentally touches an apple while saying "zero," then the total number of apples will be
off by 1.

① counting from 0　　　　　　　② numbering in reverse order
③ adding up the numbers given　　④ learning words through games
⑤ saying numbers in a loud voice

어휘 중요한 어휘를 확인하세요.

major 중대한, 주요한　　determine 판단하다, 결정하다　　object 대상, 사물　　point to ~을 가리키다　　continue 계속하다
confusing 혼란시키는　　stress 강조하다　　accidentally 우연히　　total 총계의, 전체의

구문 주요 구문을 살펴보아요.

1행 1)[To determine the number of objects by counting, such as determining 2){how many apples there are on a table}], 3)**many children would** 4)[touch or point to the first apple and say "one,"] then 5)[move on to the second apple and say "two,"] and 6)[continue in this manner 7){until all the apples are counted}].

1)은 목적의 의미를 나타내는 부사적 용법의 to부정사구이다.
2)는 determining의 목적어 역할을 하는 명사절로서 의문사 how가 이끄는 간접의문문 〈의문사＋주어＋동사〉 어순이다.
3) many children은 문장의 주어이다.
4), 5), 6)은 등위접속사 and에 의해 조동사 would에 병렬로 연결된 구조이다.
7)은 접속사 until이 이끄는 시간의 부사절이다.

How to solve 이런 방법으로 접근하세요.

Step 1 빈칸 문장 확인 및 핵심 소재 파악하기

- There is a major problem with __________________.
- ➡ __________________ 에 중대한 문제가 있다.

- To determine the number of objects by counting ~
- ➡ **핵심 소재** 수를 세어 대상의 수를 판단하는 것

Step 2 구체적 사례와 단서 파악하기

- ~ determining how many apples there are on a table ~
- ➡ **구체적 사례** 탁자 위에 몇 개의 사과가 있는지를 판단하는 것

- ~ many children would touch ~ and say "one,"
- ➡ **단서 1** 사과 숫자를 1부터 셀 경우
  - → 첫 번째 사과를 만지거나 가리킨 후 "하나"라고 말함

- If we start at 0, ~ "one, two, three" and so on.
- ➡ **단서 2** 사과 숫자를 0부터 셀 경우
  - → 0일 때는 아무것도 만지지 않아야 하며, 이후로는 만지기 시작하며 숫자를 세야 함

Step 3 단서 종합해 요지 추론하기

- This can be very confusing ~ (이것은 매우 혼란스러울 수 있다)
- ➡ **단서 종합** 사과를 1부터 셀 경우: 문제없음 / 사과를 0부터 셀 경우: 혼란스러움
- ➡ **요지** 사과를 만지며 0부터 세면 총 개수가 한 개만큼 부족해지는 혼란이 생긴다.

Step 4 정답 확인하기

① 0부터 숫자 세기 → 숫자를 0부터 셀 때의 문제점을 핵심으로 다루고 있으므로 정답!

② 역순으로 번호 매기기 → 번호 역순에 관한 글은 아님

③ 주어진 수를 더하기 → 수를 더하는 내용은 언급되지 않음

④ 게임을 통하여 어휘 배우기 → 지문 내용과 무관함

⑤ 큰 목소리로 숫자 말하기 → 숫자를 세는 목소리의 크기에 관한 글은 아님

Do It Yourself 실전 문제를 풀어보세요.

01 다음 빈칸에 들어갈 말로 가장 적절한 것은? | 고2 전국연합 |

Theseus was a great hero to the people of Athens. When he returned home after a war, the ship that had carried him and his men was so treasured that the townspeople preserved it for years and years, replacing its old, rotten planks with new pieces of wood. The question Plutarch asks philosophers is this: is the repaired ship still the same ship that Theseus had sailed? Removing one plank and replacing it might not make a difference, but can that still be true once all the planks have been replaced? Some philosophers argue that the ship must be ________________. But if this is true, then as the ship got pushed around during its journey and lost small pieces, it would already have stopped being the ship of Theseus.

*plank 널빤지

① the reminder of victory
② the sum of all its parts
③ fit for the intended use
④ the property of the country
⑤ around for a long period of time

지문에서의 어휘의 뜻을
써보고 해설에서 확인하세요.

- treasure
- townspeople
- preserve
- replace
- rotten
- philosopher
- sail
- remove
- argue
- journey

구문 주요 구문을 살펴보아요.

1행 1)[When he returned home after a war], 2)[**the ship** 3){that 4)**had carried** him and his men}] was 5)[**so** treasured **that** the townspeople preserved it for years and years, 6){**replacing** its old, rotten planks **with** new pieces of wood}].

1)은 시간의 부사절이다.
2)는 주절의 주어이고, 그 안의 3)은 the ship을 수식하는 관계절이다.
4) ⟨had+p.p.⟩는 과거완료시제로, 과거보다 이전의 때를 나타낸다.
5)는 「so ~ that ….」 구문으로, '매우 ~해서 …하다'의 의미이다.
6)은 동시상황을 나타내는 분사구문이며, 「replace A with B」는 'A를 B로 대체[교체]하다'의 의미이다.

02 다음 빈칸에 들어갈 말로 가장 적절한 것은? | 고1 전국연합 |

In the not-too-distant future, everyday objects such as shoes, carpets, and toothbrushes will contain technology that collects information. You will then be able to personalize these objects, allowing them to change physical state like color or respond to your daily mood. They will also be able to exchange data with other objects and send information to other people. For example, your toothbrush will be capable of analyzing your breath and booking an appointment with your doctor if it detects the smell of lung cancer. In other words, what were once just ordinary objects will be increasingly ________________. Manufacturers will use the information generated by these smart products to sell you other services or enhance your "ownership experience."

① changeable and dangerous
② sustainable and affordable
③ networked and intelligent
④ insecure and meaningless
⑤ complicated and isolated

지문에서의 어휘의 뜻을
써보고 해설에서 확인하세요.

- not-too-distant
- object
- contain
- personalize
- physical state
- respond to
- exchange
- be capable of
- analyze
- book
- appointment
- detect
- ordinary
- manufacturer
- generate
- enhance
- ownership

구문 주요 구문을 살펴보아요.

6행 For example, **your toothbrush** will **be capable of** 1) [analyzing your breath] and 2) [booking an appointment with your doctor] 3) [if **it detects** the smell of lung cancer].

be capable of ~는 '~할 수 있다'의 의미이며, of가 전치사이므로 뒤에는 동명사구인 1)과 2)가 왔고, 둘은 병렬을 이룬다.
3)은 조건의 부사절로서 의미는 미래이지만, 조건의 부사절에서는 미래 시제 대신 현재 시제를 쓰므로 detects가 쓰였다. it은 앞의 your toothbrush를 가리킨다.

Do It Yourself

03

다음 빈칸에 들어갈 말로 가장 적절한 것은?

Children sometimes display ___________________ . I think of five-year-old Peter watching two girls in the kindergarten using dolls to act out a scene on a tabletop. They were deeply immersed and so was he. It happened that on that day some fire-fighters came
5 to the school, because one of the teachers had called them after noticing a burning smell in her room. Three fire engines roared into the school's parking lot. Peter's friend Benjamin ran up to him, crying, "Peter, Peter, the fire engines are here!" But Peter was so intent on watching the scene the girls were acting out
10 that he did not respond. Benjamin tried again with the same result. He shrugged and rushed back to the window to watch the fire-fighters arrive.

① a lack of insight
② the habit of repeating
③ adult-like brain activity
④ a depth of concentration
⑤ changes in their behavior

지문에서의 어휘의 뜻을
써보고 해설에서 확인하세요.

• display
• kindergarten
• act out
• scene
• tabletop
• deeply
• be immersed
• notice
• roar
• intent
• result
• shrug

구문 주요 구문을 살펴보아요.

4행 [1)]**It happened that** on that day some fire-fighters **came** to the school, [2)][because one of the teachers **had called** them **after** [3)]{noticing a burning smell in her room}].

1) It happened that ~은 '공교롭게[우연히] ~했다'의 의미이다.
2)는 이유의 부사절이며, had called는 앞의 came 보다 이전에 일어난 일이므로 과거완료 시제가 쓰인 것이다.
after는 전치사로, 뒤에 동명사구인 3)이 이어졌다.

04 다음 빈칸에 들어갈 말로 가장 적절한 것은?

음성파일

Clearly some medical research is essential. Without it, we would have no vaccinations against diseases such as polio, no drugs such as antibiotics and no treatments like radiation. Nevertheless, the field of medical research is very competitive and this also
5 results in financial losses. Take, for example, the current research being conducted on the AIDS virus. In this field it is arguable that money is being wasted. The scientists are working independently towards the same ultimate goal — to find a cure for AIDS, and they have the same hope of becoming famous in
10 the process. Surely it would be more productive and less costly if these scientists ___________________ .

*polio 소아마비 **radiation 방사(선)
***AIDS[acquired immune deficiency syndrome] 에이즈, 후천성 면역 결핍증

지문에서의 어휘의 뜻을
써보고 해설에서 확인하세요.

- vaccination
- antibiotics
- treatment
- field
- competitive
- financial
- loss
- current
- independently
- conduct
- ultimate
- cure
- productive
- costly

① joined forces together
② discovered new medicines
③ challenged the fixed ideas
④ conducted a market survey
⑤ collected more medical data

구문 주요 구문을 살펴보아요.

1행 1) **Without** it, 2) [we would have 3) {no vaccinations against diseases such as polio}, 4) {no drugs such as antibiotics} and 5) {no treatments like radiation}].

1) without은 '~이 없다면(= but for = if it were not for = were it not for)'의 의미이다.
주절인 2)는 가정법 과거 시제로 쓰였으며, 3), 4), 5)는 have의 목적어로, 병렬로 연결되어 있다.

How was it?

A

다음 영어는 우리말로, 우리말은 영어로 옮겨 쓰시오.

01 species ___________________   11 brief ___________________

02 decade ___________________   12 permanent ___________________

03 translate ___________________   13 existing ___________________

04 complicated ___________________   14 secure ___________________

05 오르다, 등반하다 ___________________   15 conference ___________________

06 cliff ___________________   16 심리학자 ___________________

07 enrich ___________________   17 inspect ___________________

08 defense ___________________   18 spot ___________________

09 gather ___________________   19 속이다 ___________________

10 breakthrough ___________________   20 entertain ___________________

B

다음 각 네모 안에서 어법상 적절한 것을 고르고, 색칠된 부분을 해석하시오.

01 All of a sudden, we must face the possibility that / what our ability to be creative is not unrivaled. *Link p.112 Example*

➡ 적절한 것: ___________________   해석: ___________________

02 Suppose that your doctor said that you have six months to live and recommended that you do / had done everything you ever wanted to do. *Link p.114 01번*

➡ 적절한 것: ___________________   해석: ___________________

03 The surprising result of a nationwide inquiry among America's most famous mathematicians, including Einstein, to find out their working methods, was / were that thinking "plays only a subordinate part in the brief, decisive phase of the creative act itself." *Link p.115 02번*

➡ 적절한 것: ___________________   해석: ___________________

04 You or I, in such a situation, would immediately see the marks and probably try to touch them or rub them off, and so did / were the chimpanzees. *Link p.117 04번*

➡ 적절한 것: ___________________   해석: ___________________

C 다음 영어는 우리말로, 우리말은 영어로 옮겨 쓰시오.

01 determine   11 ordinary

02 confusing   12 manufacturer

03 stress   13 kindergarten

04 accidentally   14 be immersed

05 treasure   15 roar

06 preserve   16 shrug

07 remove   17 antibiotics

08 항해, 여행   18 competitive

09 personalize   19 conduct

10 appointment   20 최종의, 궁극적인

D 다음 각 문장의 밑줄 친 부분을 어법에 맞게 바르게 고쳐 쓰시오.

01 When he returned home after a war, the ship that had carried him and his men was so treasured **why** the townspeople preserved it for years and years, replacing its old, rotten planks with new pieces of wood. 🔗 Link p.120 01번

➡ ____

02 For example, your toothbrush will be capable of analyzing your breath and booking an appointment with your doctor if **it will detect** the smell of lung cancer.

 🔗 Link p.121 02번

➡ ____

03 It happened that on that day some fire-fighters came to the school, **because of** one of the teachers had called them after noticing a burning smell in her room.

 🔗 Link p.122 03번

➡ ____

04 Surely it would be **more productively** and less costly if these scientists joined forces together. 🔗 Link p.123 04번

➡ ____

Unit 03 빈칸 추론(긴 어구/어절)

1. 주어진 지문을 읽고, 빈칸에 들어갈 적절한 어구 또는 어절을 고른다.
2. 글의 주제 및 요지와 관련 있는 핵심어구 또는 어절이 빈칸으로 제시된다.
3. 빈칸 추론 긴 어구/어절 유형은 매년 수능에 2~3문제 정도 출제된다.

Example

다음 빈칸에 들어갈 말로 가장 적절한 것은?　　　　　| 고1 전국연합 |

We are more likely to eat in a restaurant if we know that it is usually busy. Even when
→ 주제문
nobody tells us a restaurant is good, our herd behavior determines our decision-making.
　　　　　　　　　　　　　　　　　　→ 근거 제시
Let's suppose you walk toward two empty restaurants. You do not know which one to
→ 가정을 통한 사례 제시
enter. However, you suddenly see a group of six people enter one of them. Which one are

5 you more likely to enter, the empty one or the other one? Most people would go into the
　　　　　　　　　　　　　　　　　　　　　→ 사례의 결과
restaurant with people in it. Let's suppose you and a friend go into that restaurant. Now,
　　　　　　　　　　→ 사례에 대한 추가 가정
it has eight people in it. Others see that one restaurant is empty and the other has eight

people in it. So, _______________________.
　　　　　→ 추가 가정에서 내려지는 결론

*herd 무리, 떼

① both restaurants are getting busier
② you and your friend start hesitating
③ your decision has no impact on others'
④ they reject what lots of other people do
⑤ they decide to do the same as the other eight

 중요한 어휘를 확인하세요.

be likely to ~하기 쉽다, ~할 가능성이 높다　　**determine** 결정짓다, 결심하다　　**suppose** 가정하다　　**empty** 비어 있는　　**hesitate** 망설이다, 주저하다　　**impact** 영향; 영향을 미치다　　**reject** 거부[거절]하다

 주요 구문을 살펴보아요.

4행 However, you suddenly **see** a group of six people **enter** one of them.

지각동사 see의 목적격 보어로 동사원형 enter가 쓰였다.

How to solve

Step 1 도입부에서 주제 파악하기

- We are more likely to eat in a restaurant if we know that it is usually busy.

  (어떤 식당이 대체로 붐빈다는 것을 알게 되면 우리가 그 식당에서 식사할 가능성이 더 크다.)

➡ **주제**　식당에 있는 인원과 식당 선택의 관계

Step 2 주제문을 뒷받침하는 근거 찾기

- ~ our herd behavior determines our decision-making

  (우리의 무리 행동이 우리의 의사를 결정한다)

➡ **근거**　our herd behavior (우리의 무리 행동)

Step 3 사례를 통해 빈칸에 들어갈 말 추론하기

➡ **사례(가정)**　Let's suppose you walk toward two empty restaurants.

　　　　　　　(여러분이 두 개의 텅 빈 식당 쪽으로 걸어가고 있다고 가정하자.)

➡ **결과**　Most people would go into the restaurant with people in it.

　　　　(대부분의 사람들은 사람이 있는 식당에 들어갈 것이다.)

➡ **추가 가정**　Let's suppose ~ go into that restaurant. / Now, it has eight people in it.

　　　　　　(그 식당에 들어가서 사람이 8명이 됨)

➡ **빈칸에 들어갈 결론**　So, 그들도 다른 여덟 명과 같은 행동을 하기로 결정한다.

Step 4 정답 확인하기

① 두 식당 모두 더 붐비게 된다 → 둘 중 하나를 선택하는 것과 관련 있으므로 오답

② 여러분과 여러분의 친구는 망설이기 시작한다 → 여러분과 친구가 들어간 식당을 본 다른 사람들의 결정에 관한 것이므로 오답

③ 여러분의 결정은 다른 사람의 결정에 영향을 미치지 못한다 → 무리 행동과 상반되므로 오답

④ 그들은 다른 많은 사람들이 하는 것을 거부한다 → 무리 행동과 상반되므로 오답

⑤ 그들도 다른 여덟 명과 같은 행동을 하기로 결정한다 → 무리 행동을 하는 사람들의 특성이므로 정답!

01

다음 빈칸에 들어갈 말로 가장 적절한 것은?　　　　　| 고2 전국연합 |

Sometimes a person is acclaimed as "the greatest" because ________________. For example, violinist Jan Kubelik was acclaimed as "the greatest" during his first tour of the United States, but when impresario Sol Hurok brought him back to the United States in 1923, several people thought that he had slipped a little. However, Sol Elman, the father of violinist Mischa Elman, thought differently. He said, "My dear friends, Kubelik played the Paganini concerto tonight as splendidly as ever he did. Today you have a different standard. You have Elman, Heifetz, and the rest. All of you have developed and grown in artistry, technique, and, above all, in knowledge and appreciation. The point is: you know more; not that Kubelik plays less well."

*acclaim 칭송하다 **impresario 기획자, 단장

① there are moments of inspiration
② there is little basis for comparison
③ he or she longs to be such a person
④ other people recognize his or her efforts
⑤ he or she was born with great artistic talent

구문 주요 구문을 살펴보아요.

2행 For example, violinist Jan Kubelik ¹⁾**was acclaimed** as "the greatest" during his first tour of the United States, but ²⁾[**when** impresario Sol Hurok brought him back to the United States in 1923], several people **thought** ³⁾[that he **had slipped** a little].

1) Jan Kubelik이 칭송받는 대상이기 때문에 수동태 was acclaimed가 쓰였다.
2)는 접속사 when이 이끄는 시간의 부사절이다.
3)은 thought의 목적어 역할을 하는 명사절이다. 그 안의 had slipped는 과거완료 〈had+p.p.〉의 형태로, 과거형 thought보다 한 시제 더 앞선 과거를 나타낸다.

지문에서의 어휘의 뜻을 써보고 해설에서 확인하세요.

· tour
· slip
· dear
· concerto
· splendidly
· standard
· the rest
· artistry
· above all
· appreciation

02 다음 빈칸에 들어갈 말로 가장 적절한 것은?

| 고1 전국연합 |

In philosophy, the best way to understand the concept of an argument is to contrast it with an opinion. An opinion is simply a belief or attitude about someone or something. We express our opinions all the time: We love or hate certain films or different types of food. For the most part, people's opinions are based almost always upon their feelings. They don't feel they have to support their opinions with any kind of evidence. An argument is something a bit different from this. It is made to convince others that one's claims are true. Thus, it is an attempt to _________________________. Arguments are the building blocks of philosophy, and the good philosopher is one who is able to create the best arguments based on a solid foundation.

① present reasons in support of one's claims
② develop one's own taste in each area
③ compare one's opinions with others'
④ look into a deeper meaning of a topic
⑤ build up knowledge from one's experiences

지문에서의 어휘의 뜻을 써보고 해설에서 확인하세요.

- philosophy
- argument
- contrast
- opinion
- attitude
- evidence
- convince
- claim
- create
- solid
- foundation

구문 주요 구문을 살펴보아요.

10행 1)[Arguments are the building blocks of philosophy], and 2)[the good philosopher is **one** 3){who is able to create **the best arguments** 4)(based on a solid foundation)}].

1)과 2)는 등위접속사 and로 병렬 연결되었다.
3)은 선행사 one을 수식하는 관계절이며, 4)는 과거분사구로 the best arguments를 수식한다.

Do It Yourself

03 다음 빈칸에 들어갈 말로 가장 적절한 것은?

59% of students with access to the Internet report that they use social networking sites to discuss educational topics and 50% of them say that they use the sites to talk about school assignments. After George Middle School in Portland introduced a social media program to engage students, grades went up by 50%, chronic absenteeism went down by 33%, and 20% of students voluntarily completed extra-credit assignments. A study published in the *Journal of Applied Developmental Psychology* said college freshmen use social networking sites to build networks of new friends, feel socially integrated at their new schools, and reduce their risk of dropping out. In this way, social networking sites ___________________.

*absenteeism 장기 결석 **credit 학점, 이수 단위

① help students do better at school
② prevent face-to-face communication
③ promote increased interaction with friends
④ make students share thoughts, photos, and music
⑤ spread false and potentially dangerous information

구문 주요 구문을 살펴보아요.

7행 A study ¹⁾[published in the *Journal of Applied Developmental Psychology*] said ²⁾[college freshmen use social networking sites ³⁾{to build networks of new friends}, ⁴⁾{feel socially integrated at their new schools}, and ⁵⁾{reduce their risk of dropping out}].

문장의 주어는 A study이고, 동사는 said이다.
1)은 과거분사구로 A study를 수식하고, 2)는 said의 목적어 역할을 하는 명사절이다.
2) 안의 3), 4), 5)는 각각 목적의 의미를 나타내는 to부정사구로, 등위접속사 and로 인해 병렬 연결되었다.
4)와 5)의 앞에는 to가 생략되어 있다.

04

다음 빈칸에 들어갈 말로 가장 적절한 것은?

Heating and cooling can ＿＿＿＿＿＿＿＿＿＿＿. The molecules in matter are always moving. Their speed alters when they are heated or cooled. The molecules in a solid move back and forth, but they do not move away from each other. As a solid is heated, the molecules move faster and faster until the bonds weaken and the solid melts, turning into a liquid. Altering a solid into a liquid is called melting. The temperature at which a substance changes from a solid to a liquid is called the melting point. When a liquid is cooled, its molecules slow down and it may even freeze, changing to a solid. The change from the liquid state to the solid state is called freezing. The temperature at which a substance turns into a solid from a liquid is called the freezing point.

*molecule 분자

① be more efficiently controlled
② change matter from one state to another
③ be changed to create a cleaner environment
④ keep you comfortable in your home or business
⑤ contribute to lowering the risk of future gas crises

지문에서의 어휘의 뜻을 써보고 해설에서 확인하세요.

- matter
- alter
- solid
- back and forth
- bond
- weaken
- melt
- liquid
- temperature
- substance
- freeze
- state
- crisis

구문 주요 구문을 살펴보아요.

4행 As a solid is heated, ¹⁾[the molecules move faster and faster ²⁾{until the bonds weaken}] and ³⁾[the solid melts, ⁴⁾{turning into a liquid}].

두 개의 절 **1)**과 **3)**이 and로 인해 병렬 연결되었다.
2)는 시간의 의미를 나타내는 부사절이다.
3) 안의 **4)**는 결과의 의미를 나타내는 분사구문으로, the solid를 의미상의 주어로 한다. the solid(고체)가 녹아 액체로 변한다는 뜻이다.

1. 주어진 지문을 읽고, 그 내용을 요약한 문장의 빈칸에 들어갈 말을 고른다.
2. 요약문은 글의 요지와 핵심을 종합하거나 결론을 내리는 문장이다.
3. 요약문에 들어가는 어휘는 글의 핵심어이며, 본문에 쓰인 어휘의 유의어인 경우가 많다.
4. 매년 수능에 1문제가 꾸준히 출제된다.

Example

다음 글의 내용을 한 문장으로 요약하고자 한다. 빈칸 (A), (B)에 들어갈 말로 가장 적절한 것은?

| 고1 전국연합 |

What really works to motivate people to achieve their goals? In one study, researchers looked at how people respond to life challenges including getting a job, taking an exam, or undergoing surgery. For each of these conditions, the researchers also measured how much these participants fantasized about positive outcomes and how much they actually expected a positive outcome. What's the difference really between fantasy and expectation? While fantasy involves imagining an idealized future, expectation is actually based on a person's past experiences. So what did the researchers find? The results revealed that those who had engaged in fantasizing about the desired future did worse in all three conditions. Those who had more positive expectations for success did better in the following weeks, months, and years. These individuals were more likely to have found jobs, passed their exams, or successfully recovered from their surgery.

↓

Positive expectations are more ____(A)____ than fantasizing about a desired future, and they are likely to increase your chances of ____(B)____ in achieving goals.

	(A)		(B)		(A)		(B)
①	effective	········	frustration	②	effective	········	success
③	discouraging	········	cooperation	④	discouraging	········	failure
⑤	common	········	difficulty				

How to solve 이런 방법으로 접근하세요.

Step 1 **요약문 내용 확인하기** 요약문을 먼저 읽고 글의 흐름과 방향을 예측하세요.

- **요약문** 긍정적인 기대는 바라던 미래에 대해 공상하는 것보다 더 ______(A)______ 하고, 그것은 목표를 성취하는 데 있어 ______(B)______ 의 가능성을 높여 주는 경향이 있다.

Step 2 **글의 흐름을 통해 요지 파악하기** 요지는 요약문과 직접적 관련이 있어요.

1. **화제 제시** What really works to motivate people to achieve their goals?
   (무엇이 정말 사람들로 하여금 자신의 목표를 성취하도록 동기를 부여하기 위해 효과가 있는가?)

2. **사례 제시** In one study, ~ (한 연구에서 ~)
   - ~ how people respond to life challenges (사람들이 인생의 과제에 어떻게 대응하는가)
   - ~ fantasized about positive outcomes / ~ actually expected a positive outcome
     (긍정적인 결과에 대해 공상하기 / 긍정적인 결과를 실제로 기대하기)
   - What's the difference really between fantasy and expectation?
     (공상과 기대의 차이는 진정 무엇인가?)

3. **결과** The results revealed that ~ (연구 결과는 ~을 밝혀냈다)
   - ~ those who had engaged in fantasizing ~ did worse ~
     (공상을 했던 사람들은 더 못해냈다)
   - Those who had more positive expectations ~ did better ~
     (긍정적인 기대를 더 많이 했던 사람들은 더 잘해냈다)
   ➡ **요지** 공상하는 것보다 긍정적인 기대를 하는 것이 성공 가능성을 높여준다.

Step 3 **요지와 요약문을 토대로 정답 확인하기**

- **요지** 공상하는 것보다 긍정적인 기대를 하는 것이 성공 가능성을 높여준다.
- ➡ **정답** 공상보다는 기대가 목표 성취와 성공의 가능성을 높여준다는 것이므로, (A)에는 effective(효과적인)가, (B)에는 success(성공)가 들어가는 것이 적절하다.
  (오답 선택지: ① 효과적인 – 좌절 / ③ 낙담시키는 – 협조 / ④ 낙담시키는 – 실패 / ⑤ 흔한 – 어려움)

요약문 완성 유형 지문의 특징

요약문 완성 지문은 주로 심리, 사회 현상, 철학, 과학, 예술 등 다양한 소재에 관한 내용을 연구 및 실험 등을 통해 설명하는 것이 많으므로, 흐름을 잘 파악하고 배경 지식을 기르는 것이 좋다.

Do It Yourself

01 다음 글의 내용을 한 문장으로 요약하고자 한다. 빈칸 (A), (B)에 들어갈 말로 가장 적절한 것은?

| 고1 전국연합 |

Children are much more resistant to giving something to someone else than to helping them. One can observe this difference clearly in very young children. Even though one-and-a-half-year-olds will support each other in difficult situations, they are not willing to share their own toys with others. The little ones even defend their possessions with screams and, if necessary, blows. This is the daily experience of parents troubled by constant quarreling between toddlers. There was no word I heard more frequently than "Mine!" from my daughters when they were still in diapers.

*toddler (걸음마를 배우는) 아기

> Although very young children will ______(A)______ each other in difficult situations, they are unwilling to ______(B)______ their possessions.

	(A)		(B)
①	ignore	········	share
②	help	········	hide
③	ignore	········	defend
④	understand	········	hide
⑤	help	········	share

지문에서의 어휘의 뜻을 써보고 해설에서 확인하세요.

- resistant
- observe
- support
- be willing to
- share
- defend
- possessions
- blow
- constant
- quarrel
- frequently
- diaper

 주요 구문을 살펴보아요.

1행 Children are **much** more resistant [1)][to giving something to someone else] than [2)][to helping them].

much는 비교급을 강조하는 표현으로 much more resistant는 '훨씬 더 저항하는' 정도로 해석한다.
두 개의 전치사구 1)과 2)가 than을 기준으로 비교 구조를 이루고 있다. 각각의 to는 '~에 (대해)'의 의미로 쓰인 전치사이므로 뒤에 동명사 형태가 온 것이다.

02

다음 글의 내용을 한 문장으로 요약하고자 한다. 빈칸 (A), (B)에 들어갈 말로 가장 적절한 것은?

| 고1 전국연합 |

음성파일

In one study, researchers asked students to arrange ten posters in order of beauty. They promised that afterward the students could have one of the ten posters as a reward for their participation. However, when the students finished the task, the
5 researchers said that the students were not allowed to keep the poster that they had rated as the third-most beautiful. Then, they asked the students to judge all ten posters again from the very beginning. What happened was that the poster they were unable to keep was suddenly ranked as the most beautiful. This
10 is an example of the "Romeo and Juliet effect": Just like Romeo and Juliet in the Shakespearean tragedy, people become more attached to each other when their love is prohibited.

↓

> When people find they cannot _____(A)_____ something, they begin to think it more _____(B)_____.

	(A)		(B)
①	own	………	attractive
②	own	………	forgettable
③	create	………	charming
④	create	………	romantic
⑤	accept	………	disappointing

지문에서의 어휘의 뜻을 써보고 해설에서 확인하세요.

- arrange
- order
- afterward
- reward
- task
- rate
- judge
- rank
- tragedy
- attach
- prohibit

구문 주요 구문을 살펴보아요.

8행 ¹⁾[**What** happened] was ²⁾[that **the poster** ³⁾{they were unable to keep} was suddenly ranked as the most beautiful].

1)은 관계대명사 What이 이끄는 명사절로, 문장의 주어 역할을 한다.
문장의 동사는 was이며, 2)는 보어 역할을 하는 명사절이다. 그 안의 3)은 관계절로, 앞의 the poster를 수식한다.

Do It **Yourself**

03

다음 글의 내용을 한 문장으로 요약하고자 한다. 빈칸 (A), (B)에 들어갈 말로 가장 적절한 것은?

If you were asked to memorize a passage of a text, you would probably start by reading it over and over again, expecting the act of repetition to help fix the information in your mind. However, this isn't the most efficient way to remember the information, which therefore means you have a good chance of forgetting it in the future. Ultimately, it is understanding the meaning of the text that will lead to a stronger memory of it. The more you understand the meaning of what you have read, the more connections you can make between the passage and what you already know, and as a result the better your memory of it will be.

↓

> To memorize a text better, you should _____(A)_____ its meaning rather than relying on _____(B)_____ reading it.

	(A)		(B)
①	look up	········	repetitively
②	look up	········	speedily
③	define	········	meaningfully
④	comprehend	········	repetitively
⑤	comprehend	········	meaningfully

지문에서의 어휘의 뜻을 써보고 해설에서 확인하세요.

- memorize
- passage
- repetition
- fix
- efficient
- chance
- ultimately
- lead to
- connection

구문 주요 구문을 살펴보아요.

1행 1)[If you **were asked** to memorize a passage of a text], 2)[you **would** probably **start** by reading it over and over again, 3){expecting the act of repetition 4)(to help fix the information in your mind)}].

조건절인 1)에 과거형 동사 were asked가 쓰였고, 주절인 2)에 〈과거형 조동사+동사원형(would ~ start)〉이 쓰인 것으로 보아, 전체적으로 가정의 의미를 나타내는 문장임을 알 수 있다.

3)은 분사구로 주절에 대한 추가적인 정보를 제공한다. '~ 하기를 기대하면서'라고 해석할 수 있다.

4)는 to부정사구로, expecting의 목적격 보어 역할을 한다.

04

다음 글의 내용을 한 문장으로 요약하고자 한다. 빈칸 (A), (B)에 들어갈 말로 가장 적절한 것은?

In his book *The Motivated Mind* Raj Persaud cites a client of his, whose chief goal in life was to be a novelist. The client was deeply frustrated because he could never quite finish a book. When Dr. Persaud asked him about his perfect day, it involved
5 tropical beaches, scoring the winning goal in the World Cup final and being treated like a celebrity. There was nothing literary in it whatsoever. It was clear that he didn't really want to be a novelist at all. His fantasies revealed what he really wanted. No wonder, then, that he was feeling frustrated and
10 stressed — he was setting himself the wrong goals in life and then feeling a failure because he didn't achieve them.

⬇

Dr. Persaud's would-be novelist failed to _____(A)_____ his true goal in life and ended up feeling stressed _____(B)_____ the goal he thought he ought to have.

	(A)		(B)
①	achieve	………	changing
②	identify	………	releasing
③	identify	………	chasing
④	achieve	………	abandoning
⑤	recall	………	chasing

지문에서의 어휘의 뜻을 써보고 해설에서 확인하세요.

- cite
- client
- chief
- frustrated
- involve
- tropical
- celebrity
- literary
- whatsoever
- reveal
- no wonder
- failure

구문 주요 구문을 살펴보아요.

1행 In his book *The Motivated Mind* Raj Persaud cites a client of his, **whose** chief goal in life was to be a novelist.

소유격 관계대명사의 경우. 그 앞에 콤마를 두어 계속적 용법으로 전환하면 그 의미 관계를 정확히 이해할 수 있다. 즉, '자신의 고객 중 한 명을 인용하는데, 그의 삶의 주된 목표는 소설가가 되는 것이었다' 정도로 풀어서 이해하면 된다.

How was it?

A

다음 영어는 우리말로, 우리말은 영어로 옮겨 쓰시오.

01 suppose ___________ 11 solid ___________

02 empty ___________ 12 foundation ___________

03 hesitate ___________ 13 access to ___________

04 거부[거절]하다 ___________ 14 assignment ___________

05 splendidly ___________ 15 chronic ___________

06 standard ___________ 16 integrated ___________

07 appreciation ___________ 17 alter ___________

08 contrast ___________ 18 liquid ___________

09 attitude ___________ 19 얼다 ___________

10 convince ___________ 20 crisis ___________

B

다음 각 문장의 밑줄 친 부분을 어법에 맞게 바르게 고쳐 쓰시오.

01 However, you suddenly see **a group of six people enters** one of them.

Link p.126 Example

➡ ___________

02 Arguments are the building blocks of philosophy, and the good philosopher is **one he or she is able to create** the best arguments based on a solid foundation.

Link p.129 02번

➡ ___________

03 A study published in the *Journal of Applied Developmental Psychology* said college freshmen use social networking sites to build networks of new friends, feel socially integrated at their new schools, and **reducing their risk** of dropping out.

Link p.130 03번

➡ ___________

04 As a solid is heated, the molecules move faster and faster until the bonds weaken and the solid melts, **turn into a liquid**. *Link p.131 04번*

➡ ___________

C

다음 영어는 우리말로, 우리말은 영어로 옮겨 쓰시오.

01 동기를 부여하다 _______________

02 measure _______________

03 fantasize _______________

04 reveal _______________

05 resistant _______________

06 possessions _______________

07 blow _______________

08 quarrel _______________

09 task _______________

10 judge _______________

11 tragedy _______________

12 prohibit _______________

13 암기하다 _______________

14 passage _______________

15 repetition _______________

16 cite _______________

17 chief _______________

18 involve _______________

19 celebrity _______________

20 literary _______________

D

다음 각 문장의 밑줄 친 부분을 어법에 맞게 바르게 고쳐 쓰시오.

01 Children are much more resistant to giving something to someone else than **to help them**.   🔗 Link p.134 01번

➡ _______________

02 **That happened** was that the poster they were unable to keep was suddenly ranked as the most beautiful.   🔗 Link p.135 02번

➡ _______________

03 Ultimately, it is understanding the meaning of the text **what** will lead to a stronger memory of it.   🔗 Link p.136 03번

➡ _______________

04 When Dr. Persaud asked him about his perfect day, it involved tropical beaches, scoring the winning goal in the World Cup final and **treating** like a celebrity.

🔗 Link p.137 04번

➡ _______________

Part

5

논리 추론

논리 추론은 어떤 유형인가요?

우리는 '논리에 맞다' 라는 말을 종종 쓰죠. 생각과 내용의 전개가 이치에 맞다는 것인데요, 근거를 토대로 어떤 것을 이치에 맞게 추론하는 유형을 말합니다. 수능 독해에서는 이런 논리 추론을 간접 글쓰기 영역으로 제시합니다. 글의 순서, 문장 삽입, 그리고 무관한 문장 유형 등이 이에 속합니다.

문제의 난이도는 어떤 편인가요?

간접 글쓰기 영역에 속하고 논리적인 분석을 통해 글의 흐름을 파악해야 하므로 수험생들이 꽤 어려워하는 유형이에요.

문제를 풀 때 가장 유의해야 할 점에는 무엇이 있나요?

다른 유형과 마찬가지로 글의 중심 내용을 파악하는 것이 가장 중요해요. 동시에 세부 내용과 문맥을 근거로 논리와 일관성을 판단하는 능력도 필요합니다. 답을 추론하기 위한 근거가 지문에 반드시 주어져 있는데, 가장 큰 바탕이 되는 근거가 바로 중심 내용입니다.

지문은 보통 어떤 방식으로 구성되나요?

글의 순서는 핵심을 근거로 연결어나 지시어 등을 이용하여 논리적이면서 자연스러운 글의 흐름을 파악하도록 합니다.
문장 삽입은 한 문장을 주고 글의 흐름상 단절이 있는 곳에 넣는 유형으로, 주어진 글에서 앞뒤 내용을 추론할 수 있는 단서가 제공됩니다.
무관한 문장 추론 문제는 대체로 전반부에 글의 중심 내용을 제시한 후 그 내용을 보충하는 문장이 이어지도록 구성되므로 전반부에서 내용을 확실히 파악해야 합니다.

Part 5

글의 순서

유형 특징
1. 주어진 글에 이어질 적절한 글의 순서를 추론한다.
2. 시간의 순서 또는 논리적인 순서를 파악해야 한다.
3. 글의 흐름을 유기적으로 연결해주는 지시어, 대명사 등을 잘 활용해야 한다.
4. 매년 수능에 2문제가 꾸준히 출제된다.

Example

🎧 음성파일

주어진 글 다음에 이어질 글의 순서로 가장 적절한 것은? | 고1 전국연합 |

The next time you're out under a clear, dark sky, look up. If you've picked a good spot
→ 상황 제시
for stargazing, you'll see a sky full of stars, shining and twinkling like thousands of
→ 구체적 소재 제시: 밤하늘의 별 관찰
brilliant jewels.

(A) It might be easier if you describe patterns of stars. You could say something like, "See
→ 사례 제시: 별의 패턴을 묘사하면 더 쉬움
that big triangle of bright stars there?" Or, "Do you see those five stars that look like a
big letter W?"

(B) But this amazing sight of stars can also be confusing. Try and point out a single star to
→ 역접 연결어: 앞에는 이와 상반된 내용이 있음을 전제로 함
someone. Chances are, that person will have a hard time knowing exactly which star
→ 정확히 어떤 별을 보고 있는지 알기 어려움
you're looking at.

(C) When you do that, you're doing exactly what we all do when we look at the stars. We
→ 지시어   → 주제문
look for patterns, not just so that we can point something out to someone else, but
→ 패턴 찾기: 어떤 것을 다른 사람에게 가리켜보여줄 수 있음
also because that's what we humans have always done.
→ 우리 인간이 항상 해온 것이기도 함

① (A) − (C) − (B)　　　　② (B) − (A) − (C)
③ (B) − (C) − (A)　　　　④ (C) − (A) − (B)
⑤ (C) − (B) − (A)

어휘 중요한 어휘를 확인하세요.

spot 장소　　stargaze 별을 보다　　twinkle 반짝이다　　brilliant 찬란하게 빛나는　　jewel 보석　　sight 광경, 시야
confusing 혼란시키는　　chances are (that) 아마 ~일 것이다

How to solve　

Step 1　주어진 글을 통해 지문 내용 예측하기

- The next time you're out under a clear, dark sky, look up.

  (다음에 여러분이 맑고 어두운 하늘 아래에 있다면, 위를 올려다보라.)
- If you've picked a good spot for stargazing ~ like thousands of brilliant jewels.

  (별을 보기에 좋은 장소를 골랐다면, 수천 개의 광채가 나는 보석처럼 빛나고 반짝거리는 별로 가득한 하늘을 보게 될 것이다.)

➡ **지문 내용 예측**　밤하늘의 별을 관찰하는 것에 관한 내용

Step 2　단서를 통해 이어질 단락 찾기　연결어, 지시어, 대명사 등이 가리키는 것을 잘 파악하세요.

- (B) **But** this amazing sight of stars can also be confusing.

  (하지만 이 놀라운 별들의 광경은 또한 혼란스러울 수도 있을 것이다.)

➡ **역접 연결어 But**　주어진 글의 내용과 다르게 전환 또는 상반되는 흐름 유도

Step 3　논리적 흐름 고려해 나머지 순서 추론하기

- (B) ~ that person will have a hard time knowing exactly which star you're looking at.

  (그 사람은 여러분이 어떤 별을 보고 있는지를 정확하게 알기 어려울 것이다.)

➡ **다른 방법을 유도하기 위한 근거**

- (A) It might be easier if you describe patterns of stars.

  (만약 여러분이 별의 패턴을 묘사한다면 그것은 더 쉬워질 수도 있다.)

➡ **다른 방법 제시**

- (C) When you do that, you're doing exactly what we all do when we look at the stars.

  (여러분이 그렇게 하면, 여러분은 우리가 별을 바라볼 때 우리 모두가 하는 것을 정확하게 하고 있는 것이다.)

➡ **(A)에서 언급한 방법에 대한 부연 설명**

Step 4　최종 순서 점검하기　빠른 속도로 꼭 다시 읽고 확인하세요!

➡ **최종 순서**　(주어진 글) 밤하늘의 별을 감상함 → (B) 어떤 별을 가리키는지 정확히 설명하기 어려움 → (A) 별의 패턴을 묘사하면 쉬워짐 → (C) 패턴을 찾고 보여줄 수 있음

글의 순서 문제를 풀 때 유의점

연결어, 지시어, 대명사 등이 유용한 단서일 때가 많긴 하나, 가리키는 바를 정확히 파악하지 못하면 오히려 함정이 될 수도 있다. 따라서 기본적으로 글의 핵심을 근거로 논리 관계를 따져 답을 찾아야 한다.

Do It Yourself 실전 문제를 풀어보세요.

01 주어진 글 다음에 이어질 글의 순서로 가장 적절한 것은?

| 고1 전국연합 |

> Detective work is a two-part process. First, a detective must find the clues. But the clues alone don't solve the case.

(A) The same sort of process takes place in reading. You need to look for clues and then draw conclusions based on those clues.

(B) What is the writer trying to say? Good conclusions come from good observations. To be a better reader, be more like Sherlock Holmes: be more observant.

(C) The detective must also draw conclusions based on those clues. These conclusions are also called inferences. Inferences are conclusions based on reasons, facts, or evidence.

*observant 관찰력이 있는

① (A) − (C) − (B)　　② (B) − (A) − (C)
③ (B) − (C) − (A)　　④ (C) − (A) − (B)
⑤ (C) − (B) − (A)

지문에서의 어휘의 뜻을 써보고 해설에서 확인하세요.

- detective
- clue
- take place
- draw
- conclusion
- observation
- inference
- reason
- fact
- evidence

구문 주요 구문을 살펴보아요.

3행 You need to [1)][look for clues] and then [2)][draw **conclusions** [3)]{based on those clues}].

1)과 2)는 병렬구조로 앞의 to에 연결되었다.
3)은 앞의 conclusions를 수식하며 '~을 바탕으로 한'의 뜻이다. 즉 '그러한 단서를 바탕으로 한 결론'으로 해석한다.

02 주어진 글 다음에 이어질 글의 순서로 가장 적절한 것은? | 고1 전국연합 |

음성파일

There are many situations where other people try to influence our mood by changing the atmosphere of the environment; probably you have already done the same.

지문에서의 어휘의 뜻을 써보고 해설에서 확인하세요.

- influence
- atmosphere
- relaxed
- spirit
- apology
- unfortunate
- wedding anniversary
- rescue
- candlelit
- be aware of
- aroma
- outstanding

(A) The low-level light of the candle puts her in a relaxed spirit. And finally, romantic music does the rest to make the wife willing to accept the husband's apology for the mistake.

(B) For example, let us imagine that a man is in the unfortunate situation where he forgot his wedding anniversary. The man tries to rescue the situation by preparing a self-cooked, candlelit dinner for his wife with romantic background music.

(C) Whether or not he is aware of it, a candlelit dinner is a fantastic way to influence a person's mood. When the man's wife enters the room, she is surprised by the delicious aroma of the outstanding dinner he has prepared.

① (A) − (C) − (B)
② (B) − (A) − (C)
③ (B) − (C) − (A)
④ (C) − (A) − (B)
⑤ (C) − (B) − (A)

구문 주요 구문을 살펴보아요.

12행 [1)][Whether or not he is aware of it], a candlelit dinner is **a fantastic way** [2)][to influence a person's mood].

1) 「Whether or not 주어+동사 ~」는 「Whether+주어+동사 ~ or not」과 바꿔 쓸 수 있으며 '~이든지, 그렇지 않든지'의 의미이다. 이 문장에서는 '그가 그것을 알든 모르든'으로 해석한다.
2)는 a fantastic way를 수식하는 형용사적 용법의 to부정사구이다.

Do It **Yourself**

03 주어진 글 다음에 이어질 글의 순서로 가장 적절한 것은?

Before planning a lesson, it is important that you know your students. A teacher can no more plan for a lesson without knowing the strengths and weaknesses of her students than a scientist can examine the effectiveness of a new product on the environment without knowing its strengths and weaknesses.

(A) Data should be analyzed for both trends and for gaps. If the data shows that students in your classroom tend to do significantly better in reading than in mathematics, this would be a trend.

(B) Look at your student data (i.e., state and national tests, record of attendance, and health screening). Look for both strengths and weaknesses. If you are unsure about the prerequisite skills that your students bring to your classroom, you can assess them with a pre-test or questionnaire to help you plan appropriately.

(C) The trend should be analyzed to find its cause: Are there gaps in the textbooks and other materials being used in your school? Do teachers in your school have the requisite skills and resources needed to teach mathematics?

*prerequisite (다른 과목을 취득하기 위해) 필수의

① (A) − (C) − (B)　　　② (B) − (A) − (C)
③ (B) − (C) − (A)　　　④ (C) − (A) − (B)
⑤ (C) − (B) − (A)

구문 주요 구문을 살펴보아요.

2행 A teacher can **no more** plan for a lesson without knowing the strengths and weaknesses of her students **than** a scientist can examine the effectiveness of a new product on the environment without knowing its strengths and weaknesses.

「no more ~ than ...」 구문은 '…가 아닌 것과 같이 ~도 아니다'라는 의미를 나타낸다.

지문에서의 어휘의 뜻을
써보고 해설에서 확인하세요.

- lesson
- strength
- weakness
- examine
- effectiveness
- analyze
- significantly
- attendance
- screening
- unsure
- assess
- questionnaire
- appropriately
- requisite
- resource

04 주어진 글 다음에 이어질 글의 순서로 가장 적절한 것은?

Most people agree that drugs must be tested effectively for safety, or many new lifesaving drugs might never be developed.

지문에서의 어휘의 뜻을
써보고 해설에서 확인하세요.

- drug
- effectively
- develop
- volunteer
- method
- advanced
- predict
- reaction
- prevent
- serious
- harm

(A) If drugs are not tested on animals first, they say, more human volunteers are likely to become sick or even die. However, the groups supporting animal rights express a different opinion.

(B) So they argue that new methods are needed such as the use of tissue cultures or the development of advanced computer programs to predict human reactions to new drugs.

(C) They say that testing drugs on animals does not clearly prevent serious accidents from happening when they are finally tested on humans. Chimpanzees are very close to human beings, but even so, drugs which are safe for them may still harm humans.

*tissue culture 조직 배양

① (A) − (C) − (B)　　② (B) − (A) − (C)

③ (B) − (C) − (A)　　④ (C) − (A) − (B)

⑤ (C) − (B) − (A)

구문　주요 구문을 살펴보아요.

11행 They say 1)[that testing drugs on animals does not clearly 2){**prevent** serious accidents **from happening**} 3){when they are finally tested on humans}].

1)은 say의 목적어에 해당하는 명사절이다.

2)「prevent A from -ing」는 'A가 ~하는 것을 막다'의 의미로 '심각한 사고가 일어나는 것을 막다'로 해석한다.

3)은 시간의 부사절이다.

02 문장 삽입

1. 지문을 읽고, 주어진 문장이 들어가기에 적절한 곳을 고른다.
2. 글의 핵심을 토대로 논리 관계를 파악해 흐름상 단절이 있는 곳을 찾아야 한다.
3. 연결어, 지시어 등을 활용할 수 있다.
4. 매년 수능에 2문제가 꾸준히 출제된다.

Example

글의 흐름으로 보아, 주어진 문장이 들어가기에 가장 적절한 곳은?　　　| 고1 전국연합 |

> When the boy learned that he had misspelled the word, he went to the judges and told them.
> → 철자를 틀린 것을 알게 되어 심판에게 가서 말함

Some years ago at the national spelling bee in Washington, D.C., a thirteen-year-old boy
→ 소재 제시: Washington D.C.에서 있던 전국 단어 철자 맞히기 대회　　→ 주인공: 13세 소년
was asked to spell *echolalia*, a word that means a tendency to repeat whatever one hears.
→ 상황 1: 'echolalia'의 철자를 말하도록 요청 받음
5 (①) Although he misspelled the word, the judges misheard him, told him he had
→ 상황 2: 철자를 틀렸으나 심판은 맞혔다고 착각함　　　↓: 상황 2와 3 사이에 내용 단절
spelled the word right, and allowed him to advance. (②) So he was eliminated from
→ 상황 3: 소년이 대회에서 탈락함
the competition after all. (③) Newspaper headlines the next day called the honest
young man a "spelling bee hero," and his photo appeared in *The New York Times*. (④)
"The judges said I had a lot of honesty," the boy told reporters. (⑤) He added that part
10 of his motive was, "I didn't want to feel like a liar."

*spelling bee 단어 철자 맞히기 대회

 중요한 어휘를 확인하세요.

misspell ~의 철자를 잘못 말하다　　**judge** 심판; 판단하다　　**tendency** 경향　　**repeat** 반복하다, 따라 말하다　　**advance** (다음 단계로) 진출하다, 전진시키다　　**eliminate** (예선 등에서) 실격시키다　　**competition** 대회　　**appear** 등장하다, 나타나다　　**motive** 동기

 주요 구문을 살펴보아요.

3행 Some years ago at the national spelling bee in Washington, D.C., a thirteen-year-old boy was asked to spell *echolalia*, 1)[**a word** 2){that means a tendency to repeat 3)(whatever one hears)}].

1)은 echolalia와 동격 관계를 이룬다.
2)는 a word를 수식하는 관계절이다.
3)은 repeat의 목적어로 쓰인 복합관계대명사절이다.

How to solve 이런 방법으로 접근하세요.

Step 1 주어진 문장과 도입부를 통해 소재 및 상황 파악하기

- When the boy learned that he had misspelled the word ~
  (그 소년은 자신이 단어 철자를 잘못 말했다는 것을 알았을 때 ~)
- Some years ago at the national spelling bee in Washington, D.C. ~
  (몇 년 전 Washington D.C.에서 있었던 전국 단어 철자 맞히기 대회에서 ~)

➡ **소재 및 상황** 13세 소년이 전국 단어 철자 맞히기 대회에 나감

Step 2 주어진 문장에서 단서 파악하기

- When the boy learned that he had misspelled the word, he went to the judges and told them.
  (그 소년은 자신이 단어 철자를 잘못 말했다는 것을 알았을 때, 심판에게 가서 말했다.)

➡ **단서 1** he had misspelled the word ~ (그는 철자를 잘못 말했다)
  : 철자를 말하는 상황이 앞에 제시되어야 함
➡ **단서 2** ~ he went to the judges and told them (심판에게 가서 말했다)
  : 말하고 난 뒤의 상황이 이어져야 함을 짐작 가능

Step 3 흐름상 논리적 단절이 있는 곳 찾기

- Although he misspelled the word, the judges misheard him, told him he had spelled the word right, and allowed him to advance.
  (그는 철자를 잘못 말했지만 심판은 잘못 듣고 철자를 맞혔다고 말했고, 그가 (다음 단계로) 진출하도록 허락했다.) →
  (②) → So he was eliminated from the competition after all. (그래서 그는 결국 대회에서 탈락했다.)

➡ **단절 발생** ②를 기준으로 논리적 단절 발생

Step 4 흐름 최종 확인하여 정답 찾기

- Although he misspelled the word, the judges misheard him, told him he had spelled the word right, and allowed him to advance. (그는 철자를 잘못 말했지만 심판은 잘못 듣고 철자를 맞혔다고 말했고, 그가 (다음 단계로) 진출하도록 허락했다.) → <u>When the boy learned that he had misspelled the word, he went to the judges and told them.</u> (그 소년은 자신이 단어 철자를 잘못 말했다는 것을 알았을 때, 심판에게 가서 말했다.) → So he was eliminated from the competition after all. (그래서 그는 결국 대회에서 탈락했다.)

➡ **주어진 문장이 들어가기에 가장 적절한 곳** ②

Do It Yourself

01 글의 흐름으로 보아, 주어진 문장이 들어가기에 가장 적절한 곳은? | 고1 전국연합 |

음성파일

> Instead it takes in air through its skin and an opening under its tail.

A turtle doesn't have automatic body temperature control like birds and mammals. (①) Its temperature changes according to its environment. (②) When it gets too cold, it digs a hole deep into the mud at the bottom of a pond or into the dirt of the forest. (③) How can it breathe when it's buried? (④) The turtle stops breathing air through its nose and mouth. (⑤) And when spring comes and the ground warms up, the turtle digs itself out and starts breathing normally again.

*mammal 포유류

지문에서의 어휘의 뜻을 써보고 해설에서 확인하세요.

- take in
- tail
- turtle
- automatic
- body temperature
- control
- according to
- environment
- dig
- mud
- pond
- dirt
- breathe
- bury
- normally

구문 주요 구문을 살펴보아요.

9행 And ⁱ⁾[when ²⁾{spring comes} and ³⁾{the ground warms up}], ⁴⁾[the turtle ⁵⁾{digs itself out} and ⁶⁾{starts **breathing** normally again}].

1)은 시간의 부사절이며 그 안에서 두 개의 절 2)와 3)이 병렬을 이룬다.

4)가 주절이며 그 안에서 동사구 5)와 6)이 병렬을 이룬다.

6)의 breathing은 동명사로 동사 starts의 목적어 역할을 한다.

02 글의 흐름으로 보아, 주어진 문장이 들어가기에 가장 적절한 곳은? | 고1 전국연합 |

음성파일

> In addition, there are various English reading programs such as Storytelling, Role-play, and Book Talk for users.

Delhi English Library is the only public English library in New Delhi where you can experience a public library similar to those in western countries. (①) We have an English-friendly environment and 25,000 English books. (②) Users check their reading levels before joining these programs with the English Reading Test provided by us. (③) It helps users know their appropriate reading level. (④) In this way, we support the people who do self-directed English reading. (⑤) We welcome all New Delhi citizens.

*self-directed 자기 주도적인

지문에서의 어휘의 뜻을 써보고 해설에서 확인하세요.

- in addition
- various
- role-play
- public
- similar to
- -friendly
- check
- level
- appropriate
- support
- citizen

구문 주요 구문을 살펴보아요.

3행 Delhi English Library is 1)[**the only public English library in New Delhi** 2){where you can experience **a public library similar to those** in western countries}].

1)은 문장의 보어이며, 2)는 the only public English library in New Delhi를 수식하는 관계부사절이다. similar to는 앞의 a public library를 수식하며 '~와 비슷한'의 의미이다. 형용사 similar 앞에 which is 를 넣어 생각하면 이해하기 쉽다. those는 반복되는 the public library를 내용상 복수형 the public libraries로 받아 중복되는 내용을 대신하는 대명사이다.

Do It Yourself

03 글의 흐름으로 보아, 주어진 문장이 들어가기에 가장 적절한 곳은?

> With my own kids, I can either ask them directly or check the "acceptable gifts" list taped onto the refrigerator or the duplicate electronic copy sent to me via e-mail.

Children of all ages receive presents for their birthdays, gifts during the holiday season, and "I love you" knickknacks throughout the year. (①) A quick search on the world's largest online shopping mall reveals that there are more than 500,000 toys, games, books, and video games to choose from, virtually an endless sea of possibilities. (②) With so many choices, how are well-meaning parents and grandparents supposed to find gifts that are not only suitable for their youthful recipients but desired by them as well? (③) Simple enough, but then again, how do children and adolescents actually know what they want in the first place? (④) That is where advertising comes in. (⑤) When done well, advertisements have the power to influence the objects that youth think about, desire, and ultimately purchase.

*knickknack 예쁜 장신구, 작은 장난감

구문 주요 구문을 살펴봐요.

1행 With my own kids, I can **either** ¹⁾[ask them directly] **or** ²⁾[check ³⁾{the "acceptable gifts" list taped onto the refrigerator} or ⁴⁾{the duplicate electronic copy sent to me via e-mail}].

「either A or B」는 'A 또는 B 둘 중의 하나'라는 의미의 구문이다.
1)이 A에 해당하고, 2)가 B에 해당한다.
3)과 4)는 모두 check의 목적어로, or로 병렬 연결되었다.

04

글의 흐름으로 보아, 주어진 문장이 들어가기에 가장 적절한 곳은?

음성파일

> This kind of strange sighting is called "a glory" and is very rare.

In this world there are so many unusual and spectacular things you might see. (①) One example is if you climbed up a mountain and stood on top of it and then looking down — you might see a silhouette of your head on the clouds below you. (②) This could happen only if the sun was shining behind you and the clouds below were filled with rain. (③) Then your head's shadow might have a halo surrounding it, just like the moon does at times. (④) You can increase your chances of seeing it, however, if you are ever flying in a plane and sitting in a window seat away from the sun. (⑤) If you watch closely, you may see the silhouette of your plane on the clouds below, with colored rings completely surrounding it!

*silhouette 그림자, 윤곽 **halo 후광, (해·달의) 무리

지문에서의 어휘의 뜻을
써보고 해설에서 확인하세요.

- strange
- sighting
- glory
- rare
- unusual
- spectacular
- shine
- be filled with
- shadow
- surround
- closely
- colored
- completely

구문 주요 구문을 살펴보아요.

12행 1) [If you watch closely], you may see the silhouette of your plane on the clouds below, 2) [**with** colored rings completely **surrounding** it]!

1)은 조건의 부사절이다.

2)는 동시 상황을 나타내는 분사구로, 이때 with는 '~하고서, 한 상태로'의 의미이다. colored rings가 surround의 주체이므로 능동을 나타내는 현재분사 surrounding이 쓰였다.

03 무관한 문장

유형 특징
1. 주어진 지문을 읽고, 전체 흐름과 관계 없는 문장을 고른다.
2. 글의 요지 및 핵심을 토대로 이에 어긋나는 문장을 고른다.
3. 주로 글 전반부에서 주제와 소재가 제시된다.
4. 지문의 문장들이 선택지를 구성한다.
5. 매년 수능에 1문제가 꾸준히 출제된다.

Example

🎧 음성파일

다음 글에서 전체 흐름과 관계 없는 문장은?　　　　　　　　　　| 고1 전국연합 |

Words like 'near' and 'far' can mean different things depending on where you are and
→ 주제문
what you are doing. If you were at a zoo, then you might say you are 'near' an animal if
　　　　　　　→ 구체적 사례 1
you could reach out and touch it through the bars of its cage. ① Here the word 'near'
　　　　　　　　　　　　　　　　　　　　　　　　　　→ 사례 1 부연 설명
means an arm's length away. ② If you were telling someone how to get to your local
　　　　　　　　　　　　　　→ 구체적 사례 2
shop, you might call it 'near' if it was a fiveminute walk away. ③ It seems that you had
better walk to the shop to improve your health. ④ Now the word 'near' means much
→ 앞서 나온 소재이나, 내용은 흐름에서 어긋남　　　　　　　→ 사례 2 부연 설명
longer than an arm's length away. ⑤ Words like 'near', 'far', 'small', 'big', 'hot', and 'cold'
　　　　　　　　　　　　→ 주제문 반복
all mean different things to different people at different times.

어휘 중요한 어휘를 확인하세요.

depending on ～에 따라　　reach out (손을) 뻗다　　cage (동물) 우리　　length 길이　　improve 개선하다, 향상시키다

구문 주요 구문을 살펴보아요.

1행 Words like 'near' and 'far' can mean different things depending on 1)[where you are] and 2)[what you are doing].

1)과 2)는 모두 depending on의 목적어로 쓰인 의문사절로, and로 병렬 연결되었다.

How to solve 이런 방법으로 접근하세요.

Step 1 **주제문과 주제 파악하기**

➡ **주제문** Words like 'near' and 'far' can mean different things depending on where you are and what you are doing. ('near'와 'far' 같은 단어들은 여러분이 어디에 있는지와 무엇을 하는지에 따라 여러 가지를 의미할 수 있다.)

➡ **주제** 상황에 따라 달라지는 단어의 의미

Step 2 **선택지 문장 세부적으로 이해하기**

① Here the word 'near' means an arm's length away.

(여기서 'near'라는 단어는 팔 하나 만큼의 길이를 의미한다.)

② If you were telling someone ~ if it was a fiveminute walk away.

(여러분이 누군가에게 동네 가게에 가는 방법을 말해주고 있다면, 만약 그 거리가 걸어서 5분 거리라면 그것을 '가까이'라고 말할 수도 있을 것이다.)

③ It seems that you had better walk to the shop to improve your health.

(여러분은 건강을 향상시키기 위해 그 가게로 걸어가는 것이 더 좋을 것 같다.)

④ Now the word 'near' means much longer than an arm's length away.

(이제 'near'라는 단어는 팔 하나 만큼의 길이보다 훨씬 더 길다는 것을 의미한다.)

⑤ Words like 'near', 'far', ~ mean different things to different people at different times.

('near', 'far 등과 같은 단어들은 모두 다른 때에 다른 사람들에게 다른 것을 의미한다.)

Step 3 **흐름에 어긋나는 문장 파악하기**

① → 앞서 말한 'near'의 구체적인 사례를 부연 설명하므로 흐름과 관계 있음

② → 'near'의 두 번째 구체적인 사례에 해당하므로 흐름과 관계 있음

③ → 건강 향상에 관한 내용은 전체 흐름 및 핵심과 관련 없음!

④ → 'near'의 두 번째 구체적인 사례를 부연 설명하므로 흐름과 관계 있음

⑤ → 주제문의 내용을 반복하고 있으므로 관계 있음

Step 4 **무관한 문장을 뺀 후 전체 흐름 재확인하기**

➡ 'near'와 같은 단어의 의미는 상황에 따라 달라질 수 있다는 내용이므로, ③은 전체 흐름과 관계 없다.

무관한 문장 유형의 함정

무관한 문장에도 전체 글에서 반복되는 핵심어(구) 또는 앞에서 나온 소재가 쓰인 경우가 거의 대부분이므로, 정확한 의미를 파악하지 못하면 모든 문장이 흐름과 관계 있는 것처럼 느껴질 수 있으므로 유의하자.

Do It Yourself

01 다음 글에서 전체 흐름과 관계 <u>없는</u> 문장은? | 고1 전국연합 |

The water that is embedded in our food and manufactured products is called "virtual water." For example, about 265 gallons of water is needed to produce two pounds of wheat. ① So, the virtual water of these two pounds of wheat is 265 gallons. ② Virtual water is also present in dairy products, soups, beverages, and liquid medicines. ③ However, it is necessary to drink as much water as possible to stay healthy. ④ Every day, humans consume lots of virtual water and the content of virtual water varies according to products. ⑤ For instance, to produce two pounds of meat requires about 5 to 10 times as much water as to produce two pounds of vegetables.

*virtual water 공산품·농축산물의 제조·재배에 드는 물

지문에서의 어휘의 뜻을 써보고 해설에서 확인하세요.

- embedded
- manufacture
- virtual
- wheat
- present
- dairy product
- beverage
- liquid
- consume
- content
- vary
- according to

구문 주요 구문을 살펴보아요.

9행 For instance, 1)[to produce two pounds of meat] requires 2)[about 5 to 10 times **as** much water **as** to produce two pounds of vegetables].

1)은 to부정사구로 문장의 주어이고, 동사는 requires이다.
2)는 requires의 목적어로, 「배수사+as ~ as ...」 형태의 배수 표현이 쓰였고, '…의 –배인 ~'이라고 해석한다.

02 다음 글에서 전체 흐름과 관계 없는 문장은? | 고1 전국연합 |

In an experiment, when people were asked to count three minutes in their heads, 25-year-olds were quite accurate, but 65-year-olds went over on average by 40 seconds. Time seemed to pass faster for the older group. ① This may seem meaningless, but there are a lot of benefits to perceiving time like 65-year-olds. ② For example, if you have been working on a project for eight hours, but it only feels like six, you will have more energy to keep going. ③ If you have been running for 20 minutes, and you perceive it to be only 13 minutes, you're more likely to have seven more minutes of energy. ④ One of the greatest benefits of getting older is the cooling of passion — not rushing to quick action. ⑤ So, if you want to use your energy to work longer, just change your perception of how long you have been working.

지문에서의 어휘의 뜻을
써보고 해설에서 확인하세요.

- experiment
- minute
- accurate
- on average
- second
- meaningless
- benefit
- perceive
- passion
- perception

구문 주요 구문을 살펴보아요.

8행 1)[If 2){you have been running for 20 minutes}, and 3){you perceive it to be only 13 minutes}], you're more likely to have 4)[seven more minutes of energy].

1)은 조건의 부사절이며, 그 안에서 2)와 3)이 and로 인해 병렬을 이룬다.
4)는 주절에서 have의 목적어로 쓰인 명사구이다.

Do It Yourself

03 다음 글에서 전체 흐름과 관계 <u>없는</u> 문장은?

There is much debate over whether the long-term consumption of dairy products helps bones. A good deal of evidence suggests that it does not. ① Several studies of teenagers have found that their adult bone health is related to their physical activity level earlier in life, but not to the amount of milk or calcium they consumed. ② Milk consumption is apparently no help later in life either. ③ In a 12-year Harvard study of 78,000 women, those who got the most calcium from dairy products received no benefit and actually broke more bones than the women who got little or no calcium from dairy products. ④ With low calcium intake levels during important bone growth periods, today's youth face a serious public health problem. ⑤ Similarly, a 1994 study of elderly men and women in Sydney showed that those who consumed the most dairy products had double the hip fracture rate of those who consumed the least.

*hip fracture rate 둔부 골절률

구문 주요 구문을 살펴보아요.

3행 Several studies of teenagers have found ¹⁾[that their adult bone health is related to their physical activity level earlier in life, but **not** to **the amount of milk or calcium** ²⁾{they consumed}].

1)은 문장의 동사인 have found의 목적어이다. 1) 안의 not은 is not related에서 중복되는 is related를 생략한 형태이다.

2)는 the amount of milk or calcium을 수식하는 관계절로, they 앞에는 목적격 관계대명사 that 혹은 which가 생략되었다.

04

다음 글에서 전체 흐름과 관계 <u>없는</u> 문장은?

A hybrid vehicle is a vehicle which uses two or more kinds of propulsion. Most hybrid vehicles use a conventional gasoline engine as well as an electric motor to provide power to the vehicle. These are usually called hybrid-electric-vehicles, or HEVs. ① Hybrid vehicles use two types of propulsion in order to use gasoline more efficiently than conventional vehicles do. ② Most hybrid vehicles use the gasoline engine as a generator which sends power to the electric motor. ③ Both sales of hybrid vehicles and the number of hybrid models have risen steadily since their introduction. ④ The electric motor then powers the car. ⑤ In conventional vehicles, the gasoline engine powers the vehicle directly.

*propulsion 추진(력)

구문 주요 구문을 살펴보아요.

2행 Most hybrid vehicles use ¹⁾[a conventional gasoline engine **as well as** an electric motor] ²⁾[to provide power to the vehicle].

1)은 동사 use의 목적어이고, 그 안에 'B뿐만 아니라 A도'라는 의미의 「A as well as B」 구문이 쓰였다.
2)는 to부정사구로 목적의 의미를 나타낸다.

지문에서의 어휘의 뜻을 써보고 해설에서 확인하세요.

- conventional
- gasoline
- electric motor
- power
- in order to
- efficiently
- generator
- rise
- steadily
- directly

How was it? 배운 내용을 확인해보세요.

A 다음 영어는 우리말로, 우리말은 영어로 옮겨 쓰시오.

01 spot

02 twinkle

03 chances are

04 detective

05 conclusion

06 atmosphere

07 구조하다, 구하다

08 outstanding

09 examine

10 attendance

11 requisite

12 appropriately

13 advanced

14 judge

15 eliminate

16 competition

17 mud

18 pond

19 숨쉬다, 호흡하다

20 묻다, 매장하다

B 다음 각 네모 안의 말을 어법에 맞는 순서로 고쳐 쓰시오.

01 There are many situations influence / where / our mood / try to / other people by changing the atmosphere of the environment. 🔗 Link p.145 02번

➡ ______________________________

02 They say that testing drugs on animals does not clearly from / accidents / happening / serious / prevent when they are finally tested on humans. 🔗 Link p.147 04번

➡ ______________________________

03 Users check their reading levels before joining these programs provided / us / the English Reading Test / by / with. 🔗 Link p.151 02번

➡ ______________________________

04 Then your head's shadow might have a halo surrounding it, the moon / at times / does / like / just. 🔗 Link p.153 04번

➡ ______________________________

C

다음 영어는 우리말로, 우리말은 영어로 옮겨 쓰시오.

01 duplicate _______________

02 adolescent _______________

03 드문, 희귀한 _______________

04 spectacular _______________

05 length _______________

06 improve _______________

07 embedded _______________

08 wheat _______________

09 dairy product _______________

10 vary _______________

11 accurate _______________

12 perceive _______________

13 passion _______________

14 debate _______________

15 소비, 체내 섭취 _______________

16 apparently _______________

17 intake _______________

18 elderly _______________

19 conventional _______________

20 steadily _______________

D

다음 각 네모 안의 말을 어법에 맞는 순서로 고쳐 쓰시오.

01 For instance, to produce two pounds of meat requires about 5 to 10 times much / as / water / to / as / produce two pounds of vegetables. ⬭ Link p.156 01번

➡ _______________

02 So, if you want to use your energy to work longer, just change your perception of working / long / how / been / you / have. ⬭ Link p.157 02번

➡ _______________

03 Similarly, a 1994 study of elderly men and women in Sydney showed that those who consumed the most dairy products had double the hip fracture rate of who / least / consumed / those / the. ⬭ Link p.158 03번

➡ _______________

04 Most hybrid vehicles use a conventional gasoline engine as well as an electric motor the / to / vehicle / power / provide / to. ⬭ Link p.159 04번

➡ _______________

Part

6

장문 독해

'장문' 이라는 말만 봐도 벌써 걱정이 앞서는데요, 어떤 유형인가요?

비교적 긴 글을 통해 독해 능력을 평가하는 유형입니다. 보통 2개의 단락으로 구성된 한 지문에 대해 2문항을 푸는 유형과, 4개의 단락으로 구성된 한 지문에 대해 3문항을 푸는 유형의 두 가지가 있어요.

수능에서 이 유형의 비중은 어느 정도 인가요?

매년 수능에 두 유형이 항상 출제됩니다.

읽어야 할 내용도 많은데, 문제도 여러 개라 부담돼요.

사실 장문 독해 유형은 다른 유형에 비해 난이도가 높지 않은 편임에도, 독해 시험의 마지막에 제시되기 때문에 수험생들이 부담을 가지고 있어요. 앞에서 시간 안배를 잘못하면 시간이 부족해 제대로 풀지 못할 수도 있으니 유의해야 합니다. 또 지문이 길다는 심리적 압박감으로 인해 집중력이 떨어질 수 있으니 장문 독해 문항을 먼저 빠르게 푼 후에 다른 문항들을 해결하는 것도 하나의 방법일 수 있습니다.

지문은 보통 어떤 방식으로 구성되나요?

2문항 지문의 경우, 보통 전반부에 글의 핵심 내용이 나오고, 후반부에는 결론에 이르는 내용으로 진행되는 것이 일반적입니다. 3문항 지문의 경우, 보통 네 개의 단락으로 구성되며, 주로 일화에 관한 내용을 다룹니다.

장문 독해 (1지문 2문항)

 1. 주로 두 단락으로 구성된 긴 지문을 읽고, 두 개의 문항에 답을 한다.
2. 제목을 고르는 문제와 문맥상 쓰임이 적절하지 않은 낱말을 고르는 문제로 주로 출제된다.
3. 매년 수능에 꾸준히 출제된다.

Example

[01~02] 다음 글을 읽고, 물음에 답하시오. | 고1 전국연합 |

Many advertisements cite statistical surveys. But we should be (a) cautious because we usually do not know how these surveys are conducted. For example, a toothpaste manufacturer once had a poster that said, "More than 80% of dentists recommend *Smiley Toothpaste*." This seems to say that most dentists (b) prefer *Smiley Toothpaste* to other brands. But it turns out that the survey questions allowed the dentists to recommend more than one brand, and in fact another competitor's brand was recommended just as often as *Smiley Toothpaste*! No wonder the UK Advertising Standards Authority ruled in 2007 that the poster was (c) misleading and it could no longer be displayed.

A similar case concerns a well-known cosmetics firm marketing a cream that is supposed to rapidly reduce wrinkles. But the only evidence provided is that "76% of 50 women agreed." But what this means is that the evidence is based on just the personal opinions from a small sample with no objective measurement of their skin's condition. Furthermore, we are not told how these women were selected. Without such information, the "evidence" provided is pretty much (d) useful. Unfortunately, such advertisements are quite typical, and as consumers we just have to use our own judgment and (e) avoid taking advertising claims too seriously.

01 윗글의 제목으로 가장 적절한 것은?

① The Link between Advertisements and the Economy
② Are Statistical Data in Advertisements Reliable?
③ Statistics in Advertisements Are Objective!
④ The Bright Side of Public Advertisements
⑤ Quality or Price, Which Matters More?

02 밑줄 친 (a)~(e) 중에서 문맥상 낱말의 쓰임이 적절하지 <u>않은</u> 것은?

① (a)　　② (b)　　③ (c)　　④ (d)　　⑤ (e)

How to solve 이런 방법으로 접근하세요.

Step 1 **선택지를 통해 글의 내용 예측하기**

① 광고와 경제의 관계

② 광고의 통계 자료는 믿을만한가?

③ 광고의 통계 수치는 객관적이다!

④ 공익 광고의 밝은 면

⑤ 품질 또는 가격, 어떤 것이 더 중요한가?

➡ **글의 내용** 광고와 관련 있음

Step 2 **글의 전개를 통해 요지 추론하기**

- Many advertisements cite statistical surveys. (많은 광고는 통계 조사를 인용한다.) ➡ **화제 제시**
- But we should be cautious because we usually do not know how these surveys are conducted.
  (하지만 우리는 보통 이러한 조사들이 어떻게 실시되는지를 모르기 때문에 신중해야 한다.) ➡ **주제문**
- For example, a toothpaste manufacturer ~ (예를 들면, 한 치약 제조업체가 ~) ➡ **예시 1**
- ~ a well-known cosmetics firm marketing a cream ~ (크림을 판매하는 유명 화장품 회사 ~) ➡ **예시 2**
- ~ as consumers we just have to use our own judgment ~
  (소비자로서 우리는 스스로 판단해야 하며 ~) ➡ **결론**

➡ **요지** 광고는 통계 자료를 왜곡해 인용할 수 있으므로, 소비자는 신중히 판단해야 한다.

Step 3 **요지에 부합하는 제목 고르기**

➡ **제목** ② 광고의 통계 자료는 믿을만한가?

Step 4 **요지와 문맥을 근거로 적절하지 않은 낱말 고르기**

① cautious : 광고의 통계 조사 방식을 알지 못하므로 받아들이는 데 신중해야 함 → 적절함

② prefer : 통계 조사를 왜곡하여 대부분의 치과의사들이 특정 치약 브랜드를 선호한다는 인상을 줌 → 적절함

③ misleading : 포스터가 더 이상 게시될 수 없게 된 것은 그것이 잘못된 정보를 주는 것이기 때문 → 적절함

④ useful : 표본에 대한 정보 없이 광고에서 제공되는 증거는 유용함 → 적절하지 않으며, useful을 useless 정도로 고쳐야 함!

⑤ avoid : 소비자는 잘 판단하여 광고의 주장을 너무 진지하게 받아들이는 것을 피해야 함 → 적절함

장문 독해 문제를 풀 때

지문이 길다는 점 외에는 다른 유형의 독해와 차이가 없다고 생각하면서 자신감을 갖고 차분히 글을 읽자. 시간에 쫓겨 마음이 급해지지 않도록 하는 연습이 필요하다.

Do It Yourself

On Jan. 13, 1989, the 27-year-old Italian interior designer, Stefania Follini, went down into a cave near Carlsbad, N. Mex., where she was to live for more than four months as part of an experiment aimed at examining how the stresses of long-term isolation could affect space travel. Pioneer Frontier Explorations, an Italian research foundation, had selected Follini, one of 20 volunteers for the assignment, because she was judged to have inner strength and stamina. For 131 days she lived there alone in a 6 meter by 12 meter Plexiglas module sealed 9 meters under the surface, without sunlight or any other way of measuring time.

After about four months, she returned aboveground on schedule. But by her calculations it was only mid-March. During Follini's underground stay, her sense of time seemed to be longer. Her "day" extended to 25 hours, then to 48 hours. She tended to sleep for 22 to 24 hours, then burst into activity for up to 30 hours. In short, her ___________ had gone out of order.

 주요 구문을 살펴보아요.

1행 On Jan. 13, 1989, the 27-year-old Italian interior designer, Stefania Follini, went down into a cave near Carlsbad, N. Mex., [1)] [**where** she **was to live**] for more than four months as part of **an experiment** [2)] [**aimed at examining** [3)] {how the stresses of long-term isolation could affect space travel}].

1)에서 where는 계속적 용법의 관계사이며, was to live는 「be+to부정사」의 구조로, 예정을 나타낸다. '그곳에서 그녀는 살 예정이었다'라고 해석할 수 있다.

2)는 an experiment를 수식하는 과거분사구로, an experiment가 aim(목표로 하다)의 대상이므로 수동의 의미를 나타내는 과거분사 aimed로 쓰인 것이다. 그 뒤의 at은 전치사이므로 뒤에 동명사 examining이 왔다.

3)은 동명사인 examining의 목적어이다. 결국 2)는 'how 이하를 조사하는 것을 목표로 하는'으로 해석할 수 있다.

01 윗글의 제목으로 가장 적절한 것은?

① How to Select a Volunteer
② Why Is Oversleeping Harmful?
③ Comfortable Underground Living
④ What Changes Can Isolation Cause?
⑤ Advantages of Unexpected Exploration

지문에서의 어휘의 뜻을
써보고 해설에서 확인하세요.

- aim at
- examine
- isolation
- affect
- foundation
- assignment
- inner strength
- stamina
- seal
- measure
- on schedule
- calculation
- extend
- burst into
- in short
- go out of order

02 윗글의 빈칸에 들어갈 말로 가장 적절한 것은?

① internal clock
② design tool
③ personal computer
④ electronic calculator
⑤ experimental equipment

Do It Yourself

[03~04] 다음 글을 읽고, 물음에 답하시오.

The nuns of the School Sisters of Notre Dame in a remote part of Mankato in Minnesota have (a) <u>attracted</u> quite a lot of interest from researchers into brain-ageing. And it is no wonder. Many of the nuns are over 90 and quite a few well over 100. Sister Marcella Zachman, who was featured in *LIFE* magazine, was teaching until she was 97. Sister Mary Esther Boor was working on the front desk until she decided to retire, when she was at the age of 99! Moreover, the nuns seem to suffer far (b) <u>fewer</u> and milder cases of senile dementia and other brain diseases than average.

Professor David Snowdon of the University of Kentucky believes that there is a good reason for this. The nuns take the admonition that an 'idle mind is the devil's plaything' very (c) <u>seriously</u> and go to extraordinary lengths to keep their minds occupied. All the time they compete in quizzes, solve puzzles, hold (d) <u>active</u> debates, write in their journals, run seminars and much more. Snowdon has examined the brains of over 100 nuns of Mankato, which were donated for research when they died, and he believes that intellectual stimulation makes the brain connectors that normally (e) <u>increase</u> with age branch out and make new links.

*senile dementia 노인성 치매 *admonition 충고, 경고

 **구문** 주요 구문을 살펴보아요.

6행 Moreover, the nuns seem to suffer [1)][far fewer and milder cases of senile dementia and other brain diseases than average].

1)은 suffer의 목적어 역할을 하는 명사구이다.

03 윗글의 제목으로 가장 적절한 것은?

① It's Not Age That Counts, But Mental Activity

② The Surprising Secrets of the Nuns' Physical Health

③ How Does the Brain Store Memories for a Long Time?

④ The Unexpected Results That A Professor's Bias Caused

⑤ The More Relationships We Have, the Smarter We Become

지문에서의 어휘의 뜻을
써보고 해설에서 확인하세요.

• nun
• remote
• ageing
• wonder
• feature
• retire
• mild
• idle
• plaything
• go to extraordinary
  lengths to
• keep one's mind
  occupied
• compete
• debate
• and much more
• examine
• donate
• intellectual
• stimulation
• normally
• branch out

04 밑줄 친 (a) ~ (e) 중에서 문맥상 낱말의 쓰임이 적절하지 <u>않은</u> 것은?

① (a)　　② (b)　　③ (c)　　④ (d)　　⑤ (e)

장문 독해 (1지문 3문항)

유형 특징
1. 주로 네 단락으로 구성된 긴 지문을 읽고, 세 개의 문항에 답을 한다.
2. 글의 순서, 지칭 추론, 내용의 적절성 판단이라는 세 가지 유형의 문제가 출제된다.
3. 주로 일화에 관한 내용이며, 지문은 길지만 난이도는 높지 않은 편이다.
4. 매년 수능에 꾸준히 출제된다.

Example

[01~03] 다음 글을 읽고, 물음에 답하시오. | 고1 전국연합 |

(A)

Kevin was in front of the mall wiping off his car. He had just come from the car wash and was waiting for his wife. An old man whom society would consider a beggar was coming toward him from across the parking lot. From the looks of him, (a) <u>he</u> seemed to have no home and no money. There are times when you feel generous but there are other
5 times when you just don't want to be bothered.

*wipe off 닦다

(B)

Kevin also needed help. Maybe not for bus fare or a place to sleep, but he needed help. He opened his wallet. And Kevin gave (b) <u>him</u> not only enough for bus fare, but enough to get a warm meal. No matter how much you have, no matter how much you have accomplished, you need help too. No matter how little you have, no matter how loaded
10 you are with problems, even without money or a place to sleep, you can give help.

(C)

This was one of those "don't want to be bothered" times. "I hope the old man doesn't ask me for any money," Kevin thought. He didn't. He came and sat on the bench in front of the bus stop but he didn't look like he could have enough money to even ride the bus. After a few minutes he spoke. "That's a very pretty car," he said. He was ragged but (c) <u>he</u>
15 had an air of dignity around him. Kevin said, "Thanks," and continued wiping off his car.

*dignity 위엄

(D)

He sat there quietly as Kevin worked. The expected request for money never came. As the silence between them widened, Kevin asked, "Do you need any help?" (d) <u>He</u> answered in three simple but profound words that Kevin shall never forget: "Don't we all?" Kevin was feeling successful and important until those three words hit (e) <u>him</u>.
20 Don't we all?

01 주어진 글 (A)에 이어질 내용을 순서에 맞게 배열한 것으로 가장 적절한 것은?

① (B) − (D) − (C) 　 ② (C) − (B) − (D) 　 ③ (C) − (D) − (B)

④ (D) − (B) − (C) 　 ⑤ (D) − (C) − (B)

02 밑줄 친 (a)~(e) 중에서 가리키는 대상이 나머지 넷과 다른 것은?

① (a) 　 ② (b) 　 ③ (c) 　 ④ (d) 　 ⑤ (e)

03 윗글의 Kevin에 관한 내용으로 적절하지 않은 것은?

① 아내를 기다리고 있었다.
② 자신의 지갑을 열었다.
③ 노인이 돈을 요구하지 않기를 바랐다.
④ 버스 정류장 앞 벤치에 앉아 있었다.
⑤ 노인에게 도움이 필요한지 물었다.

How to solve 이런 방법으로 접근하세요.

전문해석:
정답과 해설 p.53

Step 1 각 단락 내용 요약하기
- (A) 쇼핑몰 앞에서 차를 닦고 있던 Kevin이 걸인처럼 보이는 노인을 목격함
- (B) 누구에게나 도움이 필요하다는 깨달음을 얻은 Kevin
- (C) 방해받고 싶지 않은 Kevin과 위엄의 기운을 가진 노인의 첫 대화
- (D) 침묵 이후, 도움이 필요한지 묻는 Kevin의 질문에 우리 모두가 그렇다고 대답하는 노인

Step 2 단락 요약을 토대로 이어질 글의 순서 추론하기
- (A) Kevin이 노인 목격
- ➡ **이어질 순서** (C) Kevin과 노인의 첫 대화 → (D) 침묵 이후 이루어지는 대화 → (B) Kevin의 깨달음과 이야기의 교훈

Step 3 전체 내용을 토대로 가리키는 대상이 다른 것 찾기
- ➡ **다른 것** (e)는 Kevin, (a), (b), (c), (d)는 노인을 가리킴

Step 4 전체 내용을 토대로 적절하지 않은 것 찾기
- ➡ **Kevin에 관한 내용으로 적절하지 않은 것** 버스 정류장 앞 벤치에 앉은 것은 노인이므로 ④는 적절하지 않음

(A)

My husband David called me on my cell phone the week before our daughter's wedding and said, "We have a problem." He told me that the electric company announced a future power outage in our neighborhood to allow for a major repair. The real problem was that we were going to have the power outage on the day of the wedding.

*power outage 정전

(B)

So we got up early on Sunday morning, and found a generator parked right outside of our house — it was (a) her solution. That's right — our house was connected to electricity all day from our own private generator while the rest of the neighborhood had a blackout! It was amazing. Rosa made it clear that our happiness was important to (b) her as well. There are truly people with big hearts. Kindness is still alive.

*generator 발전기

(C)

I called the electric company to ask, or rather to beg, them to put off the repair work since we really, really needed our house to prepare for the wedding(makeup, hair, etc.). I was immediately transferred to a manager named Rosa. She understood the problem and explained that they absolutely couldn't reschedule the power outage, but (c) she would see what she could do.

(D)

Two days later, Rosa called to say that they could not let only our house keep its electricity. Then she said, "We can let you use a room in our company's building." I was surprised and asked if (d) she had ever done that. She said, "Actually, it's happened before." The next day, Rosa called again in a happy voice and said that she had found a solution. She told me that my daughter would be able to use electricity and prepare for (e) her wedding at home.

01 주어진 글 (A)에 이어질 내용을 순서에 맞게 배열한 것으로 가장 적절한 것은?

① (B) − (D) − (C)　　② (C) − (B) − (D)　　③ (C) − (D) − (B)

④ (D) − (B) − (C)　　⑤ (D) − (C) − (B)

지문에서의 어휘의 뜻을
써보고 해설에서 확인하세요.

- electric
- announce
- neighborhood
- solution
- connect
- blackout
- beg
- put off
- transfer
- absolutely
- reschedule

02 밑줄 친 (a)~(e) 중에서 가리키는 대상이 나머지 넷과 다른 것은?

① (a)　　　　② (b)　　　　③ (c)

④ (d)　　　　⑤ (e)

03 윗글의 필자에 관한 내용과 일치하지 <u>않는</u> 것은?

① 딸의 결혼식 날에 집이 정전될 예정이었다.
② 일요일에 자신의 집은 정전을 피할 수 있었다.
③ 공사를 연기해 달라고 전기 회사에 요청했다.
④ 전기 회사의 건물에서 딸의 결혼식을 치렀다.
⑤ 전기 회사 직원으로부터 해결책을 찾았다는 말을 들었다.

구문 주요 구문을 살펴보아요.

2행 He told me [1)][that [2)]{the electric company} announced a future power outage in our neighborhood [3)]{to allow for a major repair}].

1)은 문장의 동사 told의 직접목적어인 that절이다. 1) 안의 주어는 2)이고, announced가 동사이다.
3)은 to부정사구로 목적의 의미를 나타낸다.

[04~06] 다음 글을 읽고, 물음에 답하시오.

(A)

 In 1949, Ben Hogan was involved in a catastrophic automobile accident. However, before the actual collision, Hogan saved his wife, Valerie by throwing himself over her, but his own legs were crushed. Blood clots rising from his injured legs toward his lungs and brain threatened his life. When they got him to the hospital, the doctors told his wife that (a) he would not survive the night. His wife quietly said, "You obviously don't know my husband."

*blood clot 혈전

(B)

 As the months went by, Ben began to get his spirit back again. Although he was in a hospital bed with his body badly damaged, he decided that he was going to play golf again. Oschner was surprised when he learnt of his intent and (b) he said to his wife, "Mrs. Hogan, Ben now wants his golf clubs strung up on the ceiling where he can see them all day long, but he is never going to play golf again" and Mrs. Hogan said, "You obviously don't know my husband."

(C)

 He underwent a risky operation, but the next morning (c) he was still fighting for his life. That state continued for an extended period with Hogan barely clinging to life. Many times the chief surgeon, Alton Oschner felt he had lost the battle against a series of blood clots that were in Hogan's lungs. In the end, Hogan miraculously pulled through, but the doctors told his wife, "Mrs. Hogan, Ben is never going to walk again", and she said, "You obviously don't know my husband."

(D)

 After undergoing incredibly painful physical therapy, (d) he was back on the golf course. Only 10 months had passed since the accident, so his legs had to be swathed in elastic to keep the swelling down, but, incredibly, (e) he was soon winning major tournaments again. During the period of 1950-1953, Hogan scaled to the top of the player rankings again. He was even more successful than before the accident and won the bulk of his nine major titles. He remained the dominant player in the game until the dawn of the 1960s.

*swathe (붕대로) 감싸다 **scale (높은 곳에) 오르다

04 주어진 글 (A)에 이어질 내용을 순서에 맞게 배열한 것으로 가장 적절한 것은?

① (B) − (D) − (C) ② (C) − (B) − (D) ③ (C) − (D) − (B)
④ (D) − (B) − (C) ⑤ (D) − (C) − (B)

05 밑줄 친 (a)~(e) 중에서 가리키는 대상이 나머지 넷과 다른 것은?

① (a) ② (b) ③ (c) ④ (d) ⑤ (e)

06 윗글의 Ben Hogan 관한 내용으로 적절하지 않은 것은?

① 자동차 사고 당시 몸을 던져 아내를 구했다.
② 병원 천장에 골프채를 매달기를 원했다.
③ 의사들은 Ben Hogan이 다시는 걷지 못할 것이라고 여겼다.
④ 물리치료를 거부하고 골프 코스로 돌아갔다.
⑤ 사고 전보다 더 성공적인 골프 성적을 거두었다.

지문에서의 어휘의 뜻을
써보고 해설에서 확인하세요.

- involved in
- catastrophic
- automobile
- collision
- crush
- injure
- lung
- threaten
- obviously
- spirit
- intent
- golf club
- string
- ceiling
- undergo
- operation
- extended
- barely
- cling to
- chief surgeon
- pull through
- physical therapy
- elastic
- swell
- the bulk of
- dominant
- dawn

구문 주요 구문을 살펴보아요.

3행 **Blood clots** [1)][rising from his injured legs toward his lungs and brain] threatened his life.

1)은 문장의 주어인 Blood clots를 수식하는 분사구이다.

How was it?

A 다음 영어는 우리말로, 우리말은 영어로 옮겨 쓰시오.

01	statistical		11	foundation
02	conduct		12	봉인하다
03	misleading		13	burst into
04	concern		14	remote
05	firm		15	ageing
06	주름		16	특집으로 다루다
07	objective		17	은퇴하다
08	examine		18	idle
09	isolation		19	기증하다, 기부하다
10	pioneer		20	stimulation

B 다음 각 문장의 밑줄 친 부분을 어법에 맞게 바르게 고쳐 쓰시오.

01 A similar case concerns a well-known cosmetics firm marketing a cream that is supposed to **rapid reduce wrinkles**. 🔗 Link p.164 Example

➡ ____

02 Unfortunately, such advertisements are quite typical, and as consumers we just have to use our own judgment and **avoiding taking** advertising claims too seriously. 🔗 Link p.164 Example

➡ ____

03 Stefania Follini went down into a cave near Carlsbad, N. Mex., where she was to live for more than four months as part of an experiment aimed at examining **how could the stresses of long-term isolation affect** space travel. 🔗 Link p.166 01~02번

➡ ____

04 For 131 days she lived there alone in a 6 meter by 12 meter Plexiglas module **seal** 9 meters under the surface, without sunlight or any other way of measuring time. 🔗 Link p.166 01~02번

➡ ____

C

다음 영어는 우리말로, 우리말은 영어로 옮겨 쓰시오.

01 beggar	__________	**11** private	__________
02 generous	__________	**12** blackout	__________
03 bother	__________	**13** beg	__________
04 fare	__________	**14** immediately	__________
05 loaded	__________	**15** catastrophic	__________
06 ragged	__________	**16** collision	__________
07 profound	__________	**17** ceiling	__________
08 발표하다, 공표하다	__________	**18** 부어오르다	__________
09 neighborhood	__________	**19** dominant	__________
10 해결책	__________	**20** dawn	__________

D

다음 각 문장의 밑줄 친 부분을 어법에 맞게 바르게 고쳐 쓰시오.

01 Rosa made it clear **which** our happiness was important to her as well. *Link p.172 01~03번*

➡ ____

02 I called the electric company to ask, or rather **begging**, them to put off the repair work since we really, really needed our house to prepare for the wedding(makeup, hair, etc.). *Link p.172 01~03번*

➡ ____

03 Blood clots **rose** from his injured legs toward his lungs and brain threatened his life. *Link p.174 04~06번*

➡ ____

04 When they got him to the hospital, the doctors told his wife **what** he would not survive the night. *Link p.174 04~06번*

➡ ____

Memo

Memo

Memo

Memo

메가스터디
절대
평가
큐

메가스터디
절대
평가
큐

영어 1등급
프 로 젝 트

READING

메가스터디

절대
평가
큐

영어

기본

유형독해
정답과 해설

megastudy

READING

영어 1등급 프로젝트

메가스터디

절대평가 큐

영어 기본

유형독해

정답과 해설

Part 1 중심 내용 추론

Unit 01 주장 추론

Example 답 ③

pp.8~9

소재 노력을 통해 길러지는 행복

전문해석 여러분은 행복의 조건을 살 수 있지만, 행복은 살 수 없다. 그것은 테니스를 치는 것과 같다. 여러분은 가게에서 테니스를 치는 즐거움을 살 수는 없다. 여러분은 공과 라켓을 살 수 있지만, 경기를 하는 즐거움을 살 수는 없다. 테니스의 즐거움을 경험하기 위해, 여러분은 (테니스를) 치는 법을 배우고, 경기하기 위해 스스로 훈련해야만 한다. 서예 쓰기도 마찬가지이다. 여러분은 잉크, 닥종이, 붓을 살 수 있지만, 만약 여러분이 서예 기술을 함양하지 않는다면 서예를 진정으로 할 수 없다. 그래서 서예는 연습을 필요로 하고, 여러분은 스스로 훈련해야만 한다. 여러분은 서예를 할 능력이 있을 때만 서예가로서 행복하다. 행복도 역시 그러하다. 여러분은 행복을 길러가야만 한다. 여러분은 그것을 가게에서 살 수 없다.

구문풀이

[6행] You are happy [**as a calligrapher**] **only** [when you have **the capacity** {to do calligraphy}].

: 첫 번째 [ ]는 전치사구이며, as는 '~로서'의 의미이다. 부사 only 는 시간의 부사절인 두 번째 [ ]를 수식한다. { }는 the capacity를 수식하는 to부정사구이다.

Do It Yourself

pp.10~13

| 01 ① | 02 ⑤ | 03 ② | 04 ④ |

01 답 ①

소재 구어체로 간결하게 글쓰기

전문해석 대부분의 사람들이 글을 쓰기 시작할 때 그들에게 어떤 생각이 밀려온다. 그들은 친구들에게 이야기할 경우에 사용할 법한 말과는 다른 언어로 글을 쓴다. 하지만, 만약 사람들이 여러분이 쓴 것을 읽고 이해하기를 원한다면, 구어체로 글을 써라. 문어체는 더 복잡한데, 이것은 읽는 것을 더욱 수고롭게 만든다. 그것은 또한 형식적이고 거리감이 들게 하여 독자로 하여금 주의를 잃게 만든다. 생각을 표현하기 위해 복잡한 문장이 필요하지는 않다. 심지어, 어떤 복잡한 분야의 전문가들조차도 자신의 생각을 표현할 때, 그들이 점심으로 무엇을 먹을지에 대해 이야기할 때 사용하는 것보다 복잡한 문장을 사용하지는 않는다. 만약 여러분이 구어체로 글을 쓰게 된다면, 여러분은 작가로서 좋은 출발을 하는 것이다.

정답풀이 일상 대화에서 사용하는 구어체로 간결하게 글을 쓸 것을 권하는 내용이므로, 필자의 주장으로는 ①이 가장 적절하다. 주제문인 세 번째 문장에서 필자의 주장이 드러나고, 마지막 문장에서 주장을 다시 한 번 강조하고 있다.

구문풀이

[2행] They write [in **a language** {different from **the one** (**they would use if they were** talking to a friend)}].

: [ ]는 전치사구이고, { }는 a language를 뒤에서 수식하는 형용사구이다. ( )는 the one(= language)을 수식하는 관계절로, they 앞에 목적격 관계대명사 that 또는 which가 생략되어 있다. 〈주어+would+동사원형 ~, if+주어+were[과거동사] ~〉는 현재 사실의 반대를 나타내는 가정법 과거시제 구문이다.

[5행] Written language is more complex, [which {makes it more work to read}].

: [ ]는 앞 절의 내용을 부연 설명하는 관계절이다. { }는 「make+형식상의 목적어(it)+목적격 보어+내용상의 목적어(to부정사)」 구문으로, '~하는 것을 …하게 만들다'의 의미이다.

어휘풀이

- come over (생각·감정이) 밀려오다
- complex 복잡한
- distant 거리감이 있는, 먼
- express 표현하다
- complicated 복잡한
- manage to (그럭저럭·어떻게든) ~하다
- language 언어
- formal 형식적인, 공식적인
- attention 주의, 집중, 관심
- specialist 전문가
- field 분야

02 답 ⑤

소재 부정적인 감정을 있는 그대로 받아들이기

전문해석 강한 부정적인 감정은 인간임의 일부이다. 이러한 감정을 통제하거나 피하려고 지나치게 노력하면 문제가 발생한다. 강한 부정적인 감정에 대처하는 데 도움이 되는 한 가지 방법은 그 감정을 있는 그대로 받아들이는 것이다. 그 감정들은 여러분을 안전하게 지켜주기 위한 의도로 여러분의 몸과 마음이 보내는 메시지이다. 예를 들어, 여러분이 업무상의 발표를 두려워한다면, 불안을 피하려고 애쓰는 것이 여러분의 자신감을 감소시키고 두려움을 증가시킬 수도 있다. 그 대신 대부분의 다른 사람들처럼, 사람들 앞에서 말하는 것에 대해 여러분이 아마 긴장해 있다는 신호로 그 불안을 받아들이도록 노력하라. 이것은 여러분의 불안과 스트레스 수준을 낮추는 데 도움을 주어 자신감을 높이고 발표를 훨씬 더 쉽게 해 줄 것이다.

정답풀이 불안과 같은 강한 부정적인 감정을 통제하려고만 하지 말고 있는 그대로 받아들일 것을 권하는 내용의 글이므로 필자의 주장으로는 ⑤가 가장 적절하다. 세 번째 문장이 주제문으로 필자의 주장이 드러나고, 끝에서 두 번째 문장인 'Instead, ~' 부분에서 주장을 다시 드러내고 있다.

구문풀이

[7행] Instead, try to accept your anxiety as **a signal** [that you are probably nervous about public speaking — just like most other people].

: [ ]는 a signal과 동격 관계를 이루는 절이다.

[9행] This helps you lower the level of your anxiety and stress, [increasing your confidence and making the presentation **much** easier].

: [ ]는 결과의 의미를 나타내는 분사구이다. much는 비교급 앞에 쓰여 '훨씬'이라는 뜻으로 비교급의 의미를 강조한다.

어휘풀이

- negative 부정적인
- control 통제하다; 통제
- take A for B A를 B로 받아들이다
- be afraid of ~을 두려워하다
- anxiety 불안감
- confidence 자신감
- signal 신호
- public speaking 대중 앞에서 말하기, 연설
- lower 낮추다, 내리다
- occur 일어나다, 발생하다
- cope with ~에 대처하다
- intend 의도하다
- presentation 발표
- likely 가능성 있는
- fear 두려움
- nervous 긴장한, 불안한

03 답 ②

소 재 목표의 수정

전문해석 목표를 세우는 것이 쉬운 일이 아니지만, 연습함에 따라 여러분은 그것을 더 잘하게 될 수도 있다. 사람들이 변하는 것처럼 목표도 변한다. 여러분은 목표가 시간이 지나면서 변할 것이라는 것을 이해해야 하고, 그것을 새롭게 할 수 있어야 한다. 예를 들어, 여러분은 여분의 학업 시간을 수학 학습시간에 쓸 목표로 학기를 시작할 지도 모른다. 여러분은 중간고사에서 'A'를 받은 후에 이미 여러분의 목표를 성취했으니 여러분의 영어 학습시간에 그 여분의 학업 시간을 쓸 필요가 있다고 결심할 지도 모른다. 학기가 끝나기 전에 목표를 성취하면 여러분은 하기로 시작한 일을 했다는 것을 인정하고서 새로운 목표를 세울 만큼 충분히 유연성이 있어야 한다.

정답풀이 시간이 지나면서 목표는 변할 수도 있으므로 때에 따라 변경할 수 있어야 한다고 주장하고 있다. 따라서 필자가 주장하는 바로 가장 적절한 것은 ②이다. 세 번째 문장이 주제문으로, 특히 'need to ~'라는 표현에서 필자의 주장이 드러나고, 마지막 문장에서 이를 한 번 더 구체적으로 드러내고 있다.

구문풀이

[8행] If you achieve your goal [before the semester is over], you need to be **flexible enough to acknowledge** [that you have done {what you set out to do}] and then set a new goal.

: 첫 번째 [ ]는 종속절인 if절 안에서의 시간을 나타내는 절이다. 「형용사+enough+to부정사」는 '…할 만큼 충분히 ~한'의 의미이다. 두 번째 [ ]는 acknowledge의 목적어로 쓰인 명사절이며, 그 안의 { }는 have done의 목적어로 쓰인 명사절이다.

어휘풀이

- set a goal 목표를 세우다
- with practice 연습함에 따라서
- update 새롭게 하다, 갱신하다
- spend (돈·시간을) 쓰다
- get better 나아지다, 좋아지다
- over time 시간이 지나면서
- semester 학기
- extra 남는, 여분의

- midterm examination 중간고사
- be over 끝나다
- acknowledge 인정하다, 시인하다
- set out ~을 시작하다, ~을 착수하다
- achieve 성취하다
- flexible 유연성[융통성]이 있는

04 답 ④

소 재 퇴비용 호스에 투자하기

전문해석 퇴비를 만들 때, 물을 쉽게 이용할 수 있는 것은 중요하다. 수분은 성공적인 퇴비를 만드는 노력에 필수적인 요소이고, 유기물을 계속 제대로 썩히기 위해 여러분은 그것을 주기적으로 물로 적실 필요가 있을듯하다. 값싼 호스는 여러분을 끊임없이 괴롭힐 것이고, 여러분은 결국 포기하고 더 좋은 것을 살 것이다. 따라서 처음부터 좋은 품질의 호스에 더 많은 돈을 투자하라. 퇴비를 만들기 위해 좋은 분무기는 여러분이 작업할 때 물을 낭비하지 않고 모든 것을 서서히 적시는 데 큰 효과가 있다. 노즐은 다양한 스타일과 가격대에서 구입할 수 있다. 여러분은 릴(= 감아주는 장치)이 있거나 없는 호스를 살 수 있는데, 여러분이 주로 쓰는 호스를 위해서는 릴이 강력히 권장된다. 그것은 여러분이 호스를 빠르고, 쉽고, 깔끔하게 감고 보관할 수 있게 해준다. 그것은 또한 호스의 수명을 연장시킨다.

정답풀이 퇴비에 물을 잘 공급하는 것이 중요한데, 이때 값싼 호스를 쓰면 계속 불편하므로 처음부터 분무기와 릴 등을 고려해 좋은 품질의 호스를 사도록 권하는 내용이다. 따라서 필자의 주장으로는 ④가 가장 적절하다. 네 번째 문장이 주제문이다.

구문풀이

[1행] Moisture is an essential component of a successful composting effort, and [**it's likely that** you'll need to moisten the organic matter regularly {**to keep it decomposing** properly}].

: 「it's likely that ~」 구문은 '~할 것 같다'의 의미이다. 여기서 it은 형식상의 주어이며, that 이하가 내용상의 주어이다. { }는 목적을 나타내는 to부정사구이며, 「keep+목적어+현재분사」 구문은 '~을 계속 …하게하다'의 의미이다.

[11행] It **enables you to coil and store** your hose quickly, easily, and neatly.

: 「enable+목적어+to부정사(구)」 구문으로, '~가 …할 수 있게 하다'의 의미이다.

어휘풀이

- compost 퇴비를 만들다; 퇴비
- moisture 수분, 습기
- component 성분, 구성 요소
- organic matter 유기물
- trouble 괴롭히다
- from the beginning 처음부터
- available 이용할[구입할] 수 있는
- recommend 권하다, 추천하다
- coil 감다, 둘둘 말다
- extend 늘리다, 연장하다
- access 이용, 접근
- essential 필수적인
- moisten 적시다, 축축하게 하다
- properly 적절히
- invest 투자하다
- spray 분무기; 뿌리다
- a wide range of 다양한, 광범위한
- enable ~할 수 있게 하다
- store 보관하다, 저장하다

Example 답 ③   pp.14~15

소재 아이에게 칭찬과 상을 남발하는 것의 부정적 효과

전문해석 분명 칭찬은 아이의 자존감에 중요하지만, 너무 사소한 일을 너무 자주 칭찬하면, 진정한 칭찬이 필요할 때 그 칭찬의 효과가 사라진다. 모든 사람은 그들이 가치가 있고 인정받는다는 것을 알 필요가 있으며, 칭찬은 그러한 느낌을 표현하는 하나의 방법이다. 하지만 칭찬할 만한 일을 성취한 뒤여야만 한다. 상은 보상이어야 한다. 긍정적인 행동에 대한 반응, 어떤 일을 잘한 것에 대한 상. 그러한 상을 너무 가볍게 부여하는 것에 상존하는 위험은 아이들이 그것에 의존하고 상을 받을 것이라고 생각하는 일만을 하게 될 수도 있다는 것이다. 그들이 칭찬 배지를 받을 만큼 충분히 잘 할 수 있다고 확신하지 않거나, 또한 보상이 보장되지 않는다면, 아이들은 그러한 활동은 피할지도 모른다.

구문풀이

[1행] Certainly praise is [critical to a child's sense of self-esteem], but [**when given** too often for too little], it kills the impact of real praise [when it is called for].

: 첫 번째 [ ]는 보어이다. 두 번째 [ ]는 시간의 부사절로서 when given은 when it(= praise) is given에서 it is가 생략된 것으로 볼 수 있다. 세 번째 [ ] 역시 시간의 부사절이다.

Do It Yourself   pp.16~19

01 ②   02 ①   03 ④   04 ②

01 답 ②

소재 신제품 광고가 기존 제품 광고와 대비될 필요성

전문해석 너무도 많은 회사들이 마치 경쟁자들이 존재하지 않는 것처럼 신제품들을 광고한다. 그들은 (비교 대상이 없는) 공백의 상황에서 광고하고 나서 자신들의 메시지가 도달하지 못할 때 실망한다. 특히 이전 것과 대조되지 않는다면 새로운 제품 범주를 도입하는 것은 어렵다. 새롭고 특이한 것이 예전의 것과 연결되지 않는다면 소비자들은 일반적으로 관심을 주지 않는다. 그래서 여러분에게 정말로 새로운 제품이 있다면 그것이 무엇인지보다는 무엇이 아닌지를 말하는 것이 대체로 더 좋다. 예를 들어 최초의 자동차는 '말이 없는' 마차라고 불렸으며, 이 명칭은 대중이 기존의 수송 방식과 대조하여 그 개념을 이해하도록 해주었다.

정답풀이 신제품이 기존 제품과 대비되지 않는다면 소비자의 관심을 받기 어렵기 때문에 기존 제품과 대비하여 신제품 광고를 하는 것이 효과적이라는 내용이다. 따라서 글의 요지로는 ②가 가장 적절하다.

구문풀이

[6행] Consumers do not usually pay attention **to** [what's new and different] [**unless** it's related to the old].

: 첫 번째 [ ]는 전치사 to의 목적어 역할을 하는 명사절이다. 두 번째 [ ]는 접속사 unless(~하지 않으면)가 이끄는 조건의 부사절이다.

[9행] For example, [the first automobile was called **a "horseless" carriage**], [**a name** {which **allowed the public to understand** the concept against the existing mode of transportation}].

: 첫 번째 [ ]에서 「A be called B」는 'A가 B라고 불리다'의 의미이다. 두 번째 [ ]는 앞의 a "horseless" carriage와 동격을 이룬다. { }는 a name을 수식하는 관계절이다. 「allow+목적어+목적격 보어(to부정사(구))」는 '~가 …하도록 허용하다'의 뜻을 나타낸다.

어휘풀이

- advertise 광고하다
- competitor 경쟁자
- exist 존재하다
- product 제품
- vacuum 진공, 공백
- disappointed 실망한
- get through 도달하다
- category 범주, 부문
- contrast 대비[대조]시키다
- consumer 소비자
- pay attention to ~에 관심을 주다, ~에 주목하다
- be related to ~와 연결[관련]되다
- automobile 자동차
- carriage 마차
- allow ~하게 하다, 허락하다
- concept 개념
- existing 기존의, 존재하는
- transportation 수송, 운송, 교통

02 답 ①

소재 표정에 대한 문화별 인식 방식

전문해석 표정에 관한 흥미로운 연구가 최근에 미국 심리학회에 의해 발표되었다. 15명의 중국인과 15명의 스코틀랜드인이 이 연구에 참여했다. 이들은 컴퓨터 화면에서 임의로 바뀌는 감정 중립적인 얼굴을 보고, 행복한, 슬픈, 놀란, 두려운 혹은 화난 표정으로 분류했다. 그들의 반응을 통해 연구자들은, 참가자가 감정을 드러내는 얼굴 부위 중 어느 부분을 각각의 감정과 관련짓는지를 알게 되었다. 연구에 따르면 중국인 참가자들은 표정을 식별하기 위해 눈에 좀 더 의존하는 반면, 스코틀랜드인 참가자들은 눈썹과 입에 의존했다. 서로 다른 문화권 출신의 사람들은 행복한, 슬픈 또는 화난 표정을 다른 방식으로 인식한다. 즉, 표정은 "감정의 보편적인 언어"가 아니다.

정답풀이 표정에 관한 연구에서 중국인 참가자들과 스코틀랜드인 참가자들이 표정을 알기 위해 주목하는 얼굴 부위가 다르다는 결과를 소개하는 내용이다. 따라서 글의 요지로 가장 적절한 것은 ①이다.

구문풀이

[4행] They viewed **emotion-neutral faces** [that were randomly changed on a computer screen] and then categorized the facial expressions as happy, sad, surprised, fearful, or angry.

: 주어인 They에 동사 viewed와 categorized가 병렬로 연결된

구조이다. [ ]는 앞의 emotion-neutral faces를 수식하는 관계절이다.

[8행] The study found [that the Chinese participants relied more on the eyes {to tell facial expressions}, {**while** the Scottish participants relied on the eyebrows and mouth}].

: [ ]는 found의 목적어 역할을 하는 명사절이다. 그 안에서 첫 번째 { }는 목적을 나타내는 to부정사구이며, 두 번째 { }는 명사절 내의 부사절로, 접속사 while은 대조의 의미를 나타낸다.

- facial expression 표정
- publish 발표하다, 출판하다
- view 보다, 조사하다
- emotion 감정, 정서
- neutral 중립적인
- randomly 무작위로, 임의로
- categorize 분류하다
- fearful 두려워하는
- response 반응
- allow 허락하다, 허용하다
- identify 확인하다, 식별하다
- expressive (생각·감정을) 보여주는, 표정이 있는
- feature 특징
- participant 참가자
- associate 연관 짓다, 관련시키다
- perceive 인식하다, 인지하다
- eyebrow 눈썹
- universal 보편적인

03 답 ④

 작품에 대한 이해력을 높이는 연기

 위대한 희곡을 읽는 것은 대부분의 소설이 제공할 수 있는 것보다 더 강렬한 경험을 제공하고, 희곡을 보는 것은 훨씬 더 좋다. 그리고 희곡에서 연기하는 것은 그 의미와 중요성에 대한 훨씬 더 큰 이해력을 가져다준다. 그것이 셰익스피어의 비극이든 페도의 소극이든, 위대한 희곡의 내막은 여러분이 그 안에서 연기할 때 훨씬 더 분명해진다. 물론 여러분이 배우는 것이 다른 문학 작품에 대한 이해력을 높인다. 많은 대학생 연기자들은 극에 출연하는 데 시간을 보냄에도 불구하고, 고전 작품을 연습하고 공연하는 동안 그들이 얻는 지식 때문에 문학과 심지어 역사 강좌에서의 그들의 성적은 향상될 수 있다는 것을 발견했다.

 극에서 연기하는 것은 그 작품의 의미와 중요성에 대한 훨씬 더 큰 이해력을 가져다주며 극의 내막을 더 분명하게 해 준다는 내용이다. 따라서 글의 요지로 가장 적절한 것은 ④이다.

[4행] [**Whether** it's a Shakespearean tragedy **or** a Feydeau farce], the inner workings of a great play **become much clearer** when you act in it.

: 부사절 [ ]에서 「whether A or B」는 'A이든 B이든'의 의미이다. the inner workings가 주절의 주어이며 복수이므로 동사도 수 일치를 시켜 become이 되었다. much clearer는 보어이다.

[6행] [**What** you learn], of course, enhances your understanding of other works of literature.

: [ ]는 명사절인 주어이며, 여기서 what은 선행사를 포함한 관계대명사로 '~하는 것(= the thing which[that])'의 의미이다.

- play 극, 연극, 희곡
- intense 강렬한, 진지한
- novel 소설
- act 연기하다
- understanding 이해(력)
- tragedy 비극
- inner 내적인, 내부의
- enhance 높이다, 향상하다
- literature 문학
- despite ~에도 불구하고
- appear 출연하다, 나타나다
- course 강좌, 교육과정
- acquire 얻다, 습득[획득]하다
- rehearse (예행) 연습하다
- classic work 고전 작품

04 답 ②

 고가품 판매 시 훈련된 판매직원의 필요성

 판매는 모든 상점에게 중요한 기능이다. 초콜릿이나 잡지와 같은 기본적인 제품을 판매하는 상점은 판매활동을 그다지 많이 할 필요가 없다. 대부분의 고객들은 무언가를 사러 들어와서 원하는 물건을 고르고 값을 지불하고 떠난다. 하지만 고객들이 텔레비전이나 자동차와 같은 값비싼 품목을 사고자 한다면 더 많은 도움과 조언을 기대한다. 그러므로 이러한 종류의 상품을 파는 상점은 친절하고 지식을 갖춘 훈련된 판매직원들이 필요하다. 그들은 제품을 설명하고, 시연해 보일 수 있어야만 하며, 이것들을 고객의 특정한 요구와 연결시킬 수 있어야 한다. 잘 훈련 받은 판매직원을 보유하는 데에는 많은 이득이 있다. 그들은 많은 문의들을 확고한 판매로 전환하고 고객과 강한 유대관계를 형성할 수 있다.

 일반적인 물건을 파는 경우와는 달리, 고가 상품을 판매할 때는 상세한 설명과 조언을 하며 판매할 수 있는 잘 훈련된 판매직원들이 필요하며, 이것이 고객과 강한 유대관계를 형성한다는 내용이다. 따라서 글의 요지로 가장 적절한 것은 ②이다.

[4행] However, customers expect more help and advice [if they want to buy **an expensive item, such as a television or car**].

: [ ]는 조건을 나타내는 부사절이다. 「A, such as B」는 'B와 같은 A'의 의미이다.

[8행] They **must be able to** describe and demonstrate their products, and link these to the customer's specific needs.

: must와 can은 조동사로 동시에 쓰일 수 없으므로 can 대신에 같은 의미의 be able to를 쓴 것이다.

- sales 판매, 매출
- function 기능; 기능하다
- basic 기본적인
- product 제품
- customer 고객
- goods 상품, 물품
- expensive 고가의, 비싼
- item 품목
- staff 직원
- knowledgeable 지식을 갖춘
- describe 설명하다, 묘사하다
- demonstrate (실험 등으로) 시연하다, 증명하다
- link 연결하다; 연결, 연관
- specific 특정한

· need 요구, 욕구, 수요
· inquiry 문의, 질문
· benefit 이득, 혜택
· firm 견고한, 확실한

How was it?
pp.20~21

A 01 조건 02 훈련시키다 03 함양하다, 기르다, 경작하다 04 능력 05 복잡한 06 전문가 07 복잡한 08 field 09 ~에 대처하다 10 anxiety 11 두려움 12 긴장한, 불안한 13 학기 14 남는, 여분의 15 flexible 16 인정하다, 시인하다 17 이용, 접근 18 적절히 19 이용할[구입할] 수 있는 20 늘리다, 연장하다

B 01 the one they would use
02 making the presentation much easier
03 flexible enough to acknowledge
04 to keep it decomposing properly

C 01 중요한, 결정적인 02 자존감 03 벌다, 받다 04 guarantee 05 경쟁자 06 진공, 공백 07 대비[대조]시키다 08 기존의, 존재하는 09 neutral 10 무작위로, 임의로 11 확인하다, 식별하다 12 보편적인 13 비극 14 높이다, 향상하다 15 얻다, 습득[획득]하다 16 (예행)연습하다 17 기능; 기능하다 18 상품, 물품 19 설명하다, 묘사하다 20 (실험 등으로) 시연하다, 증명하다

D 01 which is often better → it is often better: 조건의 부사절 다음에 이어지는 주절에서 뒤에 내용상의 주어 to say ~가 있으므로, 관계대명사 which를 형식상의 주어 it으로 고쳐 써야 한다.
02 allowed researchers identifying → allowed researchers to identify: allow는 목적격 보어로 to부정사를 취하는 동사이므로 identifying을 to identify로 고쳐 써야 한다.
03 That you learn → What you learn: 뒤에 오는 동사 enhances에 호응하는 명사절 주어부를 이루도록 선행사를 포함한 관계대명사 what으로 고쳐 써야 한다.
04 are friendly and knowledgeably → are friendly and knowledgeable: be동사 are에 대한 보어 자리이며 형용사 friendly와 병렬을 이루도록 부사 knowledgeably를 형용사 knowledgeable로 고쳐 써야 한다.

Unit 03 주제 추론

Example 답 ①
pp.22~23

소 재 의학의 발전

전문해석 의료 행위는 모든 나라에서 사람들이 살 것이라고 기대하는 평균 연령이 역사에 기록되었던 것보다 더 높아지고, 한 개인이 암, 뇌종양, 심장병과 같은 심각한 질병에서 살아남을 가능성이 더 높아지는 결과를 낳았다. 그러나 더 길어진 수명은 사람이 늘어나는 것을 의미하고, 이는 식량과 주택 공급의 어려움을 악화시킨다. 게다가 의료 서비스는 여전히 공정하게 분배되지 않고, 의료 서비스에 대한 접근성은 세계의 여러 지역에서 문제로 남아 있다. 의학 기술의 향상은 인구 집단의 균형점을 이동시킨다(초기에는 어린아이들에게로 그리고 다음에는 노인들에게로). 그것은 또한 돈과 자원을 시설과 숙련된 사람들을 위해 쓰도록 묶어 두어, 더 많은 비용이 들게 하고, 다른 것들에 쓰일 수 있는 것에 영향을 미친다.

구문풀이
[4행] However, longer life spans mean more people, [worsening food and housing supply difficulties].
: [ ]는 앞 문장 전체 내용을 의미상의 주어로 삼아 그 결과를 설명하는 분사구이다.

Do It Yourself
pp.24~27

01 ②	02 ④	03 ①	04 ④

01 답 ②

소 재 지역마다 다르게 영어를 말하는 방식

전문해석 여러분은 외국에 나가본 적이 있는가? 여행을 많이 하는가? 그렇다면 여러분은 내가 무엇에 관해 말하고 있는지 알 것이다. 여러분은 이 지구상 어디를 가든지, 영어로 살아갈 수 있다. 대부분의 사람들이 어떤 식으로든지 영어로 말하거나, 또는 적어도 주변에 이 언어로 의사소통할 수 있는 사람이 있다. 그러나 그때, 여러분은 대체로 그곳에서 영어가 사용되는 방식에 있어 이상하다고 발견할 수 있는 무언가가 있다는 것을 깨닫게 된다. 만약 여러분이 외국에 있다면, 영어는 여러분이 말하는 방식과 다소 다를 수 있다. 만약 여러분이 그곳에 잠시 동안 머무른다면, 거기가 어디든지 간에, 여러분은 이것에 익숙하게 될 것이다. 그리고 만약 여러분이 그곳에 보다 오랫동안 머무른다면, 이러한 특징들 중 일부를 배워서 그 지역 사람들처럼 들리기 시작할지도 모른다. 이러한 사례가 우리에게 가르쳐 주는 것은 영어가 더 이상 "단일 언어"가 아니라는 것이다.

정답풀이 지구상의 어디를 가든지 영어로 의사소통을 할 수 있지만, 지역마다 사용하는 영어는 서로 다른 특징을 가진다는 내용이다. 결정적으로 마지막 문장의 '영어가 더 이상 단일 언어가 아니다'라는 말을 통해, 주제로는 ② '다양한 지역에서의 영어의 현지화'가 가장 적절함을 알 수 있다.

오답풀이
① 해외여행에 대한 찬반 양론 → 첫 두 문장으로 인해 유도될 수 있는 오답이다.
③ 체계적인 영어 교육의 필요성 → 영어 교육에 관한 글은 아니다.
④ 영어 능력을 향상하기 위한 다양한 방법 → 영어 능력 향상에 관한 글은 아니다.
⑤ 해외에서 현지 주민과 잘 지내는 방법 → 전혀 무관한 내용이다.

구문풀이
[5행] But then, you realize [that mostly there's **something** {you may find odd about the way (English is used there)}].

: [ ]는 realize의 목적어에 해당하는 명사절이며, { }는 목적격 관계대명사 that이 생략된 관계절로, something을 수식한다. ( )는 the way를 수식하는 관계절이다.

- **abroad** 외국으로, 해외로
- **get along** 살아가다, 지내다
- **odd** 이상한, 홀수의
- **pick up** 배우다
- **local** 현지인; 현지의
- **localization** 현지화
- **method** 방법
- **resident** 주민, 거주자
- **globe** 지구
- **communicate** 의사소통하다, 전달하다
- **get used to** ~에 익숙해지다
- **feature** 특징, 모습
- **pros and cons** 찬반 양론
- **systematic** 체계적인
- **get along with** ~와 잘 지내다

02 답 ④

소 재 스토리텔링을 통한 역사 교육

전문해석 스토리텔러 Syd Lieberman은 사실을 걸기 위한 못을 제공하는 것은 바로 역사 속의 이야기라고 말한다. 학생들은 역사적 사실이 이야기에 결합되어 있을 때 그것을 기억한다. 한 보고서에 따르면, Colorado주 Boulder의 한 고등학교에서 현재 역사 자료를 제시하는 것에 대한 연구를 실험하고 있다. 스토리텔러들은 학생들에게 자료를 극적인 맥락에 넣어 제시하고, 그룹 토의가 잇따른다. 학생들은 (자료를) 더 많이 읽도록 장려된다. 이와는 대조적으로, 또 다른 그룹의 학생들은 전통적인 조사/보고 기법에 참여한다. 이 연구는 스토리텔러들에 의해서 제시된 자료가 전통적인 방법을 통해서 얻은 자료보다 훨씬 더 많은 흥미와 개인적인 영향을 지닌다는 것을 보여 준다.

정답풀이 역사적 사실이 이야기와 결합되면 그것을 더 잘 기억하고, 스토리텔러들이 제시한 자료가 전통적인 방법에서 얻어진 역사 자료보다 더 많은 흥미와 개인적 영향을 지난다는 내용이다. 따라서 글의 주제로는 ④ '역사를 가르칠 때 스토리텔링의 이점'이 가장 적절하다.

① 학생들이 역사를 배워야 하는 이유 → 역사를 배우는 이유에 대한 글은 아니다.

② 사극의 필수 요소 → 사극도 역사와 관련된 것이지만 내용과 무관하다.

③ 전통적인 교수법의 장점 → 글의 내용과 상반된다.

⑤ 역사에 대한 균형 잡힌 시각을 가지는 것의 중요성 → 역사를 보는 시각에 대한 언급은 없다.

[1행] Storyteller Syd Lieberman suggests [that **it is** the story in history **that** provides the nail to hang facts on].

: [ ]는 suggests의 목적어 역할을 하는 명사절이다. 그 안에 「it is ~ that ...(…하는 것은 바로 ~이다)」 강조 구문이 쓰여 the story in history를 강조하고 있다.

- **nail** 못
- **fact** 사실
- **according to** ~에 따르면
- **presentation** 제시
- **context** 맥락, 문맥, 환경
- **indicate** 보여 주다
- **method** 방법
- **hang** 걸다, 매달다
- **tie** 결합하다, 묶다, 잇다
- **currently** 현재
- **dramatic** 극적인
- **be involved in** ~에 참여하다
- **via** ~을 통해

03 답 ①

소 재 다중 작업을 할 때 남자와 여자의 차이

전문해석 여자는 관련이 없는 여러 가지 일을 동시에 할 수 있다. 그녀는 새로운 조리법으로 요리를 하고 TV를 보면서 동시에 전화 통화를 할 수 있다. 또는 핸즈프리로 통화를 하는 동안 운전을 하고 화장을 하며 라디오를 들을 수 있다. 대조적으로, 남자가 조리법을 보면서 요리를 할 때 그에게 말을 걸면, 그는 적혀진 설명서를 따라가는 것과 듣는 것을 동시에 할 수 없기 때문에 화를 내기 쉽다. 남자가 면도를 할 때 말을 걸면 그는 면도날에 베일 것이다. 어떤 경우에는 남자는 여자가 자신에게 말을 하고 있었기 때문에 그 순간 그가 고속도로에서 방향을 바꾸지 못하게 만들었다고 여자를 비난할 수도 있다. 한 여성은 자신의 남편에게 화가 난다면 남편이 못에 망치질을 하고 있을 때, 그에게 말을 걸 거라고 농담 삼아 우리에게 말했다.

정답풀이 여자는 요리와 전화 통화, 운전, 라디오 듣기 등 서로 관련 없는 일을 동시에 할 수 있지만, 남자는 면도, 운전, 망치질을 할 때 대화를 하면 그 일을 제대로 할 수 없다는 것을 예로 들고 있다. 따라서 글의 주제로는 ① '다수의 일을 동시에 처리할 때의 성별 차이'가 가장 적절하다. 전체 내용을 포괄하는 하나의 뚜렷한 주제문이 없는 글이므로, 예시를 종합해 주제를 추론하도록 한다.

② 가사 일을 분담하는 것의 이점 → 가정에서 하는 일이 언급되었지만 가사일 분담에 관한 글은 아니다.

③ 부부의 의견 불일치를 일으키는 것들 → 부부의 의견 불일치에 관한 글은 아니다.

④ 일상에서 여성들이 가장 좋아하는 활동들 → 여성들이 동시에 하는 일들을 언급했지만 가장 좋아하는 활동에 관한 글은 아니다.

⑤ 운전하면서 집중하는 것의 중요성 → 운전의 예시는 나왔지만 운전하면서 집중하는 것의 중요성에 대한 글은 아니다.

[8행] In some cases, a man might **accuse** a woman **of making** him **miss** a turn on the highway [because she was chatting to him at the time].

: 주절에 「accuse A of B(B에 대해 A를 비난하다)」 구문이 쓰였으며, of가 전치사이므로 뒤에 동명사 making이 쓰였다. 이 making은 '~하게 하다'라는 의미의 사역동사 make의 변형이므로 뒤에는 목적격 보어로 동사원형 miss가 왔다. [ ]는 이유를 나타내는 부사절이다.

• unrelated 관련 없는　　　　　　• recipe 조리법
• put on make-up 화장하다
• hands-free 핸즈프리 방식(전화기를 손에 들지 않고 통화하는 방식)
• in contrast 반면에, 대조적으로　　• instructions 설명서, 설명
• shave 면도하다　　　　　　　　• cut oneself (칼에) 베이다
• accuse A of B B에 대해 A를 비난하다
• hammer 망치질하다; 망치　　　• gender 성, 성별
• multitasking 멀티태스킹(여러가지 일을 동시에 하는 것)
• household chores 가사일　　　• concentration 집중

04 답 ④

소 재　역사 의식을 가질 필요성

전문해석　우리는 현재와 미래에 살고 있고 그렇게 하는 것에 대해 자부심을 느낀다. 그러나 과거에 대한 강한 의식이 없다면 현재는 무의미하고 미래는 위험으로 가득할 것이다. 히틀러는 죽었지만 그가 만든 망령은 사라지지 않았으며 결코 사라지지 않을 것이다. 그 망령이 무엇을 의미하며 특정한 상황에서 그것이 어떻게 작용하는지를 알지 못한다면, 우리는 그것의 재발에 대처하지 못할 것이다. 고대 그리스는 멸망했지만 그것이 안고 있던 문제, 특히 위대한 민주주의가 풀지 못한, 어떻게 자유와 안전을 동시에 성취할 수 있는가 하는 한 가지 문제는 여전히 남아 있다. 그리스가 왜 멸망했는가를 배우는 것은 우리가 더 행복한 해결책을 찾는 것을 도와줄 수 있을 지도 모른다. 모든 개인의 삶 속에서 우리는 우리가 그것을 의식하지 못할 때조차도 과거가 여전히 활발하게 남아서 영향력을 발휘하는 것을 안다. 국가적으로도 마찬가지며, 그 파동(영향력)은 수세기 동안 계속해서 확산되고 있다.

정답풀이　두 번째 문장이 주제문으로 과거에 대한 강한 의식을 가져야 한다는 것이다. 히틀러의 망령이나 그리스 멸망의 원인과 같은 과거의 사실은 완전히 사라진 것이 아니라 현재에도 큰 영향력을 미치고 있다는 부연 설명을 통해, 과거에 대해 알아야 관련된 문제에 대처할 수 있고, 더 나은 해결책을 찾을 수 있다는 요지를 뒷받침하고 있다. 따라서 글의 주제로 가장 적절한 것은 ④ '역사에 대한 적절한 감각을 가질 필요성'이다.

오답풀이
① 미래 예측의 어려움 → 미래에 관한 내용은 일부만 언급되었다.
② 역사 해석에서의 변화 → 역사 해석의 변화에 초점을 둔 글이 아니다.
③ 민주 사회를 위해 해야 할 일 → 민주 사회를 위해 할 일에 대한 글이 아니다.
⑤ 자유와 안전 사이의 관계 → 지엽적인 예시에만 초점을 둔 오답이다.

구문풀이
[11행] We know [that {in every individual's life} the past remains active and influential, {even when we are unconscious of **it**}].
: [ ]는 know의 목적어에 해당하는 명사절이다. 첫 번째 { }는 전치사구이며, that절의 주어는 the past이고 remains가 동사이다. 두 번째 { }는 시간의 부사절이며, it은 '과거가 활발하게 남아 영향력을

발휘하는 것'을 가리킨다.

• present 현재　　　　　　　　• sense 의식, 감각
• spirit 정신, 망령　　　　　　• generate 낳다, 발생시키다
• circumstance 상황, 환경　　　• cope with ~에 대처하다
• especially 특히　　　　　　　• democracy 민주주의
• solve 해결하다　　　　　　　• security 안전, 보안
• solution 해결(책)　　　　　　• individual 개인; 개인의
• active 활발한　　　　　　　　• influential 영향력 있는
• unconscious 무의식의　　　　• be true of ~에도 적용되다[해당되다]
• wave 파동, 파도

Unit 04 제목 추론

Example　답 ⑤　　　　　　　　　　pp.28~29

소 재　누군가가 지켜본다는 신호가 주는 사회적 성과

전문해석　사람들이 커피 값을 기부하는 양심 상자 가까이에, 영국 Newcastle 대학교의 연구자들은 사람의 눈 이미지와 꽃 이미지를 번갈아 가며 놓아두었다. 각각의 이미지는 일주일씩 놓여 있었다. 꽃 이미지가 놓여 있던 주들보다 눈 이미지가 놓여 있던 모든 주에 사람들이 더 많은 기부를 했다. 연구가 이루어진 10주 동안, '눈 주간'의 기부금이 '꽃 주간'의 기부금보다 거의 세 배나 많았다. 이 실험은 '진전된 협력 심리가 누군가가 지켜보고 있다는 미묘한 신호에 아주 민감하다.'는 것과 이 연구 결과가 사회적으로 이익이 되는 성과를 내게끔 어떻게 효과적으로 넌지시 권할 것인가를 암시한다고 말했다.

구문풀이
[5행] Over the ten weeks of the study, **contributions** [during the 'eyes weeks'] were almost three times higher than **those** [made during the 'flowers weeks].'
: 두 개의 [ ]는 각각 contributions와 those를 수식하는 전치사구와 분사구이다. those는 중복되는 contributions를 대신하는 대명사이다.

Do It Yourself　　　　　　　　　　pp.30~33

　01 ⑤　　　　02 ②　　　　03 ①　　　　04 ②

01 답 ⑤

소 재　화요일이 생산적인 이유

전문해석　여러분은 직장에서 일요일로 채워진 한 달을 꿈꿀지도 모르지만, 여러분의 상사는 화요일로 채워진 일주일을 원한다. 무엇

이 화요일을 특별하게 만드는 것인가? 월요일은 '일을 진행하기 위한' 회의들로 매우 부담되는데, 그것들은 그리 생산적이지 않다. 수요일은 '힘든 날'이라서 직장인은 그냥 넘겨 버리자고 생각한다. 목요일에는 사람들이 지치게 된다. 그리고 금요일에는 모두가 주말을 생각하고 있다. **화요일에는 직장인들이 일과에 매우 집중된 상태이기 때문에 업무수행능력이 최고가 된다.** 또한 화요일은 보통 일주일 중에서 그들이 자신의 업무에 집중하게 되는 첫 번째 날이다. 그들은 10시간 동안 20시간 분량의 일을 한다.

 직장인들이 화요일에 가장 생산적인데, 화요일에는 특히 일과에 집중할 수 있고, 자신의 과업에 몰두하며, 두 배의 업무 효율이 있다고 했으므로 글의 제목으로는 ⑤ '왜 화요일이 가장 생산적인 날인가?'가 가장 적절하다.

① 더 창의적이고 싶은가? → 창의성에 대한 글이 아니다.
② 여러분의 직원들이 기다리고 있는 것 → 금요일에는 모두가 주말을 생각한다는 내용에서 유도될 수 있는 오답이다.
③ 주말은 여러분을 더 생산적으로 만든다 → 지문과 어긋나는 내용이다.
④ 여러분만의 주간 계획을 짜는 방법 → 언급되지 않은 내용이다.

[9행] Also, Tuesday is usually **the first day of the week** [that they're focused on their own task].
: [ ]는 the first day of the week을 수식하는 관계절이다.

· special 특별한
· productive 생산적인
· exhausted 지친, 고갈된
· performance 수행, 성과
· overloaded 지나치게 부담되는
· get over ~을 넘겨 버리다
· peak 최고의, 절정의; 절정, 꼭대기
· task 과업, 업무

02 답 ②

 교사의 질문의 중요성

 그저 학생에게 어려운 텍스트를 제공하는 것으로는 학습이 일어나기에 충분하지 않다. 학생에게 어려운 텍스트를 혼자 읽고 그것에 관해 생각해 보고 그것에 관한 글을 쓰게 과제를 주는 것 또한 충분하지 않다. 양질의 질문은 교사가 학생의 텍스트에 대한 이해를 확인할 수 있는 한 가지 방법이다. 질문은 또한 학생들의 이해를 심화시키기 위해 그들의 증거 탐색과 텍스트로 되돌아가야 할 필요를 촉진할 수 있다. 학생이 텍스트를 다시 읽게 하는 질문을 던져서 결국 동일한 텍스트를 여러 번 읽게 함으로써 학생의 이해를 진전시키고 심화시키는 데 있어 교사는 적극적인 역할을 한다. **다시 말해서, 텍스트에 근거한 질문은 학생에게 다시 읽어야 하는 목적을 제공해 주고, 이것은 어려운 텍스트를 이해하는 데 있어 중요하다.**

 학생 혼자 텍스트를 읽고 생각하고 연관된 글쓰기를 하도록 하는 것보다는 교사가 양질의 질문을 통해 확인하는 것이 학생이 텍스트를 반복해 읽도록 하여 결국 이해를 진전시키고 심화시킨다는 내용이다. 따라서 글의 제목으로는 ② '더 나은 이해를 위한 질문하기'가 가장 적절하다.

① 지나치게 많은 숙제는 해롭다 → 숙제에 관한 글은 아니다.
③ 너무 많은 시험은 학생을 피곤하게 한다 → 시험에 관한 글은 아니다.
④ 과학이 아직 답할 수 없는 질문들 → 질문에 관한 글이지만, 과학과는 무관하다.
⑤ 늘 하나의 정답만 있는 것은 아니다 → 질문에 관한 글이지만, 정답의 수와는 무관하다.

[2행] [Assigning students to independently read, think about, and then write about a complex text] is not enough, either.
: [ ]는 문장의 주어 역할을 하는 동명사구이며, 단수 취급되어 동사로 is가 쓰였다.

· provide A with B A에게 B를 제공하다
· complex 어려운, 복잡한
· independently 혼자서, 독립적으로
· promote 촉진하다
· deepen 심화시키다
· comprehension 이해
· multiple 여러 번의, 다양한
· purpose 목적
· assign 주다, 부여하다
· quality 양질의
· evidence 증거
· active 적극적인
· result in 결국 ~하게 되다
· text-based 텍스트에 근거한
· critical 중요한, 결정적인

03 답 ①

 프리허그

 인간들은 낯선 사람을 불신하도록 태어나면서부터 조건화되어 있는데, 특히 접촉이 연관될 경우에 그러하다. 그러므로, 낯선 사람들에게 포옹을 제공하려는 한 남자의 의도는 군중의 의심을 살만큼 충분히 특이했다. 그가 프리허그를 제공할 때 사람들은 경계심을 가지고 그를 지켜보았다. 그들이 이 낯선 사람과 그의 의도를 신뢰할 수 있었을까? 그가 그저 장난을 하고 있는 걸까? 첫 여성이 눈가리개를 한 그 남성에게 다가가 포옹을 하자 군중의 혼합된 감정과 반응이 사라졌고 다른 사람들도 그녀의 본보기를 따랐다. 몇몇은 짧은 포옹을 했고, 다른 사람들은 오랫동안 보지 못했던 친구와 인사하는 것처럼 그를 꽉 붙잡았다. **접촉의 길이와 상관없이, 서로에게 포옹하는 것은 연결과 신뢰라는 힘을 위한 환경을 만들어 냈다.**

 낯선 사람을 불신하는 것이 인간의 본능인데, 프리허그를 통해 사람들 사이에 연결과 신뢰가 생겨날 수 있었다는 내용이다. 따라서 글의 제목으로는 ① '프리허그: 연결하고자 하는 용기'가 가장 적절하다.

② 낯선 사람과 대화하기가 왜 그렇게 어려울까? → 대화에 관한 내용은 아니다.
③ 낯선 사람이 접근할 때 해야 하는 것 → 낯선 사람이 접근할 때 해야 하는 것에 대한 글은 아니다.
④ 포옹은 남을 인정하는 최고의 방법이다 → 포옹이 타인을 인정하는 최고

의 방법이라는 언급은 없다.

⑤ 의도와 동기 부여 사이의 차이는 무엇인가? → 동기 부여에 관한 내용은 전혀 없다.

구문풀이

[2행] Therefore, **one man's intention** [to give out hugs to strangers] was [unique enough to prompt the crowd to be suspicious].

: 첫 번째 [ ]는 one man's intention을 수식하는 to부정사구이다. 두 번째 [ ]는 「형용사+enough+to부정사」 구문으로 '…할 만큼 충분히 ~한'의 뜻이다.

[9행] Some gave brief hugs; others clung to him [as if greeting a long-lost friend].

: [ ]는 as if (they were) greeting a long-lost friend에서 they were가 생략된 형태이다. 부사절에서는 〈주어+be동사〉가 종종 생략된다.

어휘풀이

- **be programmed to** ~하도록 조건화되다
- **distrust** 불신하다
- **intention** 의도
- **hug** 포옹, 허그
- **unique** 특별한, 고유한
- **prompt** (어떤 일이) 일어나도록 하다, 유도하다
- **suspicious** 의심하는
- **warily** 경계하여, 방심하지 않고
- **blindfolded** 눈가리개를 한
- **lead** 본보기, 선례
- **cling to** ~을 꽉 붙잡다, ~을 고수하다
- **greet** 인사하다
- **long-lost** 오랫동안 보지 못한
- **connection** 연결
- **acknowledge** 인정하다, 인식하다
- **motivation** 동기 부여

04 답 ②

소재 체육 수업 후 샤워하기를 꺼리는 학생들

전문해석 한 보고서에 의하면, 절반이 넘는 고등학교 학생들이 체육 수업 후에 절대로 샤워를 하지 않는다고 한다. 연구원들은 학생들이 땀을 흘리고 샤워하는 것을 원치 않아서 체육 수업에 덜 적극적이라고 암시한다. 그 연구원들은 잉글랜드의 Essex에 있는 학교의 약 4,000명의 학생들에게 질문을 했다. 수석연구원인 Gavin Sandercock 박사는 학생들이 얼마나 샤워를 꺼리는지 알고 놀랐다고 한다. 그는 "만약 샤워를 꺼리는 것이 땀을 내는 것에 대한 장애가 된다면, 학교에서의 활동을 장려하기 위해 우리가 이러한 꺼림에 대해 조치를 취할 필요가 있습니다."라고 말했다. 그 보고서는 학생들이 체육 시간 후에 왜 샤워를 하지 않았는지에 대한 정확한 이유를 찾지는 않았다. 하지만 약자를 괴롭히는 것에 대한 두려움과 창피함이 일부 학생들이 샤워하기를 꺼리는 이면에 있을지도 모른다고 지적하는 다른 연구들이 있다. 또래 앞에서 옷을 벗는 것이 어떤 학생들에게는 너무 지나친 것일지도 모르며, 많은 학생들이 자신의 신체 이미지에 대해 걱정한다.

정답풀이 많은 학생들이 체육 시간이 끝난 후에 샤워를 하지 않는데, 그 이유의 이면에는 괴롭힘에 대한 두려움, 창피함 등이 있다는 내용의 글이므로, 글의 제목으로는 ② '체육 수업 후에 학생들은 그저 샤워를 하지 않는다'가 가장 적절하다.

오답풀이

① 고등학교 학생들의 동기부여 문제 → 동기 부여에 대한 내용은 아니다.

③ 학업 성과가 신체 활동에 미치는 영향 → 학업 성과에 대한 글이 아니다.

④ 운동하기의 심리적, 사회적 이점 → 운동에 관한 내용과 관련은 있지만 그것의 이점을 언급하지는 않았다.

⑤ 학습에 대한 장벽에 대처하기 위해 교실 활동 개선하기 → 지문의 내용과 무관하다.

구문풀이

[1행] A report has found [that more than half of high school students never shower after their physical education (P.E.) classes].

: [ ]는 has found의 목적어로 쓰인 명사절이다.

[12행] However, there are **other studies** [that point out {that fear of bullying and humiliation may be behind the reluctance of some students to shower}].

: [ ]는 other studies를 수식하는 관계절이고, { }는 point out의 목적어로 쓰인 명사절이다. '~를 지적하는 다른 연구들'이라는 뜻으로 해석한다.

어휘풀이

- **physical education class** 체육 수업
- **sweat** 땀을 흘리다
- **unwillingness** 꺼림, 내키지 않음
- **barrier** 장애, 장벽
- **tackle** (문제 등에) 착수하다
- **promote** 장려하다
- **humiliation** 창피(함)
- **reluctance** 꺼림, (마음이) 내키지 않음
- **undress** 옷을 벗다
- **be too much for** ~에게 너무 지나치다
- **concern** 걱정
- **academic** 학교의, 학문의
- **enhance** 개선하다, 향상시키다
- **address** 대처하다; 주소

Unit 05 함축 의미 추론

Example 답 ④   pp.34~35

소재 부족과 과잉의 중간 지점

전문해석 인생의 거의 모든 것에는, 좋은 것에도 지나침이 있을 수 있다. 심지어 인생에서 최상의 것도 지나치면 그리 좋지 않다. 이 개념은 적어도 아리스토텔레스 시대만큼 오래전부터 논의되어 왔다. 그는 미덕이 있다는 것은 균형을 찾는 것을 의미한다고 주장했다. 예를 들어, 사람들은 용감해져야 하지만, 만약 어떤 사람이 너무 용감하다면 그 사람은 무모해진다. 사람들은 (타인을) 신뢰해야 하지만, 만약 어떤 사람이 (타인을) 너무 신뢰한다면 그들은 잘 속아 넘어가는 사람으로 여겨진다. 이러한 각각의 특성에 있어, 부족과 과잉 둘 다를 피하는 것이 최상이다. 최상의 방법은 행복을 극대화하는 "sweet spot"에 머무르는 것이다. 아리스토텔레스는 미덕은 중간 지점에 있다고 말했는데, 그곳에서는 사람이 너무 관대하지도 너무 인색하지도, 너무 두려워하지도 너무 무모하게 용감하지도 않다.

구문풀이

[5행] For each of these traits, **it** is best [to avoid both deficiency and excess].

: it은 형식상의 주어이고, [ ]가 내용상의 주어이다.

Do It Yourself

pp.36~39

01 ③　　　02 ⑤　　　03 ④　　　04 ⑤

01 답 ③

소 재　정보 과다의 문제

전문해석　기술은 의문의 여지가 있는 이점을 지니고 있다. 우리는 정확한 정보만 사용해서 의사 결정 과정을 간소하게 하는 것에 맞추어 너무 많은 정보는 조절해야 한다. 인터넷은 어떤 문제에 대해서도 너무 많은 무료 정보를 이용 가능하게 만들어서 우리는 어떤 결정을 하기 위해서 그 모든 정보를 고려해야 한다고 생각한다. 그래서 우리는 계속 인터넷에서 답을 검색한다. 이것이 우리가 개인적, 사업적, 혹은 다른 결정을 하려고 애쓸 때, 전조등 불빛에 노출된 사슴처럼, 우리를 정보에 눈멀게 만든다. 오늘날 어떤 일에 있어서 성공하기 위해서는, 우리는 눈먼 사람들의 세계에서는 한 눈으로 보는 사람이 불가능해 보이는 일을 이룰 수 있다는 것을 명심해야 한다. 한 눈으로 보는 사람은 어떤 분석이든 단순하게 하는 것의 힘을 이해하고, 직관이라는 한 눈을 사용할 때 의사 결정자가 될 것이다.

정답풀이　너무 많은 정보가 인터넷에 있어서 우리가 결정을 하기 위해서는 모든 정보를 고려해야 하고, 그 결과 여러 결정을 할 때 정보에 눈이 멀게 되었다는 내용이다. 따라서 밑줄 친 말의 의미로는 ③ '너무나 많은 정보 때문에 의사 결정을 할 수 없게'가 가장 적절하다.

오답풀이
① 다른 사람들의 생각을 수용하기 꺼려하게 → 글의 내용과 무관하다.
② 무료 정보에 접근할 수 없게 → 글의 내용과 상반된다.
④ 이용 가능한 정보의 부족에 무관심하게 → 글의 내용과 상반된다.
⑤ 의사 결정에 기꺼이 위험을 무릅쓰게 → 의사 결정의 위험성에 대한 언급은 없다.

구문풀이

[3행] The Internet has made **so** much **free information** available on any issue [**that** we think we have to consider all of **it** in order to make a decision].

: 「so ~ that ...」 구문은 '너무 ~해서 …하다'라는 뜻이다. 대명사 it은 앞에 있는 free information을 가리킨다.

어휘풀이
· doubtful 의문의 여지가 있는
· balance ~ versus ... …에 맞추어 ~을 조절하다[등가로 만들다]
· decision-making process 의사 결정 과정
· consider 고려하다　　　· blinded 눈먼
· accomplish 이루다

· seemingly 겉보기에, ~인 것처럼 보이는
· analysis 분석　　　· decision maker 의사 결정자

02 답 ⑤

소 재　도미노와 비슷한 신체 작동 방식

전문해석　신체는 문제를 축적하는 경향이 있으며, 그것은 흔히 하나의 작고 사소해 보이는 불균형에서 시작한다. 이 문제는 또 다른 미묘한 불균형을 유발하고, 그것이 또 다른 불균형을, 그리고 그 다음에 몇 개의 더 많은 불균형을 유발한다. 결국 여러분은 어떤 증상을 갖게 된다. 그것은 마치 일련의 도미노를 한 줄로 세워 놓는 것과 같다. 여러분은 첫 번째 도미노를 쓰러뜨리기만 하면 되는데, 그러면 많은 다른 것들도 또한 쓰러질 것이다. 마지막 도미노를 쓰러뜨린 것은 무엇인가? 분명히, 그것은 그것의 바로 앞에 있던 것이나, 그것 앞의 앞에 있던 것이 아니라, 첫 번째 도미노이다. 신체도 같은 방식으로 작동한다. 최초의 문제는 흔히 눈에 띄지 않는다. 뒤쪽의 '도미노' 중 몇 개가 쓰러지고 나서야 비로소 좀 더 분명한 단서와 증상이 나타난다. 결국 여러분은 두통, 피로, 또는 우울증, 심지어 질병까지도 얻게 된다. 여러분이 마지막 도미노, 즉 최종 결과인 증상만을 치료하려 한다면, 그 문제의 원인은 해결되지 않는다. 최초의 도미노가 원인, 즉 가장 중요한 문제이다.

정답풀이　신체가 작동하는 방식을 도미노에 비유한 글이다. 첫 번째 도미노가 쓰러지면 나머지 것들도 모두 함께 쓰러지게 되는 것처럼, 신체 역시 두통, 피로, 또는 우울증, 심지어 질병과 같은 최종 증상은 최초의 불균형, 즉 사소한 문제에서 발생한다는 흐름이므로, 밑줄 친 말의 의미로는 ⑤ '최종 증상은 최초의 사소한 문제에서 생겨난다.'가 가장 적절하다.

오답풀이
① 질병을 치료하는 데 정해진 순서는 없다. → 질병 치료 순서에 관한 글은 아니다.
② 사소한 건강 문제는 저절로 해결된다. → 사소한 것이 최종 증상으로 이어진다고 했으므로 상반된다.
③ 여러분은 나이를 먹어가면서 점점 더 무기력해진다. → 무기력에 관해서는 언급되지 않았다.
④ 아무리 늦어도 최종 결과인 증상을 치료할 수 있다. → 글 후반부의 내용과 상반된다.

구문풀이

[9행] **It's not until** some of the later "dominoes" fall **that** more obvious clues and symptoms appear.

: 「not until ~ that ...」 구문은 '~하고서야 …하다'의 의미이다.

어휘풀이
· minor 사소한　　　· imbalance 불균형
· subtle 미묘한　　　· trigger 유발하다
· symptom 증상　　　· line up ~을 한 줄로 세우다
· a series of 일련의　　　· knock down ~을 쓰러뜨리다
· obviously 분명히　　　· initial 처음의
· unnoticed 눈에 띄지 않는　　　· clue 단서, 실마리

• **fatigue** 피로
• **end-result** 최종 결과의
• **primary** 가장 중요한, 첫 번째의
• **depression** 우울증
• **address** 해결하다, 처리하다

03 답 ④

 좋은 사고로 이어지지 않을 수도 있는 좋은 논리

 모든 사람들은 나쁜 논리가 나쁜 생각을 만든다는 것에 동의한다. 그래서 당연히 좋은 논리가 좋은 생각을 만들어준다는 것이 뒤따르게 마련이다. 물론 이것은 완전히 터무니없는 말이다. **좋은 논리는 좋은 사고를 위한 하나의 요건이지만 결코 유일한 것은 아니다.** 물은 수프의 필수조건이지만 뜨거운 물 한 그릇을 만족스러운 수프로 받아들이는 사람은 거의 없을 것이다. **완벽한 논리는 그것이 작동하도록 요구되는 인식을 제공할 뿐이다.** 만약 이것들이 불충분하다면, 논리의 완벽함이 그것들을 개선시키지 않을 것이고, 여전히 형편없는 답을 제공할 것이다. 완벽히 잘 작동하는 컴퓨터가 그것이 항상 옳은 대답을 만들어낼 수 있다고 그 누구도 시사한 적이 없다. 이것은 자료의 입력에 달려 있는 것이지, 기계 자체에 달려 있는 것이 아니다. 따라서 '쓰레기가 들어가면 쓰레기가 나온다'는 것을 뜻하는 용어, GIGO가 있는 것이다.

 논리가 완벽하다고 해서 좋은 결과물이 나오는 것이 아니라, 결과물의 질은 입력되는 자료가 어떤 것인가에 달려 있다는 내용이다. 따라서 밑줄 친 부분이 의미하는 것으로는 ④ '입력되는 것의 질이 결과물의 질을 결정한다.'가 가장 적절하다.

① 논리는 상황에 따라 다르게 적용된다. → 상황에 따른 논리 적용에 관한 글은 아니다.
② 거의 모든 사실들은 실험으로 완전히 증명될 수 없다. → 지문의 내용과 무관하다.
③ 다양한 요인들이 예상치 못한 좋은 결과를 만들 수 있다. → 좋은 결과는 입력 자료에 달려 있다고 했으므로 내용과 어긋난다.
⑤ 논리적인 사고 과정은 추론을 일관되게 사용한다. → 추론에 관한 글은 아니다.

[9행] No one has ever **suggested** [that **a computer** {that works perfectly well} can by itself always produce the correct answer].
: [ ]는 suggested의 목적어로 쓰인 명사절이다. 여기서 suggest는 '제안하다'라는 뜻이 아니라 '시사하다'의 뜻으로 쓰였다. { }는 a computer를 수식하는 관계절이다.

• **logic** 논리
• **poor** 형편없는, 좋지 않은
• **nonsense** 터무니없는 것, 말도 안 되는 것
• **requirement** 요건, 요구사항
• **satisfactory** 만족스러운
• **perception** 인식, 지각
• **reliant** 의존하는, 달려 있는
• **make for** ~에 기여하다[도움되다]
• **complete** 완전한
• **by no means** 결코 ~이 아닌
• **service** 제공하다
• **inadequate** 부적합한, 불충분한
• **input** 입력

• **hence** 따라서 (~이다)
• **output** 결과물

04 답 ⑤

 미국과 유럽의 노동 시간과 여가 시간

 미국에서는 대체적으로 일주일의 평균 노동 시간이 반세기 넘게 변하지 않은 채로 유지되었다. 사실, 많은 전문가들은 여가 시간이 실제로 감소해 왔다고 믿는다. 예를 들어, 역사가인 Juliet Schor은 평균적인 미국인에게 스스로를 위한 시간이, 그들이 20년 전에 가졌던 것보다 더 적다고 설득력 있게 주장한다. 이러한 여가 시간의 손실은 우연이 아니다. Schor은 미국의 노동조합들이 근로 시간의 문제에 대해서는 거의 관심을 기울이지 않았고, 대신 에너지를 봉급과 직업 안정성의 문제로 향하게 했다는 증거를 제시한다. 유럽에서는 근로 시간의 감소 추세가 거의 머뭇거리지 않았다. 유럽의 조직화된 노동자는 전후(戰後) 시기 내내 자신의 의제 맨 꼭대기에 더 짧은 근로 시간의 문제를 계속 유지시켰다.

 유럽의 조직화된 노동자들이 더 짧은 근로 시간의 문제를 의제의 맨 꼭대기에 두었다는, 즉 근로 시간의 감소를 중요하게 여겼다는 내용이 이어지므로, 결국 유럽에서는 미국과는 반대로 근로 시간 감소 추세가 이어졌다는 흐름이 되는 것이 자연스럽다. 따라서 밑줄 친 말의 의미로는 ⑤ '근로 시간을 줄이려는 유럽에서의 노력은 계속해서 성공했다.'가 가장 적절하다.

① 노동자들의 권리가 점점 강조되었다. → 노동자들의 권리에 관한 글은 아니다.
② 여가 시간과 생산성의 관련성은 분명하지 않다. → 생산성에 관한 내용은 언급되지 않았다.
③ 노동조합은 주로 정치적 행위를 통해 목적을 달성해왔다. → 지문의 내용과 무관하다.
④ 유럽의 전반적인 상황이 미국의 그것과 똑같다. → 지문의 내용과 상반된다.

[4행] Historian Juliet Schor, for example, argues persuasively [that the average American has less time to himself or herself than he or she **did** twenty years ago].
: [ ]는 문장의 동사인 argues의 목적어로 쓰인 명사절이다. 대동사 did는 반복되는 had time ~ herself를 대신한다.

• **expert** 전문가
• **persuasively** 설득력 있게
• **accident** 우연, 사고
• **union** 노동조합
• **direct** ~로 향하다, 지휘하다
• **job security** 직업 안정성
• **organized** 조직화된
• **agenda** 안건, 의제
• **leisure** 여가
• **loss** 손실, 상실
• **evidence** 증거
• **prefer** 선호하다
• **salary** 봉급
• **miss a beat** (순간적으로) 주저하다
• **labor** 노동자 (계급), 노동

A 01 질병, 질환 02 분배하다 03 이상한, 홀수의 04 특징, 모습 05 걸다, 매달다 06 dramatic 07 ~을 통해 08 조리법 09 성, 성별 10 낳다, 발생시키다 11 상황, 환경 12 민주주의 13 무의식의 14 번갈아 가며 15 진전된, 진화된 16 미묘한 17 최고의, 절정의; 절정, 꼭대기 18 과업, 업무 19 주다, 부여하다 20 여러 번의, 다양한

B 01 That this example teaches us is → <u>What this example teaches us is</u>: 선행사를 포함한 관계대명사로 문장의 주어인 명사절을 이끎과 동시에 teaches의 목적어 역할을 하도록 That을 What으로 고쳐야 한다.
02 making him missed → <u>making him miss</u>: making은 사역동사 make에서 나온 것이고, 목적어 him이 miss의 주체이므로 목적격 보어 자리의 missed를 동사원형 miss로 고쳐야 한다.
03 what does that spirit mean → <u>what that spirit means</u>: learn의 목적어인 명사절이 되어야 하므로 직접의문문의 어순이 아니라, 〈의문사+주어+동사〉의 간접의문문 형태를 취해야 한다.
04 three times higher than that made → <u>three times higher than those made</u>: 앞에 나온 복수 명사 contributions를 대신해 쓰인 것이므로 단수 대명사 that을 those로 고쳐야 한다.

C 01 의심하는 02 인사하다 03 인정하다, 인식하다 04 barrier 05 창피(함) 06 꺼림, (마음이) 내키지 않음 07 걱정 08 미덕이 있는 09 무모한 10 인색한 11 의문의 여지가 있는 12 눈먼 13 겉보기에, ~인 것처럼 보이는 14 유발하다 15 처음의 16 fatigue 17 가장 중요한, 첫 번째의 18 완전한 19 부적합한, 불충분한 20 여가

D 01 which, 그것들은 그리 생산적이지 않다: 계속적 용법의 관계대명사 which가 쓰이는 것이 적절하다.
02 was, 낯선 사람들에게 포옹을 제공하려는 한 남자의 의도: 주어의 핵인 one man's intention이 단수이므로 was가 적절하다.
03 that, 그들은 체육 수업에 덜 적극적이다: suggest의 목적어가 되는 명사절을 이끄는 접속사 that이 적절하다.
04 that, 일부 학생들이 샤워하기를 꺼려하는 것: point out의 목적어가 되는 명사절을 이끄는 접속사 that이 적절하다.

 Part 2 종합적 판단 및 세부 정보

Unit 01 목적 추론

Example 답 ② pp.44~45

소 재 잡지 구독 갱신

전문해석 Hane 씨께,
저희의 메시지는 간결하지만, 중요합니다. 귀하의 'Winston Magazine' 구독 기간이 곧 만료되는데 저희는 귀하로부터 갱신한다는 말을 듣지 못했습니다. 저희는 귀하가 다음의 단 한 호라도 놓치고 싶지 않을 거라고 확신합니다. 서비스를 지속하기 위해 지금 갱신하십시오. 귀하는 'Winston Magazine'을 미국에서 가장 빠르게 성장하는 잡지로 만들어 주는 훌륭한 이야기와 뉴스를 계속해서 받게 될 것입니다. 지금 가능한 한 쉽게 구독 신청을 할 수 있도록, 저희는 귀하가 작성할 회신용 카드를 보냈습니다. 오늘 보내 주기만 하시면 귀하는 월간지 'Winston Magazine'을 계속해서 받게 될 것입니다.
마음을 담아,
Thomas Strout

구문풀이
[5행] You'll get continued delivery of **the excellent stories and news** [that make *Winston Magazine* **the fastest growing magazine in America**].
: [ ]는 관계대명사절로, the excellent stories and news를 수식한다. 〈make+목적어+목적격 보어〉 구문에서 *Winston Magazine*이 목적어로, the fastest growing magazine in America가 목적격 보어로 쓰였다.

Do It Yourself pp.46~49

01 ③   02 ①   03 ⑤   04 ①

01 답 ③

소 재 아파트 도색 작업에 대한 허락 요청

전문해석 Spencer 씨께
저는 오는 4월이면 이 아파트에 10년 동안 살게 됩니다. 저는 이곳에서 즐겁게 살아 왔으며 계속해서 살기를 희망합니다. 제가 처음 Greenfield 아파트에 이사를 왔을 때, 최근에 아파트 도색 작업을 했다고 들었습니다. 그때 이후로 저는 단 한 번도 벽이나 천장에 손을 댄 적이 없습니다. 지난 한 달 동안 둘러보면서 저는 페인트가 얼마나 오래되고 흐려졌는지를 깨닫게 되었습니다. 저는 새 페인트칠로 아파트를 새롭게 하고 싶습니다. 저는 이 작업이 자비 부담이라

는 것과 임대차 계약에 따라 허락을 받아야만 한다는 것을 알고 있습니다. 형편이 되는 대로 빨리 알려 주시기 바랍니다.

Howard James 올림

정답풀이 10년 동안 살아온 아파트에 페인트칠을 하도록 허락해 달라는 내용이다. 새 페인트칠로 아파트를 새롭게 하고 싶다는 말과 임대차 계약에 따라 허락을 받으려 한다는 말에서 알 수 있듯이, 글의 목적으로 가장 적절한 것은 ③이다.

구문풀이

[9행] I understand [that this would be at my own expense], and [that I must get permission to do so as per the lease agreement].

: 두 개의 [ ]는 모두 understand의 목적어로, and로 인해 병렬 연결되었다.

어휘풀이

- as of ~일자로, ~현재로
- ceiling 천장
- update 새롭게 하다
- at one's own expense 자비로
- lease 임대
- at one's convenience 형편이 되는 대로
- recently 최근에
- dull 흐릿한, 무딘
- coat 칠
- permission 허가
- agreement 계약

02 답 ①

소 재 신용카드 결제 오류

전문해석 제 아내와 저는 지난 달 귀사의 영화관을 방문했습니다. 우리는 총액이 44달러인 두 장의 표를 샀습니다. 구입 당시, 안내소의 안내원은 신용카드 결제를 승인하는 데 몇 가지 문제가 있다고 말했습니다. 그 때 저는 제 신용카드 결제가 걱정되었지만 그 직원은 저의 결제에 아무런 문제가 없다고 말했습니다. 그러나 저는 제 계좌 입출금 내역서를 받아보고 요금이 두 번 부과되었다는 것을 발견했습니다. 귀사가 이 문제를 빠르게 해결해 주신다면 감사하겠습니다.

정답풀이 영화관 매표소에서 신용카드로 표를 산 후 요금이 두 번 부과된 것을 알게 되었고, 이 문제를 해결해 줄 것을 요청하고 있으므로, 글의 목적으로 가장 적절한 것은 ①이다.

구문풀이

[6행] However, when I received my bank statement, I discovered [that you charged my card twice].

: [ ]는 discovered의 목적어 역할을 하는 명사절이다.

어휘풀이

- purchase 사다; 구입
- information desk 안내소
- payment 결제, 지불
- receive 받다
- bank statement (은행계좌의) 입출금 내역서
- charge 요금을 부과하다
- resolve 해결하다
- attendant 안내원
- accept 승인[용인]하다
- be anxious about ~에 대해 걱정하다
- grateful 감사하는
- matter 문제

03 답 ⑤

소 재 통제 없이 동네를 돌아다니는 개들에 대한 조치 요청

전문해석 최근에 저는 동네에 많은 개들이 마음대로 돌아다니는 것을 목격했습니다. 험상궂어 보이는 개들에게는 동네를 뛰어다닐 수 있는 자격증이 주어져 있습니다. 그들은 특히 어린이와 노인에게 무섭습니다. 저는 누군가가 중상을 입기 전까지는 단지 시간문제라고 우려됩니다. 이 개들의 주인들은 자신들의 반려동물을 목줄에서 풀어주는 것의 위험성을 모르는 것으로 보이며, 무관심한 태도를 취해 왔습니다. 그들은 수많은 지역 주민들로부터 개들을 통제해 달라는 요청을 받아 왔지만 모든 요청은 무시되었고 상황은 개선되지 않았습니다. 그러므로 저는 더 심각한 문제가 생기는 것을 방지하기 위해 귀하께서 가능한 한 빨리 그 문제를 조사하고 적절한 조치를 취해 줄 것을 요청합니다.

정답풀이 통제 없이 동네를 돌아다니는 개들의 위험성을 말하면서 이에 대한 빠른 조치를 취해줄 것을 요청하는 내용이다. 따라서 글의 목적으로는 ⑤가 가장 적절하다.

구문풀이

[5행] The owners of these dogs [seem to be unaware of the dangers of letting their pets off the leash] and [have adopted an indifferent attitude].

: 두 개의 술어동사구 [ ]가 and로 병렬 연결되어 주어 The owners of these dogs에 이어진다.

어휘풀이

- witness 목격하다
- loose 마음대로 돌아다니는, 묶여 있지 않은
- neighborhood 동네, 근처, 이웃
- license 면허(증), 자격(증)
- I'm afraid ~을 걱정하다, ~하여 유감이다
- injured 부상을 입은
- leash (개) 목줄, 가죽끈
- indifferent 무관심한
- numerous 다수의, 수많은
- investigate 조사하다
- occurrence (사건의) 발생, 일어남
- fierce-looking 험상궂어 보이는
- frightening 무서운
- be unaware of ~을 모르다
- adopt 취하다, 채택하다
- attitude 태도
- local (특정 지역에 사는) 주민
- appropriate 적절한

04 답 ①

소 재 청소년 야외 활동 지도자 양성 프로그램

전문해석 여러분은 오늘 오전에 Buzan 박사의 강연을 들으셨습니다. 여러분의 관심과 열정에 감사드립니다. 오늘 오후의 훈련 프로그램 동안에 여러분은 실습을 통해 배울 것입니다. 오후 1시부터 한 시간 동안, 여러분은 텐트를 설치하는 법을 배우게 될 것입니다. 그런 다음, 오후 2시부터는 지도 사용법을 배울 것입니다. 원래, 오후 3시부터 한 시간 동안, 여러분은 심폐 소생술을 연습하도록 계획이 되어 있었지만, 그것은 강사의 개인적 사정으로 취소되었습니다. 대신에, 여러분은 나침반을 사용하는 법을 배우게 될 것입니다. 오후 4시부터는 레크리에이션 시간이 있게 될 것입니다. 저는 이러한

모든 프로그램들이 여러분이 청소년 야외 활동을 위한 훌륭한 지도자가 되는 데 도움을 줄 것이라고 확신합니다. 여러분의 참여와 노력에 미리 감사드립니다.

정답풀이 청소년 야외 활동 지도자 양성 프로그램에 참가한 참가자들에게 프로그램의 오후 일정과 내용에 대해 안내하고 있으므로, 글의 목적으로 가장 적절한 것은 ①이다.

구문풀이
[3행] For one hour from 1 p.m. you'll learn [**how to set** up a tent].
: [ ]는 「의문사+to부정사구」 구문으로, 'how you should set up a tent'처럼 절의 형태로 풀어서 이해할 수 있다.

어휘풀이
- lecture 강연, 강의
- enthusiasm 열정
- originally 원래
- be scheduled to ~하기로 계획되다
- practice 연습하다; 실습
- owing to ~때문에
- compass 나침반
- participation 참여, 참가
- attention 관심, 주목
- set up ~을 설치하다
- cancel 취소하다
- instructor 강사
- outdoor 야외의
- in advance 미리

Unit 02 심경 추론

Example 답 ⑤   pp.50~51

소 재 Rowe의 동굴 탐험

전문해석 Rowe는 거의 아무도 위험을 무릅쓰고 해보지 않은 장소에 있는 것을 좋아하기 때문에 그는 동굴을 발견하고 기쁨에 폴짝 뛴다. (동굴) 입구에서 그는 나중에 자신의 새로운 모험을 뽐내기 위해 휴대전화로 사진을 계속 찍는다. 동굴 입구로부터 몇 미터 떨어진 바위에 이르러서, 그는 얼음 동굴의 빛나는 광경을 본다. 그는 얼음으로 된 벽을 만지기 위해 손을 뻗으면서 "믿을 수 없을 정도로 아름다워!"라고 말한다. 갑자기 그는 발을 헛디뎌 어둠 속으로 미끄러져 들어간다. 그는 위를 올려다보고 대략 20미터 위에 있는 틈의 빛을 본다. '전화로 도움을 요청해야지,'라고 그는 생각한다. 하지만 그는 이렇게 깊은 지하에서는 (통화) 서비스가 되지 않는다는 것을 깨닫는다. 그는 위로 올라가려고 하지만 올라갈 수 없다. 그는 "거기 누구 있나요?"라고 외친다. 응답이 없다.

구문풀이
[3행] [Coming to a stop on a rock a few meters from the entrance], he sees the icy cave's glittering view.
: [ ]는 분사구문으로, 주절을 연속 동작으로 볼 때 이전 동작의 의미를 나타낸다.

01 ②   02 ②   03 ⑤   04 ②

01 답 ②

소 재 오디션 참가 기회

전문해석 우리 중 누가 그 말을 했는지 확실치 않지만, Montague 씨가 바로 다음날에 오디션을 받게 해주겠노라고 동의한 것으로 보아, 그 말은 꽤나 설득력이 있었음에 틀림없다. 우리는 그것을 믿을 수가 없었다. 우리는 충격을 받았다. 그 날의 예행연습이 끝났다. Jean의 지하실에서 환호성을 지르고, 부둥켜 안고, 춤을 추고 난 다음, 나는 우리의 '행운'에 관해 엄마에게 말하려고 한숨에 집으로 달려갔다. 엄마는 매우 기뻐하며, 모든 일이 순조롭게 진행될 수 있도록 확실히 하기 위한 것만큼이나 응원하기 위해서 우리와 함께 오디션에 가겠다고 고집했다. 나는 성탄절 전야의 어린 아이와 같은 기분을 느꼈다. 그날 밤 나는 잠을 한 시간도 못 잤다. 그것이 아마도 그 다음 날이 꿈처럼 보인 이유였을 것이다.

정답풀이 주인공인 'I'는 다음날 오디션을 보게 되었고, 믿을 수 없어서 환호성을 지르고, 일행들과 부둥켜 안았으며, 춤을 춘 다음 '행운'에 대해 엄마에게 말했고, 엄마도 무척 기뻐하셨다고 했다. 성탄 전야의 어린 아이처럼 기분이 들떠 있으며 기쁜 마음에 잠을 한 시간도 못 잤다고 했으므로, 'I'의 심경으로는 ② '신나고 행복한'이 가장 적절하다.

오답풀이
① 슬프고 우울한
③ 안도하고 공감하는
④ 무서워하고 겁에 질린
⑤ 부끄럽고 당황스러운

구문풀이
[4행] After we stopped [screaming] and [hugging] and [dancing around Jean's basement], I ran all the way home [to tell Mom about our "lucky break."]
: 동명사(구)인 첫 번째 ~ 세 번째 [ ]가 병렬구조로 stopped에 공통으로 연결되었다. 네 번째 [ ]는 목적을 나타내는 to부정사구이다.
[6행] She was delighted, and she insisted on going with us to the audition, [**as** much for support **as** to make sure everything was going smoothly].
: 「as ~ as ...」 구문은 '…만큼 ~한'이라는 의미의 동등 비교 구문이며, '모든 것이 순조롭게 진행될 수 있도록 확실히 하기 위한 것만큼이나 응원하기 위해서'라는 뜻으로 해석한다.

어휘풀이
- convincing 설득력 있는
- shocked 충격을 받은
- scream 환호를 지르다, 비명을 지르다
- basement 지하실
- delighted 기뻐하는
- smoothly 순조롭게, 부드럽게
- audition 오디션[심사]을 하다; 심사
- rehearsal 예행연습
- lucky break 행운
- insist 고집하다, 주장하다

02 답 ②

소 재　탈출 후에 Evelyn을 만난다는 기대감

전문해석　지금쯤 누군가가 나의 탈출을 발견했을 거라는 생각이 내 마음속에 떠올랐다. 그들이 나를 붙잡아서 다시 그 끔찍한 장소에 데려갈 것이라는 생각이 나를 매우 소름끼치게 했다. 그래서 나는 마을에서 멀리 떨어질 때까지 오로지 밤에만 걷기로 했다. 사흘 밤을 걸은 후에, 나는 그들이 나를 추적하는 것을 중단했다는 확신이 들었다. 나는 버려진 오두막을 발견했고 그 안으로 걸어 들어갔다. 지쳐서 나는 바닥에 누워 잠이 들었다. 나는 멀리 떨어진 교회에서 부드럽게 일곱 번 울려 퍼지는 시계 소리에 잠이 깼고 해가 서서히 떠오르고 있는 것을 알아차렸다. 내가 밖으로 나왔을 때, 나의 심장이 기대와 열망으로 두근거리기 시작했다. Evelyn을 곧 만날 수 있다는 생각이 나의 발걸음을 가볍게 해 주었다.

정답풀이　탈출 후에 붙잡힐 것이라는 생각이 들어 소름이 끼치고 두려웠지만 시간이 지나면서 Evelyn을 만날 수 있다는 기대감과 열망이 생겼다는 내용이다. 따라서 'I'의 심경 변화로는 ② '두려운 → 희망찬'이 가장 적절하다.

오답풀이
① 감동한 → 긴장한
③ 외로운 → 짜증난
④ 동정하는 → 즐거운
⑤ 슬픈 → 겁이 난

구문풀이
[7행] I [awoke to **the sound of a far away church clock**, {softly ringing seven times}] and [noticed {that the sun was slowly rising}].
: 두 개의 [ ]는 모두 I를 주어로 하는 술어로, and로 병렬 연결되었다. 첫 번째 { }는 the sound of a far away church clock을 수식하는 현재분사구이고, 두 번째 { }는 noticed의 목적어인 명사절이다.

어휘풀이

- escape 탈출; 탈출하다
- capture 붙잡다
- chase 추적하다, 뒤쫓다
- cottage 오두막
- ring 울리다
- pound 두근거리다, 두드리다
- longing 열망
- chill 소름끼치게 하다
- awful 끔찍한
- deserted 버려진
- fall asleep 잠들다
- step 발을 내딛다
- anticipation 기대
- lighten 가볍게 하다

03 답 ⑤

소 재　졸업 파티에서의 즉석연설

전문해석　나는 나의 가장 친한 두 친구의 졸업 파티 때 약 50명의 사람들 앞에서 그 두 친구들에게 즉석연설을 했다. 나는 일어서서 말을 시작했지만 내 두 볼이 신체적 통제력을 잃기 시작하자 멈췄다. 나는 그렇게 가까이 있지도 않은 사람들이 볼 수 있을 정도로 극심하게 위아래로 떨었다. 나는 "맙소사, 왜 내 볼이 떨리지?"라고 계속 중얼거렸다. 나는 두 볼이 너무 심하게 떨려 말을 할 수 없었기 때문에 정말로 계속할 수조차 없었다. 친구 아버지가 내게 다가와 장난스럽게 내 두 볼을 마사지하기 시작했다. 그러고 나서 그는 나에게서 마이크를 가져 갔고 내게 앉으라고 말했는데, 나는 어떻게 해서든 간신히 그렇게 했다. 공석에서 말하는 것에 관한 한 이미 존재하지 않았던 나의 자신감은 거의 망쳐졌다.

정답풀이　가장 친한 두 친구의 졸업 파티 때 즉석연설을 하며 겪은 긴장에 대한 내용이다. 즉석연설을 하던 중 볼이 극심하게 떨려 말을 계속할 수 없었다는 것과 공석에서 말하는 것에 관해 이미 존재하지 않던 자신감이 망쳐졌다는 것 등을 통해 알 수 있는 'I'의 심경으로는 ⑤ '긴장하고 당혹스러운'이 가장 적절하다.

오답풀이
① 희망에 차고 신난
② 시샘하고 분개하는
③ 감사하고 만족해하는
④ 무관심하고 지루한

구문풀이
[4행] I violently shook up and down to **the point** [where **people** {who weren't even that close} could see].
: [ ]는 관계부사절로 the point를 수식하고, { }는 관계대명사절로 people을 수식한다.

어휘풀이

- cheek 볼, 뺨
- violently 극심하게
- massage 마사지하다
- somehow 여하튼, 어쨌든
- pretty much 거의
- nonexistent 존재하지 않는
- when it comes to ~에 관한 한
- physical 신체적인, 물리적인
- jokingly 장난으로, 농담으로
- microphone 마이크
- manage to 간신히 ~하다
- ruin 망치다
- self-confidence 자신감
- public speaking 공석에서 말하기

04 답 ②

소 재　친구에게서 느낀 배신감

전문해석　어느 늦은 오후에 나는 Michael에게서 전화 한 통을 받았다. "지금 입장이 좀 곤란해."라고 그는 내게 말했다. "재무 책자를 구성해서 내일 오후까지 인쇄를 해야 해." 그는 자신의 정규 디자이너가 자리에 없어서 많은 압박을 받고 있다고 말했다. 나는 다른 프로젝트를 하는 도중이었지만, Michael은 내 친구였고, 그래서 모든 걸 뒤로 미루고 그의 책자를 위해 늦은 밤까지 일해 주었다. 다음 날 이른 아침 Michael은 그것을 출력해도 좋다는 신호를 내렸다. 나는 피곤했지만 그를 끝까지 도울 수 있어서 기분이 좋았다. 사무실에 돌아와서 Michael에게서 다음의 음성 메시지가 남겨져 있는 것을 발견했다. "그게 말야, 네가 완전히 망쳤어! Jack, 네가 시간에 쫓겨 이 일을 한 건 알아, 하지만 소득 그래프가 충분히 명확하게 제시되어 있지 않아. 큰일이야. 이 일은 정말 중요한 고객(의 일)이야. 얼른 와서 고쳐줘야겠어." 나는 배신감을 느꼈다.

정답풀이　친구의 업무를 도와줄 수 있어서 기분이 좋았다는 내용

을 통해, 처음에는 '만족한(satisfied)' 심경임을 추측할 수 있고, 열심히 해 준 일에 대해 오히려 일을 망쳤다며 자신을 질책하고 얼른 와서 고치라는 말을 통해서는 '화난(angry)' 것으로 심경이 변화했음을 알 수 있다. 따라서 'I'의 심경 변화로 가장 적절한 것은 ②이다.

오답풀이

① 신나는 → 지루해 하는

③ 걱정하는 → 안도하는

④ 놀란 → 무관심한

⑤ 기분 좋은 → 의기양양한

구문풀이

[7행] Early the next morning Michael gave the go-ahead to [have it printed].

: [ ]는 〈사역동사＋목적어＋목적격 보어〉의 어순으로, 대명사 it은 앞 문장의 his brochure를 가리키는데, 그것이 print의 대상으로 해석되므로 수동을 표현하는 과거분사 printed를 목적격 보어로 썼다.

[9행] [Getting back to my office], I discovered this voice-mail message from Michael ~

: [ ]는 시간을 나타내는 분사구문으로, 주절의 주어인 I를 의미상의 주어로 삼고 있다. '사무실에 도착했을 때' 혹은 '사무실에 도착하자마자'라는 뜻으로 해석할 수 있다.

어휘풀이

· tight spot 곤란한 입장, 힘든 상황

· brochure (소)책자

· regular 정규의, 보통의

· exhausted 지친

· earnings 소득, 수입

· client 고객

· betrayed 배신감을 느끼는

· financial 재정의, 재무상의

· lay out 구성하다, 배치하다

· pressure 압박

· screw ~ up ~을 망쳐놓다

· disaster 재난, 재앙

· assume 추정하다

How was it?

pp.56~57

A 01 간결한 02 구독 03 renew 04 issue 05 천장 06 흐릿한, 무딘 07 허가 08 임대 09 안내원 10 요금을 부과하다 11 해결하다 12 witness 13 부상을 입은 14 무관심한 15 조사하다 16 적절한 17 열정 18 cancel 19 ~ 때문에 20 미리

B 01 that, 이것은 내 자비로 부담하는 것이다: 문장의 동사인 understand의 목적어가 되는 명사절을 이끄는 접속사 that이 적절하다.

02 accepting, 그들은 신용카드 결제를 용인하는 데 어떤 문제가 있었다: 문맥상 '~하는 데 문제가 있다'라는 의미의 「have a problem -ing」 구문이므로 accepting이 적절하다.

03 seem, 그들의 반려동물을 목줄에서 풀어주는 것의 위험성을 모르는: seem은 자동사이므로, '~처럼 보이다'라는 해석상의 의미와 달리 수동태로 쓰이지 않는다. 따라서 seem이 적절하다.

04 During, 여러분은 실습을 통해 배울 것이다: 뒤에 명사구 this afternoon's training programs가 왔으므로, 전치사 During이 적절하다.

C 01 위험을 무릅쓰고 ~하다 02 ~을 과시하다 03 반짝이는, 빛나는 04 crack 05 설득력 있는 06 기뻐하는 07 고집하다, 주장하다 08 순조롭게, 부드럽게 09 소름끼치게 하다 10 끔찍한 11 버려진 12 기대 13 신체적인, 물리적인 14 극심하게 15 간신히 ~하다 16 망치다 17 (소)책자 18 지친 19 소득, 수입 20 betrayed

D 01 where so few have ventured
02 must have been pretty convincing
03 The thought that I could meet Evelyn
04 a financial brochure laid out

<table>
<tr><td>Unit
03</td><td>내용 일치</td></tr>
</table>

Example 답 ⑤ pp.58~59

소 재 James Van Der Zee의 생애

전문해석 James Van Der Zee는 1886년 6월 29일에 Massachusetts주 Lenox에서 태어났다. 여섯 명의 아이들 중 둘째였던 James는 창의적인 분위기의 집안에서 성장했다. 열네 살에 그는 그의 첫 번째 카메라를 받았고 수백 장의 가족사진과 마을 사진을 찍었다. 1906년 즈음에, 그는 결혼을 한 채, New York으로 이사했고, 늘어나는 가족을 부양하기 위해 여러 가지 일을 했다. 그는 1907년에 Virginia주 Phoetus로 이사했고, Chamberlin 호텔의 식당에서 일했다. 이 시기에 그는 또한 시간제 사진사로 일했다. 그는 1916년에 자신의 스튜디오를 열었다. 1차 세계대전이 시작되었고 많은 젊은 군인들이 사진을 찍기 위해 스튜디오로 왔다. 1969년에 'Harlem On My Mind' 전시회는 그에게 국제적인 인정을 가져다주었다. 그는 1983년에 사망하였다.

구문풀이

[5행] In 1907, he moved to **Phoetus**, **Virginia**, [where he worked in the dining room of the Hotel Chamberlin].

: [ ]는 계속적 용법의 관계부사절로, 앞에 나온 Phoetus, Virginia를 부연 설명한다.

Do It Yourself pp.60~63

01 ③   02 ⑤   03 ⑤   04 ④

01 답 ③

소 재 영화 'Star Wreck'

전문해석 핀란드 영화 제작자인 Timo Vuorensola는 원작이 'Star Trek'인, 자신의 영화 'Star Wreck'에 대한 아이디어를 생각해냈다. 그는 기존의 배급 방식을 찾는 것은 거의 불가능하다는 것을 알았다. 예산이 극히 적은 아마추어 공상 과학 코미디는 주류의 제작사들에게는 별로 매력이 없었을 것이다. 그래서 Vuorensola는 혼자서 그 일을 추진했다. 그는 소셜 네트워킹 사이트를 이용하여 온라인상의 팬 기반을 구성하였는데, 이들이 줄거리에 이바지했고, 심지어 자신들의 연기 기술까지 제공했다. 도움에 대한 보답으로 Vuorensola는 2005년 'Star Wreck'을 온라인상에 무료로 배포했다. 첫 주에만 다운로드 횟수가 70만 건이었고, 현재까지 900만 건에 이르고 있다.

정답풀이 Vuorensola는 온라인상의 팬 기반을 구성하였고, 팬들이 줄거리에 이바지했으며 연기 기술까지 제공했다고 했으므로, 글의 내용과 일치하는 것은 ③이다.

구문풀이

[2행] He knew [that {looking for conventional distribution} would be almost impossible].

: [ ]는 knew의 목적어 역할을 하는 명사절이고, { }는 동명사구로 명사절 내의 주어 역할을 한다.

[4행] **An amateur, science-fiction comedy** [with an extremely small budget] would **hardly** be attractive to mainstream studios.

: [ ]는 주어 An ~ comedy를 수식하며, hardly는 '거의 ~ 않다'는 부정의 의미의 부사이다.

어휘풀이

- come up with ~을 생각해내다
- look for ~을 찾다
- distribution 배급, 유통
- extremely 매우, 지극히
- attractive 매력적인, 마음을 끄는
- build up 구성하다, 축적하다
- storyline 줄거리
- return 보답, 반환
- copy (데이터의) 복사
- original 원작, 원본, 원서
- conventional 기존의, 재래의
- science-fiction 공상 과학의
- budget 예산
- mainstream studio 주류 제작사
- contribute 기여하다, 이바지하다
- offer 제공하다
- release 배포하다, 방출하다, 개봉하다

02 답 ⑤

소 재 상록수 Joshua tree

전문해석 Joshua tree는 그 가지 끝에 뾰족한 잎이 많이 달려 있는 상록수다. 그 독특한 모양으로 인해 Joshua tree는 장식용으로 아주 매력적이다. 다른 지역으로 옮겨 심었을 때의 낮은 생존율에도 불구하고 불행히도 많은 Joshua tree가 뽑혀져 도시 지역에 심어졌다. 아메리카 원주민들은 Joshua tree의 꽃눈을 구워서 먹었다. 어린 씨앗은 날것으로 또는 요리해서 식용으로 쓰였다. (그리고 바나나와 같은 맛이 난다고 전해진다.) 또한 그 꽃으로 알콜성 음료(술)가 만들어졌다. 하지만 Joshua tree는 오늘날의 기준으로는 먹기 힘들고, 법으로 보호되기 때문에 상업적인 식용 작물이 될 가능성은 거의 없다.

정답풀이 법으로 보호되기 때문에 상업적인 식용 작물이 될 가능성은 거의 없다고 했으므로, 글의 내용과 일치하지 않는 것은 ⑤이다.

구문풀이

[2행] [The unique appearance of the Joshua tree] makes **it a very desirable decoration**.

: 목적어(it)와 목적격 보어(a very desirable decoration)가 있는 문장의 주어(The unique appearance ~)가 사람이 아니고 무생물인 경우에는 주어를 부사구로, 목적어를 주어로, 그리고 타동사를 자동사로 해석하는 것이 자연스럽다. 즉, 여기서도 '그 독특한 모양으로 인해(주어 The unique appearance) Joshua tree는(목적어 it) 장식용으로 아주 매력적이다'라고 해석하였다.

[9행] But Joshua trees **are hard to eat** by today's standards, and **have** little possibility of ever becoming a commercial food crop [because they are protected by law].

: 「be hard to부정사구」는 '~하기 힘들다[어렵다]'의 의미이며, are와 have가 주어 Joshua trees에 병렬로 연결되어 있다. possibility와 ever becoming ~ crop이 전치사 of를 사이에 두고 동격을 이루고 있다. [ ]는 이유를 나타내는 부사절이다.

어휘풀이

- evergreen 상록수; 상록수의
- sharp-pointed 끝이 뾰족한[날카로운]
- branch (나무 등의) 가지
- appearance 모양, 겉모습
- decoration 장식
- urban 도시의
- survival 생존
- roast 굽다
- seed 씨앗, 씨
- alcoholic drink 알콜성 음료, 술
- commercial 상업적인
- numerous 많은, 다수의
- unique 독특한
- desirable 매력적인, 바람직한
- dig 파다
- rate ~율, 비율
- remove 제거하다, 없애다
- bud (식물의) 눈, 싹
- raw 날[생] 것의
- standard 기준
- crop 작물

03 답 ⑤

소 재 캐나다의 음악가 Gordon Lightfoot의 생애

전문해석 Gordon Lightfoot(1938~)은 캐나다의 가수, 작곡가, 그리고 16개의 Juno상 수상자이다. 그의 노래하는 재능은 Ontario 주 Orillia에서 그가 아직 어린 소년이었을 때 인정받았다. 1960년대와 70년대 내내 Lightfoot은 일련의 히트곡을 냈고, Toronto의 Massey Hall에서 자신의 매진된 콘서트로 기록을 깼다. 그러나 무대 뒤에서 Lightfoot은 분투하였다. 1972년 인기의 절정기에 그는 얼굴 일부를 마비시키는 심각한 질병을 앓았다. 그는 병과 끝까지 싸워 이겨내고 건강을 회복했다. 그 후 30년 동안 Gordon Lightfoot은 계속해서 앨범을 녹음하고, 콘서트를 하고, 텔레비전에 출연했다. 하지만 2002년에 그는 다시 병에 걸려 다섯 차례 수술을 받고 3개월간 병원에 입원했다. 모든 역경을 딛고,

그는 재기했고 2004년 무렵에 다시 녹음과 투어를 했다. 그가 낸 200개가 넘는 음반과 함께, 그는 동료 음악가들에게 작곡의 전설로 여겨져 왔다.

정답풀이 2002년에 다섯 차례 수술을 받고, 이후 재기해 2004년 무렵 다시 녹음과 투어를 했다고 나오므로, ⑤는 글의 내용과 일치하지 않는다.

구문풀이

[7행] In 1972, [at the height of his popularity], he suffered **a serious illness** [that paralyzed part of his face].
: 첫 번째 [ ]는 전치사구로, '그의 인기의 절정기에'로 해석할 수 있다. 두 번째 [ ]는 a serious illness를 수식하는 관계절이다.

어휘풀이

- award 상; 상을 주다
- recognize 인정하다
- a string of 일련의, 여러 개의
- sold-out 매진된
- behind the scene 무대 뒤에서
- struggle 분투하다
- at the height of ~의 절정기에
- suffer 겪다, 고생하다
- paralyze 마비시키다
- fight one's way through ~을 싸워 이겨내다
- regain 되찾다
- operation 수술
- against all (the) odds 모든 역경을 딛고
- to one's credit 공적이 ~에게 있는
- legend 전설
- fellow 동료

04 답 ④

소 재 범고래라고 불리는 돌고래 orca

전문해석 orca는 흔히 범고래라고 불리지만 돌고래과에 속한다. orca는 돌고래처럼 메아리가 물체로부터 돌아오는 데 걸리는 시간을 측정하여 물체의 위치를 결정한다. orca는 자유 의지대로 호흡하는 동물인데, 한 번에 뇌의 절반으로만 잠을 자고 나머지 절반은 정신이 초롱초롱하여 호흡하는 것을 조절한다. 그들은 매우 안정된 가족 집단 안에서 생활하고 자기들의 자식을 돌보는 수준이 높다는 것을 보여주는 매우 사회적인 동물이다. 늑대와 비슷하게, orca는 먹이를 위해 무리를 지어 협동하여 사냥한다. orca는 몇 마일 떨어져서도 자신들의 무리에게서 나오는 소리를 인식할 수 있다. 그들은 세계의 모든 바다에서 살지만 가장 흔한 서식지는 북극해와 남극해이다. 그들은 북아메리카 서해안에서도 자주 발견된다.

정답풀이 'Much like wolves, orcas hunt ~'로 보아, orca는 무리를 지어 사냥한다는 것을 알 수 있으므로, 글의 내용과 일치하지 않는 것은 ④이다.

구문풀이

[2행] Like dolphins, orcas determine the position of an object **by measuring** [how long {it takes for an echo to return from the object}].
: by -ing는 '~함으로써'의 의미이며, [ ]는 measuring의 목적어 역할을 하는 명사절이다. { }는 「it takes+시간+for 행위자+to부정사 (구)」 구문으로 '~가 …하는 데 시간이 걸리다'의 의미를 나타낸다.

[6행] They are **very social animals** [who {live in stable family groups} and {display a high level of care for their offspring}].
: [ ]는 앞의 very social animals를 수식하는 관계절이며, 두 개의 { }가 병렬로 연결되어 있다.

어휘풀이

- belong to ~에 속하다
- refer to ~라고 부르다, 지칭하다, 언급하다
- determine 결정하다
- position 위치
- object 물체, 사물
- measure 측정하다
- echo 메아리
- voluntary 자유 의지를 가진, 자발적인
- alert 정신이 초롱초롱한, 경계하는
- regulate 조절하다, 규제하다
- breathe 호흡하다, 숨을 쉬다
- stable 안정된
- display 보여주다, 전시하다
- offspring 자식, 후손
- cooperatively 협동하여
- recognize 인식하다
- habitat 거주지, 서식지
- Arctic 북극; 북극의
- Antarctic 남극; 남극의
- spot 발견하다

Unit 04 도표 및 표

Example 답 ④　　　　　　　　　　　　pp.64~65

소 재 스마트폰 평균 가격

전문해석 위 그래프는 2010년과 2015년 사이의 중국과 인도의 스마트폰 평균 가격을 같은 기간의 전 세계 스마트폰 평균 가격과 비교하여 보여준다. 전 세계 스마트폰 평균 가격은 2010년부터 2015년까지 하락했지만, 여전히 셋 중에 가장 높게 머물렀다. 중국의 스마트폰 평균 가격은 2010년과 2013년 사이에는 하락했다. 인도의 스마트폰 평균 가격은 2011년에 최고점에 도달했다. 2013년부터, 중국의 스마트폰 평균 가격은 하락했고 인도의 스마트폰 평균 가격은 상승하는, 정반대의 모습을 보였다. 전 세계 스마트폰 평균 가격과 중국의 스마트폰 평균 가격의 차이는 2015년에 가장 적었다.

구문풀이

[6행] From 2013, China and India took opposite paths, **with** China's smartphone average price **going** down and India's **going** up.
: 〈with+명사구(목적어)+분사(구)(목적격 보어)〉로 동시상황을 나타내며, '~하면서'를 뜻한다.

[7행] [**The gap** between the global smartphone average price and the smartphone average price in China] **was** the smallest in 2015.
: [ ]는 문장의 주어이며, 주어의 핵인 gap이 단수이므로 단수 동사 was가 쓰였다.

어휘풀이

- average 평균의; 평균
- compare 비교하다
- decrease 감소하다
- drop 하락하다, 떨어지다
- peak 최고점, 정상
- opposite 정반대의
- path 길, 경로

01 ⑤　　　02 ④　　　03 ⑤　　　04 ⑤

01 답 ⑤

소 재　캐나다 대학생들이 잠자는 동안 꾸는 꿈

전문해석　위의 그래프는 캐나다 대학생들이 잠자는 동안 꾸는 전형적인 꿈을 보여준다. 여섯 가지 전형적인 꿈 중에서, '(무언가에) 쫓기는 것'이 응답 빈도수가 가장 높았다. 그 다음으로는 '너무 늦게 도착하는 것'이 뒤따랐는데, 그것은 참여자의 66%가 응답했다. '맛있는 음식을 먹는 것'의 비율은 '너무 늦게 도착하는 것'의 절반이었다. '(어딘가에) 갇히는 것'과 '돈을 발견하는 것'의 비율은 같았다. 참여자의 3분의 1이 응답하여 '뱀을 보는 것'은 (응답) 빈도수가 가장 낮았다.

정답풀이　참여자 가운데 25%가 뱀을 보는 꿈을 꾼다고 했는데, 이는 4분의 1에 해당하는 비율이다. 따라서 3분의 1이라고 한 ⑤는 도표의 내용과 일치하지 않는다.

구문풀이

[3행] It was followed by "Arriving too late," **which** was reported by 66 percent of the participants.

: which는 계속적 용법의 관계대명사로 Arriving too late을 선행사로 취하고, and it이라는 의미를 나타낸다.

어휘풀이

- **typical** 전형적인
- **frequently** 자주, 빈번히
- **A is followed by B** B가 A를 뒤따르다
- **arrive late** 늦게 도착하다
- **percentage** 비율, 퍼센트
- **least** 가장 적은(little - less - least)
- **chase** 추적[추격]하다
- **participant** 참여자, 참가자
- **lock up** ～을 가두다
- **one-third** 3분의 1

02 답 ④

소 재　한국인들의 뉴질랜드 방문 목적

전문해석　이 도표는 2013년, 2014년, 2015년 10월에 뉴질랜드를 방문한 한국인들의 수를 그들의 방문 목적별로 보여준다. 주어진 기간 동안 뉴질랜드를 방문한 가장 흔한 목적은 친구와 친척 방문이었다. 2014년에 교육 목적으로 방문한 사람의 수는 2013년보다 감소했지만 그 다음해에는 증가했다. 2014년에 사업상의 관심으로 방문한 한국인의 수는 이전 해의 그것과 비교하여 감소했다. 교육은 3년 내내 가장 드문 방문 목적이었다. 2013년에 친구와 친척을 방문한 사람들의 수는 2013년에 사업 목적으로 방문한 사람들 수의 두 배보다 많았다.

정답풀이　2013년에는 교육 목적의 방문이 130명으로 가장 적었지만, 2014년에는 80명, 2015년에는 144명으로 두 해 모두 사업 목적의 방문보다는 많았다. 따라서 교육이 3년 내내 가장 드문 방문 목적이었다고 한 ④는 도표의 내용과 일치하지 않는다.

구문풀이

[9행] The number of **people** [visiting friends and relatives in 2013] was more than double the number of **those** [visiting for business purposes in 2013].

: 첫 번째 [ ]는 현재분사구로 people을 수식하고, 두 번째 [ ] 역시 현재분사구로 those를 수식하는데, 이때 those는 'people(사람들)'이라는 의미이다.

어휘풀이

- **the number of** ～의 수
- **according to** ～에 따르면
- **given period** 주어진[정해진] 기간
- **education** 교육
- **following** 다음의
- **compared with** ～와 비교하여
- **double** 두 배; 두 배의
- **visitor** 방문자
- **purpose** 목적
- **relative** 친척
- **decline** 감소하다, 줄어들다
- **drop** 떨어지다, 하락하다
- **previous** 이전의

03 답 ⑤

소 재　소매 부문에서 온라인상의 매출

전문해석　위 두 개의 원 그래프는 2005년과 2010년에 캐나다에서 서로 다른 소매 부문에 걸쳐 온라인상의 매출의 비율을 비교한다. 4개 부문 모두의 경우, 그 기간에 걸쳐 온라인상의 거래의 비율에 변화가 있었다. 2005년에 전자 기기와 전기 기구 부문은 전체 온라인 매출의 35%를 차지했으나, 그 비율이 2010년에는 30%로 떨어졌다. 그 기간 동안 늘어난 사람들의 수가 온라인상으로 식음료 구매를 선택해서 그 부문에서의 비율이 22%에서 32%로 올라갔다. 가정용 비품 산업은 2005년에 온라인상의 총매출의 25%를 차지했으나, 그 숫자가 2010년에는 15%로 떨어졌다. 비디오 게임이 시장의 23%에 상당했지만, 비디오 게임의 온라인상의 매출은 2010년에 가정용 비품의 매출을 추월하지 못했다.

정답풀이　2010년에 비디오 게임의 온라인상의 매출은 23%이고, 가정용 비품의 매출은 15%로 비디오 게임이 가정용 비품을 추월했다. 따라서 ⑤는 도표의 내용과 일치하지 않는다.

구문풀이

[7행] [As an increasing number of people chose to purchase food and beverages online during the given period], [the percentage in the sector went from 22% to 32%].

: 첫 번째 [ ]는 이유의 부사절이고, 두 번째 [ ]가 주절이다.

어휘풀이

- **pie chart** 원 그래프, 파이 도표
- **retail** 소매의
- **proportion** 비율
- **time frame** 기간
- **appliance** (가정용) 전기 기구
- **purchase** 구매하다
- **home furnishing** 가정용 비품[가구]
- **figure** 숫자, 수치
- **overtake** 따라잡다, 추월하다
- **compare** 비교하다
- **sector** 부문
- **transaction** 거래
- **electronics** 전자 기기
- **account for** ～을 차지하다
- **beverage** 음료
- **fall** 떨어지다
- **represent** 해당[상당]하다, 나타내다

04 답 ⑤

소 재 미국, 캐나다, 독일의 1인당 의료비 지출

전문해석 위 표는 2011년부터 2015년까지 미국, 캐나다, 독일의 1인당 의료비 지출을 보여준다. 매년 미국의 1인당 의료비 지출은 캐나다와 독일 각각의 그것(1인당 의료비 지출)보다 훨씬 높았다. 2013년에 소폭 감소한 것을 제외하면 미국의 1인당 의료비 지출은 매년 증가했다. 하지만 캐나다의 1인당 의료비 지출은 이 기간 동안 오르락내리락했고, 2015년에 쓰인 액수는 2011년의 액수보다 결국은 컸다. 독일의 1인당 의료비 지출은 2011년부터 2015년까지 매년 꾸준히 증가했다. 2015년 미국의 1인당 의료비 지출은 9,507달러였는데, 같은 해 독일의 그것보다 두 배가 넘었다.

정답풀이 2015년 미국의 1인당 의료비 지출은 9,507달러로, 독일의 1인당 의료비 지출 5,353달러의 두 배가 넘지 않으므로, ⑤는 표의 내용과 일치하지 않는다.

구문풀이

[10행] In 2015, per capita health care spending in the U.S. was **9,507 dollars**, [**which was** more than **twice as much as that** in Germany in the same year].

: [ ]는 앞에 나온 내용을 부연 설명하는 계속적 용법의 관계절이다. which의 선행사는 9,507 dollars로, 금액은 단수 취급하여 관계절 동사 역시 단수를 나타내는 was가 쓰였다. 배수 표현 「배수사+as+원급+as」가 쓰였고, 그 뒤의 that은 per capita health care spending을 대신하는 대명사이다.

어휘풀이

- per capita 1인당
- spending 지출
- except for ～을 제외하고
- end up -ing 결국 ～하게 되다
- twice 두 배
- health care 의료
- respectively 각각, 각기
- slight 약간의, 사소한
- steadily 꾸준히

Unit 05 실용문

Example 답 ④ pp.70~71

소 재 2019 여름 캠프

전문해석 **Summer Camp 2019**

이 캠프는 사교기술과 창의력을 발달시키기 위한 훌륭한 기회입니다!

기간 및 참가

- 7월 1일–5일(월요일–금요일)
- 8세–12세(한 반당 최대 20명)

프로그램

- 요리
- 야외 활동(하이킹, 래프팅, 그리고 캠핑)

비용

- 일반 가격: 1인당 100달러
- 할인 가격: 90달러(6월 15일까지 등록 시)

알림

- 프로그램은 기상 조건에 관계없이 진행될 것입니다.
- 등록하시려면, summercamp@standrews.com으로 이메일을 보내주세요.

더 많은 정보가 필요하시면, 우리 웹사이트(www.standrews.com)를 방문해 주세요.

구문풀이

[13행] The programs will **run** regardless of weather conditions.

: run은 '진행되다'의 의미로 자동사로 쓰였다.

Do It Yourself pp.72~75

01 ⑤   02 ⑤   03 ⑤   04 ③

01 답 ⑤

소 재 농장 체험의 날

전문해석 농장 체험의 날

오셔서 저희의 '농장 체험의 날'을 즐기세요.

여러분이 즐길 수 있는 몇 가지 활동들이 있습니다.

- 암탉의 달걀을 수거하세요.
- 소, 양, 돼지에게 먹이를 주세요.
- 농장을 돌아보며 동물에 대해 배워 보세요.

– 날씨에 따라 당일의 (체험) 활동이 변경될 수 있습니다.

– 참가비는 1인당 50달러입니다. 여기에는 정성을 들여 손수 만든 점심이 포함됩니다.

– 반드시 예약을 해야 합니다.

– 저희는 평일에만 문을 엽니다.

더 많은 정보를 원하시면 5252–7088로 전화 주십시오.

정답풀이 농장 체험의 날은 평일에만 문을 연다고 했으므로, ⑤는 안내문의 내용과 일치하지 않는다.

어휘풀이

- activity 활동
- feed 먹이를 주다, 먹이다
- include 포함하다
- homemade 손수[직접] 만든
- require 필요로 하다, 요구하다
- collect 모으다, 수거하다
- according to ～에 따라서
- hearty 정성을 들인, 마음으로부터의
- reservation 예약
- weekday 주중, 평일

02 답 ⑤

소 재 박물관에서의 밤

전문해석 **박물관에서의 밤**

여러분은 이집트 조각상과 함께 잠들거나 미라 옆에서 깨어나는 것을 상상해 보신 적이 있으신가요? '박물관에서의 밤'으로 오세요! 여러분은 해가 진 후 박물관을 탐험하면서 하룻밤을 보낼 수 있습니다!

날짜와 시간

매월 셋째 주말

(토요일 오후 6시 30분부터 일요일 오전 7시 30분까지)

입장 (요금)

8세부터 13세까지만 (1인당 40달러)

포함사항

활동을 위한 자료, 야간 숙박, 아침 식사

(주의: 아침 식사 때까지는 음식이 제공되지 않으므로 간식을 가져오세요.)

예약 정보

- 박물관 웹사이트의 '박물관에서의 밤' 페이지를 통해 온라인 으로 표를 예약하세요.
- 표를 예약하기 위해서는 박물관 웹사이트에서 회원 가입을 해야만 합니다.
- 환불은 행사 2주전까지만 가능합니다.

정답풀이 환불은 행사 2주전까지만 가능하다고 했으므로, ⑤가 안내문의 내용과 일치한다.

구문풀이

[4행] You can [**spend** a night **exploring** the museum after dark]!

: 「spend+시간+-ing」는 '…하면서 (시간을) 보내다'의 의미이다.

어휘풀이

- sculpture 조각상
- explore 탐험하다
- accommodation 숙박
- snack 간식
- sign up 가입하다
- up to ~까지
- mummy 미라
- material 자료, 재료
- provide 제공하다
- book 예약하다
- refund 환불

03 답 ⑤

소 재 Rainbow 농구 프로그램

전문해석 **Rainbow 농구 프로그램**

저희 프로그램은 1학년부터 6학년까지 모든 Rainbow 초등학교 학생들에게 열려 있습니다. 등록을 위한 밤 행사가 10월 26일 수요일 오후 5시 30분부터 오후 7시까지 Rainbow Town Hall 내의 Parks and Recreation Office에서 개최될 예정입니다.

- 모든 참가자들의 등록 마감시한은 11월 12일 토요일입니다.

- 조기 등록비는 아이 당 25달러입니다. 11월 9일 이후에는 비용 이 35달러가 될 것입니다.

저희는 항상 코치와 보조 코치, 그리고 심판을 필요로 하고 있으며 언제나 (지원을) 환영합니다.

더 많은 정보를 원하시면, (064) 432-1234로 Parks and Recreation Office에 전화를 주십시오.

정답풀이 항상 코치와 보조 코치, 심판이 필요하다고 했으므로, ⑤는 안내문의 내용과 일치하지 않는다.

어휘풀이

- elementary school 초등학교
- be held 개최되다
- participant 참가자
- assistant 조수, 보조원
- registration 등록
- deadline 마감시한
- fee 요금
- referee 심판

04 답 ③

소 재 2020년 소리 없는 책 대회

전문해석 **2020년 소리 없는 책 대회**

마감일: 2020년 2월 15일

참가 자격: 대회는 전 세계 18세 이상의 삽화가들에게 열려 있습니다.

설명

- 2020년 소리 없는 책 대회는 이탈리아 Mulazzo 타운이 조직합 니다. 이 대회는 새롭고, 출판되지 않은, 삽화만 있는 책을 위해 전적으로 마련됩니다. 이야기는 글자가 아닌, 삽화로만 전해져야 합니다. 책의 주제는 자유이며, 어떤 독자 연령층에 한정되지 않 아야 합니다.
- 작품은 디지털 파일 형태로 제출하세요.

참가비

참가비는 50유로입니다.

상

수상자는 4,000유로를 현금으로 받을 것이며, 수상 책은 상업적으 로 출판될 것입니다.

대회에 관한 더 많은 정보는 www.silentbookcontest.com을 방 문하세요.

정답풀이 책의 주제가 어떤 독자 연령층에 한정되지 않아야 한다 고 했으므로, ③은 안내문의 내용과 일치하지 않는다.

구문풀이

[9행] The subject of the book [is open] and [should not be restricted to any age of readers].

: The subject of the book을 공통의 주어로 하는 두 개의 동사구 [ ]가 and로 병렬 연결되었다.

어휘풀이

- silent 침묵의, 소리 없는
- illustrator 삽화가
- exclusively 독점적으로, 전적으로
- competition 대회, 경쟁, 경기
- organize 조직하다
- reserve 따로 마련하다

• subject 주제
• submit 제출하다
• publish 출판하다
• restrict 제한하다, 한정하다
• entry fee 참가비
• commercially 상업적으로

A 01 전시회　02 인정, 인식　03 ~을 생각해내다　04 기존의, 재래의　05 budget　06 도시의　07 날[생] 것의　08 상업적인　09 분투하다　10 마비시키다　11 동료　12 정신이 초롱초롱한, 경계하는　13 조절하다, 규제하다　14 안정된　15 자식, 후손　16 average　17 최고점, 정상　18 정반대의　19 추적[추격]하다　20 참여자, 참가자

B 01 to have their pictures taken
02 when removed and planted in other places
03 it takes for an echo to return
04 compared with that in the previous year

C 01 relative　02 감소하다, 줄어들다　03 이전의　04 소매의　05 비율　06 거래　07 ~을 차지하다　08 beverage　09 각각, 각기　10 약간의, 사소한　11 최대　12 상태, 조건　13 먹이를 주다, 먹이다　14 예약　15 미라　16 숙박　17 마감한　18 심판　19 대회, 경쟁, 경기　20 제한하다, 한정하다

D 01 wake up → waking up: 두 개의 동명사구가 등위접속사 or로 인해 병렬 연결되는 구조이므로 waking up으로 고쳐야 한다.
02 explore → exploring: 「spend+시간 -ing」 구문이므로 exploring으로 고쳐야 한다. 앞에 문장의 동사 can spend가 있으므로 동사 explore를 또 쓸 수 없다.
03 give → be given: 주어인 Refunds가 give의 대상이므로 수동태 be given으로 고쳐야 한다.
04 will hold → will be held: A registration night이 hold(개최하다)라는 동작의 주체가 아닌, 대상이므로 수동태인 be held로 고쳐야 한다.

Part 3 어법·어휘

Unit 01 어법성 판단

Example　　답 ④　　　　　　　　　　　pp.80~81

소재　조명의 질이 미치는 영향

전문해석　너무 밝은 빛이나, 눈에 직접적으로 비추는 빛처럼, 나쁜 조명은 여러분의 눈에 스트레스를 증가시킬 수 있다. 형광등 또한 피로감을 줄 수 있다. 여러분이 모를 수도 있는 것은 빛의 질 또한 중요할 수 있다는 것이다. 대부분의 사람들은 밝은 햇빛 속에서 가장 행복하다. 이것은 아마 정서적인 행복감을 주는 체내의 화학물질을 분비시킬지도 모른다. 전형적으로 단지 몇 개의 빛 파장만 있는 인공 조명이 분위기에 미치는 효과는 햇빛이 미치는 효과와 똑같지 않을 수 있다. 창가에서 작업하거나 책상 전등에 있는 모든 파장이 있는 전구를 사용하여 실험해 보아라. 이것이 여러분의 작업 환경의 질을 향상시킨다는 것을 아마도 알게 될 것이다.

구문풀이

[2행] [**What** you may not appreciate] is [that the quality of light may also be important].

: 첫 번째 [ ]는 선행사를 포함한 What이 이끄는 명사절로, 문장의 주어 역할을 한다. 두 번째 [ ]는 문장에서 보어 역할을 하는 명사절이다.

Do It Yourself　　　　　　　　　　　pp.82~85

01 ⑤　　02 ②　　03 ③　　04 ②

01　답 ⑤

소재　방 청소에 대한 어머니의 잔소리

전문해석　내가 어린 소녀였을 때, 내 방은 항상 엉망이었다. 어머니는 "가서 방 치우렴!"하고 나에게 말씀하시며 내가 방을 정돈하게 하려고 항상 노력하셨다. 그럴때마다 나는 어머니에게 저항했다. 나는 무엇을 하라고 하는 말을 듣는 것이 싫었다. 나는 단호히 내가 원하는 방식으로 방을 두었다. 내가 어질러진 방에서 지내는 것을 좋아하느냐 아니냐는 전적으로 다른 문제였다. 나는 깨끗한 방을 갖는 것의 이점들에 대해 멈추어서 생각해본 적이 결코 없었다. 내게는, 내 방식대로 하는 것이 더 중요했다. 그리고 대부분의 다른 부모님들처럼, 어머니는 내가 그 이점들을 혼자 힘으로 깨닫도록 하지 않으셨다. 대신에 그녀는 잔소리를 선택했다.

정답풀이　(A) **능동태 vs. 수동태**: 주어인 I는 tell의 주체가 아닌 대상이다. 즉, '~하라고 말하다'로 해석되는 것이 아니라, '~하라는 말을 듣다'로 해석되므로 수동태인 be told를 써야 한다.

(B) **접속사의 기능**: 동사 was의 주어부를 이끌어야 하므로 명사절을 이끄는 접속사 Whether를 써야 한다. Because가 유도하는 절은 부사절이므로 문장의 주어가 될 수 없다.

(C) **형용사/부사 vs. 전치사**: 명사구인 most other parents가 뒤따르고 있으므로 전치사 like를 써야 한다. alike는 서술적 용법으로만 쓰는 형용사 혹은 부사이므로 명사구를 동반할 수 없다.

[4행] I was determined to have my room **the way** [I wanted it].

: [ ]는 the way를 수식하는 관계절로, the way 뒤에 관계부사 how가 생략되었다. how와 the way는 항상 둘 중 하나를 생략하는 경향이 있다.

[8행] To me, **it** was more important [to get my own way].

: it은 형식상의 주어이고 to부정사구인 [ ]가 내용상의 주어이다.

- **mess** 엉망, 혼돈   - **straighten up** 정돈하다
- **resist** 저항[반항]하다   - **opportunity** 기회
- **be determined to** 단호하게 ~하다
- **subject** 문제, 주제   - **altogether** 전적으로, 완전히
- **benefit** 이점, 혜택   - **realize** 깨닫다
- **lecture** 잔소리하다, 강의하다; 강의, 잔소리

02 답 ②

 감사할 줄 아는 사람들의 결정

 감사할 줄 아는 사람들은 건전한 결정을 하는 경향이 있다. 인생과 스포츠는 중요하고 어려운 결정이 내려져야 하는 많은 상황들을 제시한다. 이기적인 어른들 혹은 아이들은 감사할 줄 아는 사람들만큼 건전한 결정을 내리지 못한다. 이는 스스로를 동기 유발시키는 결정을 포함한다. 좌절한 부모는 묻는다. "어떻게 내가 아이에게 스포츠를 하거나 스포츠를 계속하도록 동기를 부여해야 하는가? 때때로 내 아이가 낙심하여 스포츠에 필요한 노력을 기울이려 하지 않는 것은 아닐까? 부모로서 돕기 위해 내가 무엇을 하거나 말할 수 있는가?" 자기들만의 편협한 이기적인 욕구에 집중하는 아이들 또는 어른들을 동기 유발시키는 것은 어려우며 거의 불가능한 일이다. 그러나 감사할 줄 아는 사람들로서 살아가는 아이들과 어른들은 스스로를 동기 유발시킬 수 있다. 그들은 또한 다른 사람들 심지어는 부모들로부터의 제안을 환영한다.

 ② **are**: 앞에 있는 동사구 make sound decisions를 가리켜야 하므로 일반동사를 대신하는 do로 바꿔 써야 한다. are를 쓰려면 be동사로 유도되는 어구가 앞에 있어야 하는데 그럴 만한 동사구가 없다.

① **where**: 앞에 있는 명사구 many situations를 수식하는 관계절을 유도하고 있고, 뒤따르는 절이 주어와 수동태를 포함한 동사구로 이루어져 있고 완전하므로 관계부사 where는 적절하다.
③ **discouraged**: 주어인 my child가 분사의 주체가 아닌 대상으로 해석되므로 주격 보어로 쓰인 과거분사 discouraged는 적절하다. 내 아이가 낙심을 느꼈다는 의미이다.
④ **to motivate**: 형식상의 주어 It에 대한 내용상의 주어를 이끄는 to부정사이므로 적절하다.
⑤ **themselves**: 주어인 kids and adults가 목적어로 다시 사용되었으므로 재귀대명사 themselves는 적절하다.

[11행] However, **kids and adults** [who live as grateful people] are able to motivate themselves.

: [ ]는 문장의 주어인 kids and adults를 수식하는 관계절이다.

- **grateful** 고마워하는, 감사하는   - **be inclined to** ~하는 경향이 있다
- **decision** 결정
- **present** 제시하다, 제공하다; 선물, 현재
- **critical** 중요한, 결정적인   - **selfish** 이기적인
- **sound** 건전한
- **self-motivated** 스스로 동기를 유발시키는
- **frustrated** 좌절한   - **motivate** 동기를 주다
- **discouraged** 낙담한, 낙심한   - **centered on** ~에 집중하는
- **narrow** 좁은, 편협한   - **suggestion** 제안

03 답 ③

 자신에 대한 인정과 사랑

 여러분이 초인이 아니라는 것을 인정하자마자 여러분은 최고의 자아가 될 수 있을 것이다. 최고의 자아가 된다는 것은 여러분 전부를 사랑하고 받아들이는 것을, 그리고 여러분이 가장 힘든 시기에 여러분의 마음이 머무는 곳을 신뢰하는 것을 의미한다. 여러분 자신을 완전히 인식하고 그런 자아를 지원할 때 여러분은 단지 최고가 될 수 있다. 많은 장소에서 여러분이 할 수 있는 최고의 일은 건강하고, 균형 있고, 행복하게 스스로를 유지시키는 것인데, 결국 '여러분'이 하는 것을 더 많이 할 수 있게 된다. 스스로 나쁜 기분이 들도록 만드는 데 에너지를 낭비하지 말라. 스스로 좋은 기분이 들도록 하는 데에 그것의(에너지의) 전부를 사용하라. 길가의 튀어나온 부분이 실제로 느끼는 것보다 훨씬 더 작다는 것을 이해하라.

 (A) **동사 vs. 동명사**: means가 문장의 동사이므로 주어로 쓸 수 있는 동명사 Being이 적절하다.

(B) **복수 동사 vs. 단수 동사**: 단수인 주어 The best thing을 관계대명사 that이 생략된 형태의 관계절 you could do at many places가 수식하고 있으므로 단수 동사 is가 적절하다. many places는 수식어구에 해당하므로 동사의 수에 영향을 끼치지 않는다.

(C) **that vs. what**: 주어(the bumps in the road), 동사(are), 보어(much smaller than they feel)로 이루어진 완전한 절이 이어지고 있으므로, Know의 목적어로 쓰인 명사절을 이끄는 접속사 that이 적절하다. what 다음에는 불완전한 절이 이어져야 한다.

[2행] Being your best self means **loving** and **accepting** all of yourself — and **trusting** [where your heart lies in your lowest times].

: loving, accepting, trusting은 모두 동명사로, 앞에 있는 동사 means의 목적어이며 특히 loving과 accepting은 all of yourself를 공통의 목적어로 갖는다. [ ]는 trusting의 목적어로, where 앞에 선행사인 the place가 생략된 것으로 볼 수 있다.

[5행] **The best** thing you could do at many places **is keep** yourself healthy, balanced and happy, ~

: to부정사는 be동사 뒤에서 주격 보어로 쓰일 수 있는데, 여기서는 동사 is의 보어로 to를 생략한 형태로 keep이 쓰였다. 이처럼 최상급 표현(the best, the most 등)이 쓰인 주어일 경우를 포함해, all이 이끄는 주어일 경우, what이 이끄는 관계사절이 주어일 경우, 서수 표현이 쓰인 주어일 경우, 혹은 비격식적/구어적 표현일 경우에 be동사의 주격 보어로 쓰인 to부정사에서 to를 생략할 수 있다.

어휘풀이

- **super-human** 초인
- **be aware of** ~을 인식하다[알다]
- **supportive** 지원하는, 협조하는
- **waste** 낭비하다
- **trust** 신뢰하다
- **fully** 완전히, 충분히
- **balanced** 균형 있는
- **bump** 튀어나온 부분, 둔덕

04 답 ②

소 재 자연스러운 관계 형성

전문해석 여러분이 관계 속에서 자연스럽게 행동할 수 있다면 관계가 제일 잘될 것이다. 여러분이 자연스럽게 행동할 수 있는 관계는 아마 더 편안한 느낌이 들고 여러분을 더 행복하게 만들어 줄 것이다. 이것은 성질을 내고 싶을 때 성질을 내고 원하는 대로 사람들에게 무례하게 굴라는 얘기는 아니다. 또한 모든 관계가 편안해야 한다는 것을 말하는 것도 아니다. 몇몇 매우 좋은 관계는 화를 돋우고 도전적일 수 있다. 여러분이 자연스럽게 행동하지 않을 때 관계가 오히려 불안정해지고 덜 만족스러운 경향이 있다. 결론은 여러분의 관계에 대해 궁금해 하고 그것들을 이해하려고 노력하는 것은 도움이 된다는 것이다.

정답풀이 ② rudely: be동사의 보어 자리에 올 적절한 형태를 묻고 있는데, 보어 자리에는 부사는 쓰일 수 없고 형용사가 와야 하므로 rudely는 적절하지 않으며 rude로 고쳐 써야 한다. 해당 문장에 「as ~ as …: …처럼 ~한」의 비교급 표현이 쓰였다.

오답풀이

① **are**: Relationships가 주어이고 where ~ yourself는 수식어구이므로 복수형 동사 are는 적절하다.

③ **is it**: 부정어구 Nor가 문장의 맨 앞에 위치하였으므로, 주어와 동사를 도치시켜 is가 it의 앞에 오는 것은 적절하다.

④ **challenging**: 주어인 Some very good ones가 문맥상 분사의 주체이므로 현재분사 challenging은 적절하다.

⑤ **try**: 문맥상 '관계를 궁금해 하고 그것들을 이해하려고 노력하는

것이 도움이 된다'는 의미가 되어야 하므로 to be curious와 병렬을 이루는 (to) try to understand them은 적절하다.

구문풀이

[3행] This is not to say [that you should {throw tantrums when you feel like it}, and {be as rude to people as you wish}].

: [ ]는 say의 목적어 역할을 하는 명사절이다. 동사구인 두 개의 { }는 등위접속사 and에 의해 should에 공통으로 연결되었다.

어휘풀이

- **relationship** 관계
- **be likely to** 아마 ~할 것이다
- **rudely** 무례하게
- **challenging** 도전적인
- **satisfying** 만족스러운
- **be oneself** 자연스럽게 행동하다
- **comfortable** 편안한
- **provocative** 화를 돋우는, 선동적인
- **unstable** 불안정한
- **curious** 궁금해 하는

100 제로 완성하는 어법

1. 동사

p.86

001 **정답** fills
해석 잔디가 부드러운 바람에 맞춰 춤추는 동안 야생화의 향기가 공기를 채운다.
풀이 The perfume이 주어로 단수이고 of wildflowers는 주어를 꾸미는 수식어구이므로 동사는 fills가 적절하다.

002 **정답** are
해석 결코 성공하지 못하는 사람들은 너무 빨리 포기하는 사람들이다.
풀이 복수인 Those가 주어이고 who never make it은 주어를 꾸미는 수식어구이므로 동사는 those를 받는 복수 형태의 are가 적절하다.

003 **정답** are
해석 숲속에 있는 유기체의 사체는 다른 유기체에게 영양을 공급해 주는데, 분해되어 토양이 된다.
풀이 The dead bodies가 주어이고 which in turn nourishes other organisms는 삽입어구이므로 동사는 are가 적절하다.

004 **정답** destroys
해석 이미 사회적으로 고립된 사람들을 투표에서 배제하는 것은 카스트 제도(사회 계급 제도)를 만들어내어 우리의 민주주의를 파괴한다.
풀이 To exclude those from voting이 주어인데, to부정사(구)가 주어로 쓰이면 단수 동사로 받는다. who are already socially isolated는 those를 꾸미는 수식어구이다.

005 **정답** is
해석 새로운 골프 코스를 만드는 것은 세계에서 가장 빠른 종류의 토지 개발 방법이다.
풀이 동명사(구)가 주어로 쓰이면 단수로 취급한다.

006 **정답** goes
해석 미국에서 사용되는 고무의 약 5분의 3이 타이어나 튜브로 쓰인다.

풀이 비율(퍼센트)이나 분수처럼 부분을 나타내는 말이 오면 of 뒤의 명사에 동사의 수를 일치시킨다.

007 정답 think
해석 내 친구들 중의 몇 명은 자전거를 (사기) 위해 일하고 저축하는 나를 어리석다고 생각한다.
풀이 most of ~, some of ~, all of~, a lot of ~ 와 같은 표현이 주어로 쓰일 경우, 동사는 of 다음에 오는 명사(구)의 수에 일치시킨다. (ex. some of+단수/복수: ~의 일부)

008 정답 decreased
해석 코알라 수가 100년 정도 전에 감소했기 때문에, 오늘날 호주 남부에 있는 모든 코알라는 최근까지 살아남았던 몇 안 되는 코알라 조상들의 후손이다.
풀이 a century or so ago라는 과거 시점을 나타내는 어구가 왔으므로 과거 시제로 쓴다.

009 정답 leaves
해석 증기선은 겨울에는 매주 화요일에 출발하지만 여름에는 화요일과 금요일에 모두 출발한다.
풀이 주기적인 일정이나 계획 등 변하지 않는 사실은 현재 시제로 표현한다.

010 정답 had
해석 나중에 어머니가 집에 오셔서 내가 무엇을 하고 있었는지 물어보셨다.
풀이 주절이 과거(came)이고 그 이전부터 진행된 일을 묻고 있으므로 과거완료 진행형(had been -ing)으로 쓴다.

011 정답 have
해석 몇 년 동안 나는 더 많은 솔선을 보여주려고 더 나은 직장을 원하는 사람들을 자주 상담해왔다.
풀이 몇 년 동안 계속 해오고 있는 것이므로 현재완료 시제를 쓴다.

012 정답 gets
해석 Jane이 집에 도착할 무렵에는 그녀의 아버지가 시카고를 향해 떠났을 것이다.
풀이 시간과 조건을 나타내는 부사절에서는 미래 의미를 현재 시제로 나타낸다. by the time은 '~할 때까지는'의 의미로 시간을 나타내는 부사절을 이끄는 어구이다.

013 정답 to move
해석 시냇물과 달리, 빙하는 움직이는 것이 보이지 않는다.
풀이 문장의 주절은 'We cannot see a glacier move'의 수동태인데, 사역동사나 지각동사(see)의 수동태에는 원형부정사 대신 to부정사를 써야 한다.

014 정답 be written
해석 당신의 이름만 이쪽에 쓰도록 하라.
풀이 명령문의 수동태는 〈let+목적어+be p.p.〉의 형태로 쓴다. 원래의 능동태 문장은 'Write nothing but your name on this side'가 된다.

015 정답 carried
해석 나는 나의 작은 발이 자동차 대회 경기장에 있는 특별관람석으로 가는 계단으로 나를 이끌었던 5월의 그날 느꼈던 엄청난 감정을 여전히 기억한다.
풀이 접속사 when 뒤에 있는 my little feet이 주어이고 동사 carry의 목적어인 me가 있으므로, 능동형인 carried가 와야 한다.

016 정답 be proved
해석 우리의 과학 이론 중 일부는 거짓임이 판명날 것이다.
풀이 과학 이론을 판명하는 주체는 사람들 또는 과학자들일 것이고 과학 이론은 판명되는 대상이므로 주어 Some of our scientific theories에 이어지는 동사는 수동태가 적절하다.

017 정답 is believed
해석 침술은 매우 효과적이라고 믿어진다.
풀이 원래의 'It is believed that acupuncture is very effective'에서 that절의 주어를 문장의 주어로 삼아 전환된 것으로 볼 수 있다. 사람들의 말과 생각 같은 일반적인 정보를 전달할 때 자주 쓰는 형태이다.

018 정답 left
해석 William Kamkwamba는 그의 가족이 수업료를 지불할 능력이 없어지자 14살 때 학교를 떠났다.
풀이 문장의 동사가 들어갈 자리이다. as 이하는 부사절이다.

019 정답 turned
해석 엄마와 함께 있으니 그녀가 만지는 모든 것이 금으로 변했다.
풀이 everything (that) she touched를 주어로 하는 동사가 들어갈 자리이다.

020 정답 laid
해석 이집트 가정들은 고양이의 죽음을 애도했고 죽은 고양이가 마침내 눕혀져 묻히기 전에 그 몸을 천으로 쌌다.
풀이 고양이가 눕혀졌다는 뜻이므로 수동태가 와야 한다. 타동사인 lay의 과거형은 laid이고, '눕다'는 뜻의 lie는 자동사이며 과거형이 lay, 과거분사형이 lain이다.

2. 준동사
p.89

021 정답 traveling
해석 2개에서 6개까지 침대를 둘 수 있는 이러한 캐러밴들은 이동할 수 있으며, 많은 가족들은 휴일마다 여기저기 여행 다니는 것을 즐긴다.
풀이 enjoy는 목적어로 동명사를 취하는 동사이므로 traveling이 적절하다.

022 정답 living
해석 해발 1,350미터에 위치하여 반짝거리는 히말라야 산맥이 내다보이는 카트만두 시는 연중 내내 기후가 온화하여 살기 좋은 곳이다.
풀이 makes의 목적어 자리이고 목적격 보어 pleasant가 뒤에 온 구조이므로 동명사 living이 필요하다. to live를 사용하려면 'makes it pleasant to live here'의 형태로 바꾸어야 한다. 즉, it을 형식상의 목적어로 하고 내용상의 목적어 to live here를 뒤로 보내도록 하는 것이다.

023 정답 expressing
해석 우리는 음악에 대한 우리의 취향이 개성을 표현하는 좋은 방법이라고 믿는 경향이 있다.
풀이 전치사 of 뒤에 오는 자리이고 목적어인 our individuality를 취하도록 동명사를 써야 한다.

024 　정답　 to make
해석　 그들은 식량을 얻기 위해 소들을 도살하지는 않는다. 그러나 소가 죽으면 뿔은 그릇으로 쓰이고 가죽은 신발, 옷,그리고 침대 덮개를 만드는 데 사용된다.
풀이　 '~하는 데 사용되다'의 의미를 나타내도록 「be used to부정사」의 형태가 되어야 한다. 참고로 「be used to -ing」는 '~하는 데 익숙하다'라는 뜻이다.

025 　정답　 breathing
해석　 불쌍한 Simba는 두 번 총을 맞았고, 머리를 들어올리지조차 못했다. 결국 Simba는 숨 쉬는 것을 멈췄다.
풀이　 「stop -ing」는 '~하는 것을 멈추다'라는 뜻이고 「stop to부정사」는 '~하기 위해 멈추다'라는 뜻이다. 여기서는 Simba가 숨쉬기를 멈추고 죽었다는 뜻이므로 「stop -ing」 구문이 적절하다.

026 　정답　 try
해석　 나는 메트로를 탄 한 남자가 전동차에서 내리려다가 실패한 것을 지켜보았다.
풀이　 지각동사 watched의 목적격 보어 자리인데 목적어인 a man과 능동의 의미 관계이므로 원형부정사를 쓴다.

027 　정답　 waving
해석　 Clauss는 수영을 하고 있는 두 사람이 팔을 흔드는 것을 보았다.
풀이　 목적어인 a pair of swimmers가 행동을 하고 있는 경우이므로 능동의 의미를 나타내는 현재분사를 쓴다. 팔을 흔들고 있는 진행 상황을 현재분사로 표현한 것이다. waved로 쓰면 동사가 두 개가 되므로 어법에 맞지 않다.

028 　정답　 done
해석　 계획이 중요하지만, 일이 이루어지도록 하는 것은 행동이다.
풀이　 〈get+목적어+목적격 보어〉 형태에서 목적어 things와 목적격 보어 do가 수동 관계이므로 과거분사를 쓴다.

029 　정답　 known
해석　 당신은 당신의 감정을 그에게 알려야 한다.
풀이　 your feelings가 그에게 알려지는 것이므로 수동의 관계이다. 따라서 목적격 보어는 과거분사가 되어야 한다.

030 　정답　 disappointing
해석　 사람들이 아이들과 함께 시간을 보내기보다는 직장에 더 많은 시간을 보내는 것에 나는 항상 실망스러움을 느껴왔다.
풀이　 it은 형식상의 목적어이고 that이 이끄는 절이 내용상의 목적어이다. that 이하의 내용이 실망을 주는 주체이므로 능동 관계가 되도록 현재분사로 써야 한다.

031 　정답　 confusing
해석　 일부 아시아 문화에서는 주는 행위는 선물 주기의 중요한 측면이고, 이 과정은 서양인들에게는 혼란스러워 보일 수도 있다.
풀이　 주어인 this process와의 의미 관계를 살펴볼 때 일부 아시아 문화의 주는 행위가 서양인들을 혼란스럽게 만든다는 능동의 의미이므로 현재분사 confusing을 쓰는 것이 옳다.

032 　정답　 accepting
해석　 출생 순서가 가족 내에서 역할을 규정지을 수는 있지만, 여러분이 어른으로 성장해가며 다른 사회적 역할들을 받아들일 때, 출생 순서는 중요하지 않게 된다.

풀이　 'as you accept other social roles(당신이 다른 사회적인 역할을 받아들이면서)'를 분사구문으로 바꾼 형태이므로 accepting이 적절하다. 분사구문의 주체가 you로서 능동이므로 현재분사가 적절하다.

033 　정답　 Terrified
해석　 보통의 사무실 직원은 사무실을 떠나기가 두렵다. 상사가 자신들을 게으르다고 생각하는 것이 두려워서, 할 일이 별로 없어도 책상에 머무른다.
풀이　 주절의 주어인 they가 분사의 의미상 주어인데, 여기서는 they가 that 이하의 내용에 의해 두려운 감정을 느끼는 수동적 입장이므로 과거분사 terrified가 적절하다.

3. 명사, 대명사 p.91

034 　정답　 that
해석　 내가 이 정원에 들어오자마자 처음 알아차린 것은 발목 높이의 풀이 울타리 반대편의 풀보다 더 푸르다는 것이다.
풀이　 비교 대상인 단수 명사 grass를 받는 대명사이므로 단수를 받는 that이 와야 한다.

035 　정답　 their
해석　 일들은 종종 더 좋아지기 바로 직전에 최악의 상태인 것처럼 보인다.
풀이　 Things를 받는 대명사를 써야 하므로 their가 적절하다.

036 　정답　 company
해석　 우리 아빠는 훌륭한 분이며 나는 아빠의 220파운드 체중 모두를 좋아하지만, 내 친구들이 있을 때 꼭 수영복을 입고 거실에 앉아 계셔야 하는 것일까?
풀이　 company가 추상명사로 '손님. 일행'의 뜻일 때는 관사 a를 사용하지 않으며 a가 붙으면 '회사'를 의미한다.

037 　정답　 its
해석　 Kathmandu는 현재 네팔의 수도이며, 마찬가지로 네팔 정부와 경제, 그리고 문화의 중심이다.
풀이　 Nepal을 지칭하는 대명사를 it으로 받으면 그 소유격은 its가 되어야 한다. it's는 it is의 축약형이다.

038 　정답　 themselves
해석　 영국 프리미어 리그에서 활동하는 비영어권 선수들은 자신을 소개하고 기본적인 개인 신상에 관해 묻고 답하기 위해 매우 기본적인 어구들을 사용할 필요가 있다.
풀이　 주어인 Non-English players(= they)가 다시 목적어로 쓰였으므로 재귀대명사를 써야 한다.

039 　정답　 others
해석　 강사가 연속적으로 새로운 개념을 제시하면, 학생들의 얼굴에서 좌절의 표정이 보이기 시작한다. 어떤 학생들은 노트에 열심히 필기를 하고, 한편 어떤 학생들은 완전히 낙담해서 필기를 포기한다.
풀이　 some (students)과 대구를 이루며 동시에 give up의 주어가 되도록 복수 형태의 others가 적절하다.

040 　정답　 themselves
해석　 감사할 줄 아는 사람들로서 살아가는 아이들과 어른들은 스스로를 동기 유발시킬 수 있다.
풀이　 주어인 Kids and adults가 to motivate의 목적어로 다시 쓰

였으므로 재귀대명사가 적절하다.

041 정답 **write them down**
해석 아마도 당신이 정한 목표에 집중하는 가장 효과적인 방법은 그것들을 적어두는 것이다.
풀이 〈동사+부사〉 형태의 동사구에서 목적어가 대명사일 경우에는 어순이 〈동사+대명사+부사〉가 된다.

4. 형용사, 부사, 비교   p.92

042 정답 **almost**
해석 많은 사람들은 한국인들이 거의 매 식사 때마다 먹는 전통 음식인 김치가 그 비결이라고 생각한다.
풀이 every를 수식하는 '거의'라는 뜻의 부사가 필요한 자리이다. most는 주로 '대부분의'라는 뜻을 가진 형용사로 쓴다.

043 정답 **most**
해석 그녀는 깨끗하고 세련된 문체로 인해 다른 대부분의 기자들과 구별된다.
풀이 '대부분의'라는 뜻으로 other journalists를 수식하는 형용사 most가 적절하다.

044 정답 **little**
해석 여러분은 가까운 거리로 이사하는 것은 너무 쉬워서 거의 힘이 들지 않고도 금방 해치울 수 있다고 생각할지 모른다.
풀이 앞에 관사 a가 없으므로 둘 다 부정의 뜻이지만 여기서는 셀 수 없는 명사로 쓰인 effort를 수식하고 있으므로 little을 쓴다.

045 정답 **few**
해석 그는 대단한 학자는 아니었지만, 교사로서는 맞먹을 사람이 거의 없었다.
풀이 복수형인 peers를 수식하므로 few를 써야 한다.

046 정답 **much**
해석 아마도 몰두하는 오페라 관객이 되는 것에 대해 가장 위대한 것은 성장을 위한 많은 여지가 있다는 것이다.
풀이 셀 수 없는 명사 room을 수식하도록 much를 써야 한다. 여기서 room은 추상명사로 '여지'라는 뜻이다.

047 정답 **rapidly**
해석 출생률은 여성 1인당 1.8명으로 낮고 노인의 수는 급속히 증가하고 있다.
풀이 앞에 있는 진행형 동사 is growing을 수식해야 하므로 부사 rapidly가 적절하다.

048 정답 **warm**
해석 깃털은 피부 표면과 가까운 신체에서 생긴 열을 가두어 새를 따뜻하게 해 주는 것을 돕는다.
풀이 keep의 목적어인 a bird에 대한 목적격 보어가 올 자리이므로 형용사 warm이 적절하다. '따뜻하게'라고 해석된다고 해서 부사를 고르면 안 된다.

049 정답 **highly**
해석 나는 이 실험이 매우 교육적이라고 믿는다.
풀이 high는 '높은'의 뜻이고 highly는 '매우'라는 뜻이다.

050 정답 **interested enough**
해석 누군가가 가난한 마을 사람들에게 도움을 주기에 충분히 관심이 있다는 사실이 종종 기적을 일으킨다.
풀이 부사 enough는 형용사를 수식할 때 형용사의 뒤에 온다. 「형용사+enough+to부정사」 구문은 '…하기에 충분히 ~한'의 뜻이다.

051 정답 **insignificant**
해석 당신의 문제나 도전들이 갑자기 대수롭지 않게 보인다.
풀이 seem의 보어가 와야 할 자리이므로 형용사인 insignificant가 적절하다.

052 정답 **aggressive**
해석 나는 막내라서 형과 누나들보다 덜 적극적이다.
풀이 '~ and thus I am less aggressive'의 문맥이므로 be동사의 보어 역할을 할 수 있는 형용사 aggressive가 적절하다. less는 부사 little의 비교급이다.

053 정답 **as**
해석 수년에 걸친 귀하의 공헌이 없었다면 우리들은 지금까지 성공했던 것만큼 성공하지 않았을 것입니다.
풀이 동등한 성질을 비교할 때는 「as+형용사/부사의 원급 as...」 구문을 쓴다. '…만큼 ~한'의 의미이다.

054 정답 **much**
해석 사람의 기억이 긴 시간이 경과한 후에 오히려 훨씬 더 뚜렷해지는 일이 생길 수도 있다.
풀이 비교급을 강조하는 부사는 much, even, far 등이다. very는 원급을 강조한다.

055 정답 **than**
해석 종이 위에서보다 칠판 위에서 수학을 하는 것이 더 나은데, 그 이유는 분필이 좀 더 쉽게 지울 수 있고 수학적인 연구는 흔히 실수로 가득 찬 경우가 많기 때문이다.
풀이 「It is better to do ~」의 비교급 구문이므로 than을 쓴다. as는 원급 구문에 쓴다.

056 정답 **deeper**
해석 유사(流沙)에서는 발버둥 치면 칠수록 더 깊이 빠져든다.
풀이 '~하면 할수록 더욱 …하다'는 뜻의 「the+비교급 ~, the+비교급 …」 구문이다.

5. 관계사, 접속사, 전치사   p.94

057 정답 **that**
해석 많은 사회과학자들은 한동안 출생 순서가 성격과 성인이 되어서의 성공에 직접적으로 영향을 끼친다고 믿어 왔다.
풀이 have believed의 목적어가 되는 절을 이끌 수 있는 접속사 that이 적절하다. 이어지는 절이 주어, 동사, 목적어를 모두 갖추었으므로 관계대명사 what은 쓸 수 없다.

058 정답 **what**
해석 비록 아이들이 그런 결과들을 믿기는 힘들겠지만, 그들도 자신들이 먹는 것에 책임을 져야 한다는 것을 배울 필요가 있다.
풀이 선행사가 없고, 전치사 for의 목적어인 명사절을 이끌어야 하며, eat의 목적어가 없으므로 what이 적절하다.

059 정답 **they**
해석 특별히 개발된 웹 사이트를 이용하여 그들은 14,000명의 사람들에게 무료 음악을 내려 받을 수 있는 기회를 제공하였다.

풀이　먼저 Using이 분사인지 동명사인 주어인지 확인해야 하는데, 뒤에 using을 받는 동사가 나오지 않는 것으로 보아 분사이므로, 콤마(,) 뒤에는 offered의 주어이면서 동시에 Using의 의미상 주어 역할도 할 수 있는 they가 와야 한다.

060　**정답**　which

해석　어떤 의미에서 내가 기억했지만 아주 최근까지 나에게 이상하거나 흥미롭게 다가오지 않았던 일들이 있다.

풀이　앞에 선행사인 things가 있으므로 which가 적절하다. 이때 which는 관계절의 동사 remembered의 목적어 역할을 한다.

061　**정답**　where

해석　영화 세트는 영화가 촬영되는 장소이다.

풀이　선행사가 장소(the area)이고 뒤에 오는 것이 주어와 동사를 갖춘 완전한 절이므로 관계부사 where를 써야 한다.

062　**정답**　how

해석　10시쯤에, 참석한 배심원단에서 20명의 사람들이 선정되어 재판 과정이 진행되는 절차를 판사가 설명해 주는 법정으로 가게 된다.

풀이　뒤에 나오는 문장이 완벽하므로 관계대명사 what은 올 수 없고, 접속사와 부사의 역할을 동시에 수행하는 관계부사 how를 써야 한다.

063　**정답**　whatever

해석　제일 처음은 "나는 태어났다"였고, 그 다음에는 좋아하는 것은 무엇이나 적을 수 있었다.

풀이　동사 put의 목적어가 되는 명사절을 이끄는 동시에 liked의 목적어 역할을 해야 하므로 복합 관계대명사인 whatever가 적절하다. however는 복합 관계부사로서 '아무리[어떻게] ～할지라도'의 의미이다.

064　**정답**　because of

해석　우리는 그것이 우리로 하여금 발전하도록 도와주는 정신적인 기술 때문에 철학을 연구한다.

풀이　뒤에 명사구인 the mental skills가 이어지고 있기 때문에 because of가 와야 한다. it helps us develop은 the mental skills를 수식하는 관계대명사절[형용사절]이므로 접속사를 사용할 필요는 없다. it helps ～ 앞에 목적격 관계대명사 that이 생략되었다고 보면 된다.

065　**정답**　Whether

해석　그 판단이 정확하든 그렇지 않든, 일단 당신이 그것을 받아들이면, 그것은 당신이 그 이웃에 대해 반응하는 방식에 영향을 줄 것이다.

풀이　'～인지 아닌지'의 뜻을 가지면서 뒤따르는 or not과 호응할 수 있는 접속사는 Whether이다.

066　**정답**　like

해석　사랑에 빠진다는 것은 마법의 구름에 싸이는 것과 같다.

풀이　뒤에 동명사구 being wrapped가 왔으므로 전치사 like를 써야 한다. alike는 '비슷한' 또는 '마찬가지로'의 의미를 가지며, 형용사로서 보어로 쓰이거나 또는 부사로 쓰인다.

6. 가정법, 조동사　　　　p.96

067　**정답**　could not

해석　적에 대한 특별한 방어 수단이 없다면, 많은 동물들이 살아남지 못할 것이다.

풀이　「if it were not for ～(～이 없다면[아니라면])」이라는 의미의 가정법 과거 구문이므로 주절에는 〈조동사의 과거형+동사원형〉을 쓴다.

068　**정답**　had turned

해석　만약 당신이 그날 화성을 향해서 빛을 보냈다면, 그것은 186초 후에 화성에 도착했을 것이다.

풀이　that day라는 과거에 일어나지 않은 일을 가정하고 있으므로 주절에는 가정법 과거완료 시제가 쓰였으며, 조건절은 〈had p.p.〉의 형태로 쓴다.

069　**정답**　were

해석　그는 배우들이 자기 연극 작품들을 뮤지컬 작품처럼 연기해 주기를 원했다.

풀이　주절과 같은 시점을 표현하고 있으므로 as if 다음에 가정법 과거로 표현해야 한다.

070　**정답**　could help

해석　다음 주 재고 조사에 관해 당신을 도와주고 싶지만, 그때까지 나는 진열창에 상품 진열을 하고 있을 것 같다.

풀이　현재 사실의 반대를 가정하고 있으므로 가정법 과거로 표현해야 한다.

071　**정답**　are

해석　당신은 그 책을 아직 읽어보지 못한 사람들을 위해 글을 쓰고 있다는 점을 기억해야 하고, 따라서 불명확한 설명을 제공하는 것은 세부적인 내용이 포함되지 않는다면 도움이 되지 못한다.

풀이　unless가 if ～ not의 부정의 뜻을 담고 있으므로 부정어구를 또 쓰면 의미가 맞지 않는다.

072　**정답**　had taken

해석　많은 목격자들은 그 사고가 횡단보도에서 일어났다고 주장했다.

풀이　'주장하다'라는 뜻의 insisted가 쓰였지만, 당위나 가정의 뜻이 아니고 있는 그대로의 사실을 표현하고 있으므로 that절의 동사에 반드시 동사원형이 오는 것은 아니다. 사고가 일어난 것이 먼저이므로 과거완료 시제로 쓴다.

073　**정답**　give

해석　그 신사는 그가 내 정직함에 대해 10달러 보상을 해야겠다고 제안했다.

풀이　제안을 나타내는 동사(propose) 다음의 that절에 '～해야 한다(should)'라는 의미가 있으므로 that절의 동사는 주어와 상관없이 《(should)+동사원형》을 쓴다.

074　**정답**　must

해석　경찰은 Baker 씨가 어제 저녁 자신의 아파트를 떠났음에 틀림없다고 추리했다.

풀이　'～했음에 틀림없다'라는 과거 사실에 대한 추측을 표현하는 것이므로 〈must have p.p.〉로 써야 한다.

075　**정답**　might

해석　새로운 과학적 증거는 공룡들이 파충류보다는 포유동물처럼 행동했던 온혈동물이었을지도 모른다는 것을 보여준다.

풀이　'～이었을 지도 모른다'라는 의미의 과거에 대한 추측을 표현할 때는 〈might[may] have p.p.〉를 쓴다.

076　**정답**　have

해석 나는 그에게 별로 주의를 기울이지 않은 것을 후회한다. 다시 말해서, 내가 그에게 더 많은 주의를 기울였어야 했다.
풀이 '~했어야 했는데 (하지 않았다)'라는 의미이므로 과거 사실에 대한 후회나 유감을 표현하는 〈should have p.p.〉로 쓴다.

7. 특수 구문
p.98

077 정답 sliding
해석 비상시에는 단추를 누르거나 레버를 내리누르거나 문을 옆으로 밀어서 여러분 스스로 문을 열어야 한다.
풀이 내용상 by에 이어지는 pushing a button, depressing a lever와 병렬구조를 이루어야 하므로 sliding이 적절하다.

078 정답 evaluate
해석 서평가로서 당신은 그 책이 이야기를 어떻게 전개해 나가는지에 대해 분석하고 글과 구성의 질을 평가한다.
풀이 주어 you의 동사가 되는 자리이므로 analyze와 병렬을 이루도록 evaluate가 되어야 한다.

079 정답 go
해석 그의 다음 목표는 자신이 사는 마을 전체에 충분한 에너지를 공급하는 것이며, 최종적으로 대학에 가는 것이다.
풀이 to provide ~와 to go ~의 병렬구조인데, 이런 구조에서는 뒤의 to는 종종 생략할 수 있으므로 go가 적절하다.

080 정답 to trees and birds
해석 나무와 새들보다는 주차장을 위해 엄청난 공간이 할당된다.
풀이 rather than 이하가 전치사구 to parking lots와 병렬을 이루는 구조이다. 병렬구조에서 뒤에 오는 to부정사의 to는 생략할 수 있지만 전치사 to는 생략하지 않는다.

081 정답 traveling
해석 먼 외지를 여행하다가 몸이 안 좋으면 따뜻한 비눗물에 화약을 조금 떨어뜨려 마셔 보라.
풀이 when you are traveling에서 주어와 be동사를 생략한 구조이다. 주어와 be동사가 생략되면 보통 분사나 형용사, 명사 등만 남는다.

082 정답 owned
해석 소는 비록 남성의 소유이기는 하지만, 그 남성의 모든 가족에게 속하는 것으로 여겨진다.
풀이 의미상의 주어인 The cattle이 소유되는 것이므로 수동을 나타내는 과거분사가 와야 한다. though they are owned by the man에서 주어와 be동사를 생략한 구문이다.

083 정답 does this enable
해석 이것은 우리가 특정 상황에 대한 반응을 선택할 수 있게 해 줄 뿐만 아니라, 상황을 창조하도록 장려하기도 한다.
풀이 Not only라는 부정어구가 문두에 왔으므로 주어와 동사를 도치시킨다. 일반동사 enables가 쓰였으므로 조동사 does를 주어 this 앞에 쓰고 뒤에는 동사원형 enable을 쓴 것이다.

084 정답 is a life
해석 당신이 기꺼이 노력을 쏟을 때만이 가치 있는 삶이 가능하다.
풀이 Only가 문두에 쓰였으므로 주어와 동사를 도치시켜야 한다. only는 '~만이 (그리고 나머지는 아닌)'라고 해석되므로 부정의 의미가 내포되어 있다고 볼 수 있다.

085 정답 do
해석 당신은 (짐을) 꾸릴 물건들이 실제로 가지고 있는 것만큼 많지 않다는 잘못된 생각을 갖고 있다.
풀이 as you really have many items to pack에서 공통 부분을 삭제하고 대동사를 쓴 형태이다. 일반동사 have를 받는 대동사이므로 조동사 do로 쓴다.

086 정답 it was eaten
해석 의사가 제일 먼저 알아야 할 사항에는 (환자가) 어떤 종류의 유독성 식물을 얼만큼 먹었는지와 그것을 언제 먹었고 그 식물의 어느 부분을 먹었는지에 관한 것이 포함된다.
풀이 동사 includes의 목적어 자리로서, what kind and how much ~와 병렬구조를 이루는 간접의문문이 와야 한다. 간접의문문은 〈의문사+주어+동사〉의 어순을 취한다.

087 정답 what comets are
해석 거의 모든 사람이 핼리혜성에 대해 들어봤지만, 대부분의 사람들은 혜성이 무엇인지 모른다.
풀이 know의 목적어로 쓰인 간접의문문이므로 〈의문사+주어+동사〉의 어순으로 써야 한다.

088 정답 rarely
해석 그는 최근의 사건들로 인한 충격으로 의기소침해져서 가장 친한 친구들에게조차 말을 거의 하지 않았다.
풀이 rare는 '드문'의 뜻을 가진 형용사이고 rarely는 '거의 ~하지 않는'의 부정의 뜻을 가진 부사이다. 문맥상 부정어구가 필요한 상황이다.

089 정답 no
해석 모두들 기꺼이 훈련에 참가는 했지만, 아무도 그것을 열심히 하지 않았다.
풀이 no는 명사 앞에 오는 형용사로 쓸 수 있지만 not은 형용사로 쓸 수 없다. 여기서처럼 no one 또는 none으로 써야 한다.

090 정답 nor
해석 우리의 방침은 우리 회사의 홍보부에서 나오지 않은 회사 정보에 관해서는 확인이나 부인을 일체 하지 않는 것이다.
풀이 「neither A nor B」 구문은 'A와 B 둘 다 아닌'의 뜻이다.

091 정답 not
해석 우리는 전에 항상 어딘가 머물 데를 발견해 왔다. 그렇다, 하지만 우리가 항상 그렇게 운이 좋지는 않을 수도 있다.
풀이 '항상 ~한 것은 아니다'라는 의미의 부분부정은 not always 형태로 쓴다.

092 정답 necessarily
해석 전문가들은 인도가 경제를 활성화시키기 위해서는 반드시 석유와 가스에만 의존하지 않아도 된다는 것을 인식하고 있다고 말한다.
풀이 '반드시 ~인 것은 아니다'는 뜻의 부분부정은 not necessarily로 표현한다.

093 정답 it develops
해석 치즈가 고유의 맛과 색깔을 갖게 되는 것은 바로 치즈가 숙성되는 기간 동안이다.
풀이 시간의 부사절 while cheese is ripening을 강조하는 「it is ~ that ...」 강조구문이다. 주절이 필요하므로 it develops를 써야 한다.

094 　정답　 much

해석　 비록 몇몇 사람들이 다른 사람들에 비해 훨씬 더 적은 자유 시간을 가지지만, 거의 모든 사람들은 베풀 수 있는 약간의 기회를 갖고 있다.

풀이　 비교급은 much, still, even, far 등으로 강조할 수 있으므로 much가 적절하다. very는 원급을 강조한다.

8. 관용 표현　　　　　　　　　　　p.101

095 　정답　 that

해석　 아이스하키는 종종 팀의 선수 숫자가 다른 상태에서 경기를 한다는 점에서 주요 스포츠와 다르다.

풀이　 '~라는 점에서'라는 뜻은 「in that ~」으로 표현한다.

096 　정답　 helping

해석　 우리의 이전의 논의에서 윤곽이 잡힌 문제들을 귀하께서 해결하는 데 도움이 되기를 고대합니다.

풀이　 '~를 고대하다'는 뜻의 look forward to에서 to는 전치사이므로 뒤에 동명사를 써야 한다.

097 　정답　 being

해석　 나는 내 신용카드 사용에 대해 요금이 부과되는 것에 강력히 반대한다.

풀이　 '~를 반대하다'는 뜻의 object to에서 to는 전치사이므로 뒤에 동명사를 써야 한다.

098 　정답　 creating

해석　 그녀는 이 정책이 회사들이 새로운 일자리를 창출하는 것을 막을 것이라고 말했다.

풀이　 A가 '~하는 것을 막다'의 뜻은 「prevent A from -ing」 형태로 쓴다.

099 　정답　 having

해석　 무슨 말인지 알겠어. 나도 6년간이나 이탈리아어를 공부해 왔는데 간단한 대화를 하는 데 어려움이 있어.

풀이　 '~하는 데 어려움을 겪다'는 뜻은 「have difficulty [trouble/hard time] -ing」의 형태로 쓴다.

100 　정답　 as

해석　 그는 아무리 열심히 공부할지라도 더 좋은 대학에는 갈 수 없다.

풀이　 '비록 ~ 일지라도'의 양보의 뜻은 「형용사/명사+as+주어+동사」의 형태로 쓴다.

Unit 02　어휘 추론

Example　 답 ⑤　　　　　　　　pp.102~103

소재　 지도자의 자질

전문해석　 지도자는 어떻게 사람들이 (자기가) 중요하다고 느끼게 하는가? 첫 번째로, 그들의 말을 듣는 것을 통해서이다. 여러분이 그들의 생각을 존중한다는 것을 알게 하고, 그들이 자신의 의견을 소리 내어 말하게 하라. 덤으로 여러분도 뭔가를 배울지도 모른다!

내 친구 중 한 명이 나에게 대기업의 최고 경영자에 대해 말해 준 적이 있는데, 그는 자신이 거느리고 있는 관리자 중 한 명에게, "당신이 나에게 말할 수 있는 것 중에 내가 전에 이미 생각해 본 적이 없는 것은 없어요. 내가 당신에게 묻지 않으면 당신이 생각하는 것을 나에게 절대로 말하지 마세요. 내 말 알아듣겠어요?"라고 말했다고 한다. 그 관리자가 틀림없이 느꼈을 자존감의 상실을 상상해 보라. 그 일은 그를 낙담시켜서 그의 업무 수행에 부정적인 영향을 미쳤음에 틀림없다. 반면 여러분이 누군가에게 (그 자신이) 아주 중요한 사람이라는 의식을 느끼게 하면, 그 사람은 의기양양해질 것이고 활력의 수준이 빠르게 증가할 것이다.

구문풀이

[1행] Let them [know {you respect their thinking}], and let them [voice their opinions].

: 두 개의 [ ]는 각각 앞에 있는 사역동사 let의 목적격 보어이다. { }는 know의 목적어 역할을 한다.

Do It Yourself　　　　　　　　pp.104~107

01 ⑤　　　**02** ③　　　**03** ⑤　　　**04** ①

01　답 ⑤

소재　 장거리 배낭여행 준비

전문해석　 대부분의 사람들은 만약 6개월간의 탐험을 시작하려 하면, 모든 가능한 난관에 대비하기 위해 많은 장비를 가져가야 할 것이라고 생각한다. 그러나 세계의 곳곳을 탐험해 본 전문 배낭여행자의 경험은 우리에게 그 정반대를 가르쳐 준다. 배낭여행이 길수록, 짐은 더 적게 지녀야 한다. 가벼운 짐을 지니고 4일 정도마다 다시 보충하는 것이 더 낫다. 보통의 배낭여행자가 10일 이상의 음식을 가지고 다니는 것은 견딜 수 없는 일이므로, 장거리 배낭여행자는 도중에 계속 다시 보충해야 한다.

정답풀이　 (A) 머릿속의 생각과는 정반대의 정보를 가르쳐 주는 것은 전문가의 경험에서 나오는 조언일 것이므로 experience(경험)가 적절하다.

(B) 배낭여행자의 경험이 가르쳐 주는 것은 짐을 많이 가져가야 한다는 우리의 생각과 반대되는 것, 즉 배낭여행이 길수록 짐을 더 적게 지녀야 한다는 것이므로 less(더 적게)가 적절하다.

(C) 짐을 가볍게 하고 음식을 도중에 보충하라는 것은 음식을 오래 지니고 다니는 것이 어렵다는 의미이므로 unbearable(견딜 수 없는)이 적절하다.

구문풀이

[7행] Since it's unbearable [{for an average backpacker} to carry more than 10 days of food], a long distance backpacker must re-supply along the way.

: it이 형식상의 주어이고 to부정사구인 [ ]가 내용상의 주어이다. { }는 to부정사구의 의미상의 주어를 나타낸다.

- **assume** 생각하다, 가정하다
- **a ton of** 많은
- **challenge** 난관, 어려움
- **explore** 탐험하다
- **opposite** 반대; 반대의
- **re-supply** 다시 보충하다
- **distance** 거리
- **expedition** 탐험, 원정
- **gear** 장비
- **backpacker** 배낭여행자
- **exact** 정확한
- **carry** 지니다
- **average** 보통의, 평균의
- **along the way** 도중에

02 답 ③

소재 산악 등반 경험

전문해석 산악 등반가인 나의 형은 한 번은 나와 내 친구를 13,776 피트의 Grand Teton으로 데리고 갔다. 그것은 무서운 경험이었다! 우리가 올라갈수록 그 산은 가파르게 변했다. 그 지점에서 만약 우리 중 한 명이 떨어지면 우리의 목숨을 구할 수 있도록 로프로 서로를 함께 묶었다. 그 로프는 내가 1,000피트 아래로 떨어져 죽는 것을 두 번이나 막아 주었다. 서로를 방해하고(→ 돕고) 로프에 의지함으로 인해 우리는 마침내 안전하게 정상에 도착했다. 만약 당신이 로프를 붙들어 매고 다른 사람의 힘을 빌린다면 인생에서 훨씬 더 많은 것을 해 낼 것이다. 로프를 더 많이 가질수록, 성공의 가능성은 더 커질 것이다.

정답풀이 필자의 경험처럼 산 정상에 안전하게 도착하기 위해서는 서로를 돕고 로프에 의지해야만 할 것이므로 ③ 'blocking(방해하다)'을 'helping(돕다)' 정도로 바꿔야 한다.

오답풀이

① climbed(올라갔다) → 위로 올라갈수록 가파르게 변할 것이므로 적절하다.

② fell(떨어지다) → 로프로 서로를 묶는 이유이므로 적절하다.

④ borrow(빌리다) → 산악 등반의 경우처럼 인생에서 더 많은 것을 이루기 위해서는 서로 돕는 자세가 필요하므로 다른 사람의 힘을 빌리는 것은 적절하다.

⑤ better(더 커지는) → 서로 도울수록 성공 가능성은 더 커지게 마련이므로 적절하다.

구문풀이

[8행] **The more** ropes you have, **the better** your chances are for success.

: 「the+비교급 ~, the+비교급 ...」 구문으로, '~하면 할수록 더 … 하다'의 의미이다.

- **mountain climber** 산악 등반가
- **tie** 묶다, 매다
- **keep A from -ing** A가 ~하는 것을 막다
- **rope up** 밧줄을 이용해 묶다
- **strength** 힘
- **terrifying** 무서운
- **save** 구하다
- **borrow** 빌리다
- **chance** 가능성

03 답 ⑤

소재 눈물을 인정하는 자세

전문해석 우리는 위대한 지도자들이 눈물을 통해 자신들의 열정, 취약함과 연민을 보여 주는 것을 목격해왔고, 흔히 우리의 반응은 실제로 그들과 더 큰 연결성을 느끼는 것이다. 있는 그대로의 감정을 목격하는 것은 말로만으로는 이루지 못할 방식으로 우리를 함께 연결할 수 있다. 부끄러움과 취약함에 관한 연구원이자 전문가인 Brene Brown은 취약해 질 수 있는 우리의 능력이 진심어린 삶을 사는 것의 핵심이라고 말한다. 관리자, 지도자, 그리고 동료로서 여러분이 눈물과 슬픔이 괜찮다는 것을 인정하는 것이 중요하다. 다른 사람들에게 이것을 보여줄 공간을 허용하는 것을 두려워하지 말고 상황이 발생할 경우 여러분 자신의 인간다움을 감출(→ 나타내 보일) 것을 두려워하지 마라.

정답풀이 눈물로 대표되는 취약함을 보여 주는 것은 자신의 나약함을 드러내는 것이 아니라 인간다움을 보여 주는 것이라는 내용의 글이다. 따라서 그러한 취약함을 드러내는 것을 두려워해서는 안 된다는 것이므로 ⑤ 'hide(감추다)'를 'reveal(드러내다)' 또는 'unveil(드러내다)' 정도로 바꿔야 한다.

오답풀이

① display(보여 주다) → 위대한 지도자들이 드러내는 눈물을 통해 그들과 더 큰 연결성을 느낀다는 맥락이므로 적절하다.

② raw(있는 그대로의) → 눈물은 있는 그대로의 감정이므로 적절하다.

③ vulnerable(취약한) → 진심어린 삶을 사는 것은 눈물을 인정하고 드러내는 것과 일맥상통한다고 볼 수 있으며, 눈물을 드러내는 것을 흔히 취약한 것으로 인식하므로 적절하다.

④ recognise(인정하다) → 눈물과 슬픔을 인정하는 자세가 필요하다는 맥락이므로 적절하다.

구문풀이

[5행] Researcher and expert on shame and vulnerability Brene Brown suggests [that **our capacity** {to be vulnerable} is the key to living a whole-hearted life].

: [ ]로 표시된 that절은 suggests의 목적어 역할을 하는 명사절이다. { }는 to부정사구로, our capacity를 수식한다.

- **witness** 목격하다
- **passion** 열정
- **connection** 연결, 연관
- **achieve** 이루다, 달성하다
- **shame** 부끄러움
- **whole-hearted** 진심의, 전적인
- **recognise** 인정하다
- **arise** 일어나다, 발생하다
- **display** 보여 주다, 드러내다
- **compassion** 연민, 동정
- **raw** 있는 그대로의, 날것의
- **expert** 전문가
- **capacity** 능력
- **colleague** 동료
- **humanness** 인간적임

04 답 ①

소재 기억을 향상하는 방법

전문해석 그림을 보는 것은 실제로 여러분의 뇌가 더 잘 기억하게 하는 데 도움이 된다. 작동 기억이라고도 불리는 단기 기억은 주로 시각 피질에 의존한다. 읽은 단어들은 우리 뇌에 의해 아주 빠르게 처리된다. 그것들은 그다지 오랫동안 머무르지 않는다. 하지만 뇌 속에 그림을 기록하는 것은 더 오래 걸린다. 이것은 무언가를 기억

하기 위해서 시간을 투자해야만 한다는 것을 의미한다. 따라서 그림을 보는 데 사용되는 시간이 더 많으면 많을수록, 그것에 대한 여러분의 기억은 <u>더 좋아진다</u>. 어떤 단어를 크게 말하는 것은 같은 일을 한다. 한 단어를 읽는 데 걸리는 시간보다 그것을 말하는 데 <u>더 오랜</u> 시간이 걸린다. 그로 인해 여러분은 그것을 크게 말할 때 그것을 더 잘 기억하게 된다. 그러므로 여러분이 막판에 벼락치기 공부를 하고 있을 때, 그림을 보고 어떤 것을 크게 말하라. 여러분의 기억과 여러분의 시험 점수가 여러분에게 고마워할 것이다.

정답풀이　(A) 단순히 읽기만 한 단어들은 우리 뇌에 의해 아주 빠르게 처리된다고 하였고, 뒤에서는 역접의 내용으로 뇌 속에 그림을 기록하는 것은 더 오래 걸린다고 하였으므로 읽은 단어들은 오래 머무르지 않는다는 흐름이 적절하다. 따라서 (A)에는 부정어 don't와 결합하여 stick이 들어가는 것이 적절하다.
(B) 무언가를 기억하기 위해서 시간을 투자해야만 한다고 했으므로 그림을 보는 데 사용되는 시간이 더 많을수록, 기억은 더 좋아질 것이라고 볼 수 있다. 따라서 better가 적절하다.
(C) 어떤 단어를 크게 말하면 그것을 더 잘 기억할 수 있다는 것은 그 단어를 읽는 것보다 말하는 데 오랜 시간이 걸렸다는 것을 의미한다고 볼 수 있다. 따라서 longer가 적절하다.

구문풀이

[9행] [It takes longer to speak a word] than it **does** to read it.
: [ ]의 「It takes+…(시간)+to부정사구」 구문은 '~하는 데 …의 시간이 걸리다' 정도로 해석한다. does는 반복되는 takes를 대신한다.

어휘풀이

- **actually** 실제로
- **rely on** ~에 의존하다
- **process** 처리하다
- **invest** 투자하다
- **short-term** 단기간의
- **visual** 시각의, 시각적인
- **record** 기록하다

A　01 인식하다　02 배출, 분비　03 인공의　04 파장, 분포 범위　05 environment　06 엉망, 혼돈　07 정돈하다　08 저항[반항]하다　09 전적으로, 완전히　10 realize　11 고마워하는, 감사하는　12 이기적인　13 sound　14 좌절한　15 낙담한, 낙심한　16 튀어나온 부분, 둔덕　17 무례하게　18 화를 돋우는, 선동적인　19 도전적인　20 불안정한

B　01 Whether I actually liked living in a messy room or not
02 who are centered on their own narrow selfish desires
03 to make yourself feel good
04 Nor is it to suggest

C　01 자존감　02 부정적으로　03 빠르게　04 탐험, 원정　05 장비　06 explore　07 거리　08 무서운　09 묶다, 매다　10 빌리다　11 힘　12 passion　13 연민, 동정　14 이루다, 달성하다　15 expert　16 능력　17 동료　18 ~에 의존하다　19 시각의, 시각적인　20 처리하다

D　01 it's unbearable for an average backpacker to carry
02 the better your chances are
03 our capacity to be vulnerable
04 It takes longer to speak a word

Part 4 빈칸 추론

Unit 01 빈칸 추론(한 단어/두 단어)

Example 답 ①   pp.112~113

소재 인간의 창의성

전문해석 창의력은 우리가 일반적으로 인간만이 유일하게 가지고 있다고 간주하는 능력이다. 인류 역사를 통틀어, 우리는 지구상에서 가장 창의적인 존재였다. 새는 둥지를 틀 수 있고, 개미는 개미탑을 쌓을 수 있지만, 지구상의 어떤 다른 종도 우리 인간이 보여주는 창의력 수준에 가까이 도달하지는 못한다. 하지만, 불과 지난 10년 만에 우리는 로봇 개발처럼, 컴퓨터로 놀라운 것을 할 수 있는 능력을 습득하였다. 2010년대의 인공 지능의 급속한 발전으로, 컴퓨터는, 몇 가지를 언급하자면, 이제 얼굴을 인식하고, 언어를 번역하고, 여러분을 대신해 전화를 받고, 시를 쓸 수 있으며, 세계에서 가장 복잡한 보드게임에서 선수들을 이길 수 있다. 갑작스럽게, 우리는 창의적인 우리의 능력이 경쟁할 상대가 없지 않게 되는 가능성에 직면해야 할 것이다.

구문풀이

[8행] All of a sudden, we must face **the possibility** [that **our ability** {to be creative} is not unrivaled].

: [ ]는 앞의 the possibility와 동격을 이루는 명사절이다. { }는 our ability를 수식하는 형용사적 용법의 to부정사구이다.

Do It Yourself   pp.114~117

01 ①   02 ③   03 ③   04 ⑤

01 답 ①

소재 두려움을 떨쳐내고 지금 하고 싶은 일을 하는 것

전문해석 용기 있는 것에 관해 여러분의 마음을 바꿀 만한 충고를 하나 하겠다. 의사가 여러분에게 이제 살 수 있는 날이 6개월뿐이고, 이제껏 하고 싶었던 모든 일을 해보기를 권했다고 가정해 보자. 여러분은 무엇을 하겠는가? 스카이다이빙이나 절벽 등반을 하거나, 혹은 한 달 동안 숲속에서 혼자 살아 보기를 늘 원했지만 다칠까 두려웠는가? 지금 그 일들을 시도한다면 무엇이 달라지겠는가? 여러분은 거의 틀림없이 그것을 헤쳐 나갈 것이고, 그것이 남아 있는 시간을 풍요롭게 해 줄 것이다. 밖으로 나가서 모든 두려움에 용감하게 맞섰노라고 말하는 게 낫지 않겠는가? 왜 사형 선고를 받을 때까지 기다리는가? 그것이 여러분에게 그렇게 중요하다면, 지금 하라.

정답풀이 스카이다이빙, 절벽 등반, 숲속에서 한 달 동안 혼자 살

기 등을 평소에 하고 싶었지만 두려워서 하지 못했다면 모든 두려움을 떨쳐내고 지금 해보는 것이 삶을 풍요롭게 해 줄 것이라고 말하고 있으므로, 필자는 ① '용기 있는 것'에 대해 한 가지 충고를 하는 것이다.

오답풀이

② 다른 사람을 돕는 것 → 언급되지 않았다.

③ 친구를 사귀는 것 → 언급되지 않았다.

④ 건강을 되찾는 것 → 지문의 'you have six months to live'라는 내용에 의해 유도될 수 있는 오답이다.

⑤ 환자를 격려하는 것 → 의사가 하는 말을 가정해보라는 내용은 있지만 환자를 격려하는 상황은 아니다.

구문풀이

[2행] Suppose [that your doctor said {that you **have** six months to live} and **recommended** {that you **do** everything you ever wanted to do}].

: [ ]는 Suppose의 목적어에 해당하는 명사절이다. 첫 번째 { }는 said의 목적어에 해당하는 명사절이며, 과거형인 said 다음에 have가 쓰인 것은 현재에도 지속되는 일이므로 시제 일치를 시키지 않은 것이다. 두 번째 { }는 recommended의 목적어에 해당하는 명사절이다. recommend(권하다)는 주장하다(insist), 명령하다(order, command), 요구하다(demand, require), 제안하다(suggest) 등의 의미를 가진 동사들과 함께, that절의 내용이 '~해야 한다' 또는 '~하는 것이 좋겠다'라는 당위의 의미를 가질 때 〈주어+(should) 동사원형〉의 형태를 취한다. 여기서는 do 앞에 should가 생략되었고 동사원형이 쓰인 것으로 볼 수 있다. 이때, should가 생략되더라도 that절의 주어의 인칭, 수에 상관 없이 동사원형이 온다.

어휘풀이

- suppose 가정하다
- sky dive 스카이다이빙을 하다
- cliff 절벽
- harm 다치게 하다, 해를 가하다
- certainly 틀림없이
- enrich 풍요롭게 하다
- fear 두려움
- recommend 권하다, 추천하다
- climb 오르다, 등반하다
- in the woods 숲에서
- attempt 시도하다
- live through ~을 헤쳐 나가다
- face 맞서다, 대면[직면]하다

02 답 ③

소재 대다수 과학자들이 창의적이지 않은 이유

전문해석 생각은 본질적으로 생존 기계이다. 정보를 수집하고, 저장하고, 분석하며, 다른 생각에 대한 공격과 수비를 하는 것, 이것은 생각이 잘 하는 것이지만, 전혀 창의적이지는 않다. 모든 진정한 예술가들은 생각이 없는 상태, 즉 내적인 고요함 속에서 창작을 한다. 심지어 위대한 과학자들조차도 그들의 창의적인 돌파구는 마음의 정적의 시간에서 생겨났다고 말했다. 아인슈타인을 포함한 미국의 가장 유명한 수학자들을 대상으로 그들의 작업 방식을 알아내기 위한 전국적인 조사의 놀라운 결과는 생각은 "창의적인 행동의 짧고, 결정적인 단계에서 단지 부수적인 역할만 할 뿐이다."라는 것이다. 그래서 나는 대다수의 과학자들이 창의적이지 않은 단순한 이유

는 그들이 생각하는 방법을 몰라서가 아니라 생각을 멈추는 방법을 모르기 때문이라고 말하고 싶다.

 예술가들과 과학자들의 창의성은 생각이 없는 상태와 정적의 시간에서 생겨났다고 했으므로, 대다수의 과학자들이 창의적이지 않은 이유는 ③ '생각을 멈추는' 방법을 모르기 때문이라고 하는 것이 가장 적절하다.

① 자신들의 생각을 정리하다 → 글의 핵심과 상반된다.
② 사회적으로 상호작용하다 → 지문의 내용과 무관하다.
④ 정보를 모으다 → 지문의 내용과 무관하다.
⑤ 자신들의 상상력을 이용하다 → 생각을 하지 않는 것에 대한 글이므로 핵심과 상반된다.

[5행] Even great scientists have reported [that their creative breakthrough came at a time of mental quietude].
: [ ]는 have reported의 목적어로 쓰인 명사절이다.

· essentially 본질적으로
· attack 공격
· gather 수집하다, 모으다
· analyze 분석하다
· breakthrough 돌파구, 획기적인 것
· nationwide 전국적인
· brief 짧은, 간결한
· phase 단계, 국면
· survival 생존
· defense 수비, 방어
· store 저장하다
· stillness 고요함
· mental 마음의, 정신적인
· inquiry 조사, 질문
· decisive 결정적인
· majority 다수

03 답 ③

 고객 서비스 지침이 유연할 필요성

 대부분의 회사들이 거래하거나 고객에게 서비스를 제공하는 것에 대한 지침을 세워 놓았다. 하지만 지침이라는 것은 영구불변한 규칙이 아니라 단지 길잡이에 불과하다는 것을 기억해야 한다. 지침은 새로운 고객 보다는 기존의 고객을 위해 훨씬 더 쉽게 바꿀 수 있도록 허용될 필요가 있다. 고객은 여러분이 자신들의 기관 내부로부터 추가적인 거래를 확보하는 것을 더 쉽게 만들어 주므로 여러분은 그들이 여러분에게 그 거래를 주는 것을 최대한 쉽게 만들 필요가 있다. 판매 생산력을 높이기 위해서 여러분은 유연할 필요가 있다. 예를 들어, 여러분 회사의 지침이 개인적인 만남에서 제품 혹은 서비스를 선전하는 것이지만 여러분의 고객이 만날 시간이 없다고 하면, (만나는 것) 대신에 전화 회의를 가지는 것을 시도해보라.

 지침은 영구불변한 규칙이 아니라 길잡이에 불과하므로 훨씬 더 쉽게 바꿀 수 있어야 하며, 고객이 거래를 주는 것을 쉽게 만들도록 해야 한다는 내용이다. 결국 지침을 유연하고 융통성있게 적용하라는 내용이므로, 빈칸에는 ③ '유연할'이 들어가는 것이 가장 적절하다.

① 정직할 → 지문의 내용과 무관하다.
② 구체적일 → 지문의 핵심과 상반된다.
④ 창조적일 → 지문의 내용과 무관하다.
⑤ 영감을 줄 → 지문의 내용과 무관하다.

[5행] Customers [make **it** easier for you {to secure additional business from within their organizations}], so you need to [make **it** as easy as possible for them {to give you that business}].
: 두 개의 [ ]는 모두 「make+it(형식상의 목적어)+for+의미상 주어+to부정사구(내용상의 목적어)」 구문으로, 각각의 { }가 내용상의 목적어이다.

· set ~ in place ~을 지정하다
· market 거래하다, 매매하다
· permanent 영원한, 불변한
· existing 기존의
· additional 추가의
· productivity 생산력, 생산성
· instead 대신에
· guideline 지침
· customer 고객
· allow 허용[허락]하다
· secure 확보하다
· organization 기관, 조직
· conference 회의

04 답 ⑤

 침팬지가 거울에 비친 자신을 인식하는가에 대한 실험

 미국의 심리학자 Gordon Gallup은 한 무리의 어린 침팬지에게 거울 하나를 주었다. 처음에 그들은 마치 다른 침팬지들을 보고 있는 것처럼 반응했지만, 며칠 후 그들은 자신들의 입속을 들여다보거나 자신들의 몸에서 평상시에 보기 어려운 다른 부분을 점검하기 위해 그것(거울)을 사용했다. 침팬지들이 이렇게 행동하는 것을 보는 것은 분명히 인상적이었다. 그들이 자신들의 이빨을 쑤시고 우스꽝스런 얼굴을 지어 보이는 방식으로 보건대, 그들이 자신을 인식하는 것은 분명해 보였지만, 우리가 확신을 할 수 있는가? 알아내기 위해, Gallup은 그들을 마취시키고 한쪽 눈 위와 반대편 귀 위에 두 개의 빨간 색 점을 눈에 띄도록 그렸다. 그들이 깨어났을 때, 그는 그들이 거울을 볼 수 있게 하였다. 여러분과 나는 그러한 상황에서 즉시 그 표시들을 보고 아마 만지거나 문질러 지워버리려고 할 것인데, 침팬지들도 그렇게 했다.

 지문의 전반부에서는 거울을 보던 침팬지들이 자신을 관찰했다는 내용이 나오고 뒤에 나오는 실험에서는 마취에서 깨어난 침팬지들이 자신들의 얼굴에 표시된 빨간 점을 인식하고 문지르거나 지우려고 했다는 내용이 나온다. 그러므로 빈칸에는 침팬지들이 자신의 모습을 ⑤ '인식하는'이라는 말이 들어가는 것이 적절하다.

① 속이는 → 침팬지들의 행동이 자신을 속이는 것은 아니다.
② 보호하는 → 자신을 보호할 용도로 거울을 사용한 것은 아니다.
③ 아름답게 하는 → 거울을 보고 몸을 치장하는 내용은 아니다.
④ 즐겁게 하는 → 'make funny faces'로 인해 유도될 수 있는 오답이다.

[2행] At first, they reacted [**as though** they were seeing other chimpanzees], but after a few days they were using it [**to look** inside their mouths or **to inspect** other normally hard-to-see parts of their bodies].

: 첫 번째 [ ]는 '마치 ~처럼'이라는 의미의 as though가 이끄는 부사절이며, 두 번째 [ ]는 '~하기 위하여'라는 목적을 나타내는 to부정사구이다. to look과 to inspect는 병렬을 이룬다.

[6행] **It** seems obvious from the way {they pick their teeth and make funny faces} [that they recognize themselves], but can we be sure?

: It은 형식상의 주어이고 [ ]가 내용상의 주어이다. { }는 the way를 수식하는 관계절로, '~하는 방식'으로 해석한다.

어휘풀이

- psychologist 심리학자
- inspect 점검하다, 조사하다
- impressive 인상적인
- pick one's teeth 이를 쑤시다
- spot 반점, 장소
- cheat 속이다
- react 반응하다
- normally 평상시에, 보통
- obvious 눈에 띄는, 분명한
- be sure 확신하다
- rub off ~을 문질러 지우다
- entertain 즐겁게 하다

Unit 02 빈칸 추론(짧은 어구)

Example 답 ① pp.118~119

소 재 1부터 숫자 세기와 0부터 숫자 세기

전문해석 0부터 숫자를 세는 것에는 중대한 문제가 있다. 탁자에 몇 개의 사과가 있는지를 판단하는 것처럼, 수를 세어 대상의 수를 판단하기 위해, 많은 아이들은 첫 번째 사과를 만지거나 가리킨 후 "하나"라고 말하고, 그리고 나서 두 번째 사과로 옮겨가서 "둘"이라고 말하며, 모든 사과를 셀 때까지 이런 방식으로 계속 할 것이다. 만약 0부터 시작하면, 아무것도 만지지 않고 "영"이라고 말해야 하지만, 그 이후로는 사과를 만지기 시작하며 "하나, 둘, 셋" 등으로 말해야 할 것이다. 이것은 매우 혼란스러울 수 있는데, 그 이유는 언제 만지고 언제 만지지 않아야 하는지를 강조할 필요가 있을 수도 있기 때문이다. 만약 한 아이가 우연히 "영"이라고 말하며 사과 하나를 만진다면, 사과의 총 개수는 한 개만큼 부족할 것이다.

구문풀이

[4행] If we start at 0, [we would have to touch nothing and say "zero,"] but then [we would have to start {touching apples} and {calling out "one, two, three" and so on}].

: 두 개의 [ ]는 등위접속사 but에 의해 병렬로 연결된 주절이다. 두 번째 [ ] 안의 { }는 모두 start의 목적어 역할을 하는 동명사구로, and에 의해 병렬로 연결되었다.

[7행] [If a child accidentally touches an apple {while saying "zero,"}] then [the total number of apples will be off by 1].

: 첫 번째 [ ]는 조건의 부사절이고, 그 안의 { }는 분사구문으로, while과 saying 사이에 the child is가 생략되었다고 볼 수 있다. 두 번째 [ ]는 문장의 주절이다.

Do It Yourself pp.120~123

01 ②　　　02 ③　　　03 ④　　　04 ①

01 답 ②

소 재 Theseus의 배

전문해석 Theseus는 아테네 사람들에게 위대한 영웅이었다. 그가 전쟁을 마치고 집으로 돌아왔을 때, 그와 그의 병사들을 태우고 다녔던 배는 매우 소중히 여겨져, 시민들은 그 배의 낡고 썩은 널빤지를 새로운 나무 조각으로 교체하면서, 그 배를 여러 해 동안 계속 보존했다. Plutarch가 철학자들에게 하는 질문은 이것이다. 수리된 배는 여전히 Theseus가 타고 항해했던 바로 그 배인가? 널빤지 하나를 제거하여 교체하는 것은 차이가 없을 수도 있지만, 모든 널빤지가 교체되었을 때도 여전히 그러할 수 있을까? 일부 철학자들은 그 배는 모든 부분의 총합이어야 한다고 주장한다. 그러나 만일 이것이 사실이라면, 그 배가 항해하는 동안 이리저리 밀쳐져 작은 조각들을 잃었을 때, 그것은 이미 Theseus의 배가 아니게 되었을 것이다.

정답풀이 Theseus의 배에서 낡고 썩은 널빤지를 새로운 널빤지로 교체했더라도 그것이 여전히 Theseus의 그 배인지, 혹은 항해하는 동안 조각을 잃었을 때 이미 Theseus의 그 배가 아니라고 봐야 할지에 관한 철학적 접근을 다룬 내용이다. 후자는 결국 배의 모든 부분을 그 배 전체를 이루는 특성으로 보고 있는 것이므로, 빈칸에는 ② '모든 부분의 총합'이 들어가는 것이 가장 적절하다.

오답풀이

① 승리를 상기시키는 것 → Theseus에 관한 일부 내용에 불과함
③ 의도된 용도에 적합한 → 지문의 내용과 무관함
④ 국가의 재산 → 배를 소중히 여겼다는 내용은 있으나, 직접적 관련은 없음
⑤ 오랜 시간 동안 주위에 → 지문의 내용과 무관함

구문풀이

[10행] But if this is true, then [as the ship **got pushed** around during its journey and lost small pieces], [it **would** already **have stopped being** the ship of Theseus].

: 첫 번째 [ ]는 시간의 부사절이며, got pushed는 「get+과거분사」 형태로 수동임을 나타낸다. 두 번째 [ ]에 가정법 과거완료 시제 〈would have+과거분사〉가 쓰였으며, 「stop -ing」는 '~(하는 것)을 멈추다[그만두다]'의 의미이다.

어휘풀이

- Theseus 테세우스(그리스 신화 속의 영웅)

· treasure 소중히 여기다
· preserve 보존하다
· rotten 썩은
· philosopher 철학자
· sail 항해하다
· argue 주장하다
· townspeople (특정 도시의) 시민
· replace 교체하다
· Plutarch 플루타르크(그리스의 철학자)
· repaired 수리된
· remove 제거하다, 없애다
· journey 항해, 여행

02 답 ③

소 재 정보를 담은 미래의 일상용품

전문해석 머지않은 미래에 신발, 카펫, 칫솔과 같은 일상용품들이 정보를 수집하는 기술을 포함하게 될 것이다. 그러면 여러분은 이런 용품들을 개인전용으로 할 수 있는데, 그것들로 하여금 색과 같은 물리적 상태를 변화시키거나 여러분의 그날그날의 기분에 반응하게 할 것이다. 그것들은 또한 다른 물건들과 자료를 교환할 수도 있고 다른 사람들에게 정보를 보낼 수도 있을 것이다. 예를 들어, 만약 여러분의 칫솔이 폐암의 조짐을 감지하면 여러분의 호흡을 분석하고 의사와의 진료 약속을 예약할 수 있을 것이다. 다시 말해, 한때는 그저 평범한 물건이었던 것이 점차 네트워크로 연결되고 지능화될 것이다. 제조업자들은 여러분에게 다른 서비스들을 팔기 위해, 혹은 "나만의 것이라는 경험"을 높이기 위해 이런 스마트 제품들에 의해 만들어지는 정보를 사용할 것이다.

정답풀이 미래의 일상용품들은 정보를 수집하는 기술을 포함해서 자료를 교환할 수도 있고, 다른 사람들에게 정보를 보낼 수도 있는데, 그 예로 칫솔은 폐암의 조짐을 감지하여 의사와의 진료 약속을 예약할 수 있다는 내용의 글이다. 따라서 빈칸에는 ③ '네트워크로 연결되고 지능화 될'이 들어가는 것이 가장 적절하다.

오답풀이
① 변하기 쉽고 위험한 → 지문에서 미래의 일상용품에 대하여 긍정적으로 서술하고 있으므로 오답이다.
② 지속가능하고 감당할 수 있는 → 자료를 교환하고 정보를 보낼 수도 있다는 내용에서 벗어난다.
④ 불안전하고 의미 없는 → 칫솔이 폐암을 감지하면 의사와의 진료 약속을 예약할 수 있다는 예시에서 알 수 있듯, 오히려 안전하고 의미 있을 것이므로 오답이다.
⑤ 복잡하고 고립된 → 자료를 교환하고 정보를 보낼 수 있다는 것은 고립되는 것과는 거리가 멀다.

구문풀이
[3행] You will then be able to personalize these objects, [allowing them to {change physical state like color} or {respond to your daily mood}].
: [ ]는 연속동작의 분사구문으로 'and allow ~'로 바꿔 쓸 수 있다. allow 뒤에는 〈목적어+to부정사(구)〉 형태가 이어지며 두 개의 { }가 to에 병렬로 연결되어 있다.
[11행] Manufacturers will use **the information** [generated by these smart products {to (sell you other services) or (enhance your "ownership experience)}]."
: [ ]는 앞의 the information을 수식하는 과거분사구로,

generated 앞에 〈주격 관계대명사+be동사〉 which is가 생략되었다. { }는 목적을 나타내는 to부정사구이며 두 개의 ( )가 to에 병렬로 연결되어 있다.

어휘풀이
· not-too-distant 머지않은
· contain 포함하다, 담고 있다
· personalize 개인전용으로 하다, 개인화하다
· physical state 물리적 상태
· respond to ~에 반응하다
· be capable of ~할 수 있다
· book 예약하다
· detect 감지하다, 인지하다
· ordinary 평범한
· manufacturer 제조업자
· enhance 높이다, 향상하다
· object 용품, 물건, 사물
· exchange 교환하다
· analyze 분석하다
· appointment 약속
· lung cancer 폐암
· increasingly 점차, 점점
· generate 만들다, 생성하다
· ownership 소유권, 나만의 것

03 답 ④

소 재 깊이 몰두하는 아이들

전문해석 아이들은 때때로 깊은 집중력을 보여준다. 나는 다섯 살 난 Peter가 유치원에 있는 두 소녀가 탁자 위에서 연극을 하려고 인형을 갖고 노는 것을 지켜보고 있는 것을 생각한다. 그 소녀들은 깊이 몰두해 있었고 그도 그랬다. 그날따라 공교롭게도 선생님들 중 한 분이 자신의 방에서 타는 냄새를 감지한 후에 소방서에 전화를 걸어서 소방관들이 학교(유치원)에 왔다. 세 대의 소방차가 소리를 울리며 학교(유치원) 주차장으로 들어섰다. Peter의 친구 Benjamin이 "Peter, Peter, 소방차가 이곳에 왔어!"라고 소리치면서 그에게 달려왔다. 그러나 Peter는 소녀들이 연극을 하는 장면에 너무 몰두하여 반응을 하지 않았다. Benjamin이 다시 시도해 보았으나 결과는 마찬가지였다. 그는 어깨를 으쓱하고 소방관들이 도착한 것을 보기 위해 창가로 다시 달려갔다.

정답풀이 Peter가 소방차가 왔다고 소리치며 달려오는 친구 Benjamin에게 반응을 보이지 않은 것은 여자 아이들의 인형극 장면에 깊이 몰두하고 있었기 때문이다. 또한 글에 쓰인 immersed, intent 등의 어휘는 빈칸에 들어갈 concentration과 맥락이 통한다. 따라서 빈칸에는 ④ '깊은 집중력'이 들어가는 것이 가장 적절하다.

오답풀이
① 통찰력의 부족 → 통찰력에 관한 글은 아니다.
② 반복하는 습관 → 습관에 관한 글은 아니다.
③ 성인 같은 뇌 활동 → 집중력이 뇌 활동이라고 볼 수 있지만 성인과 관련된 것이라는 내용은 없다.
⑤ 행동에서의 변화 → Peter는 집중하는 행동을 지속하고 있었다고 볼 수 있으므로 글의 내용과 어긋난다.

구문풀이
[1행] I think of five-year-old Peter [**watching** two girls in the kindergarten **using** dolls to act out a scene on a tabletop].
: [ ]는 think of의 목적어로 쓰인 동명사구이며, 앞의 five-year-

old Peter는 watching의 의미상의 주어이다. 지각동사 watch 뒤에 목적격 보어로 사용되는 현재분사 using은 동작의 진행을 나타낸다.

[8행] But Peter was **so** intent on [watching the scene the girls were acting out] **that** he did not respond.

: 「so ~ that ...」 구문은 '너무 ~해서 …하다의 의미이다. [ ]는 전치사 on의 목적어로 쓰인 동명사구이다.

- **display** 보여주다, 전시하다, 발휘하다
- **act out** 행하다, (극에서) ~을 연기하다
- **tabletop** 탁자의 윗면
- **be immersed** 몰두[열중]하다
- **roar** 큰 소리를 내며 움직이다
- **result** 결과
- **kindergarten** 유치원
- **scene** 장면
- **deeply** 깊이
- **notice** 알아채다, 인지하다
- **intent** 열심인, 전념하고 있는
- **shrug** (어깨를) 으쓱하다

04 답 ①

소재 의학연구에 있어 과학자들의 협력의 필요성

전문해석 분명 어느 정도의 의학연구는 필수이다. 그것이 없다면, 우리는 소아마비와 같은 질병에 대한 예방접종이 없고, 항생제와 같은 약품도 없으며, 방사선과 같은 치료법도 없을 것이다. 그럼에도 불구하고, 의학연구 분야는 매우 경쟁이 치열하고 이것이 또한 재정의 손실을 초래하기도 한다. 예를 들어, 현재 에이즈 바이러스에 대해 행해지고 있는 연구를 보자. 이 분야에서, 돈이 낭비되고 있다는 것이 주장되고 있다. 과학자들은 똑같은 최종의 목적을 향해, 즉 에이즈에 대한 치료법을 찾기 위해 독립적으로 연구하고 있으며, 그들은 그 과정에서 유명해지려는 똑같은 희망을 갖고 있다. 만약 이런 과학자들이 힘을 합친다면, 확실히 좀 더 생산적이 될 것이며 비용도 덜 들 것이다.

정답풀이 전반부에서는 '의학연구'에 대한 필요성을 이야기하지만, 그 이후부터 경쟁적이며 독립적인 연구로 인하여 재정적인 손실이 초래된다고 지적하면서 과학자들이 힘을 모으기를 강조하고 있다. 따라서 빈칸에는 ① '힘을 합친다'가 들어가는 것이 가장 적절하다.

② 새로운 약품을 개발한다 → 약품에 관한 언급은 있지만 글의 핵심에서는 벗어난다.

③ 고정된 생각에 도전한다 → 전혀 무관한 내용이다.

④ 시장조사를 한다 → 시장조사에 대한 언급은 없다.

⑤ 더 많은 의학 자료를 수집한다 → 의학연구에 관한 글이지만 자료 수집에 대한 내용은 언급되지 않았다.

[5행] Take, for example, the current research [being conducted on the AIDS virus].

: [ ]는 앞의 the current research를 수식하는 현재분사구이다. being 앞에는 which[that] is가 생략되어 있다. the current research가 conducted의 대상이므로 수동태가 쓰인 것이다.

[7행] The scientists are working independently towards **the same ultimate goal** — [to find a cure for AIDS], and they have **the same hope** [of becoming famous in the process].

: 첫 번째 [ ]는 앞의 the same ultimate goal과 동격이고, 두 번째 [ ]는 앞의 the same hope와 동격이다.

[10행] Surely it would be more productive and less costly [if these scientists joined forces together].

: 가정법 과거 시제 〈주어+조동사의 과거형+동사원형 ~, if+주어+과거동사 ~〉의 문장이다.

- **essential** 필수의, 가장 중요한
- **antibiotics** 항생제
- **field** 분야
- **result in** ~의 결과를 낳다
- **loss** 손실
- **conduct** 수행하다, 실행하다
- **ultimate** 최종의, 궁극적인
- **productive** 생산적인, 다산의
- **vaccination** 백신접종
- **treatment** 치료, 처리
- **competitive** 경쟁의, 경쟁적인
- **financial** 재정의, 금융의
- **current** 현재의
- **independently** 독립적으로
- **cure** 치료(법)
- **costly** 비용이 많이 드는

---

  pp.124~125

A 01 (생물의) 종 02 10년 03 번역하다 04 복잡한 05 climb 06 절벽 07 풍요롭게 하다 08 수비, 방어 09 수집하다, 모으다 10 돌파구, 획기적인 것 11 짧은, 간결한 12 영원한, 불변한 13 기존의 14 확보하다 15 회의 16 psychologist 17 점검하다, 조사하다 18 반점, 장소 19 cheat 20 즐겁게 하다

B 01 that, 창의적인 우리의 능력이 경쟁할 상대가 없지 않다: the possibility와 동격을 이루는 명사절을 이끄는 접속사 that이 적절하다.

02 do, 여러분이 해보기를 권했다: 권유를 나타내는 recommend의 목적어로 쓰인 that절의 동사 형태로 《(should+) 동사원형》이 온다.

03 was, 아인슈타인을 포함한 미국의 가장 유명한 수학자들: 주어의 핵 The surprising result가 단수이므로, 동사는 수 일치시킨 was가 적절하다.

04 did, 침팬지들도 그렇게 했다: 앞에 나온 일반동사 'see ~ try ~ rub ~'을 대신하는 동사가 필요하므로 be동사 were가 아닌 did가 적절하다.

C 01 판단하다, 결정하다 02 혼란시키는 03 강조하다 04 우연히 05 소중히 여기다 06 보존하다 07 제거하다, 없애다 08 journey 09 개인전용으로 하다, 개인화하다 10 약속 11 평범한 12 제조업자 13 유치원 14 몰두[열중]하다 15 큰 소리를 내며 움직이다 16 (어깨를) 으쓱하다 17 항생제 18 경쟁의, 경쟁적인 19 수행하다, 실행하다 20 ultimate

D 01 why → that: 문맥상 「so ~ that ... (매우 ~해서 …하다)」 구문이 자연스러우므로, that으로 고쳐야 한다.

02 if it will detect → if it detects: 조건의 부사절에서는 현재 시제가 미래 시제를 대신하므로 will detect를 detects로 고쳐야 한다.

03 because of → because: 뒤에 이어지는 one of the teachers ~ in her room이 절의 형태이므로, 전치사 of가 빠진 접속사 because로 고쳐야 한다.
04 more productively → more productive: 앞에 있는 be동사의 보어 자리이므로, 형용사 productive로 고쳐야 한다. 뒤에 오는 형용사 costly와도 병렬을 이루어야 한다.

Unit 03 빈칸 추론(긴 어구/어절)

Example 답 ⑤ pp.126~127

소 재 무리를 따르는 사람들의 행동

전문해석 어떤 식당이 대체로 붐빈다는 것을 알게 되면 우리가 그 식당에서 식사할 가능성이 더 크다. 아무도 우리에게 어떤 식당이 좋다고 말하지 않을 때조차도, 우리의 무리 행동은 우리의 의사를 결정한다. 여러분이 두 개의 텅 빈 식당 쪽으로 걸어가고 있다고 가정하자. 여러분은 어느 곳에 들어가야 할지 모른다. 하지만, 갑자기 여러분은 여섯 명의 무리가 둘 중 하나의 식당으로 들어가는 것을 보게 된다. 여러분은 텅 빈 식당 혹은 나머지 식당, 둘 중 어느 식당에 들어갈 가능성이 더 높겠는가? 대부분의 사람들은 사람이 있는 식당에 들어갈 것이다. 여러분과 친구가 그 식당에 들어간다고 가정하자. 이제, 그 식당 안에는 여덟 명이 있다. 다른 사람들은 한 식당은 텅 비어 있고 다른 식당은 여덟 명이 있는 것을 보게 된다. 그래서 그들도 다른 여덟 명과 같은 행동을 하기로 결정한다.

구문풀이

[1행] We are more likely to eat in a restaurant [**if** we know {that it is usually busy}].
: [ ]는 조건을 나타내는 if가 이끄는 부사절이고, { }는 know의 목적어로 쓰인 명사절이다.

[7행] Others see [that **one** restaurant is empty and **the other** has eight people in it].
: [ ]는 see의 목적어로 쓰인 명사절이다. 두 개를 열거할 때, 하나는 one, 나머지는 the other로 표현한다.

Do It Yourself pp.128~131

01 ②   02 ①   03 ①   04 ②

01 답 ②

소 재 비교 근거의 유무에 따른 음악적 평가

전문해석 때때로 누군가는 비교할 만한 근거가 거의 없기 때문에 '가장 위대하다'고 칭송받는다. 예를 들어, 바이올리니스트 Jan Kubelik는 그의 첫 번째 미국 순회공연 기간 동안 '가장 위대하다'

고 칭송받았지만, 1923년에 기획자 Sol Hurok이 그를 미국으로 다시 데려왔을 때, 몇몇 사람들은 그가 실력이 약간 떨어졌다고 생각했다. 그러나 바이올리니스트 Mischa Elman의 아버지인 Sol Elman은 다르게 생각했다. "친애하는 친구들이여, Kubelik는 그가 늘 했던 것만큼 훌륭하게 오늘 밤 Paganini 협주곡을 연주했습니다. 오늘 여러분은 다른 기준을 가지고 있습니다. 여러분에게는 Elman, Heifetz, 그리고 그 밖의 연주자가 있습니다. 여러분 모두 예술성, 기법, 그리고 무엇보다 지식과 감상력에서 발전하고 성장했습니다. 요점은 여러분이 더 많이 알고 있는 것이지, Kubelik가 연주 실력이 더 떨어진 것이 아닙니다."라고 그는 말했다.

정답풀이 바이올리니스트 Mischa Elman의 아버지 Sol Elman이 한 말에서 빈칸의 근거를 찾을 수 있다. Kubelik의 연주는 변함없지만, 청중들이 음악에 대해 더 많이 알고 다른 판단 기준(a different standard)을 갖게 됨으로써 Kubelik의 연주 실력이 약간 떨어졌다고 느꼈다는 것을 알 수 있으며, Kubelik이 위대하다고 칭송받은 것은 결국 ② '비교할 만한 근거가 거의 없기' 때문이었던 것을 추론할 수 있다.

오답풀이

① 영감이 떠오르는 순간들이 있다 → 지문의 내용과 무관하다.
③ 그가 그러한 위대한 사람이 되기를 간절히 바란다 → 지문의 내용과 무관하다.
④ 다른 사람들이 그의 노력을 알아 본다 → 노력 여부에 관한 내용은 아니다.
⑤ 그가 위대한 예술적 재능을 갖고 태어났다 → 칭송의 이유는 재능이 아니라 비교 근거 유무라는 내용이므로 어긋난다.

구문풀이

[7행] My dear friends, Kubelik **played** the Paganini concerto tonight **as splendidly as** ever he **did**.
: 「as+부사+as」로 동등비교를 나타낸 구문이며, 동사 played를 수식하도록 부사가 쓰였다. did는 played를 대신하는 대동사이다.

어휘풀이

· tour 순회공연
· dear 친애하는
· splendidly 훌륭하게
· the rest 나머지, 기타 등등
· above all 무엇보다도
· slip (실력이) 떨어지다
· concerto 협주곡
· standard 기준
· artistry 예술성
· appreciation 감상(력), 이해(력)

02 답 ①

소 재 철학에서 논증의 개념

전문해석 철학에서 논증의 개념을 이해하는 가장 좋은 방법은 의견과 대조하는 것이다. 의견은 단순히 누군가 혹은 어떤 것에 대한 믿음이나 태도이다. 우리는 항상 의견을 표현한다. 우리는 특정 영화나 다른 종류의 음식을 좋아하기도, 매우 싫어하기도 한다. 대부분의 경우, 사람들의 의견은 거의 언제나 자신의 감정에 기반을 둔다. 사람들은 자신의 의견을 어떤 종류의 증거로도 뒷받침할 필요는 없다고 느낀다. 논증은 이것과는 좀 다르다. 이것은 자신의 주장이 사실이라는 것을 다른 사람에게 확신시키기 위하여 만들어진 것이다. 그러므로 이것은 주장을 뒷받침하는 논거를 제시하려는 시도이다. 논증은 철학을 구성하는 요소이고, 훌륭한 철학자는 확고한 토대에 기초를 둔 최고의 논증을 만들어 낼 수 있는 사람이다.

 의견은 감정에 기초하는 것이지만 철학에 있어 논증은 의견과는 다른 것인데, 그 다른 점에 대한 내용이 무엇인지에 관한 부분에 빈칸을 주었다. 첫 번째 문장에서 글의 화제를 제시한 후, 중반부 이후에 정답에 대한 단서가 구체적으로 기술된다. 결국, 의견은 감정에 기초하므로 그 증거를 제시할 필요가 없지만, 철학에서 논증은 다른 사람들에게 자신의 주장이 사실이라는 것을 확신시키기 위해 논거를 제시하는 것이라는 내용이다. 따라서 빈칸에는 ① '주장을 뒷받침하는 논거를 제시한다'가 들어감을 추론할 수 있다.

② 각 분야에서 자기 자신의 취향을 개발한다 → 영화나 음식을 좋아하거나 싫어할 수 있다는 내용에서 유도될 수 있는 오답이다.
③ 자신의 의견을 다른 사람들의 의견과 비교한다 → 의견에 대한 내용이 있지만 빈칸에 적절한 답은 아니다.
④ 어떤 주제에 관한 더 깊은 의미를 조사한다 → 전혀 무관한 내용이다.
⑤ 자신의 경험으로부터 지식을 쌓는다 → 지문과 관련 있을법한 그럴싸한 단어로 표현된 오답이다.

[8행] It is made [to **convince** others {that one's claims are true}].
: [ ]는 목적의 의미를 나타내는 to부정사구이다. 동사 convince는 「convince+목적어+that절」의 형태로 쓰여 '~에게 …을 확신시키다'라는 의미를 나타낸다. 여기서는 { }의 내용을 확신시킨다는 뜻이다.

· philosophy 철학
· argument 논증, 논쟁
· opinion 의견
· all the time 항상
· convince 확신[납득]시키다
· philosopher 철학자
· solid 확고한
· reason 논거
· concept 개념
· contrast 대조[대비]하다
· attitude 태도
· evidence 증거
· claim 주장
· create 만들어 내다
· foundation 토대, 기초
· in support of ~을 뒷받침하여

03 답 ①

 학생들의 학교생활에 도움이 되는 소셜 네트워킹 사이트

 인터넷에 접속하는 학생 중 59퍼센트는 자신들이 교육적인 주제에 대해 논의하기 위해 소셜 네트워킹 사이트를 사용한다고 말하고, 그들 중 50퍼센트는 자신들이 학교 과제에 대해 이야기하기 위해 그 사이트를 사용한다고 말한다. 포틀랜드에 있는 George 중학교에서 학생들을 사로잡기 위해 소셜 미디어 프로그램을 도입한 이후에 성적은 50퍼센트나 높아졌고, 고질적인 장기 결석은 33퍼센트나 낮아졌으며, 그리고 학생들의 20퍼센트는

자진해서 특별 이수 단위 과제를 끝마쳤다. 'Journal of Applied Developmental Psychology'에 발표된 한 연구에 따르면, 대학 신입생들은 새로운 친구의 네트워크를 구축하고, 자신들의 새로운 학교에 사회적으로 통합되는 것을 느끼며, 그리고 자신들의 탈락할 위험을 줄이기 위해 소셜 네트워킹 사이트를 사용한다는 것이다. 이러한 방식으로 소셜 네트워킹 사이트는 학생들이 학교에서 더 잘하도록 돕는다.

 인터넷에 접속한 학생의 59퍼센트와 50퍼센트가 소셜 네트워킹 사이트를 사용하는 이유, George 중학교에서의 소셜 미디어 프로그램의 긍정적인 효과, 그리고 대학 신입생들이 소셜 네트워킹 사이트를 사용하는 이유를 기술하면서 소셜 네트워킹 사이트가 학생들이 학교에서 더 잘하도록 돕는다는 내용을 말하고 있다. 따라서 빈칸에 들어갈 말로 가장 적절한 것은 ① '학생들이 학교에서 더 잘하도록 돕는다'이다.

② 서로 얼굴을 맞대고 하는 대화를 막는다 → 소셜 네트워킹 사이트의 일반적인 단점에 해당할 수 있지만, 지문에는 언급되지 않았다.
③ 친구들과의 늘어난 소통을 증진시킨다 → 소셜 네트워킹 사이트의 일반적인 장점일 수 있지만 지문에는 언급되지 않았다.
④ 학생들이 생각, 사진, 그리고 음악을 공유하도록 만든다 → 소셜 네트워킹 사이트의 일반적인 기능일 수 있지만, 지문에는 언급되지 않았다.
⑤ 잘못되고 잠재적으로 위험한 정보를 퍼뜨린다 → 소셜 네트워킹 사이트의 일반적인 단점에 해당할 수 있지만, 지문에는 언급되지 않았다.

[1행] [59% of students with access to the Internet report {that they use social networking sites to discuss educational topics}] and [50% of them say {that they use the sites to talk about school assignments}].
: 두 개의 절 [ ]이 and로 인해 병렬 연결되었다. 첫 번째 { }는 동사 report의 목적어이고, 두 번째 { }는 동사 say의 목적어이다.

· access to ~에의 접근
· social networking site 소셜 네트워킹 사이트
· discuss ~에 대해 토론[논의]하다
· assignment 과제
· chronic 고질적인, 만성의
· complete 완료하다, 끝마치다
· publish 발표하다, 출판하다
· integrated 통합된
· promote 증진시키다
· report 말하다, 알리다
· educational 교육의, 교육적인
· engage (주의 · 관심을) 사로잡다[끌다]
· voluntarily 자진해서, 자발적으로
· extra- 특별한, 추가적인, 남다른
· freshman 신입생
· drop out 탈락하다

04 답 ②

 가열과 냉각을 통한 물체의 변화

 가열과 냉각은 물질을 한 상태로부터 다른 상태로 변화게 할 수 있다. 물질 내의 분자들은 항상 움직이고 있다. 그것들이 가열되거나 냉각될 때 그것들의 속도는 변한다. 고체 내의 분자들은 이리저리 움직이지만, 그것들은 서로 멀어지지는 않는다. 고체가 가

열되면서 분자들은 점점 더 빨리 움직여서 결국 결합이 약해지고 고체가 녹아 액체로 변한다. 고체 상태에서 액체 상태로의 변화는 융해라고 불린다. 물질이 고체에서 액체로 변하는 온도는 녹는점이라고 불린다. 액체가 냉각될 때 그것의 분자들은 속도가 느려져 심지어는 얼기까지 해서 고체로 변한다. 액체 상태에서 고체 상태로의 변화는 결빙이라고 불린다. 물질이 액체에서 고체로 변하는 온도는 어는점이라고 불린다.

정답풀이 가열과 냉각에 따라 물질이 고체 상태에서 액체 상태로, 또는 그 반대로 될 수 있다는 내용이다. 첫 번째 문장이 주제문으로 핵심어구에 빈칸이 있는데, 전반부에서 고체가 액체로 변하는 것에 대한 내용이 나오고, 중반부 이후에 액체가 고체로 변하는 것에 대한 내용이 나온다. 따라서 빈칸에 들어갈 말로 가장 적절한 것은 ② '물질을 한 상태로부터 다른 상태로 변하게 하다'이다.

오답풀이
① 더 효율적으로 통제되다
③ 더 깨끗한 환경을 만들도록 변화되다
④ 집이나 회사에서 여러분을 안락하게 유지시켜주다
⑤ 미래의 가스 위기라는 위험을 낮추는 데 기여하다
→ ①, ③, ④, ⑤ 모두 지문에 언급되지 않은 전혀 무관한 내용이다.

구문풀이

[7행] **The temperature** [**at which** a substance changes from a solid to a liquid] is called the melting point.
: 문장의 주어는 The temperature이고, 동사는 is called이다. [ ]는 〈전치사+관계대명사〉로 시작하는 관계절로, 선행사인 The temperature를 수식한다.

어휘풀이

- heating 가열
- matter 물체, 물질
- solid 고체; 고체의
- bond 결합, 유대
- melt 녹다
- melting 용해
- substance 물질
- slow down (속도가) 느려지다
- state 상태
- crisis 위기
- cooling 냉각
- alter 바꾸다, 변경하다
- back and forth 앞뒤로, 이리저리
- weaken 약해지다
- liquid 액체; 액체의
- temperature 온도
- melting point 융해점, 녹는점
- freeze 얼다
- freezing point 빙점, 어는점

Unit 04 요약문 완성

Example 답 ② pp.132~133

소재 공상과 기대의 차이에 따른 목표 성취 정도

전문해석 무엇이 정말 사람들로 하여금 자신의 목표를 성취하도록 동기를 부여하기 위해 효과가 있는가? 한 연구에서, 연구자들은 사람들이 직장을 얻거나, 시험을 치거나, 수술을 받는 것과 같은 인생

의 과제에 어떻게 대응하는가를 살펴보았다. 이러한 각각의 상황에 대해, 연구자들은 또한 실험 참가자들이 긍정적인 결과에 대해 얼마나 많이 공상했는지, 그리고 그들이 실제로 긍정적인 결과를 얼마나 많이 기대했는지를 측정했다. 공상과 기대의 차이는 진정 무엇인가? 공상은 이상화된 미래를 상상하는 것을 포함하는 반면, 기대는 실제로 사람의 과거 경험에 근거한다. 그래서 연구자들은 무엇을 알아냈는가? 그 결과는 바라던 미래에 대해 공상을 했던 사람들은 세 가지 상황 모두에서 성과가 좋지 않았다는 것을 보여주었다. 성공에 대한 긍정적인 기대를 더 많이 했던 사람들은 다음 주, 다음 달, 다음 해에도 좋은 성과를 거두었다. 이 사람들은 직업을 구하고, 시험에 합격하고, 수술에서 성공적으로 회복한 가능성이 더 높았다.
⇨ 긍정적인 기대는 바라던 미래에 대해 공상하는 것보다 더 효과적이고, 그것은 목표를 성취하는 데 있어 성공의 가능성을 높여 주는 경향이 있다.

구문풀이

[3행] For each of these conditions, the researchers also measured [**how much these participants fantasized** about positive outcomes] and [**how much they** actually **expected** a positive outcome].
: 두 개의 [ ]는 모두 동사 measured의 목적어로 쓰인 명사절이며, 〈how much+주어+동사〉 어순으로 '~가 얼마나 많이 …하는지'의 의미를 나타낸다.

[7행] The results revealed [that **those** {who had engaged in fantasizing about the desired future} **did** worse in all three conditions].
: [ ]는 revealed의 목적어로 쓰인 명사절이다. { }는 명사절의 주어인 those를 수식하며, did가 동사이다.

어휘풀이

- work 효과가 있다
- challenge 과제, 도전, 어려운 일
- measure 측정하다
- fantasize 공상하다
- fantasy 공상
- idealized 이상화된
- engage in ~에 참여하다
- recover 회복하다
- motivate 동기를 부여하다
- undergo surgery 수술을 받다
- participant 참가자
- outcome 결과, 성과
- involve 포함하다, 수반하다
- reveal 드러내다, 노출시키다
- condition 상황, 조건

Do It Yourself pp.134~137

01 ⑤ **02** ① **03** ④ **04** ③

01 답 ⑤

소재 자신의 것을 주지 않으려는 아이들의 성향

전문해석 아이들은 다른 사람을 돕는 것보다는 무언가를 주는 것에 훨씬 더 저항한다. 매우 어린 아이들에게서 이러한 차이점을 확실히 관찰할 수 있다. 1년 6개월 된 아기들은 어려운 상황에서는 서로 도와주려 하지만, 그들 자신의 장난감을 다른 아기들과 기꺼이 공유하려고 하지는 않는다. 그 어린 아기들은 심지어 소리를 지르고 필요하면 주먹을 날리며 자신의 소유물을 지킨다. 이는 (걸음마를 배우는) 아기들 사이의 끊임없는 싸움으로 문제를 겪고 있는 부모들의 일상적인 경험이다. 내 딸들이 기저귀를 차고 있을 시기에도 그들에게서 "내 거야!"라는 말보다 더 자주 들었던 말은 없었다.

⇨ 매우 어린 아이들은 어려운 상황에서 서로를 <u>도우려고</u> 하지만, 그들은 자신의 소유물은 기꺼이 <u>공유하려</u> 하지는 않는다.

정답풀이　아기들은 어려운 상황에서 서로 도와주려 하지만, 자신의 물건을 다른 사람과 공유하려고 하지는 않는다는 내용의 글이다. 따라서 요약문의 빈칸 (A)에는 help(돕다)가, (B)에는 share(공유하다)가 들어가는 것이 가장 적절하다.

오답풀이
① 무시하다 – 공유하다
② 돕다 – 감추다
③ 무시하다 – 방어하다
④ 이해하다 – 감추다

구문풀이
[7행] This is the daily experience of **parents** [**troubled** by constant quarreling between toddlers].

: [ ]는 분사구이며 parents를 수식한다. 분사의 수식을 받는 parents가 괴롭히는(trouble) 동작의 대상이므로 수동태가 되어 과거분사 troubled가 쓰였다.

어휘풀이
· resistant 저항하는
· support 지지하다, 편들다
· share 공유하다, 나누다
· possessions 소유물
· if necessary 필요하면
· constant 끊임없는, 일정한
· frequently 자주
· observe 관찰하다
· be willing to 기꺼이 ~하다
· defend 지키다, 방어하다
· scream 소리침, 외침
· blow 타격, 강타
· quarrel 싸우다, 다투다
· diaper 기저귀

02 답 ①

소 재　로미오와 줄리엣 효과

전문해석　한 연구에서, 학생들은 10개의 포스터를 아름다운 순서대로 배열하도록 요구받았다. 연구자들은 학생들이 나중에 포스터 중 하나를 연구 참여에 대한 보상으로 가질 수 있다고 약속했다. 하지만 학생들이 이 과업을 끝냈을 때, 연구자들은 학생들이 3순위로 선택했던 포스터는 가질 수 없다고 말했다. 그러고 나서 그들은 학생들에게 10개의 포스터를 처음부터 다시 평가하도록 요청했다. 일어난 일은 바로 학생들이 가질 수 없었던 포스터가 갑자기 가장 아름다운 것으로 순위가 매겨졌다는 것이었다. 이것은 '로미오와 줄리엣 효과'의 한 예이다. 셰익스피어 비극에 나오는 로미오와 줄리엣처럼, 사람들은 사랑이 금지될 때 서로에게 더 애착감이 생긴다.

⇨ 사람들은 무언가를 <u>소유할</u> 수 없을 때, 그것이 더 <u>매력적</u>이라고 생각하기 시작한다.

정답풀이　한 연구를 통해 '로미오와 줄리엣 효과'를 설명하고 있는 글로, 포스터 순위 정하기 실험에서 보여지듯, 사람들은 가질 수 없는 것에 대해 더 애착을 갖게 된다는 내용의 글이다. 따라서 요약문의 빈칸 (A)에는 own(소유하다)이, (B)에는 attractive(매력적인)가 들어가는 것이 가장 적절하다.

오답풀이
② 소유하다 – 잊을 수 있는
③ 만들다 – 매력적인
④ 만들다 – 낭만적인
⑤ 받아들이다 – 실망을 주는

구문풀이
[4행] However, when the students finished the task, the researchers said [that the students were not allowed to keep **the poster** {that they had rated as the third-most beautiful}].

: [ ]로 표시된 that절은 said의 목적어 역할을 하는 명사절이다. 그 안의 that절인 { }는 선행사인 the poster를 수식하는 관계절이다.

어휘풀이
· arrange 배열하다, 정리하다
· afterward 나중에
· participation 참여
· rate 평가하다, 등급을 매기다
· suddenly 갑자기
· effect 효과
· attach 애착을 갖게 하다
· order 순서
· reward 보상
· task 과업
· judge 평가[판단]하다
· rank 위치[순위]를 정하다
· tragedy 비극
· prohibit 금지하다

03 답 ④

소 재　이해를 통한 암기

전문해석　여러분이 글의 한 구절을 암기하도록 요구받을 때, 여러분은 아마도 반복하는 행동이 여러분의 정신 속에 그 정보를 고정시키는 데 도움을 줄 것이라고 기대하면서 그것을 반복해서 읽음으로써 (암기를) 시작할 것이다. 하지만 이것은 정보를 기억하는 가장 효율적인 방법은 아니라서, 이는 장차 그것을 잊게 될 가능성은 늘어나게 됨을 의미한다. 결국, 글에 대한 더 강한 기억으로 이어지게 되는 것은 글의 의미를 이해하는 것이다. 여러분이 읽은 내용의 의미를 더 많이 이해하면 할수록, 여러분은 그 구절과 여러분이 이미 알고 있는 것 사이에 더 많은 연결고리를 만들어낼 수 있고, 결론적으로 그것에 대한 여러분의 기억은 더 좋아질 것이다.

⇨ 글을 더 잘 암기하기 위해서, 여러분은 그것을 <u>반복해서</u> 읽는 것에 의존하는 것보다는 그것의 의미를 <u>이해</u>해야 한다.

정답풀이　글의 한 구절을 암기하도록 요구받을 때, 그것을 단순히 반복해서 읽기보다는 그 내용을 이해하는 것이 암기에 더 도움이 된다는 내용의 글이다. 따라서 요약문의 빈칸 (A)에는 comprehend(이해하다)가, (B)에는 repetitively(반복적으로)가 들어가는 것이 가장 적절하다.

① (사전 등에서) 찾아 보다 – 반복적으로

② (사전 등에서) 찾아 보다 – 빠르게

③ 정의하다 – 의미 있게

⑤ 이해하다 – 의미 있게

[4행] However, this isn't **the most efficient way** [to remember the information], [which therefore means you have a good chance of forgetting it in the future].

: 첫 번째 [ ]는 to부정사구로 the most efficient way를 수식한다. 두 번째 [ ]는 관계절로 앞 내용에 대한 추가적인 설명을 제공한다.

[6행] Ultimately, **it** is [understanding the meaning of the text] **that** will lead to a stronger memory of it.

: 「it is ~ that …」 강조 구문이 쓰인 문장이며, [ ]로 표시된 부분이 강조되고 있다.

[7행] **The more** you understand the meaning of what you have read, **the more** connections you can make between the passage and what you already know, and as a result **the better** your memory of it will be.

: 「the+비교급 ~, the+비교급 …」 구문으로 '~하면 할수록, 더 … 하다'의 뜻이다.

- memorize 암기하다
- repetition 반복
- efficient 효율적인
- in the future 장차, 미래에
- lead to ~로 이어지다
- passage 구절, 단락
- fix 고정시키다
- chance 가능성, 기회
- ultimately 결국, 궁극적으로
- connection 연결, 연관, 관계

04 답 ③

 삶의 목표 인식

 자신의 책인 'The Motivated Mind'에서 Raj Persaud 는 자신의 한 고객을 인용하는데, 그의 삶의 주요 목표는 소설가가 되는 것이었다. 그 고객은 자신이 결코 책을 끝낼 수 없기 때문에 매우 좌절했다. Persaud 박사가 그에게 더할 나위 없는 날에 관해 질문했을 때, 그것에는 열대의 해변, 월드컵 결승전에서 결승골을 넣는 것, 그리고 유명 인사처럼 대우받는 것이 포함되었다. 그것 안에는 문학적인 것은 전혀 없었다. 그가 정말로 소설가가 되기를 전혀 원하지는 않는다는 것이 분명했다. 그의 상상을 통해 그가 정말로 원하고 있는 것이 드러났다. 그래서 그가 좌절감과 압박감을 느끼고 있는 것은 놀랄 일이 아니었다. 그는 삶에서 잘못된 목표를 설정하고 있어서 자신이 그것을 성취하지 못했기 때문에 실패자처럼 느끼고 있었다.

➯ Persaud 박사가 인용한 소설가 지망자는 삶에서 자신의 진정한 목표를 확인하지 못했고 결국 자신이 가져야 한다고 생각하는 목표를 좇으며 압박감을 느꼈다.

 Persaud 박사의 고객 중 소설가를 지망했던 고객은 자신이 원하는 진정한 삶의 목표를 제대로 알지 못하고 자신이 그래야

한다고 생각하는 것을 삶의 목표(소설가)로 삼음으로써 절망을 느꼈다는 내용의 글이다. 따라서 요약문의 빈칸 (A)에는 identify(확인하다)가, (B)에는 chasing(뒤쫓으면서)이 들어가는 것이 가장 적절하다.

① 달성하다 – 바꾸면서

② 확인하다 – 놓아주면서

④ 달성하다 – 포기하면서

⑤ 기억해내다 – 뒤쫓으면서

[4행] When Dr. Persaud asked him about his perfect day, **it** involved [tropical beaches], [scoring the winning goal in the World Cup final] and [**being treated** like a celebrity].

: it은 his perfect day를 대신한다. [ ]로 표시된 각각은 명사구, 동명사구, 동명사구이며 and로 병렬 연결되어 involved의 목적어 역할을 한다. 내용상 Dr. Persaud가 treat의 동작의 대상이므로 동명사의 수동형인 being treated가 쓰였다.

- cite 인용하다
- chief 최고의, 주요한
- novelist 소설가
- involve 포함하다, 수반하다
- celebrity 유명 인사
- whatsoever 전혀
- no wonder ~은 전혀 놀랍지 않다
- client 고객
- goal 목표
- frustrated 좌절한
- tropical 열대의
- literary 문학적인
- reveal 드러내다
- failure 실패(자)

<table>
<tr><td>How was it?</td><td style="text-align:right">pp.138~139</td></tr>
</table>

A 01 가정하다 02 비어 있는 03 망설이다, 주저하다 04 reject 05 훌륭하게 06 기준 07 감상(력), 이해(력) 08 대조[대비]하다 09 태도 10 확신[납득]시키다 11 확고한; 고체; 고체의 12 토대, 기초 13 ~에의 접근 14 과제 15 고질적인, 만성의 16 통합된 17 바꾸다, 변경하다 18 액체; 액체의 19 freeze 20 위기

B 01 a group of six people enters → a group of six people enter/entering: 지각동사 see의 목적격 보어 자리이므로 동사원형 enter 또는 현재분사 entering으로 고쳐야 한다.

02 one he or she is able to create → one who is able to create: one(= 사람)을 수식하는 관계절이 이어지는 구조이므로 관계대명사 who로 고쳐야 한다.

03 reducing their risk → reduce their risk: 문맥상 앞에 나오는 to부정사인 to build, (to) feel과 병렬구조를 이루어야 하므로 reducing을 reduce로 고쳐야 한다. to부정사가 병렬구조를 이루는 경우 일반적으로 뒤에 오는 to부정사에서는 to를 생략한다.

04 turn into a liquid → turning into a liquid: 결과의 의미를 나타내는 분사구문이 되어야 하므로 turn을 현재분사인 turning으로 고쳐야 한다. turn의 주체가 the solid이므로 동사 turn이 바로 쓰일 수 없다.

C 01 motivate 02 측정하다 03 공상하다 04 드러내다, 노출시키다 05 저항하는 06 소유물 07 타격, 강타 08 싸우다, 다투다 09 과업 10 평가[판단]하다 11 비극 12 금지하다 13 memorize 14 구절, 단락 15 반복 16 인용하다 17 최고의, 주요한 18 포함하다, 수반하다 19 유명 인사 20 문학적인

D 01 to help them → to helping them: 전치사 to와 그 목적어가 오는 구조이므로 동명사 helping으로 고쳐야 한다.

02 That happened → What happened: 주어 역할을 하는 명사절을 이루도록 선행사를 포함한 관계사인 What으로 고쳐야 한다.

03 what → that: 문맥상 「it ~ that ...」 강조 구문을 이루어야 하므로 that으로 고쳐야 한다.

04 treating → being treated: 내용상 Dr. Persaud(= him)이 treat의 동작의 대상이므로 수동태인 being treated로 고쳐야 한다. 또한 treat의 목적어가 없으므로 수동태가 되어야 함을 알 수 있다.

Part 5 논리 추론

Unit 01 글의 순서

Example   답 ②   pp.142~143

소 재   밤하늘의 별 관찰

전문해석   다음에 여러분이 맑고 어두운 하늘 아래에 있다면, 위를 올려다보라. 만약 여러분이 별을 보기에 좋은 장소를 골랐다면, 수천 개의 광채가 나는 보석처럼 빛나고 반짝거리는 별로 가득한 하늘을 보게 될 것이다. (B) 하지만 이 놀라운 별들의 광경은 또한 혼란스러울 수도 있을 것이다. 어떤 사람에게 별 하나를 가리켜 보여 줘 보라. 아마, 그 사람은 여러분이 어떤 별을 보고 있는지를 정확하게 알기 어려울 것이다. (A) 만약 여러분이 별의 패턴을 묘사한다면 그것은 더 쉬워질 수도 있다. "저기 큰 삼각형을 이루는 밝은 별들이 보이세요?"와 같은 말을 할 수 있을 것이다. 혹은, "대문자 W처럼 보이는 다섯 개의 별이 보이세요?"라고 말할 수도 있을 것이다. (C) 여러분이 그렇게 하면, 여러분은 우리가 별을 바라볼 때 우리 모두가 하는 것을 정확하게 하고 있는 것이다. 우리는 패턴을 찾는데, 이는 우리가 다른 사람에게 어떤 것을 가리켜 보여주기 위해서 뿐만 아니라, 그것은 우리 인간이 항상 해왔던 것이기도 하기 때문이다.

구문풀이

[1행] If you've picked a good spot for stargazing, you'll see **a sky** [full of stars, shining and twinkling like thousands of brilliant jewels].

: [ ]는 형용사구로, a sky를 뒤에서 수식한다.

[10행] We look for patterns, **not just** [so that we can point something out to someone else], **but also** [because that's what we humans have always done].

: 문장에 「not just ~ but also ... (~뿐만 아니라 …도)」 구문이 쓰였다. 첫 번째 [ ]가 ~에 해당하고, 두 번째 [ ]가 …에 해당한다.

Do It Yourself   pp.144~147

| 01 ④ | 02 ③ | 03 ② | 04 ① |

01 답 ④

소 재   탐정 일과 독서의 유사성

전문해석   탐정 일은 두 부분으로 된 과정이다. 첫째, 탐정은 단서를 찾아야 한다. 하지만 단서만으로는 사건이 해결되지 않는다. (C) 탐정은 또한 그러한 단서를 바탕으로 결론을 도출해야 한다. 이러한 결론은 추론이라고 불리기도 한다. 추론은 근거, 사실, 증거를 기반으로 한 결론이다. (A) 똑같은 종류의 과정이 독서에서도 일어난다. 여러분은 단서를 찾아야 하고 그러고 나서 그 단서를 바탕으로 한

결론을 이끌어내야 한다. (B) 필자가 무엇을 말하고자 하는가? 좋은 결론은 좋은 관찰로부터 나온다. 더 나은 독자가 되기 위해서 더 셜록 홈스처럼 돼라. 즉, 더욱 관찰력이 있도록 하라.

정답풀이 주어진 글에서 탐정은 단서(clues)를 찾는다고 했으며, (C)에서 탐정은 주어진 문장의 단서를 바탕으로 결론을 도출한다고 내용을 이어간다. (A)의 The same sort of process는 주어진 문장과 (C)에서 언급한 과정이며, 독서에도 단서를 바탕으로 결론을 낸다고 하면서 내용의 전환이 일어난다. (B)에서는 다시 (A)에서 언급한 결론에 대해 말하고 있으며, 좋은 결론은 좋은 관찰에서 나오므로 셜록 홈스처럼 관찰력을 기르라는 내용으로 마무리되고 있다. 그러므로 주어진 글 다음에 이어질 글의 순서로는 ④ '(C) – (A) – (B)'가 가장 적절하다.

구문풀이

[7행] [To be a better reader], **be** more **like** Sherlock Holmes: **be** more observant.

: [ ]는 '~하기 위해서'라는 의미로 목적을 나타내는 to부정사구이다. 뒤에 오는 두 개의 be는 명령문을 이끌고 있다. 앞에서는 be ~ like 다음에 전치사 like의 목적어로 Sherlock Holmes가 왔으며, 두 번째 be 다음에는 형용사가 보어로 쓰였다.

어휘풀이

- detective 탐정; 탐정의
- take place 발생하다
- conclusion 결론
- observation 관찰
- reason 근거, 이유
- evidence 증거
- clue 단서
- draw 도출하다, 끌다
- based on ~을 바탕으로
- inference 추론
- fact 사실

02 답 ③

소 재 주위 환경의 분위기 변화가 기분에 미치는 영향

전문해석 주위 환경의 분위기를 바꿈으로써 우리의 기분에 영향을 끼치기 위해 다른 사람들이 노력하는 많은 상황들이 있다. 아마도 여러분은 이미 그와 동일한 것을 했을 수도 있다. (B) 예를 들어 한 남자가 결혼기념일을 잊어버린 난처한 상황에 놓여 있다고 상상해 보자. 그 남자는 낭만적인 배경 음악과 함께 아내를 위해 직접 요리를 하고 촛불이 켜진 저녁식사를 준비함으로써 그 상황을 만회하려고 노력한다. (C) 그가 그것을 알든 모르든, 촛불이 켜진 저녁식사는 한 사람의 기분에 영향을 미칠 수 있는 환상적인 방법이다. 그 남자의 아내가 그 방에 들어오면, 그가 준비했던 멋진 저녁식사의 맛있는 냄새에 놀라게 된다. (A) 은은한 촛불 조명은 그녀를 편안한 기분이 들게 한다. 그리고 마침내 낭만적인 음악은 아내로 하여금 그 실수에 대한 남편의 사과를 기꺼이 받아들이게 하는 나머지 역할을 하게 된다.

정답풀이 주어진 글에서 주위 환경의 분위기 변화로 기분에 영향을 주려는 노력에 대해 언급하였으며, 이것에 대한 예시로 (B)에서 결혼기념일을 잊은 남편이 촛불이 켜진 저녁 식사를 준비하여 상황을 만회하려 하는 상황을 제시했다. (B)에 이어서 (C)에서는 아내가

방에 들어오면서 남편이 준비한 저녁식사의 냄새에 놀라게 된다고 했다. 그리고 끝으로 (A)에서 은은한 촛불 조명과 음악이 남편의 사과를 받아들이게 하는 역할을 한다는 순서로 글이 전개되므로 가장 적절한 순서는 ③ '(B) – (C) – (A)'이다.

구문풀이

[1행] There are **many situations** [**where** other people try to influence our mood by changing the atmosphere of the environment]; probably you have already done the same.

: [ ]는 many situations를 수식하는 관계부사절이다. 관계부사 where가 이끄는 절은 선행사가 장소일 때뿐만 아니라 상황일 때도 수식할 수 있다.

어휘풀이

- influence 영향을 끼치다; 영향
- atmosphere 분위기
- relaxed 편안한, 느긋한
- do the rest 나머지 역할을 다하다
- unfortunate 난처한, 불행한
- rescue 구조하다, 구하다
- be aware of ~을 알다, 인식하다
- outstanding 멋진, 두드러진
- mood 기분, 분위기
- candle 양초
- spirit 정신, 마음
- apology 사과
- wedding anniversary 결혼기념일
- candlelit 촛불이 켜진
- aroma 좋은 냄새[향기]

03 답 ②

소 재 학생들의 장단점을 파악해 수업 계획 세우기

전문해석 수업을 계획하기 전에 학생들을 아는 것이 중요하다. 과학자가 장단점을 알지 못하고 주변 환경에 대한 신제품의 효과를 검사할 수 없는 것처럼 교사는 학생들의 장단점을 알지 못하는 상태에서 수업을 계획할 수 없다. (B) 학생의 데이터(즉, 주 단위 시험과 전국 단위 시험, 출석 기록과 건강 검진)를 보라. 장점과 단점을 모두 보라. 학생이 교실에 가져오는 필수 역량에 대해 확신이 서지 않으면 사전 테스트 또는 설문지를 통해 학생들을 평가하여 적절한 계획을 세우는 데 도움이 될 수 있다. (A) 데이터는 경향과 격차에 대해 모두 분석되어야 한다. 만약 그 데이터에서 반 학생들이 수학보다 읽기를 상당히 더 잘 하는 경향이 나타난다면, 이것은 경향일 것이다. (C) 이러한 경향을 분석하여 원인을 파악해야 한다. 학교에서 쓰이고 있는 교과서와 다른 자료들에 격차가 있는가? 학교의 선생님들은 수학을 가르치는 데 요구되는 필수적인 역량과 자질을 가지고 있는가?

정답풀이 주어진 글에서 교사를 과학자에 비유하며 수업을 계획하기 전에 학생들을 아는 것이 중요하다고 언급된다. (B)에서는 그렇게 하기 위해 학생의 데이터를 보고 장단점을 파악하라는 내용이 나오며, 필요하면 사전 테스트나 설문지를 통해 평가하는 것도 도움이 된다고 기술한다. (A)에서는 (B)에서 얻은 데이터를 경향과 격차에 대해 분석해야 한다고 하면서 수학보다 읽기를 더 잘하는 경향을 예로 든다. 마지막으로 (C)에서는 (A)의 a trend를 The trend로 받으며 경향에 대한 원인을 파악해야 한다고 설명하고 있다. 따라서 주어진 글 다음에 이어질 글의 순서로 가장 적절한 것은 ② '(B) – (A) – (C)'이다.

구문풀이

[13행] If you are unsure about **the prerequisite skills** [that your students bring to your classroom], you can assess them with a pre-test or questionnaire to help you plan appropriately.

: [ ]는 관계대명사절로, the prerequisite skills를 수식한다.

어휘풀이

- **lesson** 강의, 수업
- **weakness** 약점
- **effectiveness** 유효함, 효과적임
- **significantly** 상당히
- **screening** 검사, 검진
- **assess** 평가하다
- **appropriately** 적절히
- **resource** 자원
- **strength** 장점
- **examine** 검사하다, 조사하다
- **analyze** 분석하다
- **attendance** 출석 (상황)
- **unsure** 확신하지 못하는
- **questionnaire** 질문(지)
- **requisite** 필수의

04 답 ①

소재   신약을 동물에게 실험하는 것에 대한 찬반 논쟁

전문해석   대부분의 사람들은 안전을 위해 약품이 효과적으로 테스트되어야 하며, 그렇지 않으면 생명을 살리는 많은 새로운 약품들이 개발될 수 없다는 것에 동의한다. (A) 약품이 동물에게 먼저 테스트되지 않는다면 더 많은 인간 실험지원자들이 아프거나 심지어 죽게 될 것이라고 그들은 말한다. 그러나 동물의 권리를 지지하는 단체들은 다른 의견을 표명한다. (C) 그들은 동물에 대한 약품 실험은 그 약품들이 결국 인간에게 시험되었을 때 심각한 사고가 일어나는 것을 분명하게 막지 못한다고 말한다. 침팬지는 인간과 매우 유사하지만, 그럼에도 불구하고, 그들에게 안전한 약품이 인간에게 여전히 해를 입힐 수 있다. (B) 그래서 그들은 조직 배양의 사용이나 새로운 약품에 대한 인간의 반응을 예측하기 위해 진보된 컴퓨터 프로그램의 개발과 같은 새로운 방법이 필요하다고 주장한다.

정답풀이   주어진 문장에서 약품을 효과적으로 테스트 할 필요성을 언급했다. (A)의 첫 문장에서 주어진 문장에 대한 부연 설명으로 약품이 동물에게 테스트되어야 하는 당위성을 말했고, 두 번째 문장에서는 동물의 권리를 지지하는 단체의 의견에 대해 말하고 있다. (C)의 They는 (A)에 나온 the groups supporting animal rights(동물의 권리를 지지하는 단체)를 가리키며 그들이 동물 실험을 반대하는 근거를 구체적으로 설명하고 있다. 마지막으로 (B)에서 동물의 권리를 지지하는 단체가 동물 실험에 대한 대안으로서 제시하는 내용이 언급된다. 그러므로 주어진 글에 이어질 글의 순서로는 ① '(A) − (C) − (B)'가 가장 적절하다.

구문풀이

[8행] So they argue [that **new methods** are needed {such as the use of tissue cultures or the development of **advanced computer programs** to predict human reactions to new drugs}].

: [ ]는 argue의 목적어에 해당하는 명사절이다. 그 명사절 내의 주어는 new methods이며, 동사는 are needed이다. { }는 new methods를 수식한다.

어휘풀이

- **drug** 약물
- **lifesaving** 목숨을 구하는
- **volunteer** (실험) 지원자
- **opinion** 의견
- **advanced** 진보된
- **reaction** 반응
- **serious** 심각한
- **effectively** 효과적으로
- **develop** 개발하다, 발전시키다
- **be likely to** ~할 가능성이 있다
- **method** 방법
- **predict** 예측[예상]하다
- **prevent** 막다, 예방하다
- **harm** 해를 입히다

Unit
02   문장 삽입

Example   답 ②   pp.148~149

소재   단어 철자 맞히기 대회에 나간 소년

전문해석   몇 년 전 Washington D.C.에서 있었던 전국 단어 철자 맞히기 대회에서, 한 13세 소년이 '들은 것은 무엇이든 반복하는 경향'을 의미하는 단어인 'echolalia'의 철자를 말하도록 요구받았다. 그는 철자를 잘못 말했지만 심판은 잘못 듣고 철자를 맞혔다고 말했고, 그가 (다음 단계로) 진출하도록 허락했다. 그 소년은 자신이 단어 철자를 잘못 말했다는 것을 알았을 때, 심판에게 가서 말했다. 그래서 그는 결국 대회에서 탈락했다. 다음 날 신문기사 헤드라인이 그 정직한 소년을 "단어 철자 맞히기 대회 영웅"으로 알렸고, 그의 사진이 'The New York Times'에 실렸다. "심판은 내가 아주 정직하다고 말했어요."라고 그 소년은 기자들에게 말했다. 그는 그렇게 했던 이유 중 하나를 덧붙여 말했다. "저는 거짓말쟁이가 되고 싶지 않았어요."

구문풀이

[5행] Although he misspelled the word, the judges [misheard him], [told him he had spelled the word right], and [allowed him to advance].

: 세 개의 [ ]는 모두 주어 the judges를 받는 동사구로, and로 인해 병렬을 이룬다.

Do It Yourself   pp.150~153

01 ⑤   **02** ②   **03** ③   **04** ④

01 답 ⑤

소재   체온 자동 조절 능력이 없는 거북

전문해석   거북은 조류와 포유류처럼 체온을 자동으로 조절하는 능력이 없다. 거북의 체온은 주위 환경에 따라 변화한다. 날씨가 너무 추워질 때, 거북은 연못 바닥의 진흙 또는 숲의 흙 속 깊이 구멍을 판다. (흙 속에) 묻히면 거북은 어떻게 숨을 쉴 수 있을까? 거북은

코와 입으로 숨 쉬기를 멈춘다. 대신 거북은 피부와 꼬리 아래에 있는 구멍을 통해 공기를 받아들인다. 그리고 봄이 와서 땅이 따뜻해지면, 거북은 스스로 땅을 파내고 나와 다시 보통 때처럼 숨 쉬기 시작한다.

정답풀이 체온을 자동으로 조절하는 능력이 없는 거북이 어떻게 체온을 조절하는지에 대해 설명하는 글이다. 주어진 문장의 Instead는 앞 내용과 상반된 내용을 이끌어 부연 설명을 하는 연결어이므로, 주어진 문장 이전에는 피부와 꼬리 아래에 있는 구멍을 통해 공기를 받아들인다는 내용과 상반된 내용, 즉 보통의 호흡법에 관한 내용이 언급되어야 한다. 따라서 주어진 문장은 ⑤에 들어가는 것이 가장 적절하다.

구문풀이

[5행] When it **gets** too cold, it digs a hole deep [into the mud at the bottom of a pond] or [into the dirt of the forest].
: get은 상태의 변화 동사로서 뒤에 보어로 형용사가 이어지면, '~하게 되다, ~해지다'로 해석한다. 두 개의 전치사구 [ ]가 병렬로 연결되었다.

어휘풀이

- take in ~을 받아들이다
- turtle 거북
- body temperature 체온
- according to ~에 따라, ~에 의하면
- dig 파다
- bottom 바닥
- dirt 흙, 먼지
- bury 묻다, 매장하다
- tail 꼬리
- automatic 자동적인
- control 조절(능력), 통제(력)
- environment 환경
- mud 진흙
- pond 연못
- breathe 숨쉬다, 호흡하다
- normally 평소대로, 정상적으로

02 답 ②

소재 Delhi 영어 도서관

전문해석 Delhi 영어 도서관은 서구의 공공 도서관과 유사한 공공 도서관을 경험할 수 있는 New Delhi의 유일한 공공 영어 도서관입니다. 저희는 영어 친화적 환경과 2만 5천권의 영어책을 구비하고 있습니다. 게다가, 이용자들을 위한 스토리텔링, 역할놀이, Book Talk와 같은 다양한 영어 읽기 프로그램도 있습니다. 이용자들은 이 프로그램에 참가하기 전 저희 도서관에서 제공하는 영어 읽기 시험을 통해 자신의 읽기 수준을 확인할 수 있습니다. 그것은 이용자들이 자신의 적절한 읽기 수준을 아는 데 도움을 줍니다. 이런 방법으로 저희는 자기 주도적 영어 읽기를 하는 사람들을 지원하고 있습니다. 저희는 모든 New Delhi 시민을 환영합니다.

정답풀이 주어진 문장의 In addition(게다가)은 첨가 혹은 부연의 연결어이므로 앞에도 같은 맥락의 내용이 나왔음을 추론할 수 있다. 즉, 주어진 문장에서 Delhi 영어 도서관의 여러 프로그램을 나열하고 있으므로 앞에서도 Delhi 도서관이 가지고 있는 것에 대한 내용이 나와야 한다. 또한 various English reading programs라는 내용으로 보아, 주어진 문장에서 영어 읽기 프로그램이 처음 언급되었음을 알 수 있고, 이후에 그 프로그램들에 관한 내용을 these

programs로 받고 있으므로 ②에 들어가는 것이 가장 적절하다.

구문풀이

[6행] Users check their reading levels [before joining these programs with **the English Reading Test** {provided by us}].
: Users가 주어이고, check이 동사이며, their reading levels가 목적어이다. [ ]는 전치사구이며, { }는 the English Reading Test를 수식하는 과거분사구로 provided 앞에 which is를 넣으면 이해하기 쉽다.

[9행] In this way, we support **the people** [who do {self-directed English reading}].
: [ ]는 문장의 목적어인 the people을 수식하는 관계절이며 그 안의 { }는 관계절의 동사인 do의 목적어 역할을 하는 명사구이다.

어휘풀이

- in addition 게다가
- role-play 역할 놀이
- similar to ~와 비슷한
- check 확인하다
- appropriate 적절한
- citizen 시민
- various 다양한
- public 공공의, 대중의
- -friendly ~ 친화적인
- level 수준
- support 지원하다

03 답 ③

소재 아이들을 위한 선물 선택

전문해석 모든 연령대의 아이들은 일 년 내내 생일선물, 축제 시즌 선물, 그리고 '사랑해'라는 예쁜 장신구를 받는다. 세계 최대의 온라인 쇼핑몰에서의 빠른 검색에 따르면, 50만 개가 넘는 장난감, 게임, 책, 비디오 게임을 선택할 수 있으며, 사실상 무한한 가능성의 바다라는 사실이 밝혀진다. 이렇게 많은 선택들이 있는데, 어떻게 선의의 부모와 조부모들이 젊은 수령인들에게 적합할 뿐만 아니라 그들이 바라는 선물을 찾을 수 있을까? 내 아이들에 관해서라면 나는 그들에게 직접 물어보거나 냉장고에 테이프로 붙인 '마음에 드는 선물' 목록이나 이메일로 내게 보내온 전자 복사본을 확인할 수 있다. 충분히 간단한 것이지만, 다시 말해 어떻게 아이들과 청소년들이 그들이 애초에 원하는 것이 무엇인지 아는가? 거기서 광고가 들어온다. 잘 되었을 때 광고는 젊은이들이 생각하고, 원하고, 궁극적으로 구매하는 물건에 영향을 주는 힘을 가지고 있다.

정답풀이 ③ 앞에는 무수히 많은 선물 품목 중에서 어떻게 부모와 조부모들이 자기 아이들에게 적합할 뿐만 아니라 그들도 바라는 선물을 찾을 수 있을지 질문하는 내용이 왔고, 주어진 문장은 필자가 자신의 아이들을 위한 선물을 정하는 방법을 구체적으로 답변하는 내용으로, ③ 앞 문장에 대한 답변의 흐름이 된다. 따라서 주어진 문장은 ③에 들어가는 것이 가장 적절하다.

구문풀이

[4행] Children of all ages receive [presents for their birthdays], [gifts during the holiday season], and ["I love you" knickknacks] throughout the year.

: 세 개의 [ ]는 모두 receive의 목적어로, and로 병렬 연결되었다.

[9행] With so many choices, how **are** well-meaning parents and grandparents **supposed to find gifts** [that are **not only** suitable for their youthful recipients **but** desired by them as well]?

: 「be supposed to부정사(구)」는 '~해야 하다, ~하기로 되어 있다'의 의미이다. [ ]는 gifts를 수식하는 관계절이며, 그 안에 「not only A but (also) B(A일 뿐만 아니라 B인)」 구문이 쓰였다.

어휘풀이

- **refrigerator** 냉장고
- **electronic** 전자의
- **virtually** 사실상, 실질적으로
- **youthful** 젊은, 어린
- **adolescent** 청소년
- **duplicate** 복제의, 사본[복사]의
- **via** ~을 통해
- **well-meaning** 선의[호의]의
- **recipient** 수령인
- **ultimately** 궁극적으로

04 답 ④

소 재 후광이 나타나는 현상

전문해석 이 세상에는 여러분이 볼 수 있을지도 모르는 진기하고 장관인 것들이 매우 많다. 한 가지 예는 여러분이 산에 올라가 그 꼭대기에 서서 아래를 바라볼 때 있을 수 있는 것인데, 여러분은 여러분 머리의 그림자가 여러분 아래의 구름 위에 있는 것을 볼 수 있을지도 모른다. 이것은 태양이 여러분 뒤에서 비추고 아래의 구름이 비로 가득 차 있는 경우에만 발생할 수 있다. 그 다음 여러분 머리의 그림자는 마치 달이 때때로 그러는 것처럼 그 주위에 후광을 갖고 있을지도 모른다. 이러한 종류의 이상한 목격은 '장관'이라 불리며 매우 드물다. 하지만, 여러분이 비행기를 타고 가며 태양으로부터 떨어진 창가 쪽 좌석에 앉아 있다면 그것을 볼 가능성을 높일 수 있다. 만약 자세히 보면 여러분은 아래의 구름 위에 여러분이 타고 가는 비행기의 그림자를 볼 수도 있을 것이며, 색깔 있는 고리가 그것을 완전히 둘러싸고 있을 것이다!

정답풀이 주어진 문장의 This kind of strange sighting으로 보아, 주어진 문장 앞에는 이상한 광경에 관한 내용이 이미 언급되었다는 것을 나타내고, very rare로 보아, 주어진 문장 뒤에는 이런 광경을 볼 수 있는 기회에 대한 내용이 언급될 것이라는 점을 추론할 수 있다. 즉, 주어진 문장에서는 장관을 볼 가능성이 매우 드물다고 했고, ④ 이후에는 역접의 연결어 however가 가능성을 높일 수 있다는 상반된 내용을 이끌고 있으므로 주어진 문장이 ④에 들어가는 것이 자연스러운 흐름이 된다.

구문풀이

[8행] Then your head's shadow might **have a halo** [surrounding it], just like the moon **does** at times.

: [ ]는 앞의 a halo를 수식하는 현재분사구이다. does는 대동사로 앞의 have(has) a halo surrounding it을 대신한다.

[10행] You can increase your **chances of seeing** it, however, [if you are ever {flying in a plane} and {sitting in a window seat away from the sun}].

: chances of seeing은 「명사+of -ing」 구문이 쓰인 것으로, 여기

서 of는 동격의 전치사로 쓰였으며, '볼 가능성'이라고 해석한다. [ ]는 조건의 부사절이며 두 개의 { }가 are에 병렬로 연결되어 있다.

어휘풀이

- **strange** 이상한
- **glory** 장관, 영광
- **unusual** 진기한, 이상한, 남다른
- **shine** 빛나다
- **shadow** 그림자
- **closely** 자세히, 가까이
- **completely** 완전히
- **sighting** 목격, 관측
- **rare** 드문, 희귀한
- **spectacular** 장관의, 멋진
- **be filled with** ~으로 가득 차다
- **surround** 둘레[에워]싸다
- **colored** 색깔 있는

Unit
03 **무관한 문장**

Example 답 ③
pp.154~155

소 재 상황에 따라 달라지는 단어의 의미

전문해석 'near'와 'far' 같은 단어들은 여러분이 어디에 있는지와 무엇을 하는지에 따라 여러 가지를 의미할 수 있다. 만약 여러분이 동물원에 있고, 동물 우리의 창살 사이로 손을 뻗어 동물을 만질 수 있다면 여러분은 그 동물이 '가까이'에 있다고 말할지도 모른다. 여기서 'near'라는 단어는 팔 하나 만큼의 길이를 의미한다. 여러분이 누군가에게 동네 가게에 가는 방법을 말해주고 있다면, 만약 그 거리가 걸어서 5분 거리라면 그것을 '가까이'라고 말할 수도 있을 것이다. (여러분은 건강을 향상시키기 위해 그 가게로 걸어가는 것이 더 좋을 것 같다.) 이제 'near'라는 단어는 팔 하나 만큼의 길이보다 훨씬 더 길다는 것을 의미한다. 'near', 'far', 'small', 'big', 'hot', 그리고 'cold'와 같은 단어들은 모두 다른 때에 다른 사람들에게 다른 것을 의미한다.

구문풀이

[2행] If you were at a zoo, then you might say [you are 'near' an animal {if you could reach out and touch it through the bars of its cage}].

: [ ]는 say의 목적어로 쓰인 명사절이다. { }는 조건의 의미를 나타내는 부사절이다.

Do It Yourself
pp.156~159

01 ③　　02 ④　　03 ④　　04 ③

01 답 ③

소 재 가상의 물

전문해석 우리의 음식과 제품에 내포된 물은 '가상의 물'이라고 불린다. 예를 들어, 2파운드의 밀을 생산하기 위해서 약 265갤런의

물이 필요하다. 그래서 이 2파운드의 밀의 가상의 물은 265갤런이다. 가상의 물은 또한 유제품, 수프, 음료, 그리고 액체로 된 약에서도 찾아볼 수 있다. (하지만 건강을 유지하기 위해 가능한 한 많은 물을 마시는 것이 필요하다.) 인간은 매일 많은 가상의 물을 소비하는데 가상의 물의 함유량은 제품에 따라 다르다. 예를 들어, 2파운드의 고기를 생산하려면 2파운드의 채소를 생산하는 것의 약 5배에서 10배의 물이 필요하다.

정답풀이　①, ②, ④에는 글의 핵심어구인 virtual water(가상의 물)라는 표현이 있고, ⑤에는 virtual water라는 표현은 없지만 ④의 내용을 부연하고 있으므로 결국 virtual water에 대해 설명하고 있는 데 반해, ③은 건강을 위해 물을 가능한 한 많이 마시라는 내용이므로 virtual water와는 무관하다. ②의 medicines로 인해 ③이 흐름과 관계 있는 문장이라고 착각할 수 있음에 유의한다.

구문풀이

[1행] **The water** [that is embedded in our food and manufactured products] is called "virtual water."
: [ ]는 The water를 수식하는 관계절이다.

[6행] However, **it** is necessary [to drink **as** much water **as possible** to stay healthy].
: it은 형식상의 주어이고, to부정사구인 [ ]가 내용상의 주어이다. [ ] 안의 「as ~ as possible」은 '가능한 한 ~'라는 의미이다.

어휘풀이

- **embedded** 내포된, 포함된
- **virtual** 가상의
- **pound** 〈무게 단위〉 파운드
- **present** 있는, 존재하고 있는
- **beverage** 음료, 마실 것
- **medicine** 약, 약물
- **consume** 소비하다
- **vary** 다르다, 차이가 있다
- **manufacture** 제조하다
- **gallon** 〈용량 단위〉 갤런
- **wheat** 밀
- **dairy product** 유제품
- **liquid** 액체; 액체의
- **as ~ as possible** 가능한 한 ~
- **content** 함유량
- **according to** ~에 따라

02 답 ④

소 재　시간이 가는 것에 대한 인식의 변화

전문해석　한 실험에서, 사람들이 머릿속으로 3분을 세도록 요구받았을 때 25세인 사람들은 꽤 정확했지만, 65세인 사람들은 평균적으로 40초가 더 걸렸다. 시간이 나이가 더 많은 사람들에게는 더 빨리 가는 것 같았다. 이것이 무의미해 보일 수도 있지만, 65세인 사람들처럼 시간을 인식하는 것에는 많은 이점이 있다. 예를 들어, 만약 여러분이 8시간 동안 프로젝트 작업을 하고 있지만 그것을 단지 6시간처럼 느낀다면, 여러분은 일을 계속 할 수 있는 더 많은 에너지를 얻게 될 것이다. 만약 여러분이 20분 동안 달리기를 하고 있는데 그것을 단지 13분이라고 인식한다면, 여러분은 7분의 추가적인 에너지를 얻게 될 가능성이 더 있다. (나이가 들어가는 것의 가장 큰 장점 가운데 하나는 격정(激情)을 식히고 성급하게 행동으로 옮기지 않는 것이다.) 그래서 만약 여러분이 더 오래 일하기 위해 자신의 에너지를 사용하고 싶다면, 얼마나 오래 일했는지에 대한 인식을 바꾸기만 하라.

정답풀이　나이가 들면 시간이 빨리 간다고 느끼는 것과 주어진 작업 시간을 더 짧게 느끼는 것 등 시간에 대한 인식 변화를 통해 일을 할 수 있는 에너지를 더 많이 얻을 수 있다는 내용이다. 이에 반해 ④는 시간적 측면과 무관하게, 나이가 드는 것의 장점을 언급하고 있으므로 시간의 인식에 대해 말하고 있는 글의 전체 흐름에서 벗어난다.

구문풀이

[12행] So, if you want to use your energy [to work longer], just change your perception of [how long you have been working].
: 첫 번째 [ ]는 목적을 나타내는 to부정사구이고, 두 번째 [ ]는 전치사 of의 목적어로 쓰인 의문사절이다.

어휘풀이

- **experiment** 실험
- **accurate** 정확한
- **second** 〈시간 단위〉 초
- **benefit** 이점
- **be likely to** ~할 것 같다
- **perception** 인식
- **minute** 〈시간 단위〉 분
- **on average** 평균적으로
- **meaningless** 무의미한
- **perceive** 인식하다
- **passion** 격정, 열정

03 답 ④

소 재　유제품 소비와 뼈 건강의 관련성

전문해석　유제품의 장기간 소비가 뼈에 도움이 되는지에 대한 많은 논쟁이 있다. 많은 증거가 그것은 그렇지 않다고 시사한다. 십 대에 대한 몇몇 연구는 그들이 어른이 됐을 때의 뼈의 건강은 더 젊었을 때의 신체 활동 수준과 관련이 있으며, 그들이 소비한 우유나 칼슘의 양과 관련 있는 것은 아니라는 점을 발견했다. 우유 소비는 나이가 더 들었을 때에도 마찬가지로 명백히 도움이 되지 않는다. 78,000명의 여성들에 대한 12년간에 걸친 하버드의 한 연구에서 유제품에서 가장 많은 칼슘을 얻은 사람들이 어떤 이점도 얻지 못했고, 유제품에서 칼슘을 거의 얻지 못했거나 전혀 얻지 못한 여성들보다 실제로 뼈가 더 많이 부러졌다. (뼈가 성장하는 중요한 시기의 낮은 칼슘 섭취량 수준으로 인해 오늘날의 젊은이들은 심각한 공중 보건 문제에 직면한다.) 마찬가지로, 시드니에서의 나이든 남성과 여성에 대한 1994년의 한 연구는 가장 많은 유제품을 소비한 사람들이 가장 적게 소비한 사람들보다 두 배의 둔부 골절률을 가졌다는 것을 보여주었다.

정답풀이　유제품의 장기간 소비가 뼈 건강에 미치는 영향을 조사한 연구들에 따르면 그러한 소비가 뼈 건강에 큰 도움을 주지 않는다는 내용이다. 그런데 ④는 뼈가 성장하는 시기에 칼슘 섭취량 수준이 낮아 젊은이들이 심각한 공중 보건 문제에 직면해 있다는 내용으로 전체 글의 흐름에서 벗어난다.

구문풀이

[7행] In a 12-year Harvard study of 78,000 women, **those** [who got the most calcium from dairy products] received no benefit and actually broke more bones than **the women** [who got little or no calcium from dairy products].

: 첫 번째 [ ]는 those를 수식하는 관계절이다. 문장의 동사는 received와 broke로, and로 인해 병렬을 이루고 있다. 두 번째 [ ]는 the women을 수식하는 관계절이다.

[12행] Similarly, a 1994 study of elderly men and women in Sydney showed [that **those** {who consumed the most dairy products} had double the hip fracture rate of **those** {who consumed the least}].

: [ ]는 문장의 동사인 showed의 목적어이다. 그 안에서 첫 번째 { }는 첫 번째 those를 수식하는 관계대명사절이고, 두 번째 { }는 두 번째 those를 수식하는 관계대명사절이다.

- **debate** 논쟁, 토론
- **dairy product** 유제품
- **a good deal of** 다량의
- **suggest** 시사하다
- **physical** 신체의, 육체의
- **apparently** 명백히
- **intake** 섭취(량)
- **public health** 공중 보건
- **consumption** 소비, 체내 섭취
- **bone** 뼈
- **evidence** 증거
- **be related to** ～와 관련 있다
- **consume** 소비하다
- **benefit** 이점
- **period** 기간
- **elderly** 나이든

04 답 ③

소재 하이브리드 자동차의 특징

전문해석 하이브리드 자동차는 두 가지 종류 이상의 추진력을 사용하는 차량이다. 대부분의 하이브리드 자동차는 자동차에 동력을 공급하기 위해 전동기뿐만 아니라 전통적인 휘발유 엔진도 사용한다. 이것들은 보통 하이브리드 전기 자동차, 즉 HEV로 불린다. 하이브리드 자동차는 전통적인 자동차가 하는 것보다 휘발유를 더 효율적으로 사용하기 위해 두 가지 유형의 추진력을 사용한다. 대부분의 하이브리드 자동차는 전동기에 동력을 보내는 발전기로 휘발유 엔진을 사용한다. (하이브리드 자동차의 판매와 하이브리드 모델의 수 모두 그것들이 도입된 이래로 지속적으로 증가해왔다.) 그러면 전동기는 자동차에 동력을 공급한다. 전통적인 자동차에서 휘발유 엔진은 자동차에 직접 동력을 보낸다.

정답풀이 ①, ②, ④는 모두 하이브리드 자동차의 동력과 추진력의 특징에 대해 말하고 있고, ⑤는 하이브리드 자동차와 비교하기 위해 전통적인 자동차의 동력을 전달하는 방식을 기술하지만, ③은 하이브리드 자동차의 판매와 하이브리드 모델의 수에 대한 내용이므로 전체 글의 흐름에서 벗어난다.

구문풀이

[8행] [**Both** sales of hybrid vehicles **and** the number of hybrid models] have risen steadily [since their introduction].

: 첫 번째 [ ]가 주어이고, 동사는 have risen이다. 첫 번째 [ ] 안에 쓰인 「both A and B」 구문은 'A와 B 둘 다 모두'의 의미이다. 두 번째 [ ]는 '～ 이래로'라는 의미의 since가 이끄는 전치사구이다.

- **hybrid vehicle** 하이브리드 자동차 (휘발유·전기 병용 자동차)
- **conventional** 전통적인
- **gasoline** 휘발유, 가솔린

- **A as well as B** B뿐만 아니라 A도
- **power** 동력; 동력을 공급하다
- **efficiently** 효율적으로
- **rise** 증가하다, 상승하다
- **directly** 직접
- **electric motor** 전동기
- **in order to** ～하기 위해
- **generator** 발전기
- **steadily** 지속적으로, 꾸준히

    pp.160~161

A 01 장소 02 반짝이다 03 아마 ～일 것이다 04 탐정; 탐정의 05 결론 06 분위기 07 rescue 08 멋진, 두드러진 09 검사하다, 조사하다 10 출석(상황) 11 필수의 12 적절히 13 진보된 14 심판; 판단하다 15 (예선 등에서) 실격시키다 16 대회 17 진흙 18 연못 19 breathe 20 bury

B 01 where other people try to influence our mood
02 prevent serious accidents from happening
03 with the English Reading Test provided by us
04 just like the moon does at times

C 01 복제의, 사본[복사]의 02 청소년 03 rare 04 장관의, 멋진 05 길이 06 개선하다, 향상시키다 07 내포된, 포함된 08 밀 09 유제품 10 다르다, 차이가 있다 11 정확한 12 인식하다 13 격정, 열정 14 논쟁, 토론 15 consumption 16 명백히 17 섭취(량) 18 나이든 19 전통적인 20 지속적으로, 꾸준히

D 01 as much water as to produce
02 how long you have been working
03 those who consumed the least
04 to provide power to the vehicle

Part 6 장문 독해

Unit 01 장문 독해(1지문 2문항)

Example 답 ② / ④   pp.164~165

소 재 광고의 왜곡

전문해석 많은 광고는 통계 조사를 인용한다. 하지만 우리는 보통 이러한 조사들이 어떻게 실시되는지를 모르기 때문에 신중해야 한다. 예를 들면, 한 치약 제조업체가 예전에 "80%보다 많은 치과 의사들이 *Smiley Toothpaste*를 추천한다."라고 적혀 있는 포스터를 올렸다. 이것은 대부분의 치과의사들이 다른 브랜드보다 *Smiley Toothpaste*를 선호한다고 말하는 것처럼 보인다. 하지만 그 조사 항목이 치과의사들에게 한 가지 이상의 브랜드를 추천할 수 있게 했다는 것과, 실제로 또 다른 경쟁업체의 브랜드도 *Smiley Toothpaste*만큼 많이 추천되었다는 것이 드러났다! 2007년에 영국 Advertising Standards Authority는 그 포스터가 잘못된 정보를 준다고 판결을 내렸고 그것이 더 이상 게시될 수 없었음은 당연했다.

주름을 빠른 속도로 줄여 준다는 크림을 판매하는 유명 화장품 회사의 경우도 유사하다. 그러나 주어진 유일한 증거라고는 "50명의 여성 중 76%가 동의했다."라는 것뿐이다. 하지만 이것이 의미하는 것은 그 증거가 피부 상태에 대한 객관적인 측정 없는 소수의 표본에서 얻은 개인적 의견에 근거한다는 것이다. 게다가, 우리는 이 여성들이 어떻게 선별되었는지 알 수 없다. 그런 정보 없이, 주어진 "증거"는 아주 유용하다(→ 쓸모가 없다). 불행하게도, 그러한 광고들은 아주 전형적이고, 소비자인 우리는 스스로 판단해야 하며 광고의 주장을 너무 진지하게 받아들이는 것을 피해야 한다.

구문풀이

[5행] But **it turns out that** the survey questions **allowed** the dentists [to recommend more than one brand], and in fact another competitor's brand was recommended just as often as *Smiley Toothpaste*!

: 「it turns out that ~」은 '~임이 드러나다'의 의미이다. [ ]는 allowed의 목적격 보어 역할을 하는 to부정사구이다.

[11행] But [what this means] is [that the evidence is based on just the personal opinions from a small sample with no objective measurement of their skin's condition].

: 첫 번째 [ ]는 문장의 주어 역할을 하는 명사절이다. 두 번째 [ ]는 주격 보어 역할을 하는 명사절이다.

어휘풀이

· advertisement 광고
· cite 인용하다
· statistical 통계의
· survey 조사
· cautious 신중한
· conduct 실시하다, 행하다
· manufacturer 제조업체
· prefer A to B A를 B보다 선호하다
· competitor 경쟁자
· rule 판결을 내리다
· misleading 잘못된 정보를 주는, 잘못 이끄는

· display 게시하다, 보여주다
· concern ~에 관여하다, ~와 관련 있다
· cosmetics 화장품
· firm 회사
· wrinkle 주름
· opinion 의견
· objective 객관적인
· measurement 측정(치)
· typical 전형적인
· consumer 소비자
· judgement 판단
· claim 주장, 요구

Do It Yourself   pp.166~169

01 ④   02 ①   03 ①   04 ⑤

01~02 답 ④ / ①

소 재 장기 고립으로 인한 체내 시계의 변화

전문해석 1989년 1월 13일에 27세의 이탈리아인 인테리어 디자이너 Stefania Follini가 뉴멕시코의 Carlsbad 근처에 있는 한 동굴로 내려갔다. 그리고 그곳에서 장기 고립에 대한 스트레스가 우주여행에 어떻게 영향을 미치는지를 조사하는 것을 목표로 하는 실험의 일부로써 그녀는 4개월 이상 생활할 예정이었다. 이탈리아 연구 재단인 Pioneer Frontier Explorations는 20명의 해당 과제 지원자 중 한 명인 Follini를 선정했는데, 이는 그녀가 정신력과 체력을 갖추고 있다고 판단되었기 때문이다. 131일 동안 그녀는 9미터 아래 지하에 봉인된 가로 6미터 세로 12미터의 플렉시글라스 모듈 안에서 햇빛 혹은 다른 어떠한 시간 측정 방법 없이 홀로 거주했다.

약 4개월 후, 그녀는 일정에 맞추어 지상으로 복귀했다. 그러나 그녀의 계산으로는 날짜가 단지 3월 중순이었다. Follini가 지하에서 머무는 동안, 그녀의 시간 개념이 더 길어진 것처럼 보였다. 그녀의 "하루"는 25시간, 나아가 48시간으로 늘어났다. 그녀는 22시간에서 24시간 동안 잠을 자다가 돌연 최대 30시간까지 활동하는 경향이 있었다. 간단히 말해서, 그녀의 체내 시계가 고장 나 버린 것이다.

01 **정답풀이** 장기 고립이 우주여행에 미치는 영향을 조사하기 위해 Follini라는 사람이 지하에서 고립된 채로 오랫동안 지냈으며, 그 결과로 체내 시계가 고장났다고 했으므로, 글의 제목으로는 ④ '고립이 일으킬 수 있는 변화는 무엇인가'가 가장 적절하다.

오답풀이

① 지원자를 선택하는 방법 → 일부 내용에만 해당하는 오답이다.

② 과도한 수면이 왜 해로운가 → 체내 시계의 고장으로 수면 시간이 길어졌다는 내용으로 인해 유도될 수 있는 오답이다.

③ 편안한 지하 생활 → 지하 생활을 한 실험을 다루고는 있지만 그것이 편안한 지에 대한 글은 아니다.

⑤ 예상하지 않은 탐사의 이점 → 지문에서 언급되지 않았다.

02 **정답풀이** Follini가 지하에 머무는 동안, 하루는 25~48시간으로 늘어났으며, 22~24시간 동안 잠을 자고 최대 30시간까지 활동하는 경향을 보였다는 내용을 통해 ① '체내 시계'가 고장 난 것을 추론할 수 있다.

② 디자인 도구
③ 개인용 컴퓨터
④ 전자계산기
⑤ 실험 장비

구문풀이

[6행] For 131 days she lived there alone in **a 6 meter by 12 meter Plexiglas module** [sealed 9 meters under the surface, without sunlight or any other way of measuring time].

: [ ]는 a 6 meter by 12 meter Plexiglas module을 수식한다. sealed 앞에는 which(또는 that) was가 생략된 것으로 볼 수 있다.

어휘풀이

- cave 동굴
- examine 조사하다, 검사하다
- isolation 고립
- pioneer 선구자
- exploration 탐험, 탐사
- assignment 과제
- inner strength 내면의 힘, 정신력
- module 모듈(우주선의 구성 단위)
- measure 측정하다
- on schedule 일정대로, 계획대로
- extend 연장되다, 길어지다
- up to ~까지
- go out of order 고장 나다
- aim at ~을 목표로 하다, 겨냥하다
- long-term 장기적인
- affect ~에 영향을 미치다
- frontier 미개척 영역
- foundation 재단, 협회
- be judged to ~ 하다고 판단되다
- stamina 체력
- seal 봉인하다
- aboveground 지상으로
- calculation 계산
- burst into 갑자기 ~하다
- in short 간단히 말해서

03~04 답 ① / ⑤

소 재　노화와 뇌의 능력

전문해석　미네소타 주 Mankato의 외딴 지역에 있는 School Sisters of Notre Dame의 수녀들은 연구원들의 상당히 많은 관심을 뇌의 노화로 끌어들였다. 그리고 그것은 놀랄 만한 일이 아니다. 그 수녀들 중에서 많은 이들이 90세가 넘고 상당수는 100세가 족히 넘는다. 'LIFE' 잡지에서 특집으로 다뤄진 수녀 Marcella Zachman은 97세까지 가르치는 일을 하고 있었다. Mary Esther Boor 수녀는 은퇴 결심을 할 때까지 접수대에서 일을 하고 있었는데, 그 당시 그녀의 나이는 99세였다! 게다가, 그 수녀들은 평균보다 훨씬 더 적고 더 가벼운 노인성 치매와 다른 뇌 관련 질환의 사례를 겪는 것처럼 보인다.

Kentucky 대학교의 David Snowdon 교수는 이것에 대한 타당한 이유가 있다고 믿고 있다. 그 수녀들은 '게으른 정신은 악마의 장난감이다.'라는 충고를 아주 진지하게 받아들여 자신의 정신을 계속 분주하게 하려고 대단히 애를 쓴다. 항상 그들은 퀴즈로 경쟁하고, 퍼즐을 풀고, 활발한 토론을 벌이고, 일기를 쓰며, 세미나를 운영하는 등의 활동을 한다. Snowdon은, Mankato의 100명 넘는 수녀들이 사망했을 때 기증된 뇌를 조사했고, 그는 지적 자극으로 인해 보통은 나이가 들면서 증가하는(→ 감퇴하는) 뇌의 연결 장치가 가지를 뻗어 새로운 연결을 만든다고 믿고 있다.

03　정답풀이　Mankato의 수녀들의 사례에서 알 수 있듯이, 뇌는 나이가 들면서 무조건 퇴화하는 것이 아니라 활발한 지적 자극을 통해 그 능력이 감퇴하는 것을 막을 수 있다는 것이 요지이다. 따라서 글의 제목으로는 ① '중요한 것은 나이가 아니라 정신적 활동이다'가 가장 적절하다.

오답풀이

② 수녀들의 놀라운 신체 건강 비결 → 단순한 신체 건강에 초점을 둔 글은 아니다.

③ 뇌는 어떻게 기억을 오랫동안 저장하는가? → 뇌에 관한 글은 맞지만, 기억의 저장을 다루지는 않았다.

④ 한 교수의 편견이 야기한 예기치 못한 결과 → 지문의 내용과 무관하다.

⑤ 우리가 더 많은 관계를 맺을수록, 우리는 더 똑똑해진다 → 지문의 내용과 무관하다.

04　정답풀이　David Snowdon 교수가 활발한 정신적 활동을 한 수녀들의 뇌를 조사한 결과를 설명하는 흐름에서, 뒤에 뇌의 연결 장치가 가지를 뻗어 새로운 연결을 만든 것으로 믿었다는 내용이 이어지고 있으므로, 보통은 나이가 들면서 ⑤ '증가한다(increase)'고 하는 것은 적절하지 않으며, 'decline(감퇴하다)' 정도로 고쳐야 한다.

오답풀이

① 장수하는 수녀들의 뇌와 노화의 관련성이 연구원들의 관심을 끌었다는 맥락에 쓰인 attracted(끌어들였다)는 적절하다.

② 지적 활동을 활발하게 했던 수녀들의 뇌는 치매 및 뇌 관련 질환을 덜 겪었다고 하는 것이 자연스러우므로, fewer(더 적은)는 적절하다.

③ 수녀들이 활발한 활동을 한 것은 게으름을 경계하는 충고를 진지하게 받아들인 것으로 볼 수 있으므로, seriously(진지하게)는 적절하다.

④ 정신을 분주하게 하는 활동들을 적극적이고 활발히 했다는 맥락이므로, active(활발한)는 적절하다.

구문풀이

[12행] Snowdon has examined **the brains of over 100 nuns of Mankato**, [which were donated for research when they died], and he believes [that intellectual stimulation makes {**the brain connectors** (that normally decline with age)} {branch out and make new links}].

: 첫 번째 [ ]는 the brains of over 100 nuns of Mankato를 부연 설명하는 관계절이다. 두 번째 [ ]는 believes의 목적어 역할을 하는 명사절이다. 첫 번째 { }는 makes의 목적어이고, ( )는 the brain connectors를 수식하는 관계절이다. 두 번째 { }는 원형부정사구로, makes의 목적격 보어이다.

어휘풀이

- nun 수녀
- ageing 노화
- feature 특집으로 다루다
- mild (증상이) 가벼운
- plaything 장난감
- remote 외딴, 멀리 떨어진
- wonder 놀라운 것[일]
- retire 은퇴하다
- idle 게으른

- go to extraordinary lengths to ~하기 위해 대단히 애쓰다
- keep one's mind occupied 마음을 분주하게 하다
- compete 경쟁하다
- debate 토론
- and much more 기타 등등
- examine 조사하다
- donate 기증하다, 기부하다
- intellectual 지적인
- stimulation 자극
- normally 보통
- branch out 가지를 뻗다, 진출하다

Unit 02 장문 독해(1지문 3문항)

Example 답 ③ / ⑤ / ④   pp.170~171

소 재 Kevin과 한 노인의 일화

전문해석 (A) Kevin은 차를 닦으며 쇼핑몰 앞에 있었다. 그는 방금 세차장에서 나와서 아내를 기다리고 있었다. 사회가 걸인이라고 여길 만한 한 노인이 주차장 건너편에서 다가오고 있었다. 그의 행색으로 보아, 그는 집도 돈도 없어 보였다. 여러분이 관대하다고 느낄 때도 있지만 그저 방해받고 싶지 않은 그런 때도 있다.

(C) 이번이 그런 "방해받고 싶지 않은" 때 중의 하나였다. "저 노인이 나에게 돈을 요구하지 않으면 좋겠어."라고 Kevin은 생각했다. 그는 그렇게 하지 않았다. 그는 다가와 버스 정류장 앞 벤치에 앉았지만, 심지어 버스 탈 돈도 충분히 가지고 있지 않은 것처럼 보였다. 몇 분 후 그가 입을 뗐다. 그는 "차가 참 멋지네요."라고 말했다. 그는 누더기 옷을 입고 있었지만 그는 그의 주변에 위엄의 기운을 가지고 있었다. Kevin은 "고맙습니다."라고 말하고는 자신의 차를 계속 닦았다.

(D) Kevin이 차를 닦고 있을 때 그는 잠자코 거기에 앉아 있었다. 예상했던 돈의 요구는 전혀 없었다. 그들 사이의 침묵이 길어지자, Kevin은 "혹시 도움이 필요하세요?"라고 물었다. 그는 Kevin이 결코 잊지 못할 간단하지만 심오한 세 단어로 대답했다. "우리 모두 그렇지 않나요?" Kevin은 그 세 단어가 그에게 강한 인상을 주기 전까지 자신이 성공하고 중요한 사람이라고 느끼고 있었다. 우리 모두 그렇지 않은가?

(B) Kevin 또한 도움이 필요했다. 아마 버스비나 잠 잘 곳에 대한 도움은 아니겠지만, 그는 도움이 필요했다. 그는 지갑을 열었다. 그리고 Kevin은 그에게 버스비를 낼 뿐만 아니라, 따뜻한 식사를 할 만큼 충분히 (돈을) 주었다. 여러분이 아무리 가진 것이 많아도, 여러분이 아무리 많이 이루었더라도, 여러분 역시 도움이 필요하다. 여러분이 아무리 가진 것이 없어도, 여러분이 아무리 골칫거리가 많다고 하더라도, 심지어 돈이나 잠잘 곳이 없더라도, 여러분은 도움을 줄 수 있다.

구문풀이

[2행] **An old man** [whom society would consider a beggar] was coming toward him from across the parking lot.
: [ ]는 An old man을 수식하는 관계절이다.

[8행] [No matter how much you have], [no matter how much you have accomplished], you need help too.
: 두 개의 [ ]는 모두 양보의 부사절이다.

[17행] He answered in **three simple but profound words** [that Kevin shall never forget]: ~
: [ ]는 three simple but profound words를 수식하는 관계절이다.

어휘풀이

- in front of ~의 앞에
- beggar 걸인
- generous 관대한
- bother 신경 쓰게 하다, 방해하다
- fare 요금
- accomplish 이루다, 성취하다
- loaded 가득 찬
- ragged 누더기 옷을 입은
- silence 침묵, 정적
- widen 확대되다
- profound 심오한

Do It Yourself   pp.172~175

01 ③   02 ⑤   03 ④
04 ②   05 ②   06 ④

01~03 답 ③ / ⑤ / ④

소 재 딸의 결혼식을 배려해준 전기회사 직원의 친절

전문해석 (A) 내 남편 David가 우리 딸 결혼식 한 주 전에 내 휴대전화로 전화를 걸어 "우리에게 문제가 생겼어요."라고 말했다. 그는 전기 회사에서 중요한 수리를 하기 위해서 조만간 우리가 사는 인근 지역에 정전이 있을 거라고 발표했다고 나에게 말했다. 진짜 문제는 결혼식 날에 우리가 정전을 겪을 것이라는 사실이었다.

(C) 나는 전기 회사에 전화를 걸어서 우리가 결혼식 준비(화장, 머리 (손질) 등)를 하기 위해서 정말로 집이 필요하므로 수리 작업을 연기해 달라고 그들에게 부탁, 아니 오히려 사정했다. 내 전화는 즉시 Rosa라는 관리자에게 연결되었다. 그녀는 그 문제를 이해했으며 그들은 결코 정전 계획을 다시 세울 수는 없지만 자신이 어떤 조치를 취할 수 있을지 알아보겠다고 설명했다.

(D) 이틀 후에 Rosa는 전화를 걸어 우리 집만 전기를 유지하게 해 줄 수는 없다고 말했다. 그러고 나서 그녀는 "우리 회사 건물에 있는 방을 사용할 수 있게 해드릴 수 있습니다."라고 말했다. 나는 놀라면서 그녀가 그렇게 한 적이 있었는지 물었다. 그녀는 "사실은, 전에 그런 일이 있었어요."라고 말했다. 그 다음 날에 Rosa는 기쁜 목소리로 다시 전화를 걸어 해결책을 찾았다고 말했다. 그녀는 나의 딸이 집에서 전기를 사용할 수 있고 그녀의 결혼식 준비를 할 수 있을 거라고 내게 말했다.

(B) 그리하여 우리는 일요일 아침에 일찍 일어났으며 우리 집 바로 밖에 발전기가 놓여 있는 것을 발견했는데, 그것이 그녀의 해결책이었다. 그렇다, 인근 지역의 다른 집들은 정전이 되었지만, 우리 집은 하루종일 우리의 전용 발전기에서 나오는 전기에 연결되어 있었다! 그것은 놀라웠다. Rosa는 우리의 행복이 그녀에게도 중요하다는 것을 분명히 해주었다. 진실로 넓은 마음을 지닌 사람들이 있다. 친절은 여전히 살아 있다.

01 정답풀이 남편이 정전으로 인해 딸의 결혼식을 치르는 데 문제가 생겼다고 필자에게 전하는 내용의 (A)에 이어, 필자가 전기 회사에 전화를 걸어 수리 작업을 연기해 달라고 부탁하자 전기 회사 관리자인 Rosa가 취할 수 있는 조치에 대해 알아보겠다고 하는 내용의 (C)가 이어진다. 그리고 이틀 후 Rosa가 필자에게 전화를 걸어 결혼식 날 집에서 전기를 사용할 수 있다고 말해주는 (D)가 이어지고, 결혼식 날 집에 발전기가 놓여 결혼식을 치를 수 있게 된 것에 대해 필자가 Rosa의 친절함을 생각해 보게 된 내용의 (B)가 마지막으로 오는 것이 자연스럽다.

02 정답풀이 (a), (b), (c), (d)는 모두 전기 회사의 관리자인 Rosa를 가리키지만, (e)는 필자의 딸을 가리킨다.

03 정답풀이 딸의 결혼식 날에 정전이 될 예정이었으나, 전기회사 관리자인 Rosa가 전용 발전기를 연결하여 전기를 공급해 준 덕분에 집에서 결혼식을 무사히 치를 수 있게 되었다는 내용이므로, ④는 필자에 관한 내용과 일치하지 않는다.

구문풀이

[9행] Rosa made **it** clear [that our happiness was important to her as well].

: it은 형식상의 목적어이고, that절인 [ ]가 내용상의 목적어이다.

[20행] She told me [that my daughter would be able **to use** electricity and **prepare** for her wedding at home].

: [ ]는 문장의 동사 told의 직접목적어이며, be able to 다음에 use와 prepare가 등위접속사 and로 인해 병렬구조를 이룬다.

어휘풀이

· **electric** 전기의
· **neighborhood** 인근 지역, 이웃
· **park** 두다, 주차하다
· **connect** 연결하다
· **private** 사적인, 전용의
· **beg** 사정하다, 간청하다
· **immediately** 즉시
· **transfer** (전화를) 다른 곳으로 돌리다, 옮기다
· **absolutely** 절대적으로, 단호히
· **announce** 발표하다, 공표하다
· **repair** 수리; 수리하다
· **solution** 해결책
· **electricity** 전기
· **blackout** 정전
· **put off** 미루다, 연기하다
· **reschedule** 계획을 다시 잡다

04~06 답 ② / ② / ④

소재 사고를 극복한 Ben Hogan

전문해석 (A) 1949년에 Ben Hogan은 비극적인 자동차 사고를 당했다. 하지만, 실제 충돌이 있기 전에, Hogan은 자신의 아내인 Valerie에게 몸을 던져 그녀를 구했지만, 자기 자신의 다리는 으스러졌다. 다친 다리에서 폐와 뇌로 올라가는 혈전이 그의 생명을 위협했다. 그가 병원으로 옮겨졌을 때, 의사들은 그의 아내에게, 그가 그날 밤을 넘기지 못할 것이라고 말했다. 그의 아내는 "당신들은 분명히 제 남편을 알지 못하는군요."라고 나지막이 말했다.
(C) 그는 위험한 수술을 받았으나, 다음날 아침 그는 여전히 삶을 위한 사투를 하고 있었다. Hogan이 간신히 생명을 유지하면서 그 상태는 장기간 지속되었다. 외과 과장 Alton Oschner는 자신이 Hogan의 폐에 있는 일련의 혈전과의 싸움에서 패하고 있다고 여

러 차례 느꼈다. 마침내 Hogan은 기적적으로 회복되었지만, 의사들은 그의 아내에게 "Hogan 부인, Ben은 결코 다시는 걷지 못할 것입니다."라고 말했고, 그녀는 "당신들은 분명히 제 남편을 알지 못하는군요."라고 말했다.
(B) 몇 달이 지나서, Ben은 다시 정신을 차리기 시작했다. 몸이 심하게 다친 상태로 병원 침상에 있었지만, 그는 골프를 다시 치겠다고 결심했다. Oschner는 그의 의도를 알게 되었을 때 몹시 놀라서, 그는 그의 아내에게 "Hogan 부인, Ben은 지금 자기가 하루종일 (골프채를) 볼 수 있는 천장에 골프채를 매달아 두기를 원하고 있지만, 그는 결코 다시 골프를 치지 못할 것입니다."라고 말했고, Hogan 부인은 "당신은 분명히 제 남편을 알지 못하는군요."라고 말했다.
(D) 믿기 어려울 정도로 고통스러운 물리치료를 겪은 후에, 그는 다시 골프 코스로 돌아왔다. 사고 후 겨우 10개월이 지났으므로 그의 다리는 부어오르는 것을 가라앉히기 위해 고무 밴드를 감아야 했지만, 그는 놀랍게도 곧 주요 대회에서 다시 우승하고 있었다. 1950년부터 1953년까지의 기간 동안, Hogan은 최고의 선수 순위에 다시 올랐다. 그는 사고가 있기 전보다 훨씬 더 성공적이었고, 자신의 아홉 번의 메이저 대회 우승 타이틀의 대부분을 얻었다. 그는 1960년대의 여명이 올 때까지 그 경기에서 지배적인 선수로 남았다.

04 정답풀이 Ben Hogan이 비극적인 자동차 사고를 당해 병원으로 옮겨진 후, 의사들로부터 그날 밤을 넘기지 못할 것이라는 말을 듣게 되었다는 내용의 주어진 글 다음에는, 수술 이후에 기적적으로 생명을 유지하게 되고 다소 회복하게 되지만 여전히 혈전으로 위험에 처해 있었다는 내용인 (C)가 이어진다. 이후 시간이 흘러 Hogan이 다시 골프를 치겠다는 결심을 하게 되었다는 내용의 (B)가 온 후, 골프 코스로 돌아와 메이저 타이틀을 따내며 이전보다 더 성공적이게 되었다는 내용의 (D)가 이어지는 것이 가장 적절하다.

05 정답풀이 (a), (c), (d), (e)는 모두 Ben Hogan을 가리키지만, (b)는 의사인 Alton Oschner를 가리킨다.

06 정답풀이 믿기 어려울 정도로 고통스러운 물리치료를 겪은 후에 다시 골프 코스로 돌아왔다고 했으므로, ④는 적절하지 않다.

구문풀이

[15행] Alton Oschner felt he had lost the battle against **a series of blood clots** [that were in Hogan's lungs].

: [ ]는 a series of blood clots를 수식하는 관계절이다.

어휘풀이

· **involved in** ~에 연루된
· **automobile** 자동차
· **crush** 으스러뜨리다
· **lung** 폐
· **obviously** 분명히
· **intent** 의도
· **string** 끈으로 매달다
· **undergo** 받다, 겪다
· **extended** (예상보다) 길어진
· **cling to** ~에 매달리다
· **catastrophic** 비극적인, 재난의
· **collision** 충돌
· **injure** 부상을 입히다
· **threaten** 위협하다
· **spirit** 정신, 영혼
· **golf club** 골프채
· **ceiling** 천장
· **operation** 수술
· **barely** 간신히, 겨우
· **chief surgeon** 외과 과장

· pull through 회복되다　　· physical therapy 물리치료
· elastic 고무밴드　　· swell 부어오르다
· the bulk of 대부분　　· dominant 지배적인, 주도적인
· dawn 여명, 새벽

A 01 통계의　02 실시하다, 행하다　03 잘못된 정보를 주는, 잘못 이끄는　04 ~에 관여하다, ~와 관련 있다　05 회사　06 wrinkle　07 객관적인　08 조사하다, 검사하다　09 고립　10 선구자　11 재단, 협회　12 seal　13 갑자기 ~하다　14 외딴, 멀리 떨어진　15 노화　16 feature　17 retire　18 게으른　19 donate　20 자극

B 01 rapid reduce wrinkles → <u>rapidly reduce wrinkles</u>: 동사 reduce를 수식하므로 부사 rapidly로 고쳐야 한다.
02 avoiding taking → <u>avoid taking</u>: have to에 이어지는 use와 병렬을 이루어야 하므로 avoid로 고쳐야 한다.
03 how could the stresses of long-term isolation affect → <u>how the stresses of long-term isolation could affect</u>: examining의 목적어가 되는 간접의문문을 이루도록 〈의문사+주어+동사〉 어순으로 고쳐야 한다.
04 seal → <u>sealed</u>: 명사구인 a 6 meter by 12 meter Plexiglas module을 수식하는 분사가 필요한데, 그 명사구가 seal이 나타내는 동작의 대상이므로 수동의 의미가 되도록 과거분사 sealed로 고쳐야 한다.

C 01 걸인　02 관대한　03 신경 쓰게 하다, 방해하다　04 요금　05 가득 찬　06 누더기 옷을 입은　07 심오한　08 announce　09 인근 지역, 이웃　10 solution　11 사적인, 전용의　12 정전　13 사정하다, 간청하다　14 즉시　15 비극적인, 재난의　16 충돌　17 천장　18 swell　19 지배적인, 주도적인　20 여명, 새벽

D 01 which → <u>that</u>: 형식상의 목적어인 it에 대한 내용상의 목적어를 이끄는 that으로 고쳐야 한다.
02 begging → <u>to beg</u>: 등위접속사 or로 인해 앞에 있는 to ask와 병렬로 연결되었으므로, to beg으로 고쳐야 한다.
03 rose → <u>rising</u>: 분사구를 이끌어 Blood clots를 수식하도록 현재분사 rising으로 고쳐야 한다. 뒤에 문장의 동사 threatened가 있으므로 동사 rose가 또 쓰일 수는 없다.
04 what → <u>that</u>: told의 직접목적어인 명사절을 이끌어야 하므로 접속사 that으로 고쳐야 한다.

메가스터디

절대
평가
큐

메가스터디 자격 시리즈

메가스터디 '자격 시리즈'는 본격적인 입시를 준비하기 전에 꼭 알아야 하는 교과서와 수능의 **필수 개념**을 **쉽고 빠르게 정복**해 개념이 탑재된 '**자격을 갖춘 수험생**'으로 만들어 드립니다!

무슨 '자격'이냐고요?

수능 필수 개념을
2~3주에 **마스터**하는

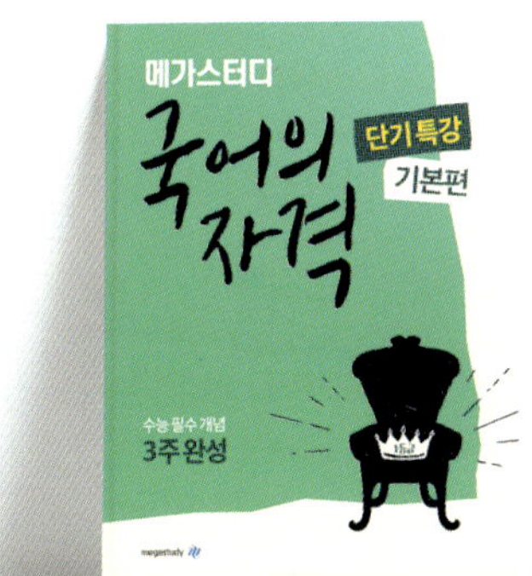

기본편, 비문학 독해, 고전시가, 문법

수능 필수 구문과 필수 어휘를
3주에 **마스터**하는

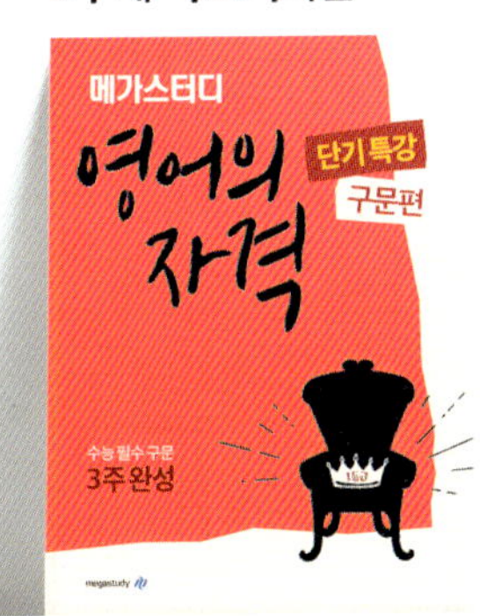

구문편, 독해편, 유형편

교과서의 모든 개념을
3주에 **마스터**하는

수학(상), 수학(하), 수학Ⅰ, 수학Ⅱ,
확률과 통계, 미적분, 기하

수능 필수 개념을
단기간에 마스터하는

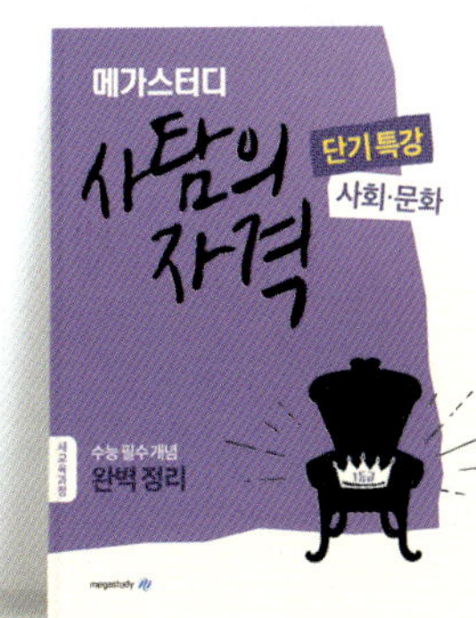

통합사회, 사회·문화, 생활과 윤리

수능 필수 개념을
단기간에 마스터하는

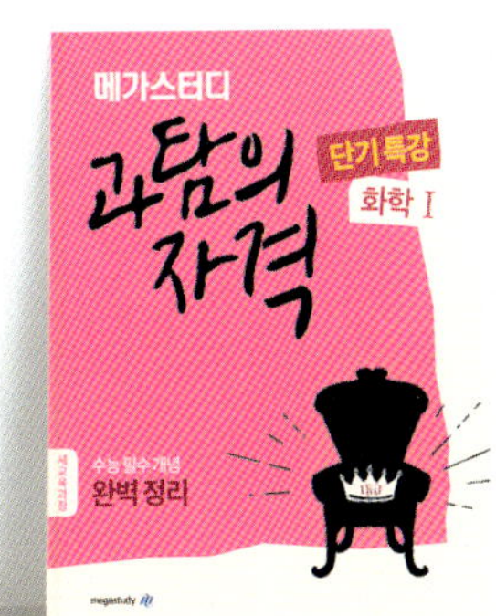

통합과학, 화학Ⅰ,
생명과학Ⅰ, 지구과학Ⅰ

수능 필수 개념을
3주에 마스터하는

한국사

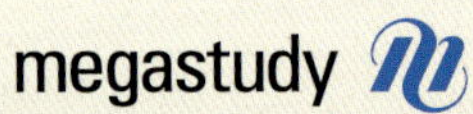

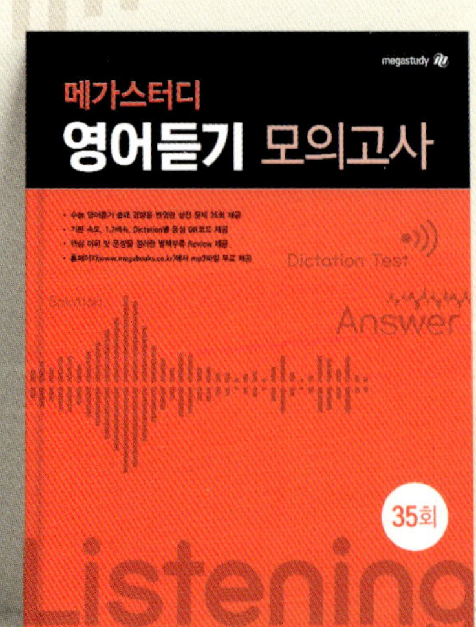

영어듣기 모의고사 유형편

영어듣기 모의고사 20회

영어듣기 모의고사 35회